Henri Bertin and the Representation of China in Eighteenth-Century France

This is an in-depth study of the intellectual, technical, and artistic encounters between Europe and China in the late eighteenth century, focusing on the purposeful acquisition of information and images that characterized a direct engagement with the idea of "China."

The central figure in this story is Henri-Léonard Bertin (1720–1792), who served as a minister of state under Louis XV and, briefly, Louis XVI. Both his official position and personal passion for all things Chinese placed him at the center of intersecting networks of like-minded individuals who shared his ideal vision of China as a nation from which France had much to learn. John Finlay examines a fascinating episode in the rich history of cross-cultural exchange between China and Europe in the early modern period, and this book will be an important and timely contribution to a very current discussion about Sino-French cultural relations.

This book will be of interest to scholars in art history, visual culture, European and Chinese history.

John Finlay is an associate scholar with the Centre d'études sur la Chine moderne et contemporaine (CECMC).

Cover image: Anonymous, Chinese, *Essai sur l'architecture chinoise*, part II, pl. 31, "Salle chez les Gens aisés," ink and color on paper, 35 × 45 cm, ca. 1773. Paris, Bibliothèque nationale de France.

Routledge Research in Art History

Routledge Research in Art History is our home for the latest scholarship in the field of art history. The series publishes research monographs and edited collections, covering areas including art history, theory, and visual culture. These high-level books focus on art and artists from around the world and from a multitude of time periods. By making these studies available to the worldwide academic community, the series aims to promote quality art history research.

Mural Painting in Britain 1630–1730
Experiencing Histories
Lydia Hamlett

Academies and Schools of Art in Latin America
Edited by Oscar E. Vázquez

The Australian Art Field
Practices, Policies, Institutions
Edited by Tony Bennett, Deborah Stevenson, Fred Myers, and Tamara Winikoff

Lower Niger Bronzes
Philip M. Peek

Art, Mobility, and Exchange in Early Modern Tuscany and Eurasia
Edited by Francesco Freddolini and Marco Musillo

The Cobra Movement in Postwar Europe
Reanimating Art
Karen Kurczynski

Emilio Sanchez in New York and Latin America
Victor Deupi

Henri Bertin and the Representation of China in Eighteenth-Century France
John Finlay

For a full list of titles in this series, please visit www.routledge.com/Routledge-Research-in-Art-History/book-series/RRAH

Henri Bertin and the Representation of China in Eighteenth-Century France

John Finlay

Routledge
Taylor & Francis Group
NEW YORK AND LONDON

First published 2020
by Routledge
605 Third Avenue, New York, NY 10017

and by Routledge
2 Park Square, Milton Park, Abingdon, Oxon, OX14 4RN

First issued in paperback 2022

Routledge is an imprint of the Taylor & Francis Group, an informa business

Publisher's Note
The publisher has gone to great lengths to ensure the quality of this reprint but points out that some imperfections in the original copies may be apparent.

Library of Congress Cataloging-in-Publication Data
A catalog record for this book has been requested

ISBN: 978-1-138-20473-7 (hbk)
ISBN: 978-0-367-51432-7 (pbk)
ISBN: 978-1-315-46736-8 (ebk)

DOI: 10.4324/9781315467368

Typeset in Sabon
by Apex CoVantage, LLC

Contents

Color Plates

13 Anonymous, "Atlas de la Seigneurie de Chatou . . .," 1780, Feuille 71 et 72, ink and watercolor on paper, 63.5 × 45 cm. Archives Municipales de Chatou.
14 *Vase Japon*, Sèvres Porcelain Manufactory, 1774, hard-paste porcelain with silver-gilt mount, h.: 26.7, diam.: 20.3 cm. Purchase in Honor of Anne L. Poulet, 2011 (2011.9.01).

Figures

Introduction

In a revealing anecdote, Friedrich Melchior Grimm and Denis Diderot tell the story of how Louis XV of France (r. 1715–1773), supposedly the "greatest philosopher of his kingdom," felt that things were not well in his domain. Speaking one day with Henri Bertin, one of his five Ministers of State, specifically on the need to reform the spirit of the nation, he asked how one might go about this. Bertin returned a few days later and replied that the solution was "Sire, to inoculate the French with the Chinese spirit."[1] The king found this idea so brilliant that he approved everything that Bertin might suggest in order to bring it about. Grimm and Diderot then briefly recount the story of how two Chinese "scholars" were brought to France at great expense, educated there, and then sent back to China to report on that ideal empire, and how their reports became the source of Bertin's grand publication project, the *Mémoires concernant les Chinois*, of which they were now announcing the appearance of the tenth volume. The authors comment ironically that perhaps "the spirit of the nation" has not yet felt the full effects of Bertin's ingenious idea, but they remind their readers that there was a time when French interiors were all decorated in the Chinese taste.[2]

Henri Bernard-Maître quotes Grimm's anecdote in full but introduces it in the context of Louis XV receiving the barbs or mockery (*brocards*) of contemporary writers, including Grimm. However reliable the story of the encounter between Bertin and the king might be, the comments bring together many of the themes—the search for accurate knowledge alongside the misunderstandings and confusions of the day—that characterized Henri Bertin's complex engagement with China. Starting in the late seventeenth to the early eighteenth century and continuing into the beginning of the nineteenth century, what has fruitfully been called the "long eighteenth century," Europeans searched for detailed knowledge of China. In this intercultural exchange, Henri-Léonard Jean-Baptiste Bertin (1720–1792) played a crucial role. In seeking to learn all that he could about China, he truly sought to improve France based on Chinese models. Bertin's official career lasted from 1753 to 1780, during which time he served most importantly as a minister of state (Secretaire d'État, 1763–1780) under Louis XV and, briefly, Louis XVI (r. 1774–1792) (Figure 0.1).

Much, although not all, of eighteenth-century thinking and writing about China is characterized by the formation of a widely shared image of an enlightened empire ruled by a wise and benevolent monarch assisted by learned scholar-officials, a model of government which Europeans hoped their own rulers could emulate—a model formulated in part to criticize elements of European monarchy and economics.[3] France had much to learn as well from China in the domain of what were called *les arts*, that is, practical or mechanical skills, crafts, manufacturing techniques, and technology,

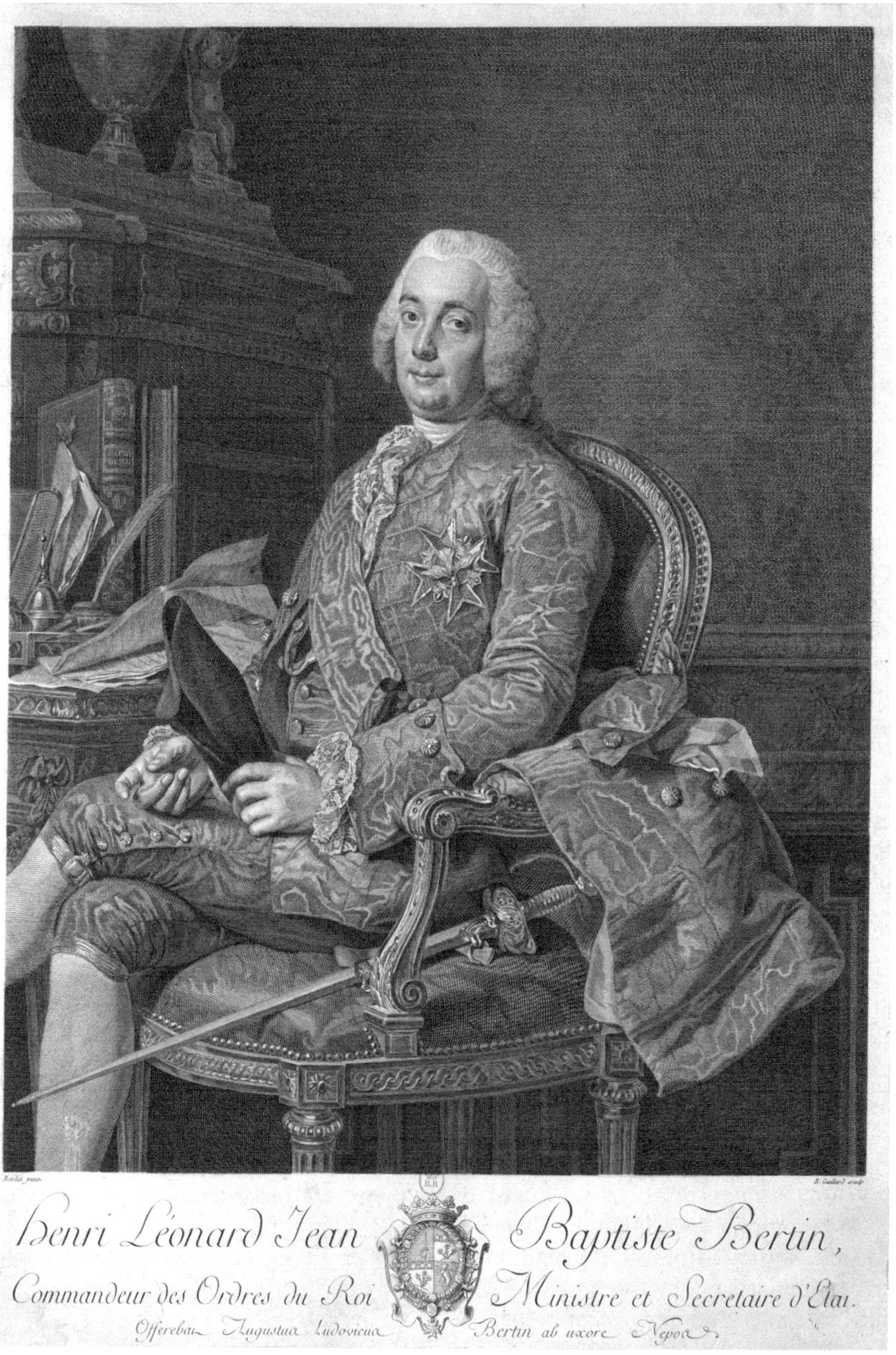

Figure 0.1 René Gaillard (1719? –1790), "Henri-Léonard-Jean-Baptiste Bertin, Commandeur des Ordres du Roi Ministre et Secrétaire d'État," after Alexandre Roslin (1718–1793), ca. 1769, engraving, 51.1 × 34.5 cm. Paris, Bibliothèque nationale de France.

as well as agriculture and other fields. For a variety of reasons, however, the term almost never referred to the fine arts when used in reference to China, and opinions of Chinese painting expressed at the time reveal both real knowledge and deep-seated European prejudices. Like his contemporaries in the late eighteenth century, Bertin believed that visual images along with objects and scientific specimens confirmed and enhanced what might be learned from texts. Frequently he wrote the phrase "see the pictures" (*voyez les peintures*) in his own hand on the pages of letters and manuscripts sent from China, a sure indication that the written text was accompanied by images and that the two must be considered together. The consciousness that words alone were not sufficient to convey complex knowledge, which must be completed or at least enhanced by visual images, is part of a distinctive eighteenth-century mentality, one that is profoundly different from how we now conceptualize learning from words and images. In a modern world saturated with information, in which pictures are but one admittedly complex, shifting, more or less reliable element, it is difficult to imagine a time when words consisted either of handwritten or printed texts, and pictures were drawings, paintings, or (multiple) printed images. Moreover, these were few in number compared to the overloaded world of images we inhabit, making them precious sources indeed and well worth close, individual study. Given the practical physical limits on the number and quality of visual images of China available in late eighteenth-century France, questions arise, too, of how much confidence was invested in such pictures, how much idealization, how much imagination went into understanding China through the medium of texts supplemented with images—or, as is often in the case of Henri Bertin's collections, images supplemented by texts.

What might be called a "commerce in images" between China and Europe begins in the mid-seventeenth century but reaches a peak of importance in late eighteenth-century Paris. The expression *commerce des images* was current in French texts in the literal sense of the "business of pictures." However, there are similar, more philosophically loaded expressions, such as the *commerce des pensées* or *commerce des idées*—both appear in Voltaire's writings, for example—which carry the sense of a free exchange of ideas in the public sphere.[4] It is the concept of an international exchange of visual images that this book seeks to highlight and explore. The beginnings of the modern encounter between Europe and China took place first principally through the media of texts and images, through the writings of explorers and Christian missionaries, and then, at approximately the same time, through the rapidly growing influx of commercial goods, especially tea, textiles, spices, and porcelain among other imports from East Asia. The dissemination of texts and—the main focus of the present study—the ever-increasing knowledge of pictures from China form part of a complex international enterprise. Visual encounters range from the dissemination of well-known and historically significant or influential pictures, often reproduced as prints and/or book illustrations, to the case of images that remained almost invisible outside of a small circle of elite connoisseurs. The phrase "commerce in images" generally presumes an active, purposeful acquisition of images that defines a direct engagement with the idea of "China," of what that far-off empire signified for Europe.

The encounters between Europe and China in the modern era (usually defined as the period after 1500) have been the theme of numerous conferences and colloquia, individual studies and group publications, as well as the subject of bibliographical overviews of the field.[5] In the broadest terms, research in the fields of history, religion, commerce, economics, and art history concentrating on the presence of China in Europe generally focuses on events in the period of the seventeenth to the early eighteenth century. Ongoing developments in Europe's encounters with China in these areas alongside new trends that only become apparent in the late eighteenth century appear to have received relatively less scholarly attention. Beginnings are, perhaps, more intriguing than what might at first appear simply as the continuation of events already underway at an earlier date. However, the European vision of China in the late eighteenth century turned more and more toward the assembly of extensive—and accurate—information from which Europe could directly profit. The sometimes unacknowledged questions here are those of how well the material that reached Europe from China was understood, how far that understanding spread, and, moving away from discussions of "influence" as too passive a term for what were very active engagements, just what impact this new knowledge of China did have for Europeans, specifically Henri Bertin and the circles around him, in the late eighteenth century. Indeed, Bertin was at the center of a network of individuals keenly interested in China. Archival documents itemizing the shipments from China include the names of over 50 individuals for whom objects or images were intended, effectively providing a register of those in the circles around Bertin, including the Bibliothèque du Roi, some directly related to him in his official capacity, and others who shared his eagerness to learn about China.[6]

The various chapters of this book deal with crucial episodes in Bertin's long search for broadly based, reliable knowledge of China. Events in his official career and his government responsibilities were linked to his evolving interest in China as well as his ever-growing collection of images, texts, Chinese objects, and even natural specimens. The evolution of Bertin's collections and his understanding of what he possessed plays out over his lifetime, and the chapters here follow a path that is largely chronological as well as thematic. What begins as a search for knowledge to be shared with all who would seek it out eventually becomes an intensely personal quest.

Chapter 1 in the present volume, "Ko and Yang and the Mission Française de Pékin," outlines how Bertin's official contact with China began. His engagement with China probably began in the 1750s in Lyon, where his earlier official positions had involved him in the importation and manufacture of silk, and this fascination continued to the end of his life. In 1764, two Chinese Christians who had been sent to France for ordination as Catholic priests, Aloys Ko and Étienne Yang, applied to Bertin for passage home on a ship of the French East India company, giving him the idea of employing them as correspondents who would report on China. Bertin was briefly administrator of the French East India company from 1763 to 1764, and the company fell under the purview of Bertin's ministry. As preparation for Ko and Yang's assignment, Bertin delayed their departure for one year and provided them with technical training in the manufacture of such things as tapestries and porcelain, in the sciences and mechanics, as well as instruction in drawing so that they could compare and report in detail on the differences between the two nations. Arriving in Beijing in 1766, Ko and Yang were taken in charge by the French Jesuits—the official Mission Française de Pékin—thus establishing the missionaries' direct contact with Bertin. His extraordinary correspondence with the Jesuits provided the material for the 15 volumes entitled *Mémoires concernant l'histoire, les sciences, les arts . . . des Chinois* (*Articles on the history, sciences, arts . . . of the Chinese*) published between 1776 and 1791.[7] The *Mémoires concernant les Chinois* represent Bertin's most active and successful effort to disseminate the knowledge that was sent to him from China, including texts that presented both translations of key historical Chinese writings and detailed reports or articles (*mémoires*) on current affairs in mid-Qing China. Engravings in the various volumes depicted many diverse subjects, including a richly illustrated life of Confucius that reflected a contemporary fascination with the evolving and sometimes contradictory depictions of the great "Chinese philosopher." The persona of Confucius was one of the main Chinese sources of the ideals of the European Enlightenment and a model for Bertin himself, as the subject dealt with in subsequent chapters in the present volume.

Chapter 2, "The Landscape of Fact and Fantasy," takes up the complex relationship between accurate representations and outright fictions in Bertin's encounters with China. The chapter deals primarily with images of Chinese imperial gardens along with other, relevant garden imagery and the contemporary theory of gardens. Archival documents list the contents of shipments from China that were destined for the French royal collections, for Bertin's own collection and those of others in the circles around him. Among the paintings received, many depict the Yuanming yuan, the "Garden of Perfect Brightness." Sometimes referred to as the Former Summer Palace, the Yuanming yuan was the garden-palace of the Qing emperors located just to the northwest of Beijing. It was already well-known in Europe from the Jesuit missionary Jean-Denis Attiret's famous letter published in 1743 in the *Lettres édifiantes et curieuses. . .*, the widely circulated volumes that are themselves a direct precedent for the *Mémoires concernant les Chinois*. Dubbed "The Versailles of Peking" by Bertin and his contemporaries, the Qing imperial garden-palace had a profound impact on garden theory and design in Europe. The French missionaries sent a surprising number of images of the Yuanming yuan, including albums of paintings and Qing imperial woodblock prints based on the Qianlong emperor's own album of "40 Views of the Yuanming yuan." The paintings the Jesuit missionaries sent to Bertin, however, contain a complex mix of reliable visual information alongside varying degrees of artistic fantasy. They raise significant questions of the Chinese and European sources of garden imagery as well as the reasons why they should include such fictions. One series of superb, large-scale paintings, for example, depicts views of the Yuanming yuan as completely reinvented, surreal landscapes. The circulation of images and knowledge of the Yuanming yuan is surprisingly well-documented in eighteenth-century sources and provides important evidence for understanding contemporary views of China. Pictures circulated within a circle of connoisseurs directly connected to Henri Bertin, and they played a key role in disseminating knowledge of Chinese gardens and Chinese architecture. And knowledge of the Yuanming yuan surely inspired Bertin's own construction projects.

Chapter 3, "Constructing an Authentic China," examines perceptions of Chinese architecture. A number of the most innovative texts and illustrations sent to Bertin by the French Jesuit missionaries dealt with Chinese architecture, a subject that had rarely been treated in European literature before this time. One representative example of interrelated paintings and texts detailed the construction and function of Chinese *serres chaudes* (greenhouses or hothouses), thus providing practical knowledge from China that might improve European practice. An album of five paintings contains highly detailed perspective views of Chinese constructions, and a corresponding article in the *Mémoires concernant les Chinois* describes in detail the advanced technology of Chinese hothouses and the advantages this expertise might provide if emulated in France. In 1775, Bertin received almost 200 paintings depicting Chinese architecture that were accompanied by a long, detailed text. Bertin had the paintings bound in two albums with the collective title *Essai sur l'architecture chinoise* (Essay on Chinese architecture). The paintings and text provided the first comprehensive presentation of Chinese architecture in Europe. In the preface to the *Essai*, the Jesuit missionaries asked the questions: "Is Chinese architecture worth being known in Europe? Would whatever knowledge we could give about it be of any use?" In France, the field of architecture was the subject of publications which spread knowledge of European historical traditions as well as architectural theory and practice, thus defining architecture as an art worthy of serious investigation. For Bertin and his contemporaries, architecture as a discursive field was broadly shaped by a classical tradition that determined what the Jesuit missionaries sent to Bertin as authentic knowledge of a non-Western architecture. Throughout the remarkable *Essai sur l'architecture chinoise*, the emphasis is on the contrasts between Chinese and European architecture, but clearly Bertin and others believed Chinese architecture was well worth knowing. And Bertin's knowledge of Chinese architecture ultimately inspired in him the desire to build something "Chinese" for himself.

Bertin's keen desire to share his knowledge of China and the materials upon which it was based is the subject of Chapter 4, "The Confucian Scholar of Enlightenment France." Bertin maintained his extensive correspondence with the missionaries in Beijing and wrote that it was specifically his purpose to assemble a collection for the benefit of savants and artists who would learn from what it contained. He established a "Cabinet de curiosités chinoises," an unparalleled library and assembly of Chinese objects, texts, and paintings, in his Paris residence, and these rooms were open to those curious to see his collection. Again, what might be learned from paintings—from visual images—is a key element in Bertin's goal of spreading precise and reliable knowledge of China, an ambition which he shared with others of his day who likewise sought to make their collections accessible in some manner to an interested public. After his retirement from government service in 1780, Bertin hoped to use the knowledge he had acquired to construct for himself a version of an authentic China, a vision that he intended to reproduce in constructions for his residence at Chatou, just west of Paris. Here he had another "cabinet chinois," where he sought to fashion himself as a kind of archetypal Chinese scholar. Father Joseph-Marie Amiot (1718–1793), one of Bertin's most prolific correspondents, wrote that he envisioned Bertin there as a kind of Chinese literatus, the Confucian ideal embodied in the scholar-officials of the Qing court, and in this role Amiot imagined Bertin as authentically Chinese. In the constructions planned at Chatou, Bertin also sought to be authentically Chinese. In contradiction to the prevailing European taste for *chinoiserie* garden follies—decorative structures in a fanciful, supposedly oriental style—Bertin hoped to include genuine Chinese landscape elements in his gardens. In this we find perhaps the most complex episode in Bertin's engagement with China, since the extant information on his actual building at Chatou and, in particular, his communications with the French Jesuits provide evidence of shifting and sometimes contradictory efforts. What Bertin had available as sources on Chinese architecture, including garden constructions and authentic Chinese interiors, is truly remarkable. What he was able to accomplish in light of his understanding of Chinese architecture is more problematic. Nevertheless, Bertin's passion for China never abated during his life, and what he planned to build at Chatou manifested his self-styling as a Confucian scholar in Enlightenment France.

Henri Bertin provides an extraordinary example of an educated and curious European who sought to learn about China through all means available to him. The Conclusion to the present volume turns in part to the end of Bertin's life and the dissemination of his collections in the wake of the French Revolution, to the issues of images from

Bertin's collection and their broader circulation, and to the Jesuit missionaries' judgments on Chinese painting, which reflect on European knowledge and reception of Chinese images. Bertin's official duties put him in a unique position to acquire knowledge from the small group of French Jesuits who would remain active in Beijing almost until the end of the eighteenth century, and they continued to respond enthusiastically to his persistent inquiries. Examining the role of a single individual in the late eighteenth-century encounter with China helps to reveal the role of personal connections and networks of like-minded figures in the collection and dissemination of the ever-growing body of knowledge of China. Bertin was a key actor in this period of history. His collections were unparalleled: There was nothing comparable in Europe in size, variety, style, and contents either to the visual imagery or the written texts in his possession.

Documenting the extent of the spread of knowledge is often challenging, and perhaps the most important evidence is that of publication. Bertin sponsored the publication of the *Mémoires concernant les Chinois* in the hope that what he printed and illustrated might likewise be widely read and studied. Other contemporary publications based on the texts and pictures in his collection were aimed at a broad European audience. Of course, knowledge of China was never complete, and what was misunderstood at the time and what we now know was missing is itself revealing. The European image of China shifted radically in the early nineteenth century, a process already begun in the eighteenth century, quickly leaving behind the idealism that characterized the views of Bertin and many of his contemporaries. The late eighteenth-century encounter between France and China—in words and, especially, visual images—had painted a very different picture, one that profited from Bertin's unprecedented contributions.

Notes

1. Friedrich Melchior Grimm and Denis Diderot, *Correspondance littéraire, philosophique et critique de Grimm et de Diderot depuis 1753 jusqu'en 1790*, vol. 12, 1784–85, Jules-Antoine Taschereau, ed. (Paris: Furne, 1830), 492–493: "Sire, c'est d'inoculer aux Français l'esprit chinois." Other versions of the anecdote are known; see Henri Bernard-Maître, "Le 'petit Ministre' Henri Bertin et la correspondance littéraire de la Chine à la fin du XVIIIe siècle,' *Comptes-rendus des séances de l'Académie des Inscriptions et Belles-Lettres*, 92nd year, no. 4 (1948), 449–451; esp. 449.
2. Henri Bernard-Maître, S.J., "Deux Chinois du XVIIIème siècle à l'école des physiocrates français," *Bulletin de l'Université l'Aurore* (1949), 151–197; see p. 153 and n. 7. Bernard-Maître is referring here to the same source as in the previous note.
3. See, among others, Frederic Wakeman, Jr., "The Chinese Mirror," *Proceedings of the Academy of Political Science* 31, no. 1, China's Developmental Experience (March 1973), 208–219, www.jstor.org/stable/1173495, accessed 30 July 2016; esp. 208–209 on the eighteenth century.
4. For the expression *commerce des pensées*, see Voltaire (François-Marie Arouet), *Dictionnaire philosophique, portatif* (London, 1765), "Liberté de Penser," 224–228; see esp. p. 225.
5. See, among others, D.E. Mungello, *The Great Encounter of China and the West, 1500–1800*, Fourth edition, revised (Plymouth: Rowman & Littlefield, 2013). See also Mungello, "Some Recent Studies on the Confluence of Chinese and Western Intellectual History," *Journal of the History of Ideas* 40, no. 4 (October–December 1979), 649–661, which is the source of some of the broader questions raised here.
6. Henri Bernard[-Maître], S.J., "Catalogue des objets envoyés de Chine par les missionnaires de 1765 à 1786," *Bulletin de l'Université l'Aurore*, series III, 9 (January–April 1948), nos. 33–34, 119–206; see esp. 201–202, Noms des destinaires, collectionneurs, etc., . . . noms propres européens.
7. The volumes are conventionally referred to as the *Mémoires concernant les Chinois*.

1 Ko and Yang and the Mission Française de Pékin

Journeys Between France and China

Just after midnight on 17 January 1765, two hours before their departure from Paris for the port of Lorient, where they would board a ship of the Compagnie des Indes to return to China, two Chinese Christians, Aloys Ko and Étienne Yang, wrote a brief record of their lives and their travel to France.[1] Their text was intended to serve as the introduction to a work entitled *Voyage et Séjour en France . . .*, which would probably have described in detail their experiences in France, their education and ordination as Catholic priests, and their official relationship with Henri Bertin. Bertin's crucial encounter with Ko and Yang would be instrumental in establishing direct contact between Bertin and the French Jesuit mission in Beijing.[2] Having enlisted them in what would become his lifelong project to secure accurate knowledge of China, Bertin sought to provide Ko and Yang with the training and education they would need to participate in this undertaking.

The French Jesuit mission in Beijing had its beginnings some 80 years earlier with the decision by Louis XIV in 1684 to send to China five Jesuits trained in the sciences, especially mathematics and astronomy, a group which was officially designated the Mathématiciens du Roi in letters patent issued by the king.[3] Appointed correspondents of the Académie Royale des Sciences (Academy of sciences), the five missionaries left France in 1685 and finally reached China in 1688, where they were first attached to the Portuguese Jesuit Vice-Province of China, from which they became independent in 1700.[4] After the final suppression of the Jesuit order by Pope Clement XIV in 1773 (the Papal Brief *Dominus ac Redemptor* reached Beijing in November 1775), the French Jesuit mission survived under royal patronage until the French Revolution in 1789. The mission was finally ceded to the Congrégation de la Mission in 1804, and, among the last of the former Jesuits, the Brother Coadjutor Giuseppe Panzi (b. 1734), who served as a painter, died in Beijing in 1811 or 1812; Father Louis Antoine de Poirot (b. 1735) died in 1813.[5]

From the beginning, the Jesuit mission was envisioned as a combination of Christian proselytizing in conjunction with careful observation and accurate reporting on China. The first Father Superior of the mission, Jean de Fontaney (1643–1710), wrote of the goals of the missionaries as he had discussed them, probably in 1681, with the minister Jean-Baptiste Colbert (1619–1683), who had founded the Académie des Sciences in 1666.[6] In a letter published in 1707, Fontaney recalled the occasion when Colbert told him that, if the missionaries were going to China, they should take advantage of the occasion and that "in the times when they were not so busy preaching the Gospel, that they should make a quantity of observations in the field, which we are lacking for the perfection of the sciences and the arts."[7] That France could profit from knowledge of China in the perfection of science and the arts—which in this context meant technology and the mechanical arts, especially advanced handicraft skills, and the methods of production of all kinds—would be repeated in many succeeding statements about the objectives of the encounters with China.[8] The Jesuits of the French mission dedicated their efforts to the production, transmission, and publication of accurate knowledge of China, an effort that would characterize Henri Bertin's direct communications with the missionaries, which began with the arrival of Ko and Yang in China.[9] By far the most comprehensive reports on China from the French mission appear in the 34 volumes of the *Lettres édifiantes et curieuses*, published in Paris from 1703 to 1776.[10] Jean-Baptiste Du Halde (1674–1743), one of the editors of the *Lettres édifiantes et curieuses*, published his own highly successful and widely circulated *Description de la Chine* in 1735.[11] When the first missionaries departed for China, the members of the Académie des Sciences provided a detailed list of questions on a broad range of subjects, a strategy that would be employed in other official inquiries into the civilization of China, and one that would be repeated by Bertin as well.[12]

The French missionaries, who arrived in Beijing in February 1688, were accorded a certain protection by the Kangxi emperor (康熙, r. 1662–1722).[13] Jesuit missionaries also served as artists in the Qing court workshops, in part reflecting parallel elements of the Christian proselytizing mission, to convince the emperor of China of the superiority of the European arts and sciences and thus the superiority of the Christian religion.[14] Missionary-painters, the most famous being Giuseppe Castiglione (Lang Shining 郎世寧, 1688–1766, arr. in China 1715), trained court artists in addition to working alongside them in the production of all kinds of painting, and on occasion prints, for the court.[15] A key element of this artistic interaction was the introduction of European linear perspective into the Qing court painting practice.[16] For the Jesuit missionary-artists, single-point European linear perspective, which provided the visual structure for the majority of their paintings for the Qing court as well as the mural decorations the three main churches in the capital, also contained a Christian religious aspect.[17] Many of these painters, especially Castiglione, had been trained in linear perspective specifically according to the instructions of the Jesuit lay brother Andrea Pozzo (1642–1709). Castiglione styled himself a "disciple" of Pozzo,[18] and Pozzo's widely circulated illustrated treatise on linear perspective, *Perspectiva Pictorum et Architectorum*, contained a key statement on its theological interpretation.[19] As rendered in the English-language edition of his book, Andrea Pozzo had admonished his students:

> Therefore, Reader, my Advice is that you cheerfully begin your Work, and with Resolution to draw all the Points thereof to that true Point, the Glory of God; and I dare predict, and promise you good Success in so honorable an Undertaking.[20]

For the Jesuit missionaries, the viewer's correct position in relation to the illusions created by linear perspective was analogous to the correct relation to the Christian religion.[21] The present discussion only suggests the importance of the role of European painters—the Jesuit missionary-artists—in the Qing court and their effect on court painting. But as we shall see, early Qing court painting in hybrid Chinese-European styles had an impact beyond the imperial court and contributed directly to the format of paintings produced in Beijing to be sent to Henri Bertin in France.[22]

An Education in France

According to the account in the *Voyage et Séjour*, Ko and Yang were the sons of Chinese Christian families.[23] As young men they were under the tutelage of the French Jesuit missionaries, who taught them Latin and provided additional instruction in the Christian religion. As a result, they were encouraged to go to France, ultimately for ordination as Roman Catholic priests, and they left China when Yang was 18 and Ko was 19 years old. They sailed on a ship of the Compagnie des Indes, the French East India Company, which left the port of Canton (Guangzhou 廣州) in January 1754 on a voyage that would last six months. They would spend nine and a half years under the auspices of the Jesuits in France, followed by another year and a half after the official suppression of the order; Yang would be 29 and Ko 30 years old when they finally returned to China. In 1762 the Paris Parliament ended the Jesuit jurisdiction over some 80 colleges, and Ko and Yang were admitted in March of that year to the Seminary of Saint-Firmin, maintained by Congrégation de la Mission, where they were ultimately ordained in 1763 as Lazarist fathers.[24] Hoping to return to China on a ship of the Compagnie des Indes, they were put in contact with Bertin, whose ministry at the time included the supervision of the French East India Company.[25] According to the *Voyage et Séjour*: "Monseigneur Bertin, Minister and Secretary of State, disposed in our favor, wanted to make us useful to France and, at the same time, to China; consequently, we were committed to delaying our voyage by one year."[26] The king, on the recommendation of Bertin—surely at his instigation—ordered that Ko and Yang should visit various royal manufactures, the official studios and workshops in Paris, and the surrounding districts that produced goods for the court and the French state. Here they would learn what differences there might be between the arts, *les arts*, of France and China.[27] Then they would travel, principally to the regions around Lyon, where they would continue their observations of manufacturing, agriculture, and the production of silk, among other activities. As always, the goal was to observe a particular selection of technical and agricultural processes with the aim of preparing detailed reports to be sent from China on these and other manufacturing and craft techniques from which France could benefit. Ko and Yang agreed that they would follow the instructions of the king as presented to them by his minister Bertin.[28]

Ko and Yang's education in the arts and sciences was planned in great detail, documents specified what they should observe and study, and they reported at length on what they had seen in written "remarks" supplemented by their "reflections," which consisted of notes on what they already knew about Chinese practice. Two members of the Royal Academy of Sciences were chosen to direct their instruction: Mathurin-Jacques Brisson (1723–1806), who would give lessons in physics and natural history, and Louis-Claude Cadet de Gassicourt (1731–1799), who gave lessons in chemistry.[29] In September of 1764, on their arrival in Lyon, Ko and Yang were welcomed by Bertin's influential colleague and correspondent Pierre Poivre (1719–1786), who supervised much of their training and education there.[30] Characteristically, Bertin laid out instructions in great detail on what he wanted Ko and Yang to observe and where he arranged for them to travel in pursuit of their technical and scientific education.[31] In his 1764 "Memoir on what the Chinese should see in France before returning to China," Bertin specified that in their travel to Lyon and surrounding regions Ko and Yang should first study the manufacture of silk textiles.[32] The instructions were based on—and concentrated on—European products. Since their journey coincided with the annual harvest of silkworm cocoons, they traveled in the Dauphiné region in southeastern France to observe the essential processes for producing silk thread. In addition to observations related to the textile industry, they were to examine the production of iron, steel, and copper and their use in various kinds of tools as well as the manufacture of arms.

One section of Bertin's memoir is signaled as a "very important article."[33] In the town of Annonay, south of Lyon, they were to carefully observe the four paper-making factories there, which were the largest and finest in France.[34] Bertin noted the extraordinary size of sheets of Chinese paper, which were not possible to produce with contemporary French manufacturing methods.[35] Ko and Yang should also familiarize themselves with the techniques of agriculture, mining, and the production of enamel and glass, ordinary ceramics and tiles, and even the science of chemistry in order to analyze what they might examine in China. Finally, Bertin noted the great importance of carefully observing the locks and their function along the Canal de Briare, one of the most important canals in France, which connects the Loire and the Seine valleys. Bertin remarked that Du Halde's *Description de la Chine* included information on magnificent canals in China, and the subject was clearly something France should know more about.[36]

Before their travel to Lyon at Bertin's instruction, Ko and Yang's practical training in the arts and sciences began with visits to the royal tapestry workshops of the Manufacture des Gobelins in Paris and included similarly instructive tours of the carpet manufactory of Savonnerie, also in Paris, of the porcelain manufactory of Sèvres, just across the Seine to the west of Paris, and the Imprimerie Royale du Louvre, the printing presses located within the French royal palace.[37] Entitled "Remarks on different manufactures," Ko and Yang's report to Bertin contains their detailed notes on what they observed and what they learned about the techniques of production of the finest luxury goods for the royal court, and these are accompanied by their "reflections" on what they saw.[38] Here as in the other sections of their reflections, French practice is compared with the comparable art or technology in China. On tapestries, they add that two or three tapestries from France in the palace of the emperor would give him more pleasure than all the magnificent thrones with which he decorates his court and that he would be surprised by the brightness of the colors and the beauty of their design. The suggestion that tapestries might make a fitting gift to the emperor of China—a suggestion repeated in Ko and Yang's comments on Savonnerie tapestries—raises the question of the extraordinary gift of a set of six tapestries that would be sent to China and ultimately presented to the Qianlong emperor. This remarkable episode is discussed in detail later.

Ko and Yang's remarks on the production of porcelain focus on the French use of models for plaster molds that are then used to shape porcelain sculptures as well as vessels. Five numbered reflections express hopes that Chinese workers could improve their representations of human figures, that indeed the Chinese should learn how to use models and the resulting molds for production, they should improve the designs of their porcelains beyond what is ordinarily seen in their production, their porcelains should be thicker and more solid, and finally while the materials the Chinese for their porcelain is finer than that of France, French taste is superior—and perhaps the

Chinese should imitate the French. It is clear that Ko and Yang's knowledge of Chinese porcelain is severely limited and represents current European thinking based on the quantities of ordinary-quality porcelains exported to the European market. Even the acknowledgment that the clay body of Chinese porcelain is indeed superior to French porcelains reflects the very real French desire to pursue knowledge of Chinese porcelain manufacture technology and to discover for France the components of Chinese porcelain, a goal that would be obtained around 1765 under Bertin's supervision of the royal manufacture at Sèvres.[39]

Ko and Yang's second report to Bertin, on the details of what they observed during their travel to Lyon and the surrounding region—the report in response to the instructions and questions from Bertin discussed previously—contains much of the same mix of accurate technical detail complemented by only a rudimentary knowledge of the state of comparable technologies in China.[40] Much of their study in the Lyon region focused on the production of silk and silk textiles, and their notes on metal-working, cannons and firearms, various kinds of hardware, and paper-making are very brief, with only occasional references to Chinese technologies. In response to Bertin's instructions on the importance of observing the locks on the Canal de Briare, Ko and Yang noted only that they examined them carefully and that in leaving China they had traveled along the "imperial canal"—the Grand Canal—where there were more than 30 locks, better built and more spacious than those on the Briare.

Instruction in Drawing and Etching

In addition to their technical training, Ko and Yang were also provided with instruction in the arts of drawing and etching. Bertin maintained in the preface to the first volume of the *Mémoires concernant les Chinois*—the series of publications on China that he sponsored beginning in 1776—that training in drawing and etching was an integral part of Ko and Yang's preparation and would make it possible to provide illustrations that could complement what words alone did not completely describe:

> We thought then that it would be important to have them take a certain introduction to drawing and the art of engraving, given that in the great distances of such a correspondence as interesting as that for which we had established the foundations, the drawing of a machine, of a loom, of an instrument, or a plant would supplement what was missing in the most detailed descriptions, and indeed infinitely surpass them. At the end of several months, they were both able to engrave by means of etching views of Chinese landscapes.[41]

It is clear that Bertin wanted Ko and Yang to be able to send images—drawings, paintings, or prints—from China, since images were crucial to the communication of accurate information. But it is less clear why they should study etching, which requires a well-equipped studio, including a large, specialized printing press and European-style paper in order to produce a satisfactory image. However, the four known examples of Ko and Yang's etchings, produced during their training in France, are intriguing for several reasons.[42] Like the extant drawings from the time of their instruction in 1764, the prints are copies of prints or drawings, not objects or views directly observed. The European images are taken from what in one case seem to be botanical illustrations, and three of their drawings and two of the etchings copy conventional images of European landscapes. These show figures and animals in the landscape, rivers, buildings, boats, and even windmills, and indeed from the details of the buildings especially they all appear to be copied from Dutch or at least northern European sources.

For instruction in what Bertin referred to as "Chinese landscapes," however, the models for Ko and Yang's etchings are clearly identifiable. These are the paintings and woodblock prints entitled the "Imperially Commissioned Illustrations of Agriculture and Sericulture," *Yuzhi Gengzhi tu* 御製耕織圖.[43] The Chinese images and accompanying sets of poems have a long and complex history, beginning with the poems composed for the Southern Song dynasty court around 1145. From their inception, the poems were understood to have a political content, to admonish the emperor not to demand too much in taxes or corvée labor from his people, and they were reproduced for distribution to local officials to disseminate that message.[44] In 1696 the Kangxi emperor commissioned a new, slightly expanded version of the original series, accompanied by his own poetry, to be illustrated with paintings by the artist Jiao Bingzhen (焦秉貞, act. 1680–1720) and reproduced as an imperial woodblock edition with the blocks cut by Zhu Gui (朱圭, act. late seventeenth to early eighteenth century). One distinguishing feature of the Kangxi imperial album is the use of European linear perspective in Jiao Bingzhen's resetting of the Song dynasty illustrations, one of the first important manifestations of the use of linear perspective in China, which had only recently been introduced by Jesuit missionary-artists into the court painting workshops. The Kangxi *Gengzhi tu* series was subsequently copied, imitated, and reproduced throughout the Qing dynasty in various versions, as paintings and woodcuts.

Given the significance of the "Illustrations of Agriculture and Sericulture," it is not surprising that the Jesuit missionaries sent a version of the album to France. In the same volume of archival documents that contains Ko and Yang's etchings and drawings is a list dated 1767 of the contents of crates sent to Bertin, which includes a "[book] of ploughing and silkworms."[45] Next to the listing are the initials "B.R.," which stand for Bibliothèque du Roi, the royal library and forerunner of the modern national library, the Bibliothèque Nationale de France (BnF). In the inventories of books and objects sent to Bertin, the initials B.R. indicate that the item was intended for presentation to the royal library, but it is not clear from modern records if this particular version of the *Gengzhi tu* is now in the BnF. However, the BnF does hold two copies of the *Gengzhi tu* that come from Bertin's own collection, which entered the library with the nationalization of his property after the Revolution.[46] The date 1767, however, which may be the date of the list and not the shipment, still leaves it unclear if this is specifically the model copied by Ko and Yang, whose education in printing and drawing took place in 1764 before they left France in 1765. Nevertheless, the two etchings in question are based directly on this Qing imperial series of illustrations, proof that a copy of the album was already in France at this time.

One of the etchings made by Ko or Yang (it is not clear which one actually produced the print) shows an old man leaning on a staff, accompanied by a small boy, along with a young man who is pointing at the rice paddy, where newly sprouted plants are emerging. The figures are silhouetted against a body of water, behind them on the bank is a small group of buildings, and the view extends to a simple bridge and a distant mountain landscape. The etching reproduces the seventh image from the Kangxi imperial album, a picture added to the original Song-dynasty series and entitled "First Seedlings" (Chuyang 初秧). The original image is reversed in the etching process, and

Ko or Yang's print has also changed the vertical, almost square format of the original to a horizontal composition, at the same time simplifying certain details of the landscape. The rendering of the three figures is rather amateurish. The other etching is a more complex composition, one which combines parts of two prints from the Kangxi album (Figure 1.1). In the foreground is the figure of a man wearing a straw cloak, a kind of raincoat, standing on a flat wooden platform being pulled by an ox. This would be a type of harrow, a farm implement with rows of spikes on the bottom to grade the muddy earth in the rice paddy, and the print from which this figure is taken is number three in the Kangxi series, a composition derived from the Southern Song original, entitled "Harrowing" or "Tilling" (Pa'nou 耙耨). The landscape in the background of the etching is copied from the second image of the Kangxi series, entitled "Ploughing" (Geng 耕). Here the Chinese student-printmaker has reproduced the two trees and the group of buildings along the shore; he also copied a tiny figure with a pole over his shoulder and the prow of a boat sticking out from behind a rock.

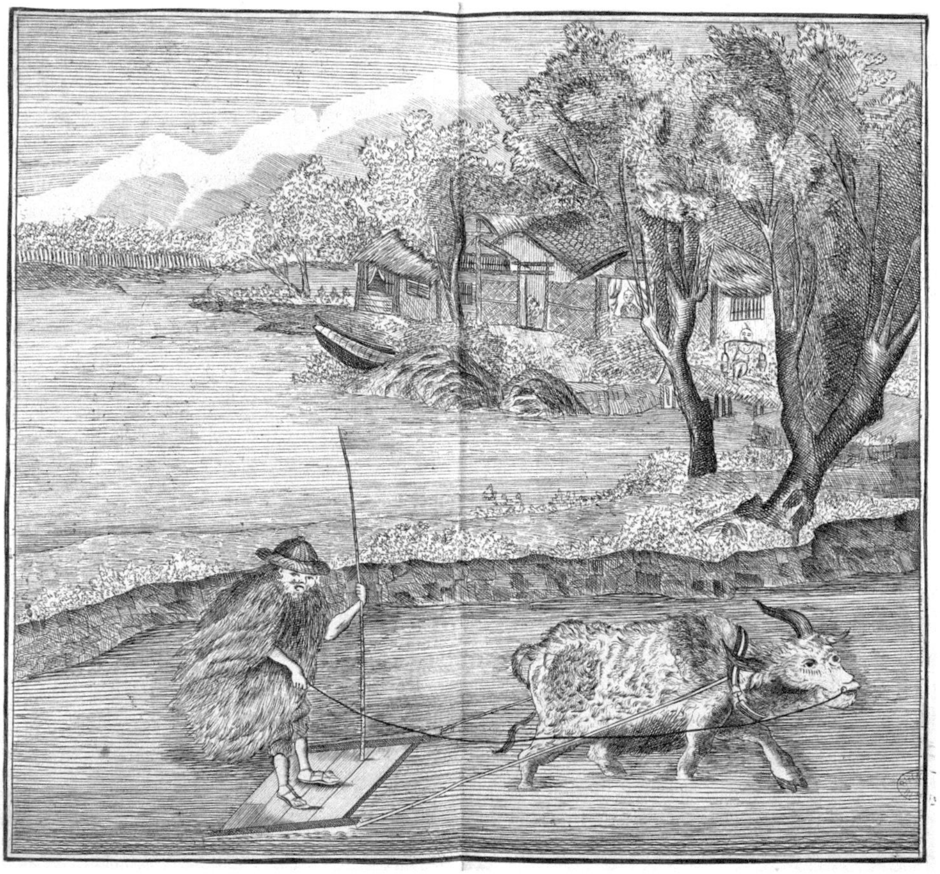

Figure 1.1 Anonymous (Aloys Kao or Étienne Yang), hybrid image based on the *Gengzhi tu*, ca. 1764, etching. Paris, Bibliothèque de l'Institut de France, Ms 1520, fol. 10.

Source: Photo ©RMN-Grand Palais (Institut de France)/Mathieu Rabeau.

In these adaptations, however, what is lost is the distinctly European single-point perspective that characterized Jiao Bingzhen's original paintings for the Kangxi emperor, a Qing imperial court style merging European and Chinese painting elements that is generally reproduced in the woodcut versions of the album of "Illustrations of Agriculture and Sericulture."[47] In order to learn how to accurately render Chinese subjects and, of particular interest for Bertin, Chinese agriculture, the two Chinese clerics who were soon to be sent back to China were assigned to copy Chinese prints depicting what were surely considered accurate representations of Chinese farming techniques. The poetic idealizations of farm life and agricultural production embodied in the poems of the *Gengzhi tu*—not to mention the implications for imperial propaganda legitimizing the Manchu Qing dynasty's right to rule the Chinese empire—would have been invisible to Bertin and his contemporaries and most likely to Ko and Yang themselves.[48]

Turgot's "Questions" to Ko and Yang: Agriculture and Economy

The presence of Ko and Yang in France and the opportunities for detailed information that they might provide also led Bertin's friend and colleague Anne-Robert-Jacques Turgot (1727–1781), who was the Intendant of the *généralité* of Limoges[49] from 1761 to 1774 and later the Controller-General of Finances, to seek specific information on the foundations and workings of China's economy. Turgot's own list of "Questions" addressed to Ko and Yang led directly to the publication of his *Réflexions sur la formation et la distribution des richesses*, a text which had an enormous influence on European thinking on economy.[50] Turgot's *Réflexions* was the direct inspiration for Adam Smith's (1723–1790) *An Inquiry into the Nature and Causes of the Wealth of Nations*, published in 1776.[51] The relationship between Turgot's two related texts, the questions for Ko and Yang and the *Réflexions*, is a complex one. The text of his 52 questions was ostensibly prepared for Ko and Yang to take back to China with them when they left France in January 1765, and like Bertin he had the same ultimate goal, to secure accurate and detailed information about China.

Turgot's questions are quite specific and limited to certain topics, and clarifications of what Turgot sees as their broader context appear in a number of "Observations" in the published text.[52] The questions are divided into three general groups: the first on wealth, the distribution of land, and agriculture (questions 1–30); the second on the arts, that is, practical questions on papermaking, printing, and textiles (questions 31–45); and finally on natural history or natural science, which also includes three brief questions on history and various peoples in the Chinese empire (questions 46–52). The questions on wealth, the largest group of questions, are formed very much in the context of Turgot's thinking on European economic models, not only of agriculture as the ultimate source of wealth, but also of the role played in China by members of the nobility (presumably the Qing imperial clan and the Manchu elite), the military, and other high government officials.

In the questions on the arts of China, which are the most relevant to the discussion here, it is especially paper and the techniques of papermaking that attracted Turgot's keen interest. He demonstrates a remarkably sophisticated knowledge of Chinese paper and papermaking technology. Much of Turgot's information may have been derived from Du Halde's *Description de la Chine*, which contains an essay on Chinese paper, ink, brushes, printing, and the binding of books.[53] Turgot is struck, like Bertin, by the size of Chinese paper, which is much larger than standard European sizes, and Du Halde also remarks a number of times on the size of the paper and the screens used to make such sheets. In question number 37, Turgot cites the title of a book, *Art du Papetier* (Art of the papermaker), which is actually the *Art de faire le papier* of Jérôme de La Lande (1732–1807).[54] The relevant pages give a description of Chinese paper and papermaking, citing a number of Chinese terms. The information here, however, is almost entirely derived from Du Halde's text, copied verbatim in a few instances, although La Lande does cite Du Halde's name at least twice. The information on European papermaking is far more comprehensive. The book, which is illustrated with engraved plates accompanied by detailed explanations, is part of a long series on the arts, handicrafts, and manufacturing sponsored by the Royal Academy of Sciences.[55] The combination here of texts and illustrations detailing the craft of papermaking is yet another example of a European Enlightenment strategy for the diffusion of technical knowledge in the form of texts accompanied by illustrations, of which Diderot and D'Alembert's project for the *Encyclopédie* is the best known example. Turgot's pursuit of knowledge of Chinese papermaking, and specifically of scientific specimens, is fully consistent with this contemporary mentality.

While Turgot's questions on paper and papermaking are remarkable for their number and detail, the questions on printing, three in all, and on textiles, another three, are far more summary. Still, what he asks indicates a knowledge of Chinese printing techniques but is framed more in terms of comparisons with European printmaking or printing technology. The questions on textiles are similarly limited, addressing only one or two basic issues. And the few questions on natural history again only deal with certain related subjects. One specific request, question number 47, is for large samples of the raw materials used for making porcelain. Here Turgot is engaging in a crucial European search for knowledge from China, part of a long quest to learn all the secrets of producing genuine hard-paste porcelain, and he refers to the 1712 letter from the French Jesuit François Xavier d'Entrecolles (1664–1741), which contained the first detailed descriptions of the manufacture of porcelain. D'Entrecolles's letter was published in 1741 in the *Lettres édifiantes et curieuses*, and the text was quickly disseminated throughout Europe.[56] What Turgot is seeking from Ko and Yang are the unprocessed, natural raw materials of porcelain, surely with the aim of determining their actual composition and, no doubt, of helping to identify the same materials in France. The final three questions of Turgot's text for Ko and Yang deal with historical evidence for the Jews in China, with the identity and situation of the Miao people in southern China, and with the Manchu Tartars, the name frequently applied to the Manchu in the eighteenth century. On the Manchu, the Qing dynasty rulers of China, given the distance in time and space from their origins and their continued presence in China, Turgot wonders if they are adopting Chinese customs and losing their original identity. No observations provide any further context for why these particular questions should have attracted Turgot's attention, but the inquiry on Manchu identity is a perceptive one. Again, although no source is immediately evident, Turgot must have been aware of this question, almost surely from the writings of Jesuit missionaries at the Qing imperial court in Beijing, where maintaining Manchu identity was, for example, a concern of the Qianlong emperor.[57]

Bertin's "Questions" to Ko and Yang: the Return to China

Like Turgot, Bertin prepared an extensive, detailed set of questions that Ko and Yang were to take back with them to China, a document or documents that would guide their research in their homeland. While the contents and history of Turgot's questions are relatively straightforward, the story of Bertin's instructions to the two Chinese priests he hoped would be his agents in China remains incomplete. One archival document, however, provides an idea of what Bertin expected of Ko and Yang, and it provides, too, evidence of the ample detail in which he expressed his objectives.[58] Dated to 16 January 1765, the day before Ko and Yang's departure from Paris for the port of Lorient, it contains numerous notes and additions in the margins written in Bertin's own distinctive handwriting. Entitled "Instruction for Mr. Ko and for Mr. Yang," it begins with a summary of the training they had received over the past year. This education is put into a global context with the statement that all the people of the world share the same origin, a Christian belief that underlies much of what was presumed about China in general and framed much of what is presented to Ko and Yang in their instructions. Thus, Ko and Yang can make comparisons in China between the arts of France and China, knowledge from which France could profit, and belief in the commensurability between the two great nations is expressed directly here. After a brief listing of the gifts presented by the king of France—a subject that is discussed later—the instruction continues with a series of numbered sections,[59] which deal with how Ko and Yang are to conduct themselves on their return, the subjects on which they will be expected to report, and the very real complexities of communicating between France and China.

The first section is a brief statement of Ko and Yang's reliability and how they should conduct themselves on the ship of the Compagnie des Indes. In the second section, they are given instructions on how they are to act on their arrival in Canton, dressing in Chinese clothes but effectively remaining out of sight. Bertin is clearly aware of the challenges that faced any Chinese who have traveled abroad, travel which was strictly forbidden by Chinese laws and severely punished. Sections three and four deal with the establishment of a contact person on whom Ko and Yang could rely to forward their letters and packages to Bertin.[60] Section five states that there is no reason for Ko and Yang to pursue their research in Canton, which might only raise suspicions about them. In section six, they are directed to write a detailed letter to Bertin on their voyage to China, on how they conducted themselves in Canton and what they think of their chances of success in their undertaking, on the person who would be their permanent contact or correspondent in Canton, and on the details of how they have arranged for their "effects"—surely the gifts from the king—to be dealt with for the present. In section eight,[61] they are encouraged to write again from Beijing as soon as possible so that their letter should be on the ship returning from Canton. Section seven again repeats instructions to study canals, bridges, and highways, but Bertin also inquires about Ko and Yang's families in China, recalling that Aloys Ko's parents had passed away while he was in France, and encouraging Étienne Yang to reconnect with his own family.

Section nine, which takes up both sides of some four pages, contains the descriptions of the three independent instructions that Bertin has provided—or will provide—to guide Ko and Yang's investigations in China.[62] The text repeats the aspiration that what Ko and Yang have learned can be mutually beneficial to France and China and that to fulfill their goals they should undertake further studies in China in order to compare this new knowledge with what they have learned in France. The text here includes a long insertion in Bertin's own handwriting where he encourages them to send information, too, on subjects not included in their previous training, and where he states his gratitude for whatever Ko and Yang might send back to France. The text then turns to the three detailed instructions that have apparently already been given to them, instructions that are divided into chapters each composed of several questions. The summaries here are apparently the only evidence for the contents of these three documents, which are lost or remain unidentified. The first concerns the *droit public*, the body of law that governs the political, administrative, and financial function of society, as well as relations between states. In order for Ko and Yang to compare the two different systems of France and China, the first instruction is accompanied by three *mémoires*, articles in the form of letters describing the creation of the world, the biblical account of the Flood, the history of the first generations and their population of different parts of the world, the origin of languages, writing, and so forth.[63] Ko and Yang are encouraged to pay the closest possible attention to these questions of both sacred and profane history so that comparisons can be made between the Chinese system and that which has been established by the savants of Europe.[64]

The second instruction prepared for Ko and Yang is only briefly summarized. It concerns the *droit civil*, the laws that govern individuals and how in China they affect private individuals and their possessions in the ordering of society. The third instruction contained several chapters on the sciences, the mechanical arts, and what is necessary for mankind, including food, clothing, and shelter; what is useful for mankind, especially commerce or trade in all its forms; and those things that would provide for such practical matters and their implementation. In general, Bertin writes that implementing these three instructions would require that Ko and Yang make contact with distinguished and important individuals who can provide the answers to his questions. As for the third instruction, the field is truly broad but at the same time critically important. Here, Ko and Yang are encouraged to identify first those subjects that are the most significant, but to be sure to put their answers in order and then to send the materials they do find in the course of their research by each annual return voyage of the ships of the Compagnie des Indes. This is an acknowledgment of the difficulties of communications between France and China as well as a sign of Bertin's eagerness for his project for the acquisition of knowledge from China to proceed as efficiently as possible.

Bertin then writes that Ko and Yang should take every opportunity to present to the Chinese a lofty idea of the virtues, greatness, and magnificence of the king of France, a statement to which Bertin adds that the dynasty has lasted for nine centuries and that Louis XV is the longest reigning monarch in Europe, having ruled for some 50 years, and is praised by both his own people and by foreigners. Ko and Yang were given maps that would show the distance between France and China and demonstrate that the French were capable of maintaining trade between the two nations. The maps serve, too, to compare the size of China in relation to France and the other nations of Europe, and the inclusion of plans of Paris, the Louvre, Versailles, and other royal residences would give an idea of the magnificence of the king of France. Bertin also sent articles written by the members of the Royal Academy of Sciences, thus demonstrating the support and protection that the king of France provides to literature, science, and the arts, as does the emperor of China.

And, at the end of his long letter to Ko and Yang, Bertin repeats his firm conviction that France and China are directly comparable:

> Finally, Ko and Yang should seize every opportunity where they will be able to demonstrate the correspondence that they have observed between the French and the Chinese in the national spirit and character, the two nations that can be seen as the best regulated and the most naturally civilized in the world.[65]

This is Bertin's clearest statement that France and China are truly commensurate, that they can be directly compared as civilizations on an equal footing.

Présents to Impress China

The text at the beginning of Bertin's long letter of 16 January 1765 detailing his instructions to Ko and Yang lists some of the gifts that the king of France had ordered to be delivered to them. Other sources provide a more complete list.[66] These included:

> A set of six tapestries of the Chinese.[67]
> Two portraits by Vigée, with glass and frames.[68]
> A case of twelve panes of glass, 30 by 24 inches.[69]
> A portable printing press "with all of its equipment and four cases of French type."[70]
> A set (or selection) of Sèvres porcelain.[71]
> Brisson's electrical apparatus.[72]
> A collection of spyglasses.[73]
> A telescope.[74]
> A camera obscura.[75]
> A "solar" microscope.[76]
> A hand-held microscope.[77]
> A selection of twenty-three booklets on the arts from the bookseller Saillant.[78]
> Books from the bookseller Vallat.[79]
> Geographical maps. . ., plans of Paris, the Louvre, Versailles and other royal residences [which] will give an idea of the magnificence of the King).[80]
> Added to this list are two gold watches.[81]

The first item on the list, the set of six tapestries, the so-called second *Tenture chinoise*, commissioned from François Boucher (1703–1770) in the early 1740s and produced by the royal manufacture of Beauvais, is the most remarkable part of this royal gift, and the tapestries as well as the question of the royal gifts themselves have been the object of significant scholarly inquiry.[82] The subjects depicted in the six tapestries—idealized, *chinoiserie* views of China, including scenes with supposedly imperial figures—would at first seem to be a curious gift to present to the emperor of China, but their scale and magnificence signaled the well-established role of tapestries as gifts from the king of France.[83] However, the gifts placed in Ko and Yang's care were not originally for presentation directly to the emperor, something Bertin himself made clear in his instructions to the young Chinese Christian clerics. The section numbered ten in his 1765 instruction deals specifically with how the royal gifts from

France were intended to be used.[84] These are of themselves not things that would be personally useful to Ko and Yang, but Bertin envisioned that they should be presented to those carefully chosen mandarins or noblemen from whom they might receive the greatest encouragement and official support in their research. Added comments in Bertin's own handwriting state that gifts should be given, too, to those persons where they might bring about a taste for the arts of France in China. However, while the king, through Bertin, specifies that these are the uses of the gifts, he also permits Ko and Yang to dispose of some of the presents if they should find themselves in a difficult situation and in need of help. Whatever the case, they are to report back to Bertin exactly how the gifts have been distributed and to whom. And in the text of the *Voyage et Séjour*, Ko and Yang agree to follow the king's instructions as they have been transmitted by his minister in regard to the gifts.[85]

When it was time for Ko and Yang to leave France and return to China, they used their remaining time to put in order the journals they had kept on their instruction and training in various arts and techniques; they took with them the texts (*mémoires*) and lists of questions concerning the subjects for which Bertin desired further information, texts that are described previously; they left Paris on 17 January 1765 for the port of Lorient, from where they sailed for China sometime after 25 January on the ship *Duc de Choiseul*.[86] On their return to China, however, Ko and Yang immediately confronted the very real differences between France, the nation they perhaps knew best, and China, their homeland from which they had been absent for so many years. In a long letter dated 12 October 1766, Father Michel Benoist (Jiang Youren 蔣友仁, 1715–1774, arr. China 1744) wrote to Bertin from the French Jesuit Residence in Beijing and described in detail what awaited Ko and Yang at the beginning of their new lives in China.[87] They had originally been under Benoist's supervision in Beijing, but they were so young when they left that they knew little of China, and their education was essentially French. Chinese law strictly regulated and severely punished any contact between Europeans and Chinese, and it was necessary for Father Joseph-Louis Le Febvre (Deng Leisi 鄧類思, 1706-after 1783, act. China 1737–1775), Superior General of the French mission, who by chance was in Canton, to accompany Ko and Yang with as much secrecy as possible to the French Jesuit residence in Beijing.[88] For the French missionaries, their role as privileged foreigners allowed them a certain limited access to the Chinese literati and other distinguished persons, but for Ko and Yang—both as native Chinese Christians and as men poorly educated in any traditional Chinese sense—such contacts would be effectively impossible. If they were to continue their studies and to reply to the many questions that Bertin had prepared for them, Ko and Yang were obliged to remain mostly within the confines of the French mission, where, in any case, they had access to the books in the Jesuits' libraries and from which they would be able to send Bertin the notes and articles he hoped he might obtain from them.[89] Nevertheless, they were able to send a number of texts and letters to Bertin, some of which were eventually published, and their contributions to Bertin's knowledge of China are discussed later.

Much of Benoist's letter from Beijing of October 1766 is taken up with the question of the tapestries Bertin had sent to China with Ko and Yang along with the other fine gifts that ultimately came from Louis XV. In a letter sent from France at about the same time but surely not received until many months later, Bertin wrote to the Ko and Yang in Beijing on 31 December 1766 repeating the king's intentions for the use of the tapestries:

In this case, Gentlemen, the intention of the King is that you take every action so that the tapestries from his Majesty's manufacture, of which he has made you the bearers and which have remained in the storehouses in Canton, should be presented to the Emperor of China, not as a gift from the King, but simply to try to determine by this experiment what the taste of the Emperor might be for the objects from our manufactures and the products of our arts.[90]

The tapestries would become part of a complex negotiation between the French Jesuit missionaries, officials in the port of Canton, and the Qianlong emperor. Benoist noted that part of their original purpose had been to help Ko and Yang establish relationships with those who could further their investigations in China, but not being members of the literati class they could not approach such persons. Access to country estates, manufactures, and other supposedly public spaces was forbidden to those who do not have specific reasons to be there, and Ko and Yang's attempts to go and gather information would surely lead to their arrest and punishment. The possession of valuable European goods would immediately arouse suspicions as well, and such gifts could only be presented to the emperor or imperial princes by those who had official access to them. On their arrival in China, the gifts from France were seized by the Zongdu, the Governor-General of Guangdong, the province that included the city of Canton, who refused to allow them to be sent to Beijing.[91] This was the latest manifestation of an official policy that since 1760 had strictly restricted all communications between the missionaries in Beijing and Canton, including the delivery of letters and books sent from Europe as well as the travels of any new members for the French mission. Benoist detailed the complex negotiations with various court officials necessary to resolve this situation, negotiations which began with a petition to the Qianlong emperor himself. His efforts eventually led to the emperor ordering the reopening of the avenues of communication between Canton and Beijing. As in many of his letters, Benoist expressed his profound gratitude to Bertin and the monarchy for their continued support of the French mission and his hopes that the replies to Bertin's questions sent from China will in some way demonstrate the missionaries' appreciation.[92]

One year later, in a letter dated 10 November 1767, Benoist confirmed the fortunate outcome of the official negotiations in response to his petition, and he described the way in which the tapestries along with Ko and Yang's other "magnificent presents" were ultimately given to the emperor.[93] The tapestries had arrived in Beijing on 8 December 1766, and they were immediately examined and much admired by the Qianlong emperor, who first thought he would display them in an imperial temple. Apparently (we must presume from Benoist's letter) the emperor was aware that the Jesuits would be offended by their use in temples to gods they did not recognize, and he ordered that they be used to decorate the European Palaces of the Yuanming yuan.[94] On learning that none of his European-style buildings was large enough to display them, the emperor ordered the construction of a new building for the tapestries. Plans for the structure called the Yuanying guan 遠瀛觀 (the View of Distant Seas) were completed in 1767, and construction would begin in the spring of the next year, with Benoist taking charge of the hydraulic works and fountains as he had in the earlier constructions on the site. Benoist described the complex court etiquette observed in the presentation of gifts to the Qianlong emperor and, in what he reports as a question-and-answer exchange, relates how he informed the emperor that, although the tapestries were of royal manufacture, they were not a gift from the king of France but from the French Jesuit missionaries.[95] Underlying this distinction was the recognition that a gift from the king of France would be understood as tribute from a vassal state to the emperor of China, a diplomatic relationship that was of course impossible.

Toward the end of the letter of 12 October 1766, Father Benoist had written about the set of questions—the instructions—Bertin had given to Ko and Yang:

> We have the instructions that they brought with them, we will work together little by little to fulfil them. These instructions having arrived late in Beijing, the time does not permit us to send much this year. Father Amiot has worked for a long enough time to bring together what the ancient and contemporary Chinese have written on the art of war; he is taking the liberty of offering Y[our] Exc[ellency] what he has prepared.[96] In the years to come we will send each year as much as time and circumstances permit.[97]

Fully aware of the challenges and limitations posed by Chinese law and custom to Ko and Yang reporting extensively from China, Father Benoist promised that the Jesuits in Beijing would work to fulfill what Bertin had requested. In fact, Ko and Yang would send a significant number of letters and articles to Bertin, but what the French missionaries themselves would send would be truly extraordinary.

Mémoires concernant les Chinois: Images and Texts

The crucial encounter with Ko and Yang established Henri Bertin's direct contact with the French Jesuit missionaries in Beijing and began what he what he would refer to as the "Correspondance littéraire de la Mission française de Pékin."[98] The letters, translations, and articles that Bertin received provided the material for at least two significant books on China. The first was the publication in 1770 of a long poem by the Qianlong emperor, *Éloge de la ville de Moukden*, the "Ode to the city of Mukden," a text translated from the original Manchu by Father Joseph-Marie Amiot (Qian Deming 錢德明, 1718–1793, arr. China 1749), a missionary who would become one of Bertin's most prolific and learned correspondents.[99] The imperial poem is effectively a hymn of praise for the homeland of the Manchu dynasty that would conquer the Ming and establish the Qing dynasty in China in 1644. This text even came to the attention of Voltaire.[100] Father Amiot was also the translator and author of the *Art militaire des Chinois*, literally the "Military art of the Chinese."[101] The book contains translations of a number of important historical texts on the arts of warfare in China as well as an illustrated essay, "Instruction on military exercises," compiled by Amiot himself.[102] The 33 engraved plates are clearly copied from Chinese sources. In the preface to this section, Amiot wrote that those who know military matters would understand better than he what is in the descriptions and that "the simple inspection of the illustrations would perhaps tell them more that all his explanations."[103]

But in 1776, a decade after Ko and Yang's return to China, Bertin sponsored the publication of the first volume of the *Mémoires concernant les Chinois*, the series of books based on what the Ko and Yang and the French missionaries sent from Beijing—the Correspondance littéraire—which would eventually include 15 volumes published in Bertin's lifetime.[104] From the beginning, Henri Bertin had stated his goal that both nations—France and China—would benefit from the direct exchange of knowledge that Ko and Yang could provide. In the preface to the first volume of the *Mémoires*,

Bertin, the ostensible author,[105] asserts that Ko and Yang had come to France as young men because of their desire to make themselves useful to their homeland, and that on their return they could "maintain a correspondence with us that would become reciprocally advantageous to both nations."[106] His words echo many of the objectives of the founders of the French Jesuit mission, the men referred to as the Mathématiciens du Roi. Since 1766, the missionaries and Ko and Yang had almost never failed to send texts each year that would answer what Bertin himself admits are the questions that might indeed have overwhelmed them.[107] As noted earlier, Father Benoist wrote to say that the French missionaries would step in and help fulfill Bertin's requests for knowledge about China. In the preface to the first volume, Bertin also lays out his goals for the subsequent volumes of the *Mémoires concernant les Chinois*. He briefly states that, having already received numerous *mémoires*—the contemporary term for articles, essays, or texts—on the arts and sciences of China, and expecting considerable numbers of such writings to arrive in the future, he has decided that these should be made available to the public. In future issues of the *Mémoires*, articles are to be published as they are received, without distinction among the subjects or the contents, since that is indeed the general practice of the learned journals produced by the various French academies.[108] This statement is followed by a detailed introduction to the contents of the current volume as well as what might be found in future volumes, and, at the end of the preface, Bertin outlines what he hopes France might learn from what is clearly seen as an ideal nation.[109]

Bertin asserts that when the first descriptions of China—he refers specifically to them as observations of facts and events—had been sent to Europe, if they had actually been carefully collected and presented to the public, then Europe would have been in a better position to compare itself with China in the fields of the arts, industry, customs, and government. Clearly, Bertin believed this was not the case with earlier writers, and much of the first volume is dedicated to correcting what are seen as errors in other published sources, although specific titles are not named here. Europe would have seen that this nation, so distant in so many ways, was no less rich or happy, and that Europe might have found something useful to gain from this knowledge. Bertin speculated that the paternal government of imperial China, which reflected the customs and principles of the Chinese nation, was perhaps the one that would most surely lead to the happiness of the people and the true glory of their rulers. It is implicit in Bertin's statements that these are the lessons Europe could learn from China.

The preface ends with a quotation from one of the Jesuit authors of the *Mémoires*, who in all modesty beg the indulgence of their readers. They protest that they are, first of all, missionaries devoted to a goal infinitely more important than these articles, without stating specifically that this goal is the conversion of the ruling elite and emperor of China to the Christian faith. They claim that they are not "savants"—not specialists in any particular field—and here they will provide information on such subjects as physics, natural history, law and government, the practice of arts and crafts, mechanics, gardening, and so forth. Concerned that their work might not be up to the standards of European scholars, they are all the more obliged to be certain that what they send should be as complete and accurate as possible, thus making them worthy of the confidence of those who support them and honor them with their generosity. The accuracy of what the Jesuit missionaries should provide was also described by Yang in a letter to Bertin dated 10 October 1772.[110] He hoped that with time he and the missionaries would have sent many articles that presented a clear and precise idea of China, which up until then had appeared as if through a thick veil. But Yang states that Bertin has spurred on the missionaries, and they are eager to comply with his intentions. Soon it will be clear that the most outstanding previously published works are at least in some respects simply imaginary, and that even the *Description de la Chine* of Du Halde, which Yang considers to be the best among them, has proposed much that might be retracted or at least corrected.[111] This might be accomplished by those among the missionaries who are "lovers of truth" (*amateurs de la vérité*).

The education of Ko and Yang in France and their instructions from Bertin set the stage for the first article in the first volume of *Mémoires concernant les Chinois*, the extended "Essai sur l'Antiquité de la nation Chinoise."[112] Bertin had provided Ko and Yang with three *mémoires*, the letters discussed previously that described what were supposedly the key links between ancient China and a specifically Christian view of history. The "Essai" begins with a brief message to Bertin signed "Ko, Jés[uit]," ostensibly identifying Aloys Ko as the author.[113] The preface to the volume also introduces the contents of this important essay by first summarizing in some detail the questions to which it is addressed, that of the origins of Chinese civilization, and specifically of the sometimes bitter disputes among writers of the seventeenth and eighteenth centuries centering on the supposed relationship between ancient China and ancient Egypt. Even Bertin refers to this as a "literary war,"[114] one which might strike modern readers as absurd, but which was treated with utmost seriousness and scholarly attention at the time.[115] This supposed relationship between ancient civilizations raised three interconnected questions. Was China somehow linked to Egypt? Was an imagined Chinese "monotheism" somehow the result of China being the place where people had settled after the Biblical flood? Could this be proven by linking Chinese characters to Egyptian hieroglyphs?

The controversy involved the assertion by the English scholar, Roman Catholic priest, and member of the Royal Society, John Turberville Needham (1713–1781), that what was supposedly a bust of the Egyptian goddess Isis in Turin was inscribed with hieroglyphs that could be compared with Chinese characters. Needham's research, first published in 1761 in his *De Inscriptione quâdam Ægyptiacâ Taurini*,[116] was sent to the Jesuits in Beijing, and Father Amiot responded to his assertions by maintaining the unique history of Chinese writing. His thinking is contained in a long letter of 20 October 1764, first published in 1765 and that was reprinted in this first volume of the *Mémoires*.[117] The publication in the *Mémoires* even included a note from Needham himself explaining how he had conducted his original research, working with, among others, a "Chinese born in Peking" and attached to the Vatican Library.[118] A set of engraved plates at the end of the volume illustrates Chinese characters in various ancient forms, including three plates (VI, VII, and VIII) that include direct comparisons with Egyptian "figures," as well as a plate showing the so-called bust of Isis (the last plate, not numbered). The plates are integral to the discussion of the question at hand, and they are referred to in Amiot's letter on the true nature and sources of Chinese writing. Given the lack of any but the most basic knowledge of Egyptian hieroglyphic writing, Amiot, like others before him, was obliged to rely on assumptions based on visual images—what he perceived in the pictorial Egyptian script.

The foreword (*Avant-propos*) to the second volume of the *Mémoires concernant les Chinois* notes that the main content here is a long dissertation entitled "The Antiquity of the Chinese Proved by their Monuments," where "monuments" has the eighteenth-century sense of literary monuments, works of history, and the classics. Given that some of the discussion here differs from what had been published in the first volume, this is cited as a demonstration that the contributors had not worked in concert but had pursued their own research, and that "the Savants of Europe can compare the facts and the proofs, and derive from them their own results."[119] The text is followed by a large number of plates, some 37 in all, with their extensive explanations and commentaries, which effectively make up a little more than half of the volume.[120] The foreword also describes Amiot as finding suggestive parallels with Christian tradition, a recurring theme that is not surprising given the role of the author, Father Amiot, as a Jesuit missionary.[121] It describes the article as perhaps a bit "arid" but maintains that savants will find it fascinating, and even Amiot himself in the introduction to his writing fears that all the detail might be a bit dull, but he feels it is necessary to present the minimum of information that would support his assertions. The plates themselves are a mixture of charts, diagrams, illustrations, maps, and a substantial number of tables or lists of names and terms. The schematic illustrations and maps are clearly based on Chinese sources—manuscripts, books, or woodblock prints—and it is likely that most of these were copied or redrawn by Bertin's Jesuit correspondents. And a few include Chinese characters.

The question of illustrations is crucial to the communication of knowledge from China in the *Mémoires concernant les Chinois*, underscoring the repetition in texts sent to Bertin of assertions that whatever written words might fail to communicate would be made clear by illustrations. On many of the documents sent to Bertin is the note, often in his own distinctive handwriting, "see the paintings" (*voyez les peintures*), which indicates that the text was accompanied by illustrations, and we will see that these covered a remarkable range of styles and quality. In the broadest terms, illustrations in the earlier volumes tend to be closer to their original Chinese sources, and perhaps the clearest example of the direct reproduction of Chinese images in the *Mémoires concernant les Chinois* is provided by the illustrations that accompany the "Portraits of celebrated Chinese figures" in Volume 3. The portraits are mostly short texts assembled by Father Amiot, but six of them are illustrated by engravings that replicate Chinese paintings.[122] In the preface to Volume 1 of the *Mémoires*, Bertin had already announced that he had "portraits or brief lives" of famous Chinese figures throughout history that had been prepared by Father Amiot. The first selection of some 52 of these biographies appeared in Volume 3 of the *Mémoires* in 1778, and one of them is a short biography of Confucius, which was illustrated by an engraved portrait (Figure 1.2). The biography emphasizes Confucius' efforts to bring virtue and good morals to the various kingdoms of ancient China, it describes what were traditionally believed to be Confucius' compilations or commentaries on classical texts, and it tells of the role of his many disciples in compiling the "Great Learning," the "Doctrine of the Mean," and the *Analects*. Two footnotes in this biography refer the reader to Volume 1, where translations of these two crucial Confucian texts, the "Great Learning" (the *Daxue* 大學) and the "Doctrine of the Mean" (*Zhongyong* 中庸), had already been published.[123] However, the biography itself is very brief, just two pages long, and contains only the bare outline of Confucius' life and career, but it ends with a statement from Amiot that he will provide a biography of this sage in greater detail.[124]

Amiot had originally obtained a Chinese album that contained mostly bust-length portraits of famous historical figures facing short biographical texts in Chinese.[125] That album, dated to 1685, was intended by Amiot to be presented to the Bibliothèque

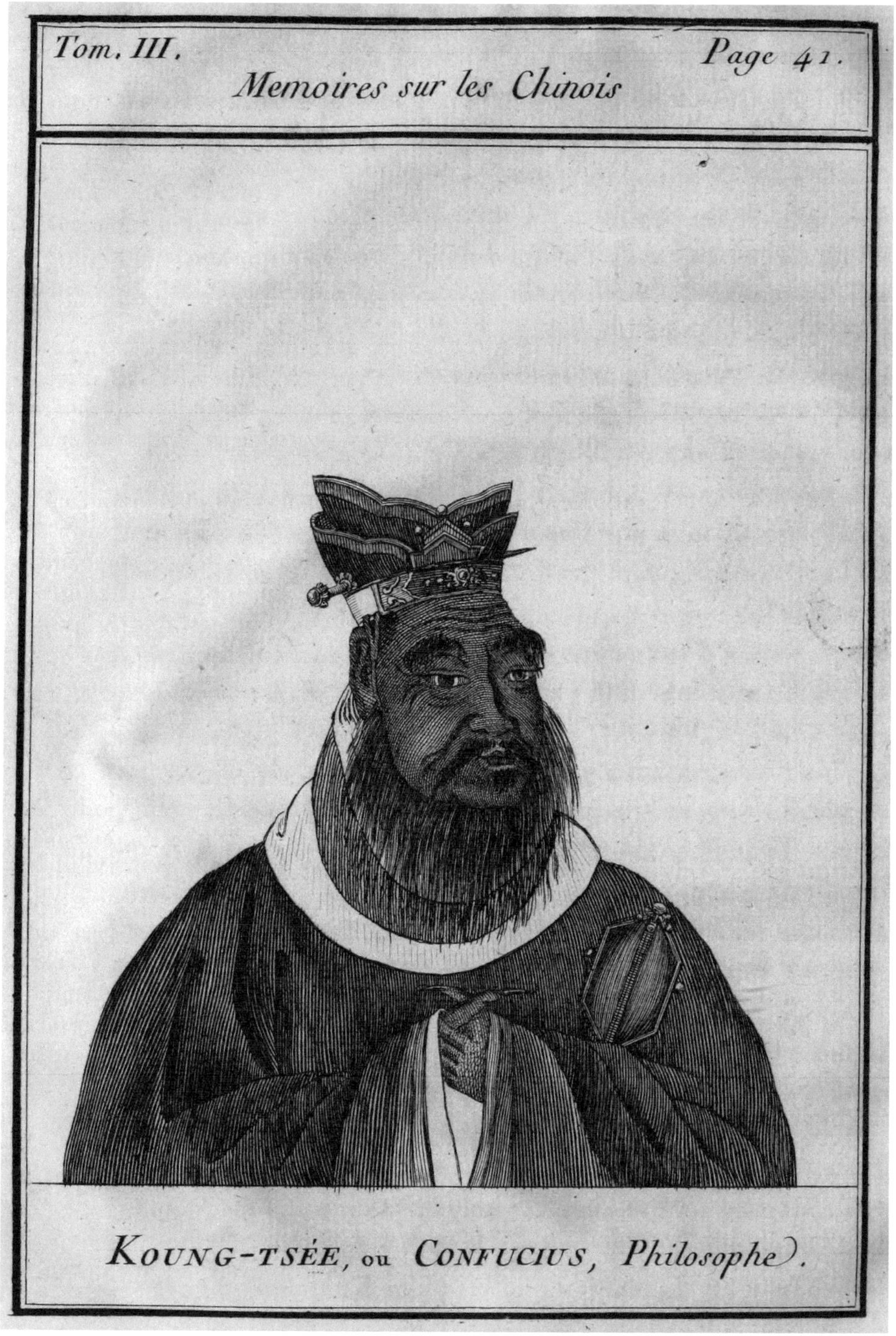

Figure 1.2 Anonymous, "*Koung-tsee*, ou Confucius, Philosophe," engraving, overall 25 × 20 cm, *Mémoires concernant les Chinois*, vol. 3 (1778), facing p. 41. Paris, Bibliothèque nationale de France.

du Roi, the French royal library. But he realized that the subjects would be of great interest to Bertin, so he wrote in October of 1771 that he was also sending a set of copies of the paintings from the 1685 album.[126] Those copies, now bound in ten volumes, contain painted portraits and Amiot's biographies, and they are the source of the publications in the *Mémoires concernant les Chinois*.[127] The engraved portrait of Confucius closely follows the format and details of the Chinese painting (Plate 1). The work of an anonymous Chinese artist, the portrait of Confucius is inscribed in Amiot's distinctive handwriting "Koung-Tsée, ou Confucius," with the number 22 and the Chinese characters Kongzi 孔子.[128] This small painting on paper is now detached from the album in which it was originally included.[129] Details of the costume and the pose identify this image as a portrait of Confucius as the Minister of Justice in the ancient state of Lu.[130] The figure of Confucius would later take on much greater significance for Bertin. The extended "Life of Confucius" accompanied by 18 engraved illustrations that appeared in Volume 12 of the *Mémoires* in 1783, a text discussed in Chapter 4 of the present volume, is central to understanding Henri Bertin's own self-perception.

Fidelity to their Chinese sources also distinguishes the 12 engravings published in 1783 in Volume 9 of the *Mémoires*, which reproduce a selection of paintings from a Chinese album sent to Bertin in 1767.[131] In one of the rare instances where Chinese paintings are discussed as art, the album was described by the missionary who sent it to Bertin as an original work, something a Chinese would purchase in the same way a European would purchase paintings by great masters, as one of the finest parts of his heritage.[132] The missionary's notes and the translation of the Chinese texts identify the subject of the album: the flooding of the city of Yanzhou fu[133] in Zhejiang province in 1742 and the Qianlong emperor's response in relieving the suffering of the region's inhabitants. The emperor's benevolence is situated in a historical context going back to ancient times, in terms of both immediate aid to flood victims and the construction of water projects that would prevent flooding and the ravages of drought in the long term. The 1742 flood was particularly devastating, and the emperor ordered the distribution of rice to the people, the reconstruction of their homes and fields, and other long-term measures. The Chinese text at the beginning of the album praises a nation that is so well governed in what is surely meant to be understood as an implicit model for France.[134] Details of the text facing the 12 paintings chosen for reproduction are also carefully translated.

The painting reproduced as plate I shows the general situation of Yanzhou fu, with the walled city on the banks of the Xin'an River and surrounded by mountains. The composition is based on a visual convention that merges a landscape painting seen from an elevated viewpoint with what is effectively a map of the region. The explanation of the plate notes that it is necessary to see this to understand how truly unbelievable the flooding was. Plate II (Figure 1.3) depicts the inundated city with many people rescued from the waters taking refuge on the city walls, others fleeing in boats, and more people across the river on the high ground around a pagoda. The following plates show such subjects as boats rescuing people in the flooded countryside and the distribution of as much rice as could be immediately saved. Most, however, concentrate on the long-term actions of the government, including rebuilding of houses, replanting of the rice fields, distribution of rice to all the people, the visit of the provincial governor to see that his orders were being carried out, the reconstruction of the city walls and bridges, and finally an assembly of the citizens before the governor

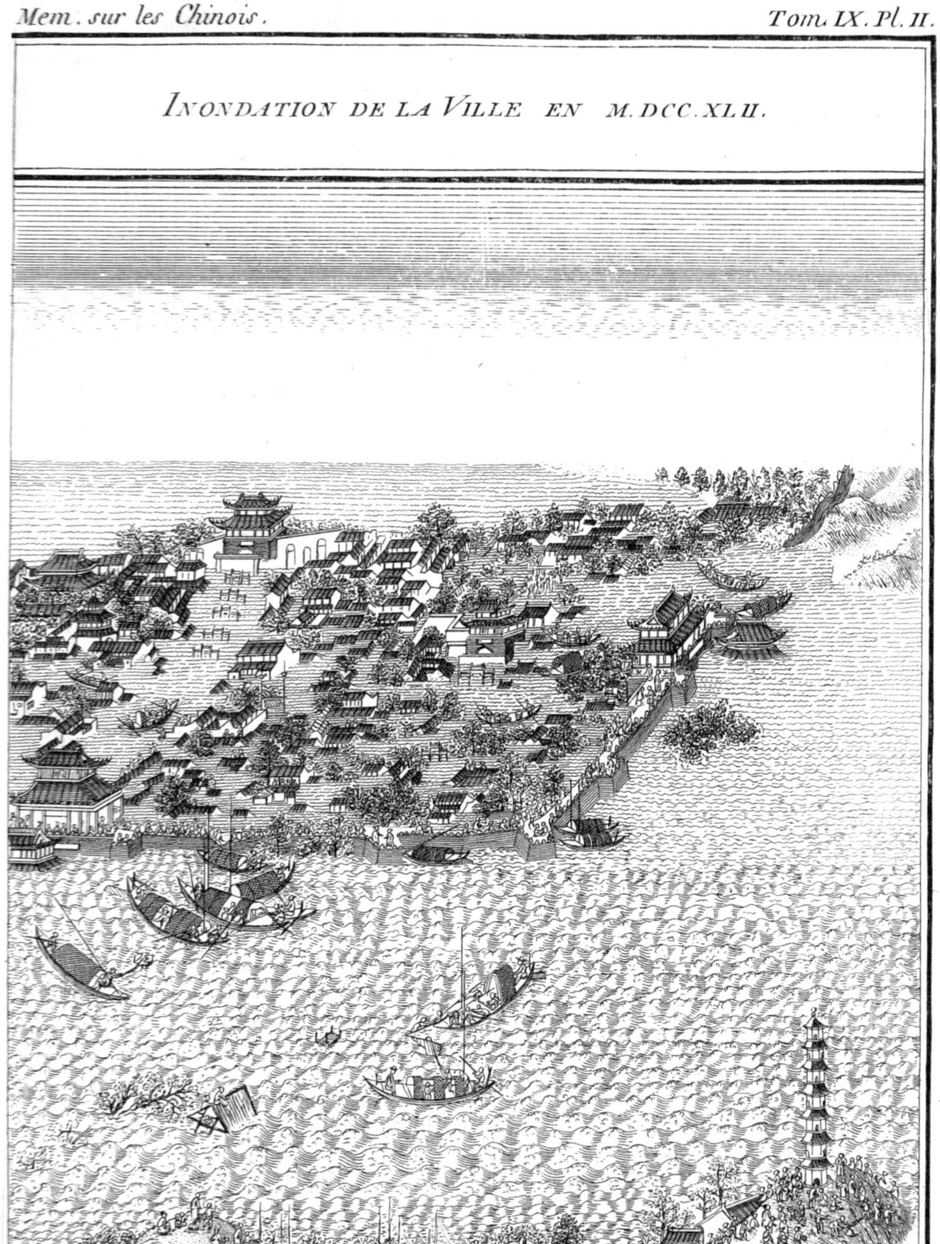

Figure 1.3 "Flooding of Yanzhou fu in 1742," engraving, ca. 1783, overall 25 × 20 cm, *Mémoires concernant les Chinois*, vol. 9, pl. II. Getty Research Institute, Los Angeles (41–499).

of the city to ask that their extraordinary gratitude be communicated to the emperor by a special document. While the engraved plates appear to closely copy the Chinese originals, the style of the paintings would appear in general to reflect an eighteenth-century pictorial idiom seen in official, imperial paintings such as the handscrolls that represent the Kangxi and Qianlong emperors' Southern Inspection Tours.[135] In the broadest terms, such paintings combine Chinese characteristics like the elevated viewpoint that provides an overview of the landscape with a European sense of perspective where figures and buildings diminish in scale in the distance.

The conclusion of the Chinese text at the beginning of the album contains an elaborate statement on how this essay, attributed to a member of the Hanlin Academy named Songnan,[136] might not fully express the horrors of the flood or the depth of the people's gratitude for the bountiful goodwill of the emperor for all of the empire to know. Thus the people of Yanzhou fu had recourse to a set of paintings that would "speak to the eyes" and present as fully as possible the true picture of these events, with the hope that they would inspire in all who saw them feelings of respect and love for the emperor. This statement of the role of painted images in the communication of knowledge beyond what words alone could convey is a surprising parallel with statements repeated a number of times by the Jesuit missionaries in the texts sent to Bertin which accompanied painted illustrations. In the following chapters we shall see how crucial images—paintings and prints—were to the transfer of knowledge of all kinds between Qing China and late eighteenth-century France.

Notes

1. Bib. Inst. Ms 1520, fols. 50–55, *Voyage et Séjour en France par Ordre du Roi de deux particuliers Chinois, les Sieurs Kô & Yang*. The text is an incomplete 12-page printer's proof with a note asking if the proof is acceptable, in which case the printer will produce 20 copies. Described as an *ouvrage*, it may have been a booklet or book.
2. Ko and Yang is one way of referring to these two men, but there are a number of variants of their names in contemporary and modern sources. Birthdates cited for the two are also inconsistent. Ko is the equivalent of Kao or the pinyin Gao, and his Chinese name is given as Gao Ren 高仁 (b. 1732) or Gao Leisi 高類思. He is variously referred to as Louis, Aloys, or Aloïs Kô. Étienne Yang's Chinese name is Yang Zhide 楊 執 德 (1733–1798?) or Yang Dewang 楊 德望. See Joseph Dehergne, S.J., *Répertoire des Jésuites de Chine de 1552 à 1800* (Roma: Institutum Historicum; Paris: Letouzey & Ané, 1973), nos. 425, 911. Notes on p. 1 of the *Voyage et Séjour* give their names as Ko Gin (i.e., Gao Ren) and Yang Tche Te (Yang Zhide) and provide translations of what the Chinese characters mean.
3. The Jesuit mission in Beijing that was first established under Louis XIV in 1684–1685 is discussed in Nathalie Monnet, "Le Jeune duc du Maine, Protecteur des premières missions françaises en Chine," in Marie-Laure de Rochebrune, ed., *La Chine à Versailles: Art et diplomatie au XVIIIe siècle* (Paris: Somogy Éditions d'Art, 2014), 36–43. See also Isabelle Landry-Deron, "Les Mathématiciens envoyés en Chine par Louis XIV en 1685," *Archive for History of Exact Sciences* 55, no. 5 (April 2001), 423–463; especially the "Introduction," 423–424. Administration of the French Jesuit mission was one responsibility of Bertin's ministry and, after the suppression of the Jesuit order in 1773, Louis XVI guaranteed the financial support of the French missionaries still in Beijing. See Camille de Rochemonteix, S.J., *Joseph Amiot et les derniers survivants de la mission française à Pékin (1750–1795)* (Paris: Librairie Alphonse Picard et fils, 1915), 216ff. On the official designation as Mathématiciens du Roi, see Catherine Marin, "La mission française de Pékin après la suppression de la compagnie de Jésus en 1773," *Transversalités* 107

(2008/3), 9–28; see esp. 14–15, n. 10, where Marin cites Henri Bernard-Maître, S.J., "Le voyage du père de Fontaney au Siam et à la Chine, 1685–1687, d'après des lettres inédites," *Bulletin de l'Université l'Aurore* (1942), 227–280.

4. Landry-Deron, "Les Mathématiciens envoyés en Chine," 424.
5. See Marin, "La mission française de Pékin." See also Henri Cordier, "La Suppression de la Compagnie de Jésus et la mission de Peking," *T'oung Pao* 17, no. 3 (July 1916), 271–347; and 17, no. 4/5 (October–December 1916), 561–623.
6. See the official site of the Académie des Sciences, www.academie-sciences.fr/fr/Histoire-de-l-Academie-des-sciences/histoire-de-l-academie-des-sciences.html, accessed 10 February 2017. Colbert at the time was Surintendant et ordonnateur général des bâtiments, arts, tapisseries et manufactures de France, among other official functions.
7. Isabelle Landry-Deron, "'Pour la perfection des sciences et des arts': La Mission Jésuite française en Chine sous le patronage de l'Académie royale," in Pierre-Sylvain Filliozat and others, eds., *L'œuvre scientifique des missionnaires en Asie* (Paris: Académie des Inscriptions et Belles-Lettres, 2011), 77–96; see esp. 77 and n. 1. Fontaney's letter from China appeared in vol. 7 of the *Lettres édifiantes et curieuses* (Paris, 1707), 65–66; it records parts of the conversation he had with Colbert: "dans le temps où ils ne sont pas si occupés à la Prédication de l'Évangile, il fissent sur les lieux quantié d'observations, qui nous manquent pour la perfection des Sciences & des Arts." See the reference to the *Lettres édifiantes et curieuses* in n. 10. Unless otherwise indicated, all translations are my own.
8. See Dictionnaire Littré online, http://littre.reverso.net/dictionnaire-francais/: *arts* [1], for the many meanings of the term, including the definition "Arts mécaniques, ceux qui exigent surtout le travail de la main." The interpretation here is broadly based on the requests sent from France and the materials the Jesuit missionaries sent in return.
9. For an in-depth discussion of the French Jesuit mission to China in relation to the Royal Academy, see Landry-Deron, "'Pour la perfection des sciences et des arts'."
10. The *Lettres édifiantes et curieuses, écrites des Missions étrangères, par quelques missionnaires de la Compagnie de Jésus* were edited by several different Jesuits over this period; additional editions and selections appeared in 1780–1783, 1810–1811, 1819, 1829–1832, and so forth, and selections have been translated into English, German, Italian, and other languages. See the basic bibliographic information on the website of the Bibliothèque nationale de France (BnF), http://catalogue.bnf.fr/ark:/12148/cb328061927, accessed 28 August 2016.
11. Jean-Baptiste Du Halde, *Description géographique, historique, chronologique, politique et physique de l'Empire de la Chine et de la Tartarie chinoise. . .*, 4 vols. (Paris: P.-G. Le Mercier, 1735); for a superb study of Du Halde's achievement, see Isabelle Landry-Deron, *La preuve par la Chine: la "Description" de J.-B. Du Halde, jésuite, 1735* (Paris: Éd. de l'École des hautes études en sciences sociales, 2002). Henri Bertin's publication of the first volume of the *Mémoires concernant les Chinois* in 1776 refers to Du Halde's work; see the following discussion.
12. For the list of questions to take back to China, see "Questions à proposer au R.P. Couplet sur le royaume de la Chine," in Virgile Pinot, *Documents inédits relatifs à la connaissance de la Chine en France de 1685 à 1740* (Paris: P. Geuthner, 1932; reprint Geneva: Slatkine, 1971), 7–9. Pinot, ibid., n. 1, provides information on his archival sources. See also Landry-Deron, *La preuve par la Chine*; in Chap. 5, Annexe V, 176–179, "Mise en regard du questionnaire de l'Académie des Sciences de 1684 avec les passages de la *Description* qui lui founissent des réponses." Landry-Deron notes here the passages of Du Halde's *Description* that respond to the questions from the Académie des Sciences.
13. Landry-Deron, "Les Mathématiciens envoyés en Chine," esp. 444–450, and see Landry-Deron, "'Pour la perfection des sciences et des arts'," 95–96.
14. Landry-Deron, *La preuve par la Chine*, Chap. III.3, "La pénétration de l'Empire chinois," 74–77. See also Virgile Pinot, *La Chine et la formation de l'esprit philosophique en France: 1640–1740* (Paris: P. Geuthner, 1932; reprint Geneva: Slatkine, 1971), 24–25, 40–41, 48–49 passim.
15. For a recent study of the training and careers of the most important Italian painters in Qing China with numerous references to archival documentation, see Marco Musillo, *The Shining Inheritance: Italian Painters at the Qing Court, 1699–1812* (Los Angeles: Getty Research Institute, 2016).

16. The literature on Jesuit missionary painters in China is extensive. For a seminal study, see Michel Beurdeley, *Peintres jésuites en Chine au XVIIIe siècle* (Arcueil: Anthèse, 1997). On the role of European painters in the uses of perspective and the production of trompe-l'oeil paintings for the Qianlong emperor, see Kristina Kleutghen, *Imperial Illusions: Crossing Pictorial Boundaries in the Qing Palaces* (Seattle and London: University of Washington Press, 2015).
17. Research on the early churches in Beijing is wide-ranging, and there remain questions of historical details and the identification of images of specific church buildings. For a very brief summary of the three main Christian Churches in Beijing in the eighteenth century, see Gauvin Alexander Bailey, *Art on the Jesuit Missions in Asia and Latin America, 1542–1773* (Toronto: University of Toronto Press, 1999), 109–111. Each of the churches had an elaborately painted interior. The North Church (Beitang 北堂, built 1703) belonged to the French mission and was decorated by Giovanni Gherardini, briefly active in China in the years 1699–1704, who painted a false dome and the high altar. The South Church (Nantang 南堂) was founded in 1650 and rebuilt in 1703 and again included a trompe-l'oeil dome. The East Church (Dongtang 東堂, built in 1729) housed the Jesuit library and the vault and illusionistic cupola were painted by Castiglione.
18. Marco Musillo, "Bridging Europe and China: The Professional Life of Giuseppe Castiglione (1688–1766)," PhD diss., School of World Art and Museology, University of East Anglia, United Kingdom, April 2006; see esp. 90ff. My thanks to Musillo for making the thesis available to me. See also Musillo, *The Shining Inheritance*.
19. See the references to the *Shixue* in Chap. 3 of the present volume. See also Musillo, *The Shining Inheritance*, 118–120.
20. Andrea Pozzo, *Perspectiva Pictorum et Architectorum* (first Roman edition, 1693), English ed., *Rules and Examples of Perspective Proper for Painters and Architects* (London, 1707, reprint, *Perspective in Architecture and Painting*, New York: Dover Books, 1989), 12, here substituting "dare" for "durst" for clarity, and other minor changes.
21. Musillo, "Bridging Europe and China," 136–137, interprets the single vanishing point of *quadratura* painting, the specific illusionistic perspective rendering techniques that are the subject of Pozzo's treatise, not as a direct analogy but rather as an implication that God is behind all geometry and, thus, all reality.
22. The diffusion of painting styles outside the court workshops is a little-studied phenomenon. On the formation of a so-called Northern school of figure painters whose style was derived from court painting in the early Qing, see James Cahill, "A Group of Anonymous Northern Figure Paintings from the Qianlong Period," http://jamescahill.info/the-writings-of-james-cahill/a-group-of-anonymous-northern-figure-paintings-from-the-qianlong, accessed 31 October 2015. And see also Cahill, *Pictures for Use and Pleasure: Vernacular Painting in High Qing China* (Berkeley: University of California Press, 2010); esp. Chap. 2, "Studio Artists in Cities and Court," 31–65.
23. Ko and Yang's parents all have French names, an indication of their faith; brief characterizations of them indicate their social class and education; see *Voyage et Séjour*, 2. For a detailed description of Ko and Yang and their family background, see Bernard-Maître, "Deux Chinois du XVIIIème siècle à l'école des physiocrates français"; see esp. 154ff., nn. 10–13. Bernard-Maître describes Ko as the son of former Christians of modest background and Yang as coming from the countryside outside Beijing. Father Michel Benoist (see the references to Benoist later) wrote to Bertin in 1766, describing Ko and Yang as young and without knowledge of the world when they were first in contact with the French Jesuit mission.
24. Joseph Dehergne, S.J., "Voyageurs chinois venus à Paris au temps de la marine à voiles et l'influence de la Chine sur la littérature française du XVIIIe siècle," *Monumenta Serica* 23 (1964), 372–397, see esp. 381–382.
25. The Compagnie des Indes was only briefly attached to Bertin's ministry, in 1763–1764, as cited by the BnF, http://catalogue.bnf.fr/ark:/12148/cb124915923.public, accessed 28 October 2016. Jacques Silvestre de Sacy, *Henri Bertin dans le sillage de la Chine: 1720–1792* (Paris: Editions Cathasia; les Belles lettres, 1970), 48–49, cites Bertin's jurisdiction as lasting only briefly in 1764.
26. "M.gr Bertin, Ministre & Secrétaire d'Etat, prévenu en notre faveur, a voulu nous rendre utiles à la France & en même temps à la Chine: en conséquence nous avons été engagés à différer notre voyage à un an." See p. 10 of the *Voyage et Séjour*, Bib. Inst. Ms 1520.

27. This phase of Ko and Yang's instruction is described in Bernard-Maître, "Deux Chinois," 157–160.
28. Ko and Yang then express their gratitude to Bertin and the king of France in the *Voyage et Séjour*, but the printer's proof only includes the first 12 pages of the work and ends here in mid-sentence.
29. For Mathurin-Jacques Brisson, see Bernard-Maître, "Deux Chinois," 165ff.; for Cadet de Gassicourt, see ibid., 181.
30. Pierre Poivre led an adventurous life, including travel to China beginning in 1741, where he became deeply interested in questions of agriculture. See the website dedicated to Pierre Poivre, www.pierre-poivre.fr/, accessed 31 October 2016. See also the *Oeuvres complettes de P. Poivre, . . . Précédées de sa vie, et accompagnées de notes* (Paris: Fuchs, 1797).
31. *Instructions*, like *mémoire* ("article" or "memorandum"), is the term used for documents prepared for Ko and Yang, including the directions on how they should maintain their correspondence with Bertin, which are described later. The text here, dated only to the year 1764, is found in Bib. Inst. Ms 1520, fols. 23–33, where it is entitled "Mémoire sur ce que les chinois doivent voir en France avant retournée [*sic*] en Chine"; it is transcribed in Bernard-Maître, "Deux Chinois," 167–174, where Bernard-Maître corrects the grammatical errors in the original French.
32. The document was drafted under the direction of Melchior-François Parent (1716–1782), who served as *premier commis*, kind of high-level clerk or assistant, for finances under Bertin; he also functioned as Bertin's secretary in his correspondence with the Jesuit missionaries. See Silvestre de Sacy, *Sillage*, 51–52.
33. Bib. Inst. Ms 1520, fols. 29–30, marked "Article très important!"
34. Annonay is still the center of fine handmade paper manufacture in France.
35. The subject of paper is one that also raised in Turgot's famous "Questions" to Ko and Yang; see the following discussion.
36. Bib. Inst. Ms 1520, fol. 32.
37. See Bernard-Maître, "Deux Chinois," 160. For the Imprimerie royale, which functioned from 1640–1797, see Auguste Bernard, *Histoire de l'imprimerie royale du Louvre* (Paris: Imprimerie impériale, 1867).
38. The "Remarques sur différentes manufactures" are found in Bib. Inst. Ms 1520, fols. 40–47; see Bernard-Maître, "Deux Chinois," 161–165, for a complete transcription of the manuscript. The descriptions of each of the manufactures are followed by comments entitled "Réflections." However, no document from Bertin setting out what they should examine at these royal manufactures seems to have survived.
39. The first object of hard-paste porcelain, manufactured in 1765 or possibly slightly later, was a small sculpture of Bacchus as a child; damaged by Allied bombing in 1942, only the head remains in the collection of Sèvres Cité de la Céramique, acc. no. MNC 1830. See Silvestre de Sacy, *Sillage*, chap. IX, "La Manufacture de porcelaine de Sèvres," 113.
40. The manuscript containing their second set of replies to Bertin is found in Bib. Inst. Ms 1520, fols. 34–39; the complete text is transcribed in Bernard-Maître, "Deux Chinois," 176–180.
41. See the following detailed discussion of the *Mémoires concernant les Chinois*; the citation here is from vol. 1, Préface, p. iii: "On crut ensuite qu'il étoit important de leur faire prendre quelque teinture du dessein & de l'art de graver; puisque dans l'éloignement d'une correspondance aussi intéressante que celle dont on jettoit les fondemens, le dessein d'une machine, d'un métier d'étoffe, d'un instrument, d'une plante, devoit suppléer ce qui manque aux descriptions les plus détaillées, & les surpasser infiniment. Au bout de quelques mois ils furent l'un & l'autre en état de graver eux-mêmes à l'eau-forte, des vues de paysages Chinois." Much of the Préface is taken up with the story of Ko and Yang. See Chao-Ying Lee, *Visions de l'Empire du Milieu au 18e siècle en France: Illustrations des* Mémoires concernant les Chinois *(1776–1791)* (Paris: L'Harmattan, 2016), 32, n. 77, where the author discusses Ko and Yang's training and cites this same passage.
42. It is unclear which one is the actual artist of the individual prints, since they bear no signature and there are only a few indications on the prints and drawings, which are bound into Bib. Inst. Ms 1520, fols. 8–13. Three pencil sketches based on Dutch sources

(showing a windmill, for example) are pasted together as fol. 9 are inscribed "Mr. Kao," "Yang fecit," and "Mr. Yang." Two careful copies of botanical illustrations in pencil and ink wash form fol. 8, and they are each inscribed "Mr. Yang." The etchings on fols. 10–13 are unsigned.

43. The series is also known by names such as the "Illustrations of Tilling and Weaving." For the genesis and early history of the series, see Roslyn Lee Hammers, *Pictures of Tilling and Weaving: Art, Labor and Technology in Song and Yuan China* (Hong Kong: Hong Kong University Press, 2011). For a concise description of the Kangxi-era woodcut edition, see Philip K. Hu, ed., *Visible Traces: Rare Book and Special Collections from the National Library of China* (New York: Queens Borough Public Library; Beijing: National Library of China, 2000), cat. 17. See also Nathalie Monnet, *Le Gengzhitu: Le livre du riz et de la soie* (Paris: J.C. Lattès, 2003); and Nathalie Monnet, *Chine: l'Empire du trait: calligraphies et dessins du Ve au XIXe siècle* (Paris: Bibliothèque nationale de France, 2004), cat. 115, "*Yuzhi Gengzhitu*," 181–184.
44. See John Lagerwey and Pierre Marsone, eds., *Modern Chinese Religion I: Song-Liao-Jin-Yuan (960–1368 AD)* (Leiden: Brill, 2015), Introduction, 33.
45. Bib. Inst. Ms 1520, fol. 130, "[livre] de labourage et vers à soie."
46. Both albums are listed in an inventory of "prints and engraved plates" from the Émigré Bertin, dated in accordance with 16 April 1796, Département des Estampes et de la photographie, Réserves, document no. 397, recto. Item no. 12 is "La Culture du Riz en dessins de Figures. in fol°. Dessin." It is followed by no. 14, "Riz et Vers à Soye. in fol°." The two albums are currently catalogued as Reserve Oe-89–4 and Reserve Oe-90-Pet Fol.
47. On the role of European linear perspective and its specific application to technological imagery and the *Gengzhi tu*, see Roslyn Lee Hammers, "Perspectives in Early Qing-Dynasty *Pictures of Tilling and Weaving* and *Pictures of Cotton*," *Historia Scientiarum* 21, no. 1 (2011), 3–19.
48. For an in-depth presentation and analysis of the political context and implications of the creation of the *Gengzhi tu*, see Francesca Bray, "Agricultural Illustrations: Blueprint or Icon?" In Francesca Bray et al., eds., *Graphics and Text in the Production of Technical Knowledge in China: The Warp and the Weft* (Leiden and Boston: Brill, 2007), 521–567. Bray also considers in detail questions of the transmission of knowledge by means of texts and images.
49. That is, he functioned as tax collector for the central government's administrative region centered on Limoges. For a brief note on Turgot's relationship to Bertin, see Silvestre de Sacy, *Sillage*, 58.
50. The list is generally entitled "Questions sur la Chine, addressées à MM. Ko et Yang." The *Réflexions* and Turgot's "Questions" have been frequently published; see Anne-Robert-Jacques Turgot, *Oeuvres de M. Turgot, Ministre d'État, . . . Précédées et accompagnées de Mémoires et de Notes sur sa Vie, son Administration, et ses Ouvrages*, Pierre Samuel Du Pont de Nemours, ed., 9 vols. (Paris: Imprimerie de Delance, 1808–1811); see esp. vol. 5, "Questions," 140–165.
51. On the question of Adam Smith's relationship to Turgot's *Réflexions*, see "Observations sur les points dans lequels Smith est d'accord avec la théorie de M. Turgot, et sur ceux dans lesquels il s'en est écarté," *Oeuvres de M. Turgot, Ministre d'État* 5 (1808), 130–139.
52. A succinct discussion of Turgot's questions to Ko and Yang is found in Isabelle Landry-Deron, "La curiosité de Turgot à l'égard de la Chine: Regard sur ses cinquante-deux questions à Ko et Yang," paper for the *Colloque International Turgot (1727–1780), Notre Contemporain? Économie, Administration et Gouvernement au Siècle des Lumières* (Université de Caen, 14–16 May 2003). I am grateful to Prof. Landry-Deron for providing me a copy of the presentation, and the discussion here is indebted to Landry-Deron's research.
53. "Du Papier, de l'encre, des pinceaux, de l'imprimerie, et de la relieure des livres de la Chine," Du Halde, *Description de la Chine*, vol. 2, 286–301.
54. Jérôme de La Lande, *Art de faire le papier* (Paris: Saillant et Nyon, 1761); see esp. "Du Papier de la Chine," 115–120.
55. *Descriptions des arts et métiers, faites ou approuvées par messieurs de l'Académie royale des sciences, avec figures en taille douce*, 113 vols. (Paris, 1761–1788). The *Encyclopédie*

of D'Alembert and Diderot was in direct competition with this series, and the *Encyclopédie* copied many illustrations and edited texts from the *Descriptions des Arts et Métiers*. The articles on *papétrie* appeared in vol. 11 of the *Encyclopédie* in 1765; the corresponding plates appeared in vol. 22 in 1767.

56. D'Entrecolles letter was actually first published in the *Recueil de voyages au nord: contenant divers mémoires très utiles au commerce & à la navigation*, Jean-Frédéric Bernard, ed., vol. 10, the last volume of the series (Amsterdam: Jean Frédéric Bernard, 1738), 305–376. However, the publication in the *Lettres édifiantes et curieuses: écrite des missions etrangères*, vol. 12 (Paris, 1741), 253–365, is widely cited as the first publication, and this edition is apparently the source of the many later reprints and translations.
57. A striking statement of Manchu identity was published in Amiot's translation of the Qianlong emperor's *Éloge de la ville de Moukden et de ses environs . . .* (Paris: N.M. Tilliard, 1770). This lyric poem in praise of Mukden, considered the heart of the Manchu nation before the Qing conquest of China, was published in Manchu and Chinese in 1748, and Amiot's preface as translator and the emperor's preface to his poem refer to the unique qualities of the Manchu people. On the Qianlong emperor's poem, the "Yuzhi Shengjing fu" 御制盛京赋, see Mark C. Elliott, "The Limits of Tartary: Manchuria in Imperial and National Geographies," *The Journal of Asian Studies* 59, no. 3 (August 2000), 603–646; see esp. 614–617.
58. Bib. Inst. Ms 1521, fols. 60–71; the text is briefly referred to in Bernard-Maître, "Deux Chinois," 158–159, n. 33; and 185, n. 119. The manuscript bears the date "16 janvier 1765" on the first and the last sheet, but in both cases it is written in a different handwriting from the rest and it is not clear who added the dates. The title reads: "Instruction pour M. Ko et pour M. Yang."
59. The 11 sections are numbered in roman numerals added in the margin of the original document; it is not immediately clear when the numbering was added.
60. The text here is supplemented by a note in Bertin's handwriting providing additional details on the choice of a correspondent, including the superior of the French mission or someone associated with the French East India Company.
61. The section numbers VII. and VIII. are switched in the manuscript.
62. Bib. Inst. Ms 1521, fols. 66 verso–69 verso. A significant part of the "Instruction" to Ko and Yang is transcribed in Henri Cordier, "Les Chinois de Turgot," in Cordier, *Mélanges d'histoire et de géographie orientales*, vol. 2 (Paris: J. Maisonneuve, 1920), 31–39; see esp. 35–39, where the transcriptions appear without citing a source.
63. Two documents exactly match this description, especially for the history of origin of the world, the first generations, the deluge, and so forth; see Bib. Inst. Ms 1521, fols. 29–46, and fols. 47–56.
64. See ibid., fol. 67 recto-verso.
65. Bib. Inst. Ms 1521, fol. 71 verso: "Enfin le Sr. Ko et le Sr. Yang saisiront toutes les circonstance où ils pourront démontrer la conformité des mœurs de génie et de caractère qu'ils ont observé entre les chinois et les françois, les deux nations pouvant être considérée comme les plus policés et les plus sociables de l'univers."
66. An abbreviated reference to some of the gifts appears in Bib. Inst. Ms 1521, fol. 62 recto-verso. Bernard-Maître, "Deux Chinois," 184, includes the complete list of gifts, citing in n. 101 that it appears in the Department of Manuscripts of the BnF in the documents contained in the BnF Fonds Bréquigny, vol. 1, fols. 6–7. These volumes contain the papers of Louis-Georges Oudart Feudrix de Bréquigny (1715–1795), the second editor of the *Mémoires concernant les Chinois*. Bernard-Maître also refers to the version of the list in *Voyage et Séjour*, 11. Bernard-Maître's n. 102, on the tapestries, however, cites a different set of tapestries following a source that runs counter to most scholarship on the subject. Silvestre de Sacy, *Sillage*, 164, also provides the list of gifts, apparently citing Bernard-Maître, "Deux Chinois," 184.
67. "Une Tenture des six Tapisseries des Chinois."
68. "Deux portraits par Vigée, avec glaces et bordures." Bernard-Maître, "Deux Chinois," 184, n. 103, cites Bib. Inst. Ms 1526, fol. 118 verso, for the payment of 262 livres to the painter, who was surely Louis Vigée (1715–1767), father of Élisabeth Louise Vigée-Lebrun (1755–1842).

69. "Une caisse de douze glaces de 30 sur 24 pouces." The traditional French *pouce* or inch measured approximately 2.7 cm; thus these large panes would have measured 81 × 64.8 cm or 31-7/8 × 25-1/2 in.
70. Dehergne, "Voyageurs chinois venus à Paris," see esp. 384, n. 46. Dehergne describes it as *garnie de ses ustensiles et de 4 casiers de caractères françois*, citing Bertin's "Instruction" of 16 January 1765 for Ko and Yang, Bib. Inst. MS 1521: fols. 60–71.
71. "Un ensemble de porcelaine de Sèvres." On the selection of porcelains, see Marie-Laure de Rochebrune, "Les porcelaines de Sèvres envoyées en guise de cadeaux diplomatiques à l'empereur de Chine par les souverains français dans la seconde moitié du XVIIIe siècle," in Zhao Bing, Isabelle Landry-Deron, and Fabien Simon, eds., *Extrême-Orient Extrême-Occident*, Des arts diplomatiques: Échanges de présents entre la Chine et l'Europe, XVIIe-XVIIIe siècles, vol. 43 (2019), 81–92.
72. "La machine d'électricité de Brisson." Bernard-Maître, "Deux Chinois," 184, n. 107, refers to the citation on 166, n. 52, Bib. Inst. Ms 1520, fols. 17–18, Brisson's letter to Bertin dated 7 September 1764, that this small electric generator was ready with all the necessary equipment for electrical experiments. Brisson is probably referring to an electrostatic mechanism called a Leyden Jar.
73. "Une collection de lunettes d'approche."
74. "Un télescope."
75. "Une chambre noire." This is an optical drawing device, a box mounted with a lens that projected an image onto a sheet of paper inside the darkened box. An accurate drawing was produced by tracing the image.
76. "Un microscope solaire." A microscope where the specimen is illuminated by sunlight reflected off a mirror.
77. "Un microscope à liqueur." Apparently this simple microscope consisted of two parts held together by a screw mechanism, one of which had a lens, the other with a diaphragm on which a drop of water served as the second lens above the specimen holder.
78. The bookseller Charles Saillant (1716–86) was one of the publishers of the extended series of illustrated volumes entitled *Descriptions des arts et métiers. . .*, some 113 titles authored or sponsored by the Royal Academy of Sciences, between 1761 and 1789, published by Saillant and, later, his nephew Jean-Luc III Nyon.
79. I am currently unable to locate further extant references to the titles from the printer and bookseller Pierre Vallat-la-Chapelle (d. 1772).
80. These are noted in Bertin's "Instruction" of 16 January 1765; Bib. Inst. MS 1521, fol. 71 verso: "Cartes géographiques. . ., plans de Paris, du Louvre, de Versailles et des autres maisons royales donneront une idée de la magnificence du Roy."
81. Bernard-Maître, "Deux Chinois," 183, "deux montres en or de chez Balthazar [à Paris] valant chacune 300 livres"; see ibid., n. 100, Bib. Inst. Ms 1526, fol. 118; in the abbreviated list of the presents from the King in Bib. Inst. Ms 1521, Bertin's instruction of January 1765, fol. 62 recto-verso, is a note added in the left margin: "à chacun une montre d'or de Balthazar horloger de Paris." On the gifts sent to China, see John Finlay, "Henri Bertin and the Louis XV's Gifts to the Qianlong Emperor," in Zhao Bing, Isabelle Landry-Deron, and Fabien Simon, eds., *Extrême-Orient Extrême-Occident* 43 (2019), Des arts diplomatiques: Échanges de présents entre la Chine et l'Europe, XVIIe-XVIIIe siècles, 93–111.
82. Boucher's original oil sketches were first exhibited in the Louvre at the Salon of 1742, six were prepared as full-scale cartoons for the tapestry series, and all of Boucher's relevant paintings for the set (a total of 10) are in the Musée des Beaux-arts et d'Archaéologie de Besançon. On their first exhibition, see Jean-Baptiste Reydellet, comp., *Explication des peintures, sculptures, et autres ouvrages de Messieurs de l'Académie royale . . .* (Paris: Jacques Colombat, 1742), 8–9, no. 21.
83. The best recent discussion of the tapestries is Kristel Smentek, "Chinoiseries for the Qing: A French Gift of Tapestries to the Qianlong Emperor," *Journal of Early Modern History* 20 (2016), 87–109. Smentek also refers to a number of the archival documents that are discussed in the present chapter. See Henri Bernard-Maître, S.J., *Les Tapisseries chinoises de Boucher au Palais Yuen-Min-Yuen de Pékin*, Variétés d'orientalisme, Fasc. 1 (Paris and Lille: Editions Cathasia, n.d. [1950]). And see Mei Mei Rado, "Qing Court's Encounters

with European Tapestries: The *Tenture Chinoise* and Beyond," in Pascal-François Bertrand and Audrey N. Maupas, eds., *Arachné: un regard critique sur l'histoire de la tapisserie* (Rennes: Presses Universitaires de Rennes, 2017); my thanks to Mei Mei Rado for providing me a draft of the essay.

84. Bib. Inst. Ms 1521, fols. 69 verso–70 verso.
85. *Voyage et Séjour*, 12: "[N]ous nous conformerons, pour ces présens, aux Instructions que le Roi nous a données par son Ministre."
86. Silvestre de Sacy, *Sillage*, 164. Ko and Yang wrote separately to Bertin from Lorient about their final preparations on 25 January 1765; see Bib. Inst. Ms 1520, fols. 122–124.
87. Henri Cordier, "Les Correspondants de Bertin, Secrétaire d'État au XVIIIe siècle," *T'oung Pao*, Second Series, 18, no. 4/5 (October–December 1917), 295–379; see part VII, letters from Benoist (whose name also appears as Benoît in a number of sources), 295–349. Cordier's source for Benoist's letters is Bib. Inst. Ms 1515. Three letters concern us here; for the first, dated 12 October 1766, see Cordier, Part VII, 295–318.
88. Le Febvre's name appears as Lefevre, Lefèvre, Le Febure, and other variants.
89. Benoist was able to arrange brief trips to various missions in northern China for Ko and Yang, but always in the company of someone who could help avoid any trouble with local officials; Cordier, "Correspondants de Bertin," 1917, 302–303.
90. Bib. Inst. Ms 1521, fol. 10 recto–verso, Bertin's letter to Ko and Yang, 31 December 1766: "Dans cet état, Messieurs, l'intention du Roy est que vous mettiés tout en œuvre pour que les tapisseries de la manufacture de sa Majesté et dont elle vous a rendu porteurs, et qui sont restées dans les magazins de Canton, soient présentées à l'Empereur de la Chine, non comme un présent du Roy, mais seulement pour tacher de connoitre par cet essay quel seroit le goût de l'Empereur pour les objets de nos manufactures et les productions de nos arts."
91. For Zongdu, see Charles O. Hucker, *A Dictionary of Official Titles in Imperial China* (Stanford, CA: Stanford University Press, 1985), no. 7158, *tsung-tu* 總督.
92. Isabelle Landry-Deron, "La curiosité de Turgot," 8–9, briefly refers to Benoist's letter, citing Cordier and the original source, Bib. Inst. Ms 1515.
93. See Cordier, "Les Correspondants de Bertin," 1917, 318–331, esp. 319–325. Bernard-Maître, "Tapisseries chinoises de François Boucher à Pékin," 6–7, gives a precise narration of the history of the tapestries, citing Benoist's letter of 10 November 1767 as published in Cordier, "Les Correspondants de Bertin," 1917, 319–320.
94. For a reliable introduction to the European Palaces of the Yuanming yuan, the hybrid Sino-Baroque buildings, and gardens built for the Qianlong emperor by Jesuit missionary-artists, see Michèle Pirazzoli-t' Serstevens, ed., *Le Yuanmingyuan: jeux d'eau et palais européens du XVIIIème siècle à la cour de Chine* (Paris: Editions Recherche sur les civilisations, 1987).
95. Benoist's letter of 10 November 1767 is cited in full in Cordier, "Les Correspondants de Bertin," 1917; see previous note. Extended citations of the same letter appear in Paul Leroy, "Notes sur les relations artistiques entre la France et la Chine aux XVIIe et XVIIIe siècles," *Réunion des sociétés des beaux-arts des départements*, Salle de l'hémicycle, à l'École nationale des beaux-arts, 1900, 413–430, along with long citations from other relevant letters in the Bibliothèque de l'Institut without, however, noting specific volumes. Another version of the same letter is found in the BnF Fonds Bréquigny, vol. 3, fols. 8ff.
96. See the following discussion of Amiot's *Art militaire des Chinois*.
97. Cordier, "Correspondants de Bertin," 1917, 315: "Nous avons les instructions qu'ils ont apportées, nous travaillerons peu à peu de concert à les remplir. Ces instructions étant arrivées tard à Pe King, le temps ne nous permet d'envoyer beaucoup cette année. Le P. Amiot depuis assez longtemps travaille à ramasser ce que les anciens et nouveaux Chinois ont écrit sur l'art de la guerre; il prend la liberté d'offrir à V. Exc. ce qu'il a de préparé. Les années suivantes nous envoyerons chaque année autant que le temps et les circonstances nous le permettent."
98. Silvestre de Sacy, *Sillage*, 164.
99. The Qianlong emperor and Father Joseph-Marie Amiot, S.J., *Éloge de la ville de Moukden et de ses environs . . .* (Paris: N.M. Tilliard, 1770); see the reference to this volume previously. The text is supplemented by Amiot's translation of a Qianlong imperial poem

on tea, a poem which was most likely inscribed on a porcelain cup or cups sent by Amiot to Bertin; see Kee Il Choi, Jr., "Father Amiot's Cup: A Qing Imperial Porcelain Sent to the Court of Louis XV," in Anne Gerritsen and Giorgio Riello, eds., *Writing Material Culture History* (London and New York: Bloomsbury Academic, 2014), Chap. 3, 33–41. The cups are discussed in the Conclusion to the present volume.

100. See François Jacob, "Kien-Long, poète d'empire," *Text Presented on Academia.edu*, www.academia.edu/14040787/Kien-Long_po%C3%A8te_dempire, accessed 24 November 2016. François Jacob is the director of the Musée Voltaire of the Bibliothèque de Genève, Geneva, Switzerland.
101. *Art militaire des Chinois, ou Recueil d'anciens traités sur la guerre, composés avant l'ere chrétienne, par différents généraux chinois* . . . Traduit en françois, par le P. Amiot, missionnaire à Pe-king, revu & publié par M. Deguignes (Paris: Didot l'Ainé, 1772). See Adam Parr, "John Clarke's *Military Institutions of Vegetius* and Joseph Amiot's *Art Militaire des Chinois*: Translating Classical Military Theory in the Aftermath of the Seven Years' War," PhD diss., University College London, 2016, http://discovery.ucl.ac.uk/1485839/7/Adam%20Parr%20Translating%20Classical%20Military%20Theory%202016.pdf, accessed 30 November 2016; see esp. Chap. 4, "Amiot's *Art Militaire des Chinois*," 136–152.
102. Amiot, *Art militaire des Chinois*, "Instruction sur l'Exercice Militaire," 317–387.
103. Ibid., 319: "La seule inspection des figures leur dira peut-être plus que toute mon explication." The source or sources of the images remain unidentified at present.
104. The full title is Joseph Amiot, François Bourgeois, Pierre-Martial Cibot, Aloys Kao, Aloys de Poirot, et al., comp., *Mémoires concernant l'histoire, les sciences, les arts, les moeurs, les usages, &c. des Chinois: Par les missionnaires de Pekin*, 15 vols. (Paris: Nyon, 1776–1791), and the series is conventionally referred to as *Mémoires concernant les Chinois*. Two posthumous volumes would both be published in 1814, one with the title *Mémoires concernant les Chinois* (Paris and Strasbourg: Treuttel et Würtz), the other entitled *Traité de la chronologie chinoise*, authored by Antoine Gaubil (Paris and Strasbourg: Treuttel et Würtz) and described as a supplement to the series. Note that bibliographic information on various library websites tends to be incomplete or inaccurate, especially in reference to the last two volumes. For a detailed bibliographic study of the series, see Joseph Dehergne, "Une grande collection: Mémoires concernant les Chinois (1776–1814)," *Bulletin de l'École française d'Extrême-Orient* 72 (1983), 267–298. Dehergne himself misrepresents the so-called Tome XVII.
105. Volume 7 of the *Mémoires* contains an "Avis de l'Éditeur," iii–vi, with a note identifying the editor as Joseph de Guignes, member of the Académie des Inscriptions et Belles Lettres. Joseph Dehergne, "Une grande collection," 275, describes Bertin as charging l'Abbé Charles Batteux (1713–1780) and, after his death, Louis-Georges Oudard Feudrix de Bréquigny (1714–1794) with the publication of the *Mémoires*. Dehergne identifies the often unnamed authors of various articles and he notes the few occasions where the writers of the various Avis, Avertissements, Préfaces, and so forth are identified.
106. *Mémoires concernant les Chinois*, vol. 1, Préface, i: "deux Chinois . . . que l'envie de se rendre utliles à leur Patrie en fit sortir. . ."; and ii: "entretenir avec nous une correspondance qui deviendroit avantageuse réciproquement aux deux Nations."
107. Ibid., xiv–xv, the last pages of the Préface, which contain a long quotation from one of the Jesuit missionaries' writing to Bertin.
108. Ibid., iv–v.
109. Ibid., xiii–xv.
110. *La Chine en Miniature*, vol. 1, Préface, xv–xvii. The six small volumes of *La Chine en miniature, ou Choix de costumes, arts et métiers de cet Empire*, . . . (Paris: Nepveu, 4 vols., 1811, 2 vols. 1812), edited by Jean Baptiste Joseph Breton de La Martinière (1777–1852) are a further publication of Bertin's papers. Acquired by the publisher and bookseller August Nepveu (n.d.), the documents were sold to François-Marie Delessert (1780–1868) and ultimately bequeathed in 1874 to the Bibliothèque de l'Institut de France, Bib. Inst. Mss. 1515–1526.
111. The sense of text is not exactly clear here; it reads: "on verra que les ouvrages les mieux *sortis* [emph. in original] sur la Chine, ne sont que des songes et des rêveries," *La Chine*

en Miniature, vol. 1, Préface, xvi. See also the brief discussion of Du Halde, *Description géographique, historique, chronologique, politique et physique de l'Empire de la Chine . . .* above; it was considered a ground-breaking encyclopedic text on China when it was first published.

112. *Mémoires concernant les Chinois*, vol. 1, 1–271.
113. But see Dehergne, "Une grande collection," 269, where Dehergne states his goal of establishing the actual authors of the contents of the *Mémoires* from the archival sources of the published versions. For the "Essai sur l'antiquité des Chinois," Dehergne identifies Ko, possibly Yang, and Father Pierre-Martial Cibot (Han Guoying 韓國英, 1727–1780, arr. in China 1758) as the authors, and his footnote 2 on p. 270 provides additional proof.
114. A "guerre littéraire"; *Mémoires concernant les Chinois*, vol. 1, vii.
115. Dehergne, "Une grande collection," deals with the important questions that motivated much of the eighteenth-century inquiry into China, and the supposed links between China and ancient Egypt, Chinese characters, and Egyptian hieroglyphs are one of these; see esp. 272, 275, 291–293, and the various references to the contents of the *Mémoires concernant les Chinois*.
116. *De Inscriptione quâdam Ægyptiacâ Taurini inventâ, et Characteribus Ægyptiacis, olim Sinis communibus . . .* (Rome: Nicolai, 1761).
117. "Lettre sur les Caractères Chinois, par le Révérend Père ****, de la Compagnie de Jésus, à Pékin, ce 20 Octobre 1764." *Mémoires*, vol. 1, 275–323; the table of contents, 484, identifies Amiot as the author. On the earlier publication, *Mémoires* vol. 1, Préface, x, simply notes that the letter was published with the accompanying plates in Brussels in 1765 by a publisher named Boubers.
118. Ibid., Avis, 273–274.
119. *Mémoires concernant les Chinois*, vol. 2, v: "Les Savans d'Europe pourront comparer les faits & les preuves, & en tirer les résultats."
120. Ibid., the text and its introduction (Avertissement) is contained on 1–150; the plates facing their explanations take up 151–364.
121. Ibid., Avant-propos, v, vii, where Amiot is identified as P.A. (Père Amiot).
122. "Portraits des Chinois célèbres," 1–386. See Dehergne, "Grande Collection," 276, which does not cite the plates specifically but does note the subsequent publications of portraits in *Mémoires*, vols. 5, 8, and 10.
123. *Mémoires*, vol. 3, 42, nn. 1 and 2, referring to the *Tchoung-young* (the *Zhongyong*), published in vol. 1, 436–458, and the *Ta-hio* (the *Daxue*), in vol. 1, 459–481. The *Daxue* was previously published in *Confucius sinarum philosophus* with translations of Chinese commentaries on the text; see Thierry Meynard, S.J., trans. and ed., *Confucius Sinarum Philosophus (1687): The First Translation of the Confucian Classics*, Monumenta Historica Societatis Iesu Nova Series, vol. 6 (Rome: Institutum Historicum Societatis Iesu, 2011), 331–422. Du Halde's earlier *Description de la Chine* includes, among the accounts of the various Confucian classics, descriptions of the *Daxue* (*L'École des adultes*), *Zhongyong* (*Le Milieu immuable*), and the *Lunyu* (*Livre des sentences*); see Du Halde, *Description*, vol. 2 (1736), 389–399. The only other extended text on Confucian teaching in the *Mémoires* is contained in Father Cibot's "Doctrine ancienne et nouvelle des Chinois sur la piété filiale," *Mémoires*, vol. 4, 1–298, based on excerpts from Confucian classics, historical documents, and contemporary Qing texts.
124. *Mémoires concernant les Chinois*, vol. 3, 43–45.
125. A very few of the paintings show full figures. See *Portraits de quelques uns d'entre les principaux chinois qui se sont rendus célèbres . . .* ("Portraits of certain figures among the most important Chinese who have become famous in government, letters, and the military"). The title is adapted from Amiot's note attached to the album, BnF, Dept. des Manuscrits, Chinois 1236. Amiot's translation of the Chinese preface provides the date, 1685, and the name of the artist, Bo Jie (or Bojie) 勃碣, whose *zi* 字 or *hao* 號 is Changxiu 常岫, who is also the author of the biographies. I have not been able to find any additional information on the artist. See also Rochebrune, ed., *La Chine à Versailles*, cat. 49.
126. See Dehergne, "Une grande collection," 276, the notes to *Mémoires*, vol. 3, citing the BnF manuscripts, NAF 4421–4431 (the albums of biographies and paintings, 1771), and the letters from Amiot to Bertin concerning the portraits, dated 5 October 1771 to September 1773.

127. The key letter from Amiot, dated 5 October 1771, is contained in Bib. Inst. Ms 1515, fols. 7–11. From what Amiot wrote, it appears that he sent the 1685 album and the set of copies at the same time. Amiot further states that he is sending 52 from 110 of the first group of "portraits" or biographies, the same number that Bertin published in Volume 3 of the *Mémoires concernant les Chinois*. The second group of biographies, with three illustrations, was published in vol. 5 in 1780, another group appeared in vol. 8 in 1782, and the final group of biographies, without illustrations, was published in 1784 in vol. 10.
128. Confucius' short biography in the *Mémoires* is actually number 21 (XXI), but the number here is that of Confucius' biography in the first version of the Chinese album of portraits acquired by Amiot.
129. I would like to thank Kee Il Choi, Jr., for sharing information on the BnF albums NAF 4421–4431.
130. See Lu Wensheng and Julia K. Murray, *Confucius: His Life and Legacy in Art* (New York: China Institute Gallery, 2010), cat. 1, "Portrait of Confucius as Minister of Justice in Lu," 32–35. See also Lee, *Visions de l'Empire du Milieu*, 77–78.
131. *Mémoires*, vol. 9 (1783); the brief description of the album appears on p. 454, the translation of the Chinese text on pp. 455–459, and the translations of the commentaries accompanying each plate on pp. 460–470; the 12 plates selected from the original 16 paintings are bound at the end of the volume.
132. Ibid., 454; see the discussion of the status of this album and the relevant text from *Mémoires*, vol. 9, in the Conclusion to the present volume.
133. The commentary to the first plate, ibid., 459, locates *Yen-tcheou-fou* (Yanzhou fu 嚴州府) on the banks of the *Sin-nan-kiang* (Xin'an River 新安江), a tributary of the Qiantang River 錢塘江, which flows into the Fuchun River 富春江.
134. Lee Chao-ying discusses the moral aspects of the Yanzhou fu album; see "L'enjeu politique," 89–92, and *Visions de l'Empire du Milieu*, 109–112.
135. On the history and depictions of the Kangxi emperor's Southern Inspection Tour, see Maxwell K. Hearn, ed., *Landscapes Clear and Radiant: The Art of Wang Hui (1632–1717)* (New York: Metropolitan Museum of Art; and New Haven: Yale University Press, 2008).
136. I have not been able to identify this person.

2 The Landscape of Fact and Fantasy

There was in France, and in Europe in general in the eighteenth century, a remarkable knowledge of Chinese gardens. Publications of descriptions, including eye-witness accounts as well as the circulation of illustrations, had a profound influence on European garden design and construction. While this phenomenon is the subject of an extensive and exhaustive literature, the focus of the present chapter is the knowledge of Chinese gardens that would have been generally available to Henri Bertin, what we can reasonably assume that he knew, along with the actual materials sent from China that we know he possessed, and, ultimately, the effect this knowledge might have had on the construction of his own garden at Chatou—itself the subject of Chapter 4. Much of the discussion here revolves around knowledge of the Yuanming yuan, the Qing imperial "Garden of Perfect Brightness," but it also includes European accounts of other Chinese gardens and translations of Chinese texts on gardens that were available in the eighteenth century. These define an image of the Chinese garden as an artful simulacrum of nature in contrast to the earlier European ideal of formal gardens—epitomized in the French royal gardens of Versailles—as artificial, lavish, and especially wasteful constructions. Along with presenting nature as an ideal, such texts also marvel at the strange rocks and grottos that were key elements in Chinese gardens, elements that had few precedents in European practice. Texts sent to Bertin by the Jesuit missionaries and other related texts contain echoes of Qing imperial statements on the supposed frugality of imperial garden construction.[1]

Indeed, a Jesuit account of the Kangxi emperor's (康熙, r. 1644–1722) gardens, describing a visit to the imperial gardens and published in French in 1735, provides the earliest statements of these issues in the encounters between the European imagination and Chinese gardens. Jean-François Gerbillon (1654–1707, Zhang Cheng 張誠, arr. China 1687), a Jesuit missionary who was part of the first official French mission to China in 1685,[2] recorded in his diary for March 1690 his visits to the Kangxi emperor's imperial residence on the Yingtai 瀛台 island in the Nanhai 南海, one of the lakes in the gardens west of the Forbidden City, and the Kangxi emperor's Changchun yuan 暢春園, the Garden of Joyful Springtime, northwest of Beijing.[3] In his descriptions of details of the emperor's gardens, Gerbillon notes the emperor's frugality in respect to his own expenditures, the supposed modesty and simplicity of the imperial residences, and his generosity in terms of government and the public expense. While Gerbillon is somewhat mystified by Chinese rocks, his descriptions, however brief, are something that Bertin might well have been aware of in view of the great success and wide circulation of Jean-Baptiste Du Halde's (1674–1743) *Description de la Chine*, the volumes where Gerbillon's text was first published.[4]

Given that landscape and garden design in England was arguably impacted by knowledge of Chinese gardens to a greater degree and at an earlier date than in France, it is worth noting that important English publications on the subject were available in France—and often republished in French-language editions, and these would be what Bertin most likely would have known. One particularly revealing example of this exchange between England and France is that of Thomas Whately's (1726–1772) *Observations on Modern Gardening*, first published in 1770, a book that was an important source on the contemporary theory of landscape and gardening.[5] The volume was reviewed in the September 1770 edition of the *Journal Encyclopédique*, which would have brought Whately's book to the attention of an educated French audience.[6] It was almost immediately translated into French and published in 1771 as *L'Art de former les jardins modernes*, a volume to which the translator, François de Paule Latapie (1739–1823), added an extensive "Discours Préliminaire."[7] This introductory text noted the review in the *Journal Encyclopédique*, and Latapie, the translator, also wrote that he had communicated his comments and criticisms directly to Whately. Whately's reply in a letter dated December 1770 is translated and reprinted here as well, in which he discussed the reasons why his volume did not include engraved plates. And he added comments on symmetry in architecture in contrast to other ideals for gardens. Latapie's "Discours Préliminaire" further included a reference and a short citation on the accounts of Chinese gardens from Du Halde's *Description de la Chine*, where Chinese gardens are described as ornamented with woods, lakes, and other recreations of natural features, including rocks and artificial mountains.[8] As proof of the resemblances between English and Chinese gardens, the "Discours Préliminaire" also contains the French translation of the complete chapter "Of the Art of Laying out Gardens among the Chinese" from William Chambers' (1723–1796) *Designs of Chinese Buildings, Furniture, Dresses, Machines and Utensils* of 1757, another one of the key texts in the transmission of knowledge of Chinese gardens to Europe.[9] On the last pages of his "Discours Préliminaire" Latapie asserted that the best thing is to present an accurate translation of Whatley's English edition, without re-editing it in "French" style.[10] The extent of the exchange of texts on Chinese gardens between England and France is well illustrated by the appearance of editions of Whately's book and its reception in France, although this is only one example of such cultural contacts.

Yuanming yuan: The Versailles of Beijing

The Yuanming yuan 圓明園, sometimes referred to as the "Former Summer Palace," while the name is more accurately translated as the "Garden of Perfect Brightness," was the largest of the garden-palaces of the Qing emperors located in an area just northwest of Beijing that was long known for garden retreats. Sometime around 1707, the Kangxi emperor presented the garden's site to the Prince Yinzhen 胤禛, the future Yongzheng emperor (雍正, r. 1723–1735), who built the original, central areas of the Yuanming yuan. Greatly enlarged by his successor, the Qianlong emperor (乾隆, r. 1736–1795), it would become the most important Qing imperial garden-palace. A letter describing the Yuanming yuan from the Jesuit missionary Jean-Denis Attiret (Wang Zhicheng 王致誠, 1702–1768, arr. China 1738)[11] was written in 1743 and subsequently published in 1749 in the *Lettres édifiantes et curieuses. . .*, the volumes that are themselves a direct precedent for the *Mémoires concernant les Chinois*.[12]

Translated into a number of languages and widely circulated, Attiret's text had a profound impact on garden theory and design in Europe, and Bertin himself surely knew of this letter, which described in great detail the buildings, waterways, and other landscape elements, frequently comparing and contrasting Chinese practice with European gardens.[13] In one important passage, Attiret stated the basic principles that govern imperial and princely gardens, noting the contrast between what is ostensibly natural and what is a strictly formal design. The translation here is the text as it appeared in the first English translation, which was published in London in 1752:

> But in their Pleasure-houses, they rather chuse* a beautiful Disorder, and a wandering as far a possible from all the Rules of Art. They go entirely on this Principle, "That what they are to represent there, is a natural and wild View of the Country; a rural Retirement, and not a Palace form'd according to all the Rules of Art."[14]

The translation, by Joseph Spence, is not strictly literal, and what is described as a "wandering as far as possible from all the Rules of Art" is an expansion on the French term *une anti-symmétrie.*[15] Anti-symmetry is a concept that appears in eighteenth-century French texts on gardens and garden theory, a selection of which are considered in the following. It is applied specifically in contrast to the formal, geometric symmetry that had characterized garden design, and anti-symmetry is one of the key features of what is considered a more natural style of gardening.

In his translation, Spence inserted a long footnote (marked in the text by the asterisk*) in which he states that Attiret had formed his opinions only on observations of the Yuanming yuan, but Spence himself had recently seen prints illustrating a different imperial garden that show the layout of the landscape and water elements, described as indeed "quite irregular," in contrast to the architectural elements, which are more formal and regular. The prints he is referring to are the engravings of the Bishu shanzhuang 避暑山莊, the "Mountain Estate for Escaping the Summer Heat" in Richard Strassberg's translation, which was constructed by the Kangxi emperor (康熙, r. 1661–1722) at Chengde 承德 (Jehol) in the Manchu homeland north of the Great Wall.[16] The emperor had commissioned from his court artists a set of paintings entitled "Thirty-six Views of the Bishu shanzhuang" (Bishu shanzhuang sanshiliu jing 避暑山庄三十六景), which was reproduced as an imperial album of woodblock prints accompanying the emperor's poems on each view or site in the garden-park. The missionary from the Propaganda Fide, Matteo Ripa (Ma Guoxian 馬國賢, 1682–1746, act. in China 1710–1724), who served the Kangxi emperor as an artist, among other duties, was asked by the emperor to reproduce the woodblock prints as engravings, and by 1713 he had produced a number of copies, these being the first copperplate engravings produced in China.[17] On his return to Europe, Ripa apparently took impressions of his prints with him, and 18 of them were reproduced most famously in a set published by four London booksellers entitled *The Emperor of China's Palace at Pekin. . .*, which appeared in 1753. This is the album of prints that Spence described in his footnote, with the remark that the prints "will very soon be publish'd here."[18] Ripa's engravings took the compositions of the original Qing imperial woodcuts and effectively translated them into a more European visual idiom, adding modeling in the water, the sky, and other landscape elements, effectively making the landscape details more complex, more specific, and less generic than the Kangxi woodcuts.[19] Ripa even added birds in the sky and fish in the water to some of the engravings. The engraved copies published in *The Emperor of China's Palace at Pekin* generally adhered to Ripa's compositions and the hybrid Chinese-European style of his engravings, but they added significant details. The view entitled in Chinese "Viewing the Fish from a Waterside Rock" (Shiji guanyu 石磯觀魚) (Figure 2.1), no. 31 in the Kangxi album, shows a pavilion beside an overhanging rock. Identified as one of Ripa's own engravings, it exemplifies these changes.[20] In the reproduction, no. 4 in the English edition, entitled "The Hanging Rock, that looks down on the Fishes," the plants and trees are given additional detail, the dramatic nature of the looming rock as Ripa engraved it is retained here, but three boats, including one with a lowered sail, have been inserted into the composition. The anonymous English engravers have added a number of

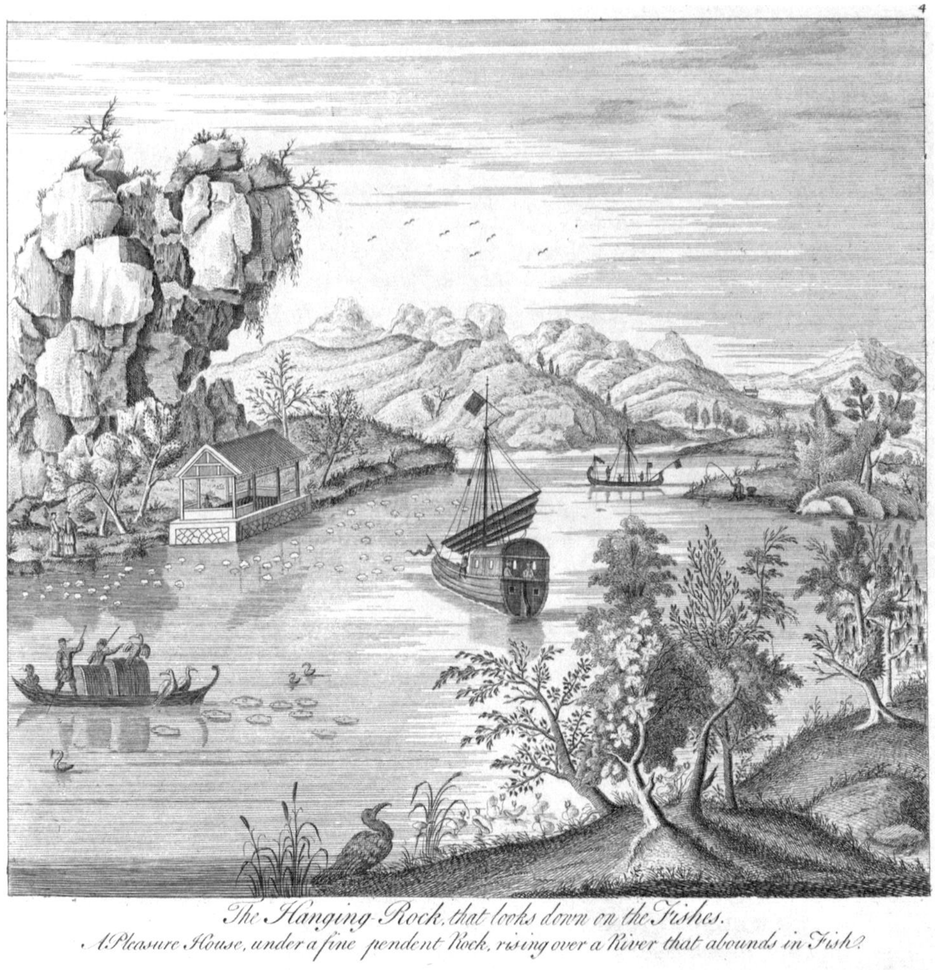

Figure 2.1 Anonymous, *The Emperor of China's Palace at Pekin* (London 1753), no. 4, "The Hanging Rock, that looks down on the Fishes," engraving, 40 × 51 cm. Getty Research Institute, Los Angeles (92-B26685).

figures, both on the boats and on the shore, where there are two women and, in the distance, a single fisherman. These engravings, surely among the first to illustrate for a broader European audience the details of the Qing imperial park, show the landscape filled with natural detail and human activity.

In his letter describing the Yuanming yuan, Attiret asked rhetorically why he had written such a long description of the Yuanming yuan when it would be better to draw plans of the garden and send these to Europe. But he immediately stated that this would have taken him at least three years, even if he had no other obligations, and in any case access to most of the garden was forbidden to all but the emperor and a chosen few.[21] Attiret eventually did send a copy of a Qing imperial woodblock album containing illustrations of the Yuanming yuan to a certain Abbé Viguier in Besançon, although this particular album was not recognized at the time for what it was, and it was Attiret's detailed written description of the imperial garden-palace that remained so broadly influential.[22] However, the album Attiret sent is one of a group of visual images that are key to understanding the circulation of knowledge of the Yuanmingyuan between France and China. Chief among them is the album entitled "40 Views of the Yuanmingyuan."[23]

In 1738, the Qianlong emperor commissioned an album of paintings, the "40 Views of the Yuanming yuan" (Yuanming yuan sishi jing tu yong 圓明園四十景圖詠), to accompany his 40 poems on "views" or sites in the garden-palace.[24] While the album was based on the model of the Kangxi "36 Views of the Bishu shanzhuang," the Qianlong paintings were rendered in a hybrid Chinese-European style that the emperor particularly favored. A typical view is no. 18, the "Studio for Assembled Worthies" (Huifang shuyuan 彙芳書院) (Plate 2). Each folio of the album includes the Qianlong emperor's preface and poem facing the paintings. Depicted from an elevated viewpoint, the architecture is laid out on a strict, single-point perspective grid, and the constructions and landscape features are rendered with a subtle sense of light and shade. One distinctive, curved building with a flat roof, the "Crescent Moon Terrace" (Meiyue xuan 眉月軒), provided views of the distant hills.[25] Completed in 1744, the finished album was kept at the Yuanming yuan, where it would have been rarely seen and never exhibited in any modern sense of the term.[26] However, a Qing imperial woodblock edition of the "40 Views" was finished and printed in 1745, and it contains black-and-white illustrations that largely reproduce the compositions of the original 40 paintings.[27] These are followed by the emperor's poems along with a massive commentary composed of citations from classical literature. Although the woodcut edition was not published or officially available to the public—copies would have been presented as imperial gifts, and many were kept in various imperial palace buildings—it soon spread beyond court circles, and examples reached Europe surprisingly quickly.

An album in the Bibliothèque nationale de France that contains only the prints from the woodblock edition of the "40 Views" bears the bookplate of the sixth Duc de Chaulnes (Michel-Ferdinand d'Albert d'Ailly, 1714–1769) and was included in the posthumous sale of his collection in 1770. The title on the album, "Various palaces and temples of China, drawn and engraved in China," and the lack of any other contemporary inscriptions indicate that de Chaulnes was not aware of the identity of the images.[28] The prints are in random order, and their condition clearly identifies them as printers' proofs that had never been trimmed and bound in a Chinese book. The print of the Huifang shuyuan scene (Figure 2.2), the same as the painting illustrated

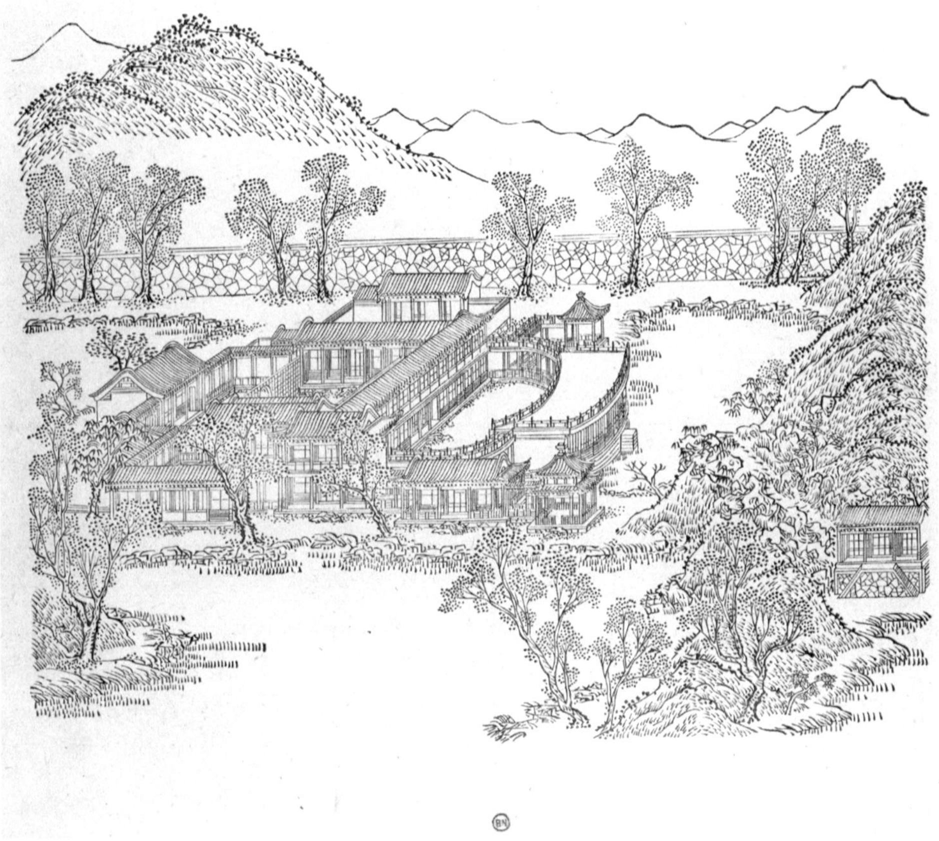

Figure 2.2 *Différents Palais & Temples de la Chine, dessinés & gravés a la Chine*, plate 4, Sun Hu and Shen Yuan, "Huifang shuyuan," woodcut, 1745, 31.5 × 39.1 cm. Paris, Bibliothèque nationale de France.

previously, plate 4 in the Chaulnes album, shows how, in general, the woodblock illustrations carefully reproduce the original paintings but bring the viewer closer to the scene, eliminating some landscape details. Bertin himself was one of the executors of the estate of the sixth Duc de Chaulnes—a man whose son was also an avid collector of Chinese objects and images.[29] Among the archival documents related to Bertin, inventory lists of material sent from China include objects destined for the Duc de Chaulnes, and from the dates, almost all after the father's death in 1769, the majority of them surely refer to the son, the seventh duke.[30] The two Ducs de Chaulnes were important figures in the network of like-minded men directly linked to Henri Bertin.

The copy of the "40 Views" that is, however, usually cited as the first to reach Europe is the one provided to Georges-Louis Le Rouge (ca. 1707–1793/94) by the Swedish Count Carl Fredrik Scheffer (1715–1786).[31] Le Rouge carefully reproduced the "40 Views" as etchings in Portfolios (*Cahiers*) 15 and 16 of his series *Jardins anglo-chinois à la mode*, both of which were published in 1786. Le Rouge acknowledged

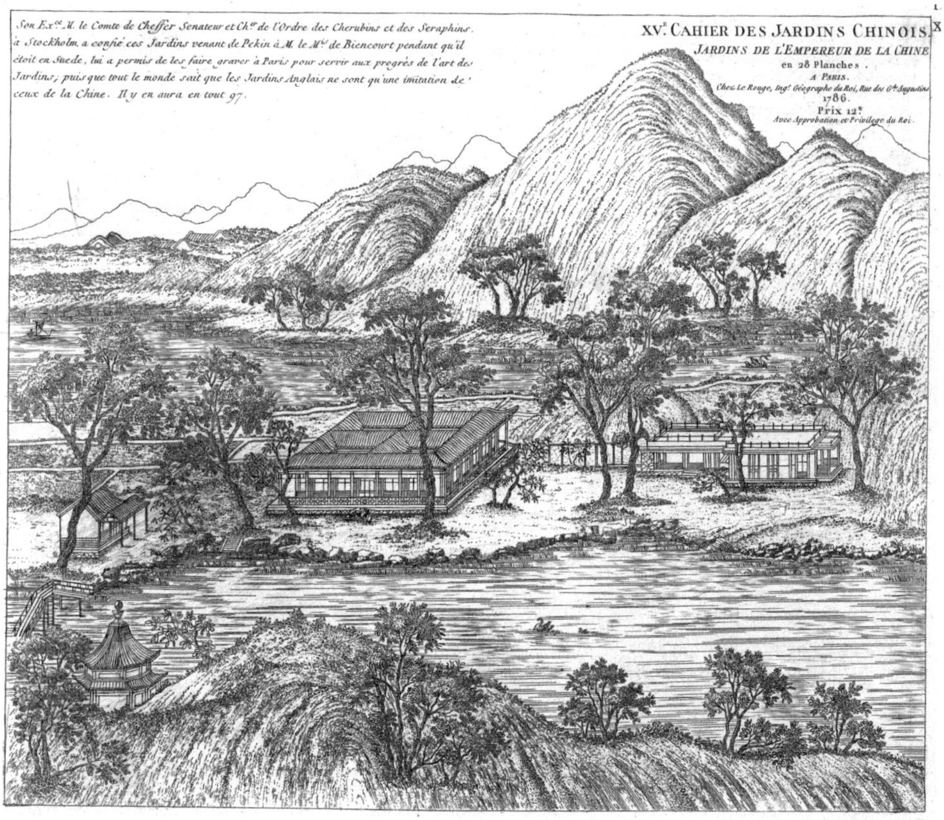

Figure 2.3 Georges-Louis Le Rouge, *Detail des nouveaux jardins à la mode*. A Paris: Chez Le Rouge. Cahier XV "Des jardins chinois: Jardins de l'Empereur de la Chine," engraving, 34 × 52 cm, 1786. Getty Research Institute, Los Angeles (88-B1922).

Cheffer (*sic*) as his source on the title page of Portfolio 15 (Figure 2.3), which reproduces no. 20 of the "40 Views," the scene entitled Danbo ningjing 澹泊寧靜 (the name means "Detachment and serenity"). The inscription on the title page notes that the prints were loaned to be engraved in Paris "in order to serve the progress of the art of Gardens; since everyone knows that English gardens are only an imitation of those of China."[32] The images copied by Le Rouge were most likely from a copy of the Qing imperial woodblock album of the "40 Views." Although the order is effectively reversed, the images generally follow the original order of the "40 Views."[33] Le Rouge, however, noted on the title page of Portfolio 17 (also published in 1786) that Chinese books "begin where ours end" and thus the pages he had reproduced were indeed in reverse order. Between 1775 and 1789 Le Rouge published 21 portfolios of prints that include in all some 490 illustrations and plans of the newly fashionable English or English-style gardens, which were supposedly in the Chinese manner.[34] A number of the plates have only a marginal connection with China or Chinoiserie-style garden designs and related architecture, but Portfolios 14 to 17, published in 1785–1786, are faithful copies of Chinese sources, carefully reproducing images from various albums loaned to Le Rouge, including the "detached palaces" (*xinggong* 行宮) used by the Qianlong emperor and illustrated in his Southern Inspection Tours, the *Nanxun shengdian tu* 南巡盛典圖, alongside the "40 Views of the Yuanming yuan."[35] Le Rouge's publications of the *Jardins anglo-chinois* are a crucial source in the circulation of images between China and Europe, and circulation of images of the Yuanmingyuan is part of a broader encounter between France and China—the result of a purposeful acquisition of knowledge.

While Le Rouge's reproductions of the "40 Views" were published relatively late in the eighteenth century, the Qing imperial garden-palace was already well-known and was often enough referred to as "the Versailles of Peking" by Bertin and his contemporaries. Indeed, two different lists of the contents of shipments to Bertin from the Jesuits in Beijing, both dated 1770, specifically refer to the "Versailles de Pékin."[36] Among Bertin's own papers is an article entitled "Jardin de *yuen-ming-yuen*" (the *Yuanming yuan* garden),[37] which, although unsigned, is likely the work of the Jesuit missionary Pierre-Martial Cibot (Han Guoying 韓國英, 1727–1780, arr. China 1759), who was one of Bertin's most prolific correspondents.[38] The article opens with the statement that "Haidian, which is two great leagues from Peking, is the Versailles of China, and the Yuanming yuan the residence and pleasure garden of the Emperor."[39] Haidian 海淀 was the city northwest of Beijing[40] that is the location of the Yuanming yuan, as Versailles is the city southwest of Paris that is the site of the great French royal palace and gardens. The text, which Bertin probably received in 1770,[41] begins with a reference to Attiret's famous letter of 1743 describing the Yuanming yuan. The article echoes Attiret's assertion that images would provide what words alone could not, and thus this text accompanies a shipment to Bertin that included two versions of the "40 Views of the Yuanming yuan." The paintings being sent to France would give a sense of the Chinese imperial garden that make the viewer

> first feel how it is so varied in its plans for the bridges and gateways, lakes and ponds, expanses of water and canals, hills and plains, woods and groves, caverns and rocks, its wandering paths and avenues, etc. Their distribution and their assemblage adhere to ideas that subordinate art to models taken from nature and only permit the choice of imitation.[42]

While the writer admits that, at first glance, the Yuanming yuan might not appear as magnificent as a European palace, it is farther away from the cares of this world than its European counterparts and always changing with the seasons.

The first painted version of the "40 Views" sent to Bertin—surely the complete set of views described in the "Jardin de *yuen-ming-yuen*"—consists of simplified copies of the original 40 imperial images rendered in watercolor on Chinese paper. Based on the imperial woodcut edition—again, as noted in the "Jardin" text—it consists of a set of paintings that was bound as an album after its arrival in France.[43] The second set of views, also referred to in this text, is described as an "album of the Chinese names of all the buildings that are represented there and the poems which the reigning Emperor has composed."[44] This was surely a copy of the imperially commissioned woodblock edition of the "40 Views," the imperial publication completed in 1745 that is discussed previously. The text of the "Jardin de *yuen-ming-yuen*" describes the contents of the album and the Chinese woodblock book, noting in particular that the names of the various views and buildings all signify examples of morality, virtue, politics, philosophy, religion, and the like.[45] While flattering in its judgments of the book's contents and the Qianlong emperor's poetry, the discussion is remarkably accurate and perceptive, obviously the work of someone who had paid close attention to the woodblock edition and wished to inspire a similar appreciation in his correspondent.

Bertin's album of paintings, the ones described in the "Jardin de *yuen-ming-yuen*," is entitled *Haitien, Maison de Plaisance de l'Empereur de Chine* (Haidian, pleasure palace of the emperor of China).[46] It is the product of a small group of painters working in a hybrid Chinese-European style in opaque and transparent watercolors on smooth white paper, almost certainly a Chinese paper. A closely related album, now in the National Museum of Ethnology in Leiden, comes from the collection of the Dutch antiquarian and sinologist Jean Theodore Royer (1737–1807).[47] While the painters of the two albums generally respected the overall compositions of the "40 Views," they altered the landscapes and occasionally added details not found in other versions such as the Qianlong imperial woodcut illustrations, which are, however, their ultimate source. The versions of the painting entitled Shuimu mingse 水木明瑟 (the name means "Clear water and soughing trees") provide a good example of the transformations of the image as they were communicated to Europe in the eighteenth century. The painting is number 22 of the "40 Views" (Plate 3), and the Qianlong emperor's preface and poem on the view celebrate a retreat of natural beauty. The preface notes that one of the buildings, the Fengshan shi 風扇室 (literally the "Wind-fan chamber"), sat over a channel where the water powered a European-style mechanism that turned a fan.[48] In the Qianlong album painting we see buildings along a narrow canal with high banks and buildings on elevated terraces around a waterway or pool, reminding us that many places in the Yuanming yuan were accessible particularly by boat. Small fields fill up much of the space, waterways lead off into the distance, and the site appears to be surrounded by hills and mountains. In Bertin's painting (Plate 4), which closely follows the composition of the imperial woodcut illustration, the point of view is closer to the scene and cuts off a large part of the building and the plank bridge over the waterway at the lower left. The fields and the building in the distance are reduced and brought closer together, making a more intimate scene, and the painter adds a tall, thin pagoda, just visible standing on the blue hills at the upper right.

Four additional paintings from Bertin's collection—paintings whose compositions radically transform their Qing imperial models—are also derived from the "40 Views." They are quite large (approximately 68 × 68 cm), and the four paintings are bound together as the pages of an album inscribed with the title "Paysages Chinois Tirés des Jardins de l'Empereur, et autres" (Chinese landscapes taken from the gardens of the Emperor and others).[49] The third painting in the album (Plate 5), which is based on the Shuimu mingsi composition, returns in many ways to the more open format of the original painting in the imperial album of the "40 Views," although how the painter of this extraordinary image might have known the original composition is not clear. There are, however, significant differences between these representations. The painting in Bertin's collection shows buildings with brightly colored tile roofs whereas the original Qing buildings had gray tiles. The season has been changed and the trees no longer have leaves; their bare branches contrast with the pines at the lower left. But the greatest changes are to the landscape setting. Here the bright sunlight and exaggerated effects of light and shade define a landscape of fantastic rocks, which are closer to illustrations of Chinese garden rocks (*jiashan* 假山, literally "false mountains") than any natural formation. (And the subject of garden rocks is discussed in the following.) The misty distance of the imperial painting has been replaced with a clear view of a lake across which we can see a shoreline with at least one small building. Along the left-hand side of the painting, the artist has added a fictitious view of rocks and hills, where steps lead up to the massive gate of a temple complex. Silhouetted against the mountains and blue sky is a tall, red pagoda with small bells hanging from the corners of the roofs. None of these appear in the Qianlong emperor's painting.

Related to the four paintings in the large-scale album is a single painting that was part of Bertin's collection, a painting based on the view entitled Qinzheng qinxian 勤政親賢 (number 2 of the "40 Views"; the name means "Diligent in affairs and keeping the worthy close"). The large painting (80 × 88 cm) is simply inscribed with the title *Maison de plaisance* (pleasure palace), but it demonstrates how far Chinese artists could go in interpreting their Qing imperial sources.[50] The painting takes the original composition from the "40 Views" and greatly extends it, adding a number of buildings along the right-hand side. The architecture is rendered in precise, accurate detail—a fine example of the traditional genre of "ruled-line" painting (*jiehua* 界畫). The painting is unquestionably the work of a Chinese artist or artists who have been trained in European techniques of perspective and modeling with light and shade. Together these five paintings raise questions on the accuracy and significance of images based on Qing imperial originals but which add varying elements of fantasy. They preserve representations of the actual structures but alter the landscapes that were, ultimately, themselves painterly fictions. We will return in the succeeding chapters to what knowledge could actually be transmitted by these and other paintings in Bertin's collection.

Chinese Gardens in the *Mémoires concernant les Chinois*

The subject of Chinese gardens first appears in the *Mémoires concernant les Chinois* in the second volume, published in 1777, and important translations and texts on the subject are contained in later volumes. The first two notes on gardens in Volume 2 are parts of an extended article entitled "Remarques sur un Écrit de M. P**, intitulé: Recherches sur les Égyptiens & les Chinois."[51] The article is a long and acerbic refutation of the *Recherches philosophiques sur les Egyptiens et les Chinois* by Cornelius de Pauw (1739–1799), published in 1773 and severely criticized at the time, especially by the Jesuits.[52] The article consists of a series of numbered "remarks" which are intended to demolish what are seen as the false assertions made by de Pauw and to provide the readers of the *Mémoires* with accurate information on many aspects of China.[53] The first remark on gardens disputes de Pauw's assertion that only a "depraved imagination" could have given rise to the idea of Chinese gardens.[54] However, in view of the current knowledge among the English, French, and others, it is clear to the authors of the remark that he has no understanding of the subject.[55] The text includes a brief listing of the many features of Chinese gardens, which is followed by contrasting the effort, material, and expense in the production and maintenance of formal European gardens, and whether this is indeed justified for the pleasure of a very few. The second remark on gardens challenges de Pauw's statement that it is unusual to see Chinese architects erecting artificial rocks in what they call "gardens."[56] In reply, reference is made to the discussion of the ruinous expenses entailed by European garden design, which is contrasted with the imitation of nature as the guiding principle of Chinese gardens. Gardens should reflect local conditions, and the rocks, grottoes, and caverns criticized by de Pauw actually require great artistic skill in order to appear natural. The wasteful expense of formal, symmetrical European garden design—especially that of France—and the supposed freedom from luxury and magnificence, and the implied economies of Chinese garden design, based as it is on natural forms, are subjects that recur in a number of French texts on garden design dating to the late eighteenth century.

The same volume of the *Mémoires*, Volume 2, also includes a translation entitled "Le Jardin de Sée-ma-kouang."[57] Although described here as a poem, the "Record of the Garden of Solitary Enjoyment" (Dule yuan ji 獨樂園記) is actually a short essay composed by Sima Guang 司馬光 (1019–1086), a scholar and government official who served at times in the imperial court of the Northern Song dynasty in the eleventh century. He is best known for the composition of the highly influential *Zizhi tongjian* 資治通鑑, the *Comprehensive Mirror for Aid in Government*, completed in 1084.[58] Retiring from court service, Sima Guang moved to the city of Luoyang in 1071, a city with a rich garden tradition. Here he built his Garden of Solitary Enjoyment in 1073, and he remained in Luoyang for the next 12 years, the time during which he compiled the *Comprehensive Mirror*. From the text of the "Record of the Garden of Solitary Enjoyment," it is clear that his garden was small and rustic in design. The names of the garden's features and constructions all reflect historical figures, poetic allusions, or Confucian moral values. For example, the phrase *dule* 獨樂, "solitary pleasure," is derived from *Mencius* and cited in the first line of the essay.[59] The translation in the *Mémoires* begins with a brief introduction that provides a context for understanding Chinese gardens as they are described in Sima Guang's text:

> The gardens of China are a studied imitation, but natural, of the different beauties of the countryside, in hills, valleys, gorges, basins, small lakes, expanses of water, islands, rocks, grottoes, ancient caverns, plants and flowers. The great achievement of their art is to extend a small space by the multitude, variety, and surprise of the scenes; to lift from nature all its resources, and to do them honor.[60]

The text makes reference to "drawings" that show all the variety of the garden elements and the architectural constructions one sees there, which indeed exist as they appear. The editors of the *Mémoires* insert two notes into this text, which provide clues to its source and its accuracy in describing Chinese gardens.[61] The first comment cites the source of the text before noting that the original then continues. It reads: "This note is taken from the Description of the Yuanming yuan Garden, sent from Peking a few years ago with the drawings. The Author of the Description then adds: To imagine more or less the effect of all these elements. . . ."[62] That is, the text here describing Chinese gardens and Sima Guang's essay would have been sent from China along with the text of the "Jardin de *yuen-ming-yuen*," which is discussed previously, and the "drawings" are the versions of the "40 Views" which Bertin had bound in the album *Haitien, Maison de Plaisance de l'Empereur de Chine*. Given that the essay on the Yuanming yuan along with the paintings arrived in France about 1770, and that the translation of Sima Guang's essay was printed in the *Mémoires* in 1777, the direct link between these crucial sources on Chinese gardens seems highly likely.[63]

There are, however, serious questions about the actual text published in the *Mémoires* as Sima Guang's "Record of the Garden of Solitary Enjoyment." Bianca

Rinaldi discusses these issues along with her translation of the introduction to what is supposedly Sima Guang's text and refers to the present poem or record itself as "far more elaborate than the original."[64] The French text of the "Jardin de Sée-ma-kouang" is indeed much longer than its supposed eleventh-century source, and only a few phrases, more or less in the same order in both texts, are shared in common.[65] What was published in the *Mémoires* in 1777 as Cibot's translation is a much longer article filled with descriptions of what is ostensibly Sima Guang's garden along with a remarkable body of details on this particular garden and Chinese gardens in general. Plants and physical features of all kinds are listed, and just one of the many additional descriptions here details something not described in Sima Guang's original. A path lined with willows leads to the bank of a stream, where

> [t]he surroundings present only a barrier of pointed rocks strangely arranged, which rise like an amphitheater, in a wild and rustic manner. When one arrives at the bottom, one finds a deep grotto which extends, widening little by little, and forms a kind of irregular room whose vault rises like a dome.[66]

While the text is highly evocative of the features of Chinese gardens, including grottos, which were also a feature of European gardens, along with other elements that clearly distinguish Chinese from French gardens, the Chinese source or sources still remain unclear. Robert Harrist notes that Sima Guang also wrote seven poems on his garden, the "Dule yuan qi ti" 獨樂園七題, each describing and extolling an individual site.[67] The poems may themselves be part of the inspiration for Cibot's text, which is indeed identified here as the translation of a poem, not an essay. Further complicating the issue is the fact that the complete, identical text had already been published in France, in Claude-Henri Watelet's (1718–1786) *Essai sur les Jardins* in 1774.[68] Watelet correctly summarizes the essay, noting that for all times and in all places wisdom is the consolation of educated men, men who are described in the text in heartfelt terms as sharing their companionship in the garden. One final note in the *Essai sur les Jardins* adds some uncertainty to what the editors of the *Mémoires* referred to as "the drawings" that accompanied the text. Watelet refers to a painting, a pleasant, faithful image drawn by an unknown hand,[69] raising the question of whether he actually saw the 40 paintings I believe accompanied the original text and thus entered Henri Bertin's collection.

The longest and surely the most important text on Chinese gardens in the *Mémoires concernant les Chinois* was published in Volume 8 in 1782.[70] Some 26 pages long, the "Essai sur les jardins de plaisance des Chinois" (Essay on the pleasure gardens of the Chinese) is also the work of Father Cibot, and it was composed and sent to Europe as early as 1774–1775.[71] The essay begins with a note on the lack of knowledge of the gardens of European Classical antiquity in contrast with China, where the history of gardens is documented in detail in China's unbroken written historical tradition. Throughout his essay, Cibot cites ancient legends, the Confucian classics, important writers, and key historical sources, and he includes translations of a number of original texts.[72] And as Rinaldi points out, Cibot's text is the first European essay on the theory of Chinese garden aesthetics.[73] The essay is divided into two parts, and the narrative of the history of Chinese gardens in the first section presents an ideal view in which, at first, only the size of the emperor's gardens distinguished them from those of the common people—indeed they were effectively fields and orchards for agricultural production. However, a century after the reign of the first two kings of the Zhou dynasty,[74] princely gardens began to take over more and more of the agricultural land of the common people, beginning a long history of Chinese gardens as a history of imperial repression. The theme is clearly an implicit lesson for the present, both for China and for Europe, and it is one to which Cibot's essay repeatedly returns in describing the increasingly extravagant and wasteful imperial gardens of the succeeding dynasties over some nineteen centuries of recorded history.

Cibot details the many natural and architectural features that were manipulated and distorted to enhance the splendor of princely gardens, and he notes that the Chinese did this long before the construction of comparably extravagant gardens began in Europe.[75] With the passage of time, the pleasure gardens of wealthy private individuals more and more came to imitate the example of princely gardens in their excess, until the rulers of the Ming dynasty (1368–1644) reevaluated imperial pleasure gardens in the context of their own supposedly enlightened and benevolent politics, forming principles that the succeeding Qing dynasty adopted. At the end of the first half of his essay, Cibot stated the lessons Ming and Qing China might have for France:

> Let wise men examine just to what extent Europe herself should adopt [these principles]. We will restrict ourselves here to saying that they succeeded in restoring pleasure gardens in China to the purposes of their first creation, even more so by the natural and pleasant form that they have taken than by the little care and expense that their upkeep requires.[76]

The second half of the "Essai sur les jardins de plaisance des Chinois" begins with the statement that the West should put aside all the false ideas of pleasure gardens in contemporary China. What follows is a detailed exposition of the many components that make up a Chinese pleasure garden—the layout of the garden, the features of the landscape and waters, the architectural elements, and the conventions of a garden art that imitates nature without appearing artificial. In support of his description of Chinese gardens, Cibot includes a long citation from a Tang-dynasty text by Liu Zongyuan (柳宗元, 773–819), a famous poet and writer on landscape,[77] where Liu seems to presage the ideal of the natural garden that Cibot has attributed first to ancient times and now to the current Qing dynasty:

> The art of laying out [gardens] thus consists of bringing together in them with such simplicity the serenity, the green, the shade, the points of view, the variety and solitude of the fields, such that the eye is fooled and taken in by their simple and rural appearance, the ear by their silence, or by what might disturb it, and all the senses by the impression of enjoyment and peace which make the time spent there so sweet. This variety, which is the eternal and dominant beauty of the countryside, must be the first thing to which one should aspire in the layout of the landscape of a garden.[78]

Cibot's comments on Liu Zongyuan's text signal the criticisms of excessive display and magnificence of the "ornaments"—the landscape features and the constructions—of an imperial garden. In continuing his presentation of the ideals of Chinese gardens, Cibot repeatedly notes that the formal alignments and symmetry characteristic of European garden features, including plantings, waterways, and the layout of the landscape, are foreign to Chinese gardens. But he admits that, given as much accurate detail as he can provide here, he only describes part of what he has seen,

> and the ideas of Europe are still so distant from Chinese taste that we almost despair that you should believe only in part in the fidelity of our descriptions. It would take an entire work to give a description that encompassed all of the details.[79]

Cibot's essay ends with an admonition that wise men should reflect on the subject of Chinese gardens, and that following in the footsteps of the Chinese in the decoration of gardens would bring to the fore the pleasures of the local climate and diminish only the expenses needed for their maintenance. His critique of waste and expense informs the moralistic tone of the entire essay, including the final statement:

> The more they [i.e., wise men] follow Chinese taste, the easier that will become for them; and they would be able to adopt such a system which would have cost agriculture so many thousands of arms so uselessly occupied with raking paths that no one walks upon and trimming or shaping trees that no one sees.[80]

Garden Theory in Eighteenth-Century France

In the last paragraph of the "Essai sur les jardins des Chinois," Cibot invokes two important figures in the history—and theory—of gardens in eighteenth-century France. The first, described simply as a "fine wit of the last century," Rinaldi perceptively identifies as the writer Saint-Simon (Louis de Rouvroy, duc de Saint-Simon, 1675–1755), who, in his memoirs for the year 1715, sharply criticized the bad taste (literally, *mauvais goût*) of Louis XIV's palace and gardens at Versailles, where the king sought to triumph over nature, an effort that was only partly successful and ruinously expensive.[81] Cibot then mentions the ideas which the

> ingenious Author of an *Essai sur l'Architecture*, who had since proposed that, in making a fortunate combination of Chinese ideas and European ideas, it would be possible to have gay and delightful gardens, where beautiful nature would be found with all it's graces.[82]

The author of the *Essai sur l'Architecture* is Marc-Antoine Laugier (1713–1769), whose essay on architecture appeared in two editions, in 1753 and 1755.[83] It is one of the crucial documents of eighteenth-century architectural theory, and it contains a chapter entitled "De l'Embellissement des Jardins" ("On the ornamentation of gardens") that discusses Chinese gardens in some detail.[84]

Laugier, himself a Jesuit priest, emphasized the role of nature and natural beauty in the inspiration of garden design.[85] He saw the art of gardens in France reaching a supreme moment under Louis XIV, for whom André le Nôtre (1613–1700) designed the gardens of Versailles and other royal palaces. Laugier invokes an ideal of the countryside as a model for gardens, looking to nature for shade and greenery, pleasant views, and describing even the "pleasant strangeness" of nature. Much of the same discourse was used by Cibot to describe Chinese gardens while criticizing the sterile formality of European gardens, and while Laugier first praises Versailles as the masterpiece of

French gardens, soon he moves on to condemning what he sees as a series of "failings" (*défauts*). At Versailles, nature is buried under an apparatus of symmetry and magnificence, resulting in sadness and boredom in a place that has cost vast sums to construct. The gardens are badly sited, with no consideration of the advantages of the surrounding landscape, and filled with useless decorations. In discussing what he lists as the second failing of the gardens of Versailles, Laugier invokes Chinese taste (*le goût des Chinois*), referring to Attiret's letter on the Yuanming yuan although without naming it specifically.[86] For Laugier, the Chinese taste in this case seems preferable to French taste. He noted the anti-symmetry of the Qing gardens, and the term *anti-symmétrie* appears in other texts on gardens as well, arguing for the superiority of what is simple and natural. Laugier even expressed the wish that Attiret's text had been accompanied by a plan of the gardens of the Yuanming yuan. He wrote:

> There is no doubt that this plan would have furnished us with a good model, and that in making an inspired mix of Chinese ideas with our own, we would in the end have come to make gardens where nature would find itself again in all its beauty.[87]

Bertin, Paintings and Practice: Rocks and Other Images

Images of Chinese gardens, and especially of the Yuanming yuan, which were received by Bertin or passed through his hands to others, surely reinforce the role of nature in the construction of Chinese gardens. Nature is invoked as an ideal or ultimate source, all the while the art of the garden designer uses nature as an inspiration where the art should, in theory, not be visible. Rocks (commonly cited as *pierres* or *rochers*) are frequently included among the distinctive features noted in texts on Chinese gardens in the eighteenth century, and their qualities are conventionally contrasted with the role of sculptures or other man-made ornaments in more traditional European gardens. In Bertin's collection, images of rocks appeared in paintings such as those which reproduced or transformed the landscapes of the Yuanming yuan, and these paintings made what was supposedly a natural landscape take on the attributes of a carefully crafted Chinese garden, despite the incongruous scale.

In Bertin's case, Chinese garden rocks had a particular significance. In 1778, he had received a Chinese rock along with what was surely its carved wood mount. The entry in the inventory of the shipment reads: "Rock, with its pedestal. When they are small, like this one, they are placed in residences; when they are large, they are placed in gardens, where they take the place of statues."[88] What the missionaries had sent to Bertin was the type now commonly referred to as a scholar's rock, sometimes fantastically contorted stones which would have been an indispensable fixture of a Chinese scholar's studio.[89] Such rocks are the subject of a long literary, artistic, and collecting tradition in China, which encompasses poetry and essays on rocks as well as paintings and albums illustrating typical or famous examples. Albums dedicated to the subject of rocks, many of which circulated in woodblock editions, were inevitably accompanied by texts, either poems and/or descriptions of the rocks depicted on the album pages. Among the best known and widely circulated albums are the "Yunlin shipu" 雲林石譜 (Album of rocks by the master Cloudy Forest) authored by Du Wan (杜綰, act. 11th century), and the "Suyuan shipu" 素園石譜 (Suyuan album of rocks), compiled by the Ming scholar-collector Lin Youlin (林友麟) in 1613.[90]

Bertin himself possessed a group of paintings of Chinese garden rocks, which he had mounted in an album entitled *Pierres employées pour ornemens [sic] dans les jardins chinois* (Rocks used for ornaments in Chinese gardens).[91] The Jesuit missionaries had sent Bertin a total of 42 paintings, all of which follow the same format. In each, a tall, slender garden rock is shown standing in a carved stone basin—itself a typical Chinese arrangement for displaying scholars rocks. The images are rendered in bright colors against a blank background and employ European modes of shading and perspective. Each is carefully painted on what is apparently a sheet of Chinese paper that often has a pencil or chalk outline around the trimmed edge as well as a faint vertical line that divides the sheet into two sections. The illustration of the rock takes up the larger section, the Chinese name for the rock is written in standard script toward the bottom of the other section, and a small identification number is written below the Chinese. Other than the title, the album contains no additional text, but the group of paintings was accompanied by a "notice," a detailed description of what it illustrates.[92] As with so many texts sent from China, this one also bears a note (in a different hand) on the first page, "See the paintings, which number 42." The notice itself, in a small, sometimes illegible handwriting, is not signed or dated.[93] It begins with a general statement that France has turned away from gardens characterized by carefully, even excessively, pruned trees and costly statues that sometimes depict indecent subjects. In their place, gardens are now more natural, and the missionaries invite their readers, presumably Bertin and others with access to his collections, to examine the Chinese model of rocks as garden ornaments. These are created with artful skill where the art or artifice is not visible, and they are just one part of overall garden designs characterized by anti-symmetry.[94]

The artist of the 42 paintings, as noted in the text, did not paint the rocks as they would appear in actual gardens but showed them in vases or basins, which is common practice for rocks in residences or in garden courtyards in cities. The missionaries realize that it would be of great interest if they could provide extensive scientific detail on all of the rocks, but that is beyond their skills, and all they can report is what they have learned from their experience in China and from certain books. Unfortunately, they cite no specific titles, but they hope that what they have to say will in some way contribute to European knowledge of the sciences and the arts, a theme that is central to the communications exchanged between Bertin and the missionaries in Beijing. Referring to the numbers on each of the illustrations, the text describes the rocks individually or, more often, in groups. The notes are generally short, identifying the general type of rock with comments on where they are found or how they are produced, since many of what appear to be natural formations are actually enhanced by carving. Color and size are also described, and, even though all the illustrations appear to show rocks of the same size, individual examples are cited as being between two and ten or more feet (*pieds*) in height, with some of the largest, rarest, and most valuable being found in imperial gardens. The illustration of one well-known type of rock is representative of the entries in the notice:

> Number 15 is famous in the history of China for the passion of one emperor for this type of stone. A prodigious quantity has been taken from Taihu or the Great Lake, at the bottom of which they have been hollowed out and pierced by the waters. It has ever since had the name of "rock from the Great Lake" and has continued to be fashionable in gardens. Those pieces that truly come from the

lake are more carefully worked, more pleasant to look at and more [illeg.] than those one finds elsewhere.[95]

The label on the painting of no. 15 (Figure 2.4) reads Nan Taihu shi 南太湖石 or "Southern Taihu rock." The association of Lake Tai (Taihu, lit., Great Lake), adjacent to the city of Suzhou 蘇州—itself long known for its scenery and gardens—with

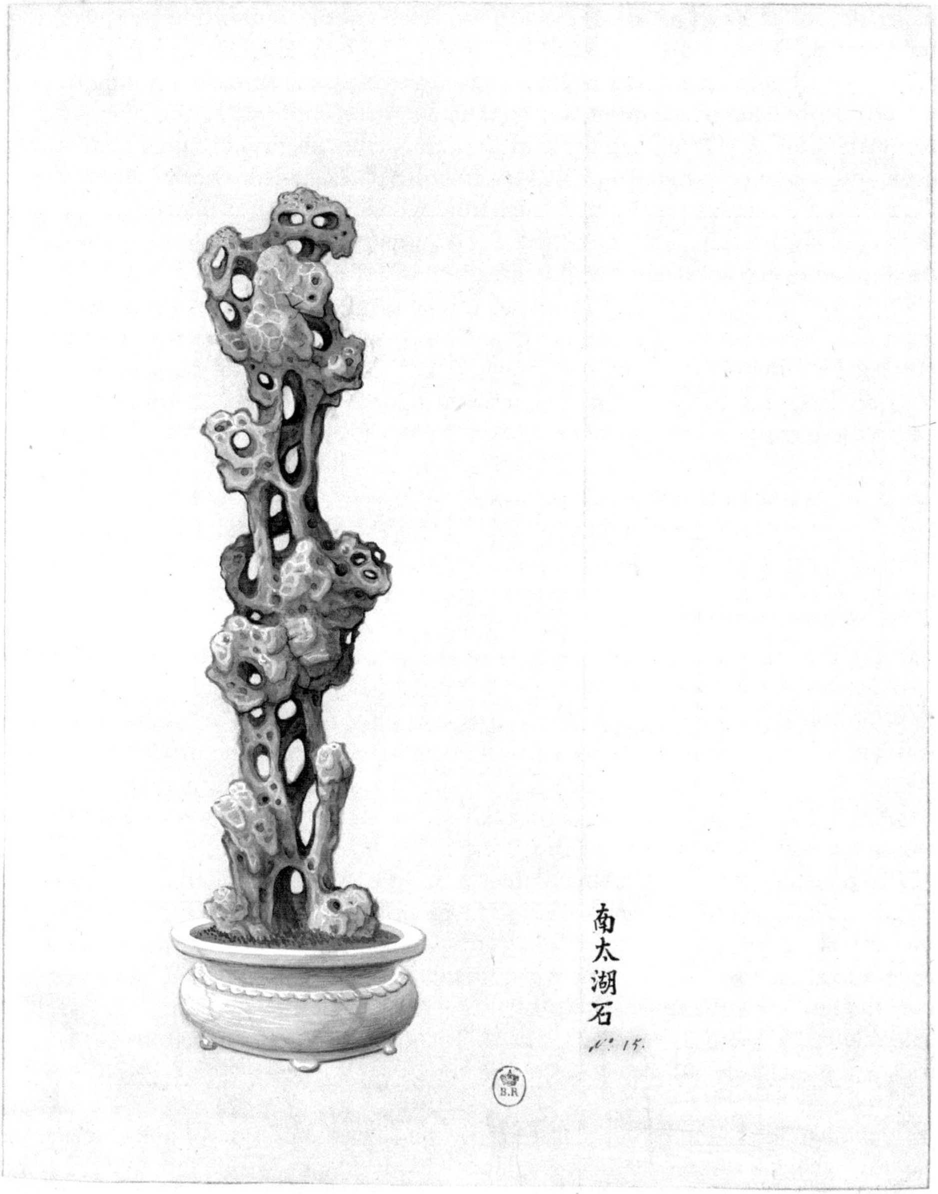

Figure 2.4 Anonymous, Chinese, *Pierres employées pour ornemens*, no. 15, "Nan Taihu shi," ink and color on paper, 40 × 33 cm. Paris, Bibliothèque nationale de France.

the most famous or desirable Chinese garden and scholar rocks is part of an ancient tradition. The description of the Taihu rock continues with a note that they can also be found in the Bei Zhili 北直隸 region (the area around the capital, Beijing), although these are not as fine. Because of the qualities of such rocks, the Chinese use them to construct garden features, including grottoes, caverns, and piles of rocks which represent mountains in miniature. Chinese workers assemble them with such skill that an entire grotto can appear to consist of one single rock. The "one emperor" mentioned in the missionaries' text is surely the Huizong emperor (徽宗, r. 1100–1126), whose Genyue Garden in Kaifeng 開封, the Northern Song capital, contained an artificial mountain called the Genyue 艮嶽 or "Northeast Marchmount," which gave its name to this legendary garden built at the end of the Northern Song (960–1127). Among the countless rocks transported to Huizong's garden, the most famous was the so-called "Divine Conveyance Rock" (Shenyun shi 神運石) a massive stone from Lake Tai that supposedly measured some 49 feet (14.9 meters) tall.[96] The extravagant expenditures on the rocks, trees, and other garden elements shipped to Kaifeng, the corruption and waste, and the burdens on the common people are traditionally cited as a major cause of the downfall of the Northern Song in 1127.[97]

The text of the notice that accompanied Bertin's album *Pierres employées pour ornemens* continues with descriptions of the various types of rocks illustrated, their characteristics, and where they might be found. The description for no. 32 contains the following statement: "Even though we have already sent a few pieces, since no reply has made mention of them, we will send others this year; the certainty we have in our ignorance will not deter our good will."[98] It is possible that this is a reference to the rock with its display pedestal noted previously, which was received in 1778. Delays in replies to letters and/or requests are noted often enough in the Jesuit missionaries' correspondence, but the reference also suggests a date for the detailed description of the contents of Bertin's album. The text concludes with more general comments on Chinese rocks. The missionaries regret that they cannot provide a complete catalogue of all the kinds of rocks seen in gardens in the capital or the provinces since this is beyond their capacities. It would require additional expenditures, but they acknowledge that such information would extend into the sphere of the sciences and the arts. And they return once more to the question of the expenses necessary for the construction and decoration of gardens as well as the burdens they impose on the people—themes that again reflect contemporary writings on garden theory in France.

Representations of Chinese gardens are relatively rare in the *Mémoires concernant les Chinois*, but in the series of illustrations illustrating the "Life of Koung-tsée, commonly called Confucius," published in Volume 12 of the *Mémoires* in 1786, there are a number of garden views.[99] The engraving most relevant to the discussion here shows an episode from the childhood of Confucius (Figure 2.5), and its content is described in an appended "Explanation."[100] The text there gives a brief description of the garden with a view of the countryside and states that the rough stones or rocks in the garden are exactly what one sees in China. The illustrations of the life of Confucius include four additional plates where garden rocks are prominently featured in the compositions, but the explanations for these plates do not mention the garden settings.[101] This crucial biography of Confucius and the illustrations that accompany it are discussed in additional detail in Chapter 4.

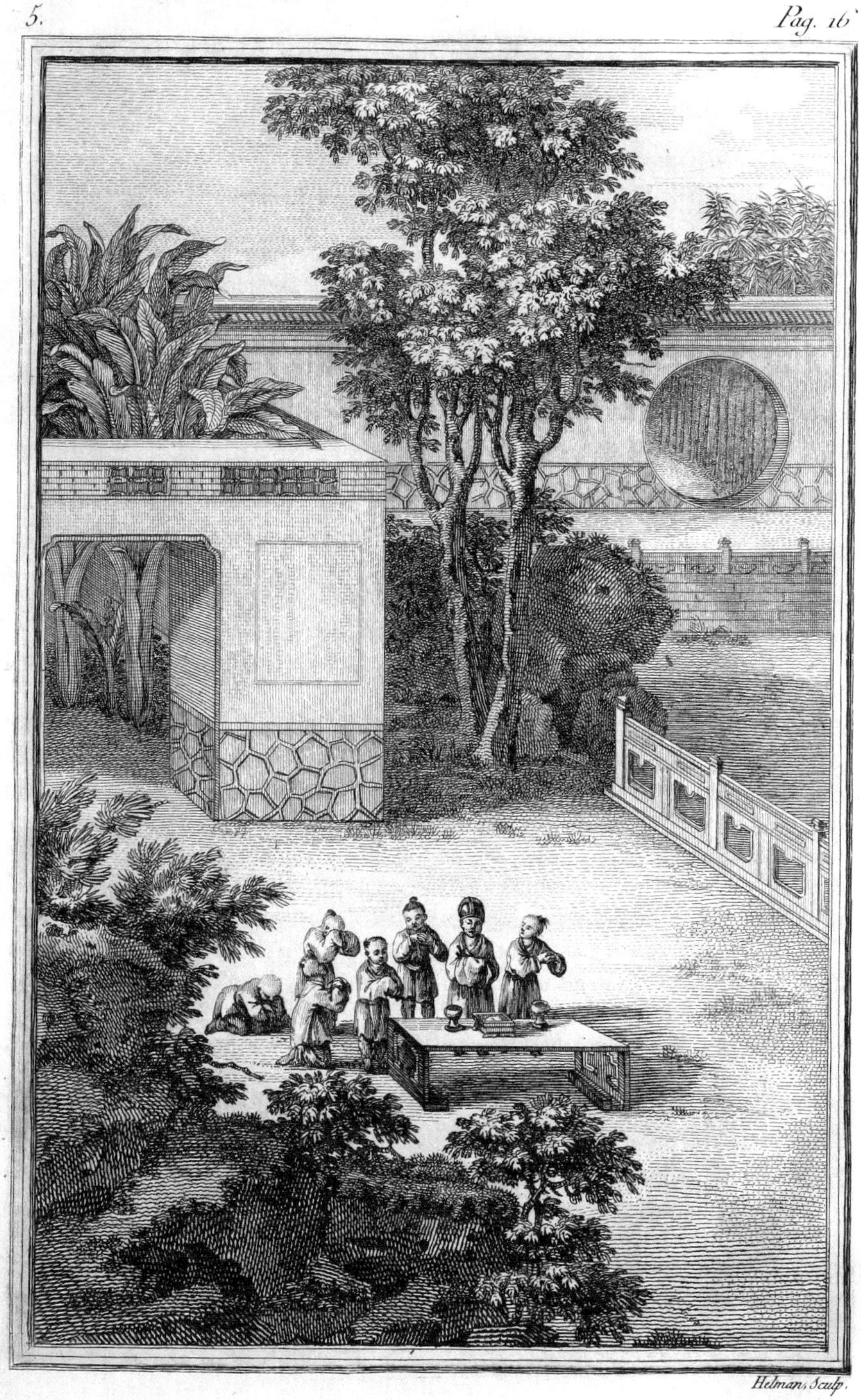

Figure 2.5 Isidore-Stanislas Helman, *Mémoires concernant les Chinois*, vol. 12, "Vie de *Koung-tsée*, Appellé vulgairement Confucius, . . ." engraving, 21 × 14.5 cm, 1786, pl. 5, facing p. 16, Confucius as a child. Getty Research Institute, Los Angeles (41–499).

Numerous publications in French and English provided a wealth of information on Chinese gardens, and a relatively limited number of illustrations—both those that were published and available to a broader public as well as prints and paintings held in private collections, which were visible to a more limited audience—formed the basis of the transfer of knowledge of Chinese gardens between China and eighteenth-century Europe. Certain themes, such as the ideal of nature as the ultimate source of Chinese garden design and the supposedly related avoidance of excessive expense, are shared by many of the sources to which Henri Bertin would have had access. Ideas of Chinese gardens fascinated European elites, and the understanding of Chinese architecture, the subject of the following chapter, was intimately related to garden design and construction.

Notes

1. On the crucial role of the Jesuit missionaries in China, see Bianca Maria Rinaldi, *The "Chinese Garden in Good Taste": Jesuits and Europe's Knowledge of Chinese Flora and Art of the Garden in the 17th and 18th Centuries* (Munich: Martin Meidenbauer, 2006); see esp. Chap. 6, "The Jesuit Contribution to Knowledge About Chinese Gardens," 171–240.
2. On the official mission dispatched to China by Louis XIV, see, among other sources, Landry-Deron, "Les Mathématiciens envoyés en Chine par Louis XIV en 1685."
3. Jean-François Gerbillon, "Seconde voyage fait par ordre del l'Empereur de la Chine en Tartarie par les Pères Gerbillon et Pereira en l'année 1689," in Du Halde, *Description de la Chine*, vol. 4, 163–251.
4. On Gerbillon's text, see the comments and selected translations in Bianca Maria Rinaldi, *Ideas of Chinese Gardens: Western Accounts, 1300–1860* (Philadelphia: University of Pennsylvania Press, 2016), Chap. 5, "Jean-François Gerbillon" (1654–1707), 66–73.
5. Thomas Whately, *Observations on Modern Gardening, Illustrated by Descriptions . . .* (London: Printed for T. Payne, at the Mews-gate, 1770); note that Whately's name does not appear on the first edition.
6. *Journal encyclopédique*, 1770, vol. 6, part 2, 229–237. The review is cited in the "Discours Préliminaire" of the French edition of Whately, xlix; see the following note.
7. *L'Art de former les jardins modernes, ou L'art des jardins anglois. . .*, François de Paule Latapie, trans. (Paris: Charles-Antoine Jombert, Père, 1771); for the "Discours Préliminaire," see i–lix.
8. Ibid., viii, citing Du Halde, *Description de la Chine*, vol. 2, 101.
9. Sir William Chambers, *Designs of Chinese Buildings, Furniture, Dresses, Machines and Utensils . . .* (London: Published for the Author. . ., 1757); for the chapter in question, see 14–19. The French translation, published in the same year, is entitled "De l'Art de distribuer les jardins selons l'usage des Chinois," *Desseins des édifices, meubles, habits, machines, et ustenciles* [*sic*] *des Chinois* (London: J. Haberkorn, 1757), 15–19.
10. *L'art de former les jardins modernes*, lii–lix.
11. Attiret's biography is contained in a letter from Jean-Joseph-Marie Amiot dated 1 March 1769. See Henri Bernard[-Maître], S.J., "Le Frère Attiret au service de K'ien-long (1739–1768)," *Bulletin de l'Université l'Aurore* (1943), series III, 4, no. 1 (2013), 30–82; 4, no. 2 (2014), 435–474. Attiret's letter and a number of other eighteenth-century texts discussed later are listed on the website History of Gardens in East Asia: Bibliography China (chronological), http://inside.bard.edu/~louis/gardens/bibliochina.html, accessed 1 July 2017. I would like to thank François Louis and the Bard Graduate Center for compiling this list and making it available online.
12. For Attiret's letter on the Yuanming yuan, see *Lettres édifiantes et curieuses*, vol. 27 (Paris: chez les Frères Guérin, 1749), 1–57.
13. Hugh Honour notes that Attiret's descriptions of "artificially natural hills and lakes and winding walks" essentially confirmed what were already features of English parks. See the

"Introduction" to Osvald Sirén, *China and Gardens of Europe of the Eighteenth Century* (New York: Roland Press, 1949; reprint Washington, DC: Dumbarton Oaks Research Library and Collection, 1990).

14. *Lettres édifiantes et curieuses*, vol. 27, 34–35 (italics as in the original): "Mais dans les maisons de plaisance, on veut que presque partout il règne un beau désordre, une anti-symmétrie. Tout roule sur ce principe: *C'est une campagne rustique & naturelle, qu'on veut représenter; une solitude, non pas un Palais bien ordonné dans toutes les règles de la symmétrie & du rapport.*" The English translation is *A Particular Account of the Emperor of China's Gardens Near Pekin. . .*, Translated from the French by Sir Harry Beaumont (London: R. Dodsley, 1752), 38–39. Sir Harry Beaumont is the pseudonym of Joseph Spence, and Spence puts quotation marks around the text in italics in the French.
15. Rinaldi, *Ideas of Chinese Gardens*, Chap. 9, "Jean-Denis Attiret (1702–68)," 91–111, cites Spence's translation in its entirety; see esp. 91–92, and 102, nn. 22–24.
16. The discussion here relies on the comprehensive article by Richard E. Strassberg, "Transmitting a Qing Imperial Garden: Kangxi's Thirty-Six Views of Bishu Shanzhuang and Their Journey to the West," published in Chinese and English, *Fengjing yuanlin* 风景园林 [Landscape architecture] no. 83 (June 2009), 93–103. For the footnote, see Spence, *A Particular Account*, 38.
17. Apparently Ripa was not the only artist who engraved the copper plates, since at least two other artists were involved in this task, although the name of only one, Zhang Kui 張奎 (dates unknown), is recorded on proofs of the prints. See Michele Fatica and Yue Zhuang, "Copperplates Controversy: Matteo Ripa's *Thirty-Six Views of Jehol* and the Chinese Rites Controversy," in Yue Zhuang and Andrea M. Riemenschnitter, eds., *Entangled Landscapes: Early Modern China and Europe* (Singapore: National University of Singapore Press, 2017), 144–186. Note that Ripa is occasionally identified as a Jesuit missionary; on Ripa as a missionary of the Propaganda Fide, see "Copperplates Controversy," 145 and n. 14; on the Chinese artists engraving plates for the *Thirty-Six Views*, see ibid., 150 and n. 41.
18. The very long title of the anonymous publication begins *The Emperor of China's Palace at Pekin, and His Principal Gardens, as Well in Tartary, as at Pekin, Gehol and the Adjacent Countries . . .* (London: Printed and Sold by Robert Sayer, Henry Overton, Thomas Bowles, and John Bowles and Son, 1753). Richard Strassberg, in Marcia Reed and Paola Demattè, eds., *China on Paper: European and Chinese Works from the Late Sixteenth to the Early Nineteenth Century* (Los Angeles: Getty Research Institute, 2007), 122–123, discusses *The Emperor of China's Palace at Pekin* as part of the chapter "War and Peace: Four Intercultural Landscapes," 89–137. See also *China on Paper*, cat. 31, 206–207.
19. See Yue Zhuang, "Hatchings in the Void: Ritual and Order in *Bishu Shanzhuang Shi* and Matteo Ripa's *Views of Jehol*," in Petra ten-Doesschate Chu and Ning Ding, eds., *Qing Encounters Artistic Exchanges between China and the West* (Los Angeles: Getty Research Institute, 2015), 142–157. The process of the "translation" of Chinese images into European modes is discussed further in the Conclusion.
20. Fatica and Zhuang, "Copperplates Controversy," 150ff., discusses the stylistic details of the engravings attributed to Ripa himself, including hatching and clouds in the sky and similar details in the water, elements that are mostly left blank in Chinese style by the Chinese engravers. For "Viewing the Fish from a Waterside Rock," see 179, n. 43.
21. *Lettres édifiantes et curieuses*, vol. 27, 40–41.
22. See Paul Pelliot, "Les 'Conquêtes de l'empereur de la Chine'," *T'oung Pao* 20 (1921), 183–274; the discussion of the images of the Yuanming yuan, a version of the album of the "40 Views of the Yuanming yuan" that Attiret eventually sent is discussed on 206–207 in the text, and n. 3. Viguier offered the album for sale with other documents in a letter dated January 1770, but when he received them is not clear. On the album, see the discussion immediately below.
23. For a detailed discussion of the "40 Views," the album generally referred to as the "20 Engravings of the European Palaces," and related images, see John Finlay, "Henri Bertin (1720–1792) and Images of the Yuanmingyuan in Eighteenth-Century France," in *Collecting and Displaying China's "Summer Palace" in the West: The Yuanmingyuan in Britain and France*, edited by Louise Tythacott (Abingdon, Oxford, UK: Routledge, 2018), Chap. 8, 123–137.

24. Taken by a French officer in the 1860 looting of the Yuanmingyuan, the album is now in the Bibliothèque nationale de France (BnF), Département des Estampes et Photographie, Réserve B-9-FT 6. See the BnF website, http://catalogue.bnf.fr/ark:/12148/cb438054446.public, *Yuanming Yuan si shi jing*, accessed 5 August 2017, for catalogue information and access to digital images of the "40 Views."
25. See He Zhongyi and Zeng Zhaofen, *Yuanming yuan yuanlin yishu* (Garden art of the Yuanming yuan) (Beijing: Kexue chubanshe, 1995), 229–233; and Chiu Che Bing, *Yuanming Yuan: Le jardin de la Clarté parfaite* (Besançon: Les Éditions de l'Imprimeur, 2000), 232.
26. See the second Qing imperial catalogue of paintings and calligraphy, *Shiqu baoji xubian* 石渠寶笈續編 (1793), *juan* 78, reprint vol. 7, 3755–3759 (Taipei: National Palace Museum, 1971). An inscription gives the date, equivalent to October–early November 1744, and the names of the painters, Tangdai (唐岱, 1673-after 1751) and Shen Yuan (沈源, act. ca. 1728–1748).
27. Qing imperial editions were produced by the Imperial Printing Office (Xiushu chu, 修書處), located in the Wuying dian 武英殿 complex in the Forbidden City. See Shiow-jyu Lu Shaw, *The Imperial Printing of Early Ch'ing China, 1644–1805* (Taipei: Chinese Materials Center, 1983), 9–17. The Wuying dian edition of the "40 Views" and the imperial edict of 1745 that ordered its creation are noted in the 1769 *Guochao gongshi* (國朝宮史, History of the palaces of the present [Qing] dynasty); see E'ertai鄂爾泰 and others, *Guochao gongshi*, Reprint edition (Beijing: Guji chubanshe, 2000). This would have been the album which Attiret sent to the Abbé Viguier; see n. 17 above.
28. *Différents Palais & Temples de la Chine, dessinés & gravés a la Chine*. The album is in the BnF, Département des Estampes et de la photographie, Réserve OE-21 (C)-Pet Fol.
29. See Constance Bienaimé, "Les objets 'de la Chine' dans les collections des ducs de Chaulnes," in Florence Boulerie, and others, eds., *L'Extrême-Orient dans la culture européenne des XVIIe et XVIIIe siècles* (Tübingen: Narr, 2009), 151–165.
30. On the inventories of objects, texts and images sent by the French Jesuits in Beijing, see Bernard[-Maître], "Catalogue des objets envoyés de Chine," nos. 33–34: 119–206. For the relevant inventory lists, see Bib. Inst. Ms 1524.
31. On Count Scheffer, see Sirén, *China and Gardens of Europe*, Chap. 18, "Swedish Interest in China: Carl Fredrik Scheffer, It's Chief Representative. . . ." On Scheffer and his connections to William Chambers, see Yue Zhuang, "Fear and Pride: Sir William Chambers' *Dissertation on Oriental Gardening*, Burke's Sublime and China," 56–114, in Zhuang and Riemenschnitter, eds., *Entangled Landscapes*; see esp. 60, 69.
32. "pour servir aux progrès de l'art des Jardins; puisque tout le monde sait que les Jardins Anglais ne sont qu'une imitation de ceux de la Chine."
33. The Qing woodblock album consisted of two volumes (*ce* 冊) contained in one wrapper (*han* 函); see the catalogue information on the website of the National Palace Museum, Taipei, http://npmhost.npm.gov.tw/ttscgi/ttsqueryxml?0:0:npmrbxml:000016023, accessed 5 December 2017. Cahier XV reproduces 28 views of the Yuanming yuan in the following order: nos. 20, 19, 18, . . ., 1, 40, 39, 38, . . ., 33. Cahier XV contains the remaining 12 views: nos. 32, 31, 30, . . ., 21. Le Rouge thus consistently reproduced the prints from the two volumes, albeit in reverse order. Scheffer is also credited as the source of prints for Portfolio 17 (October 1786). See Véronique Royet and others, comp., *Georges Louis Le Rouge: Jardins anglo-chinois* (Paris: Bibliothèque nationale de France, 2004), cats. 317, 345, 375.
34. Le Rouge's magnum opus is the subject of numerous studies. The most complete, which is the source of much of the information here, is Royet and others, comp., *Georges Louis Le Rouge*. The number of plates differs according to different sources, from 488 to 492. Le Rouge's prints are variously etchings, engravings, or combinations of the two techniques; see Royet, *Le Rouge*, 76–77, for references to the BnF website for specific catalogue details, now accessible online in searches for "Jardins anglo-chinois" with links to "Documents iconographiques."
35. Royet, *George Louis Le Rouge*, 202, cites the BnF cataloguing information for each of the Chinese sources reproduced here, and Appendix II, 274–276, is a concordance of the images in Le Rouge with various Chinese sources in the BnF that are identical to Le Rouge's sources. See Richard Strassberg, in Reed and Demattè, eds., *China on Paper*, for

a detailed discussion of images of Chinese gardens and the sources for Le Rouge's portfolios; see esp. "The Landscape of Intercultural Citation: The Chinese-Style Garden in Europe," 121–132.

36. The first is from Bib. Inst. Ms 1524, "Catalogue des objets venus de Chine depuis 1765 à 1769," fol. 133 verso, a document dated 1770 listing "41 [*sic*] dessins des maisons de l'Empereur ou du Versailles de PéKing." A note in the margin indicates that they were destined for a M. Heurtault [de Lammerville]. This is most likely Jean-Marie Heurtault de Lammerville (1740–1810); see the sale catalogue of his estate, *Catalogue de tableaux, dessins et estampes. . . . Composant le cabinet de feu M. Hurtault* [*sic*], . . . (Paris: Imprimerie Moreau, February 1825); see esp. 15–16. The second is from a document in the same vol., fol. 136 recto, listing "une boëte de carton où sont diverses peintures. au dessus sont les vües de ge ho eul plus bas sont les 40 peintures du Versailles de Péking." That is, along with 40 paintings of the Versailles of Beijing, the box contained views of Jehol or Rehe, the location of the Bishu shanzhuang at Chengde, and the subject here is surely a version of the Kangxi emperor's 1712 "36 views of the Bishu shanzhuang" (see the discussion of the Bishu shanzhuang beginning on p. 42 above). See also Bernard[-Maître], "Catalogue des objets envoyés de Chine," 135, 139.
37. BnF, Fonds Bréquigny, vol. 123, fols. 243–246.
38. On the question of authorship and the date of the manuscript, see the following discussion of Cibot's published translation of the "Jardin de Sée-Ma-Kouang." See also n. 30 above.
39. Fonds Bréquigny, vol. 123, fol. 243: "Hai-tien qui est a deux grandes lieux de Pe-King est le versaille [*sic*] de Chine et Yuen-ming-yuen la maison et jardin de plaisance de l'Empereur."
40. Haidian is now a district of the municipality of Beijing.
41. See n. 36 above.
42. Fonds Bréquigny, vol. 123, fol. 244 recto: "il sentira d'abord qu'elle est très variée dans ses plans pour les ponts et les arcs de triomphe les lacs et les Étangs, les napes d'eaux et les canaux, les collines et les plaines, les bois et les bosquets, les cavernes et les rochers. Les sentiers perdus et les avenües &c. Leur distribution et leur ensemble tiennent a des idées qui assujettissent l'art au modelles de la nature et ne lui permettent que le choix de l'imitation." The French term *arcs de triomphe* is used to describe the various gateways (*pailou* 牌樓), often with signboards or inscriptions, at the entrance to Chinese imperial buildings.
43. The album is entitled *Haitien. Maison de Plaisance, de l'Empereur de Chine* (Haidian, pleasure palace of the emperor of China); it was acquired by the BnF in the nationalization of Bertin's collections in 1792 and is kept in the Département des Estampes et de la photographie, Réserve Oe-21-Pet Fol. For a detailed discussion of images of the Yuanming yuan in Henri Bertin's collection, see Finlay "Henri Bertin (1720–1792) and the *40 Views of the Yuanming yuan.*"
44. Fonds Bréquigny, vol. 123, fol. 244 verso: "Recueil des noms chinois de toutes les maisons qu'elle représente et des vers que l'Empereur Reignant a composé."
45. My thesis, John Finlay, "'40 Views of the Yuanming yuan': Image and Ideology in a Qianlong Imperial Album of Poetry and Paintings," PhD diss., Yale University, New Haven, CT, 2011, deals at length with the ideological content of the names of sites and structures in the Yuanming yuan.
46. See n. 43 above.
47. Royer Collection/Zeldzaamheden, Rijksmuseum voor Volkenkunde, Leiden, The Netherlands (1883, accession no. 360–364). See Jan van Campen, "A Chinese Collection in the Netherlands," *The Magazine Antiques*, September 2000, 360–371. The relationship between the two albums is briefly discussed in Finlay, "Henri Bertin (1720–1792) and the *40 Views of the Yuanming yuan.*"
48. Chiu, *Yuanming Yuan: Le jardin de la Clarté parfaite*, 253–254; Chiu provides a translation of the preface and poem. See also He and Zeng, *Yuanming yuan yuanlin yishu*, 230.
49. BnF, Département des Estampes et de la photographie, Réserve OE-26-FT 4, listed simply as *Recueil. Paysages chinois*. It is not clear when Bertin received these and other related paintings.

50. See John Finlay, "Henri Bertin and the Commerce in Images," 79–94 in Chu and Ding, eds., *Qing Encounters*; see esp. 84, 86, and Fig. 5. The image has previously been published at least twice. See Hendrik Budde et al., eds., *Europa und die Kaiser von China (1240–1816)* (Frankfurt am Main: Insel-Verlag, 1985), 261; and Anita Chung, *Drawing Boundaries: Architectural Images in Qing China* (Honolulu: University of Hawai'i Press, 2004), 61, color pl. 4.
51. *Mémoires*, vol. 2, 365–574. The original date "À Pe-king, ce 27 Juillet 1775" appears on 574. Although the "Remarks" are variously attributed to Amiot or Cibot (see, for example, Rinaldi, *Ideas of Chinese Gardens*, Chap. 17, "Jean-Joseph-Marie Amiot (1718–93) or Pierre-Martial Cibot (1727–80) (attributed)," 149–154). Dehergne "Grande Collection," 274, ultimately attributes these responses to Cibot with Aloïs Ko (Gao), citing a letter from Bertin to Cibot dated 30 September 1777 as well as other sources. However, the "Table Générale des Matières," the index published in *Mémoires*, vol. 10, lists texts written by Amiot; see 184–185, citing Amiot's writings in vol. 2, 365ff., specifically the refutation of Cornelius de Pauw: "Remarques sur un écrit de M. Paw, intitulé, *Recherches sur les Egyptiens & les Chinois*, dont M. Amiot combat les erreurs & les faussetés, 365 & suiv." On De Pauw, see the following note. And see the Fonds Bréquigny, vol. 12, which contains the original, unsigned manuscript, dated 27 July 1775, in a folder labeled "Réponses aux *Recherches philosophiques* de M. de P[auw] sur les Chinois, par le P. Amiot."
52. Cornélius De Pauw, *Recherches philosophiques sur les Égyptiens et les Chinois, par l'auteur des recherches sur les Amériquains*, 2 vols. (Berlin: C.J. Decker, 1773).
53. The text is briefly described in *Mémoires*, vol. 2, *Avant-propos*, viii.
54. Ibid., XXXIXe Rem. (no. 39), 435–436.
55. Rinaldi, *Ideas of Chinese Gardens*, Chap. 17. The "remarks" and a number of other texts cited below are translated and discussed by Bianca Rinaldi, herself a practicing garden architect, in *Ideas of Chinese Gardens*. While I rely on my own readings of the French sources, the discussion here also reflects Rinaldi's many thoughtful insights.
56. *Mémoires*, vol. 2, CIV[e] Rem. (no. 104), 569–570.
57. Ibid., 643–650, including two pages of introduction.
58. On Sima Guang, see Robert E. Harrist, Jr., *Painting and Private Life in Eleventh-Century China: Mountain Villa by Li Gonglin* (Princeton: Princeton University Press, 1998); Chapter 3, "The Transformed Landscape: *Place and Persona in Northern Song Gardens*;" see esp. 50–54, "Virtuous Retirement: Sima Guang and the Garden of Solitary Enjoyment."
59. James Legge, *The Works of Mencius Translated, with Critical and Exegetical Notes, Prolegomena, and Copious Indexes by James Legge*, The Chinese Classics, vol. 2 (reprint, New York: Dover Publications, 1970), "King Hui of Liang, Part II," 151.
60. *Mémoires*, vol. 2, 643: "Les Jardins de Chine sont une imitation étudiée, mais naturelle, des différentes beautés de la campagne, en collines, vallées, gorges, bassins, petites plaines, nappes d'eau, ruisseaux, îles, rochers, grottes, vieux antres, plantes & fleurs. Le grand ouvrage de l'art est d'étendre une petit espace, par la multitude, la variété, la surpises des aspects; de dérober à la nature toutes ses resources, & de lui en faire honneur."
61. Rinaldi, *Ideas of Chinese Gardens*, Chap. 16, "Pierre-Martial Cibot (1727–80)," 146–148, translates this introductory text but leaves out the editor's reference that provides the source of the translation.
62. *Mémoires*, vol. 2, 643: "Cette Note est *extraite d'une Description du Jardin de* Yuen-ming-yuen, *envoyée de* Pé-king, *il y a quelques années, avec les dessins. L'Auteur de la Description ajoute:* Pour imaginer à-peu-près l'effet de toutes ces parties. . . ." The italics are as in the original.
63. As discussed later, the text of the "Record of the Garden of Solitary Enjoyment" was published in France before it appeared in the *Mémoires*; see also Rinaldi, *Ideas of Chinese Gardens*, Chap. 16, 147.
64. Ibid.
65. My analysis of the Sima Guang's "Record" is based on the translation published in Edwin T. Morris, *The Gardens of China: History, Art, and Meanings* (New York: Charles Scribner's Sons, 1983), Chap. 4, "The Garden of the Scholar: Principles and Elements of Design," 69–96; see esp. 78ff. on "Naming." Morris's translation appears on 80–81, and

note 6, citing his reliance on the translation's first published source in Sirén, *China and Gardens of Europe*, 77–78, with Morris's revisions. The English version here seems to faithfully follow the original Chinese text; see http://ctext.org/wiki.pl?if=gb&chapter=101475, accessed 15 August 2017.

66. *Mémoires*, vol. 2, 647: "Les environs n'offrent qu'une barrière de rochers pointus bizarrement assemblées, qui s'élèvent en amphithéâtre, d'une manière sauvage & rustique. Quand on arrive au bas, on trouve une grotte profonde qui va en s'élargissant peu-à-peu, & forme une espèce de sallon irrégulier dont la voûte s'élève en dôme."
67. Harrist, *Painting and Private Life in Eleventh-Century China*, 50–54.
68. Claude-Henri Watelet, *Essai sur les Jardins* (Paris: Impr. de Prault, 1774); see 125–137, "Le Jardin Chinois." Some copies of the *Essai sur les Jardins* have the mistaken date M.DCC.LXIV (1764) on the title page, although the volume first appeared in 1774. See the reference material from the Getty Research Institute, http://primo.getty.edu/GRI:GETTY_ALMA21135428900001551, accessed 15 August 2017.
69. Watelet, *Essai sur les Jardins*, 136–137: "Le tableau qui suit n'est qu'un simple paysage dessiné d'après une nature agréable; mais ceux qui aiment ce genre de peinture, ne dédaignent pas quelquefois une étude fidelle, tracée même par une main inconnue."
70. *Mémoires*, vol. 8 (1782), "Essai sur les Jardins de Plaisance des Chinois," 301–326.
71. Cibot's name does not appear on the "Essay" in vol. 8, but the "Table générale des Matières," *Mémoires*, vol. 10, 224–225, credits Cibot. A document in Bib. Inst. Ms 1524, fol. 176 recto, includes the following listing of objects and documents sent from China, which provides the early date: "No. O. Essai sur les jardins de plaisance de Chine. Notice sur la Culture des Champignons. Les deux pieces ont êté [*sic*] Envoyées à l'Académie impériale de St. Petersbourg en 1774 et 1775." Cibot is credited with a *Notice* on mushrooms accompanied by an illustration, *Mémoires*, vol. 4 (1779), 500–503.
72. See Rinaldi, *Ideas of Chinese Gardens*, Chap. 18, Cibot, "Essai sur les Jardins de Plaisance des Chinois," 155–181, where the notes on pp. 175–181 identify the many writers and historical sources quoted in the essay.
73. Ibid., 155.
74. Divided between the Western Zhou (1046–771 BCE) and the Eastern Zhou (770–256 BCE); Cibot, "Essai," 304, cites the first emperor, Wu Wang (武王, r. ca. 1046–1043 BCE), as having become master of the empire in 1222 BCE, although the date is not correct. Cibot describes King Mu (Mu Wang 穆王, r. 976–921 BCE) as the first to begin construction of elaborate, decorative imperial gardens.
75. See esp. *Mémoires*, vol. 8, "Essai," 312: "Que l'Europe revienne de ses présmptions, & renonce à la gloire d'avoir la première vaincu ou suplée les saisons, subjugué ou surpassé la fertilité de la terre. . . ."
76. Ibid., 316: "Que les sages examinent jusqu'où l'Europe se doit à elle-même de les adopter. Nous nous bornons à dire qu'on a réussi à ramener en Chine les jardins de plaisance à la fin de leur première institution, encore plus par la forme naturelle & agréable qu'ils ont prise, que par le peu de soin & de dépenses que demande leur entretien."
77. Rinaldi, *Ideas of Chinese Gardens*, 169, n. 52. Liu Zongyuan's poetry is deeply imbued with a sense of nature; see Stephen Owen, *The End of the Chinese 'Middle Ages': Essays in Mid-Tang Literary Culture* (Stanford, CA: Stanford University Press, 1996), esp. "Reading the Landscape," 34–54. Liu is famous as an essayist and a key figure of the *guwen* 古文 (ancient prose) literary movement of the mid-Tang.
78. *Mémoires*, vol. 8, "Essai," 318: "L'art de les tracer consiste donc à y rassembler si naïvement la sérénité, la verdure, l'ombrage, les points de vue, la variété & la solitude des champs, que l'oeil trompé se méprenne à leur air simple & champêtre, l'oreille à leur silence, ou à ce qui le trouble, & tous les sens à l'impression de jouissance & de paix qui en rend le séjour si doux. Ainsi la variété, qui est la beauté dominante & éternelle de la campagne, doit être la première à laquelle il faille viser dans la distribution du terrein d'un jardin." I have not been able to locate Liu Zongyuan's text which Cibot presents here.
79. Ibid., 325: "& les pensées de l'Europe sont si loin encore du goût chinois, que nous désespérons presque qu'on croie une partie sur la foi de nos récits. Il faudroit un ouvrage entier pour en donner une description que embrassât tous les détails."

80. Ibid., 326: "Plus ils suivront le goût chinois, plus cela leur deviendra facile; & ils pourroient faire adopter tel systême qui vaudroit à l'agriculture des milliers de bras si inutilement occupés à ratisser des allées où personne ne passe, & à tondre ou façonner des arbres que personne ne voit."
81. Rinaldi, *Ideas of Chinese Gardens*, 174, n. 58, citing the *Mémoires complets et authentique du duc de Saint-Simon sur le siècle de Louis XIV*, second edition (Paris: Buisson, 1789), vol. 1, 129–130.
82. *Mémoires*, vol. 8, "Essai," 326: "que l'ingénieux Auteur d'un Essai sur l'architecture, a avancé depuis, qu'en faisant un heureux mélange des idées chinoises & des idées européennes, on réussiroit à avoir des jardins gais & rians, où la belle nature se trouveroit avec toutes ses graces."
83. Marc-Antoine Laugier, *Essai sur l'Architecture* (Paris: Chez Duchesne, 1753); idem, *Nouvelle édition, Revue, corrigée, & augmentée* . . . (Paris: Chez Duchesne, 1755).
84. Laugier, *Essai sur l'Architecture*, Chap. 6, 272–293 in the 1753 edition, 233–252 in the 1755 edition. See Rinaldi, *Ideas of Chinese Gardens*, 174, for the reference to Laugier and 181, n. 59 for a brief discussion of his importance in the history of French garden theory.
85. See the short biographical notice in Rinaldi, *The "Chinese Garden in Good Taste"*, 264; Rinaldi's sources are cited on p. 261.
86. The section in question appears on 279–282 of the 1753 edition and 240–243 of the 1755 edition. Other parts of Laugier's *Essai* were substantially rewritten for the second edition.
87. The quote is on 281–282 of the 1753 edition; 241–242 of the 1755 edition: "Sans doute que ce plan nous fourniroit un bon modèle, & qu'en faisant un ingénieux mêlange des idées Chinoises avec les nôtres, nous viendrons à bout de faire des Jardins où la nature se retrouveroit avec toutes ses graces." The translation here is my own; Rinaldi, *Ideas of Chinese Gardens*, 181, n. 59, also translates part of this statement; and Rinaldi, ibid., refers to the English-language edition, *An Essay on Architecture by Marc-Antoine Laugier*, Wolfgang and Anni Herrmann, trans. (Los Angeles: Hennessey & Ingalls, 1977).
88. Bib Inst Ms 1524, fol. 168 verso, Extrait d'une Notice, intitulée, Envoi de 1778: "Pierre, avec son pied d'Estal [*sic*]. Quand elles sont petites, comme celle-ci, on les met dans les appartements; quand elle sont grandes, on les met dans les Jardins, et elles tiennent lieu des statues."
89. For a good introduction to the subject, see Robert D. Mowry, *Worlds Within Worlds: The Richard Rosenblum Collection of Chinese Scholars' Rocks*, with contributions by Claudia Brown and others (Cambridge, MA: Harvard University Art Museums, 1997).
90. On Du Wan, see Edward H. Schafer, *Tu Wan's Stone Catalogue of Cloudy Forest: A Commentary and Synopsis* (Berkeley: University of California Press, 1961; reprint, Warren, CT: Floating World Editions, 2005).
91. BnF, Département des Estampes et de la photographie, Réserve OE-44-Pet Fol.
92. BnF, Fonds Bréquigny 126, fols. 100–105. The text is entitled "Notice des pierres dont on orne les jardins en Chine." A note added on the first page reads: "Voy. les peintures au nombre de 42."
93. The documents in Bréquigny 126 are described on fol. 2 as "No. 8 Carton 18 . . . [*sic*] 14. articles. Manuscrits concernant la Chine non employés dans les Memoires chinois. Architecture, Jardins, Vases, Ornemens." None of the documents is signed or dated, although all are written in the same hand as the "Notices des pierres. . . ."
94. The phrase "ces jardins dont le dessein est plein d'anticimetrie [*sic*]" appears on the second page of the text, ibid., fol. 100 verso.
95. Ibid., fol. 102 recto (p. 5 of the original document): "Le No. 15 est fameux dans l'histoire de Chine par la passion d'un empereur pour cette espèce de pierres. On en tira alors une quantité prodigieuse du tai hou ou Grand Lac au fond du quel elles avoient été vuidées et cavernées par les eaux. Elle a porté depuis le nom de pierre du Grand Lac et a continüé d'être à la mode dans les jardins. Les morceaux qui sortent véritablement de ce lac sont plus travaillés, plus agréables à voir et plus [illeg.] que ceux qu'on tire d'ailleurs."
96. See James M. Hargett, "Huizong's Magic Marchmount: The Genyue Pleasure Park of Kaifeng," *Monumenta Serica* 38 (1988–1989), 1–48; for the reference here, see p. 12, n. 37.
97. Ibid., 5ff.

98. Fonds Bréquigny 126, fol. 104 recto: "Quoique nous en ayons déjà envoyé quelques morceaux, comme aucune réponse n'en a fait mention, nous en Envoyerons Encore d'autres cette année, La Conviction que nous avons de notre ignorance n'intimide pas notre Bonne volonté."
99. *Mémoires*, vol. 12 (1786), 1–403, "Vie de *Koung-tsée*, Appellé vulgairement Confucius, . . ." Koung-tsée is the eighteenth-century French transcription of Kongzi 孔子.
100. Ibid.; the illustration, pl. V, faces p. 16 of the biography, and the description in the "Explication des planches" appears on 439–440.
101. *Mémoires*, vol. 12 (1786), pl. 7, facing 153; pl. 12, 333; pl. 15, 379; and pl. 17, 398.

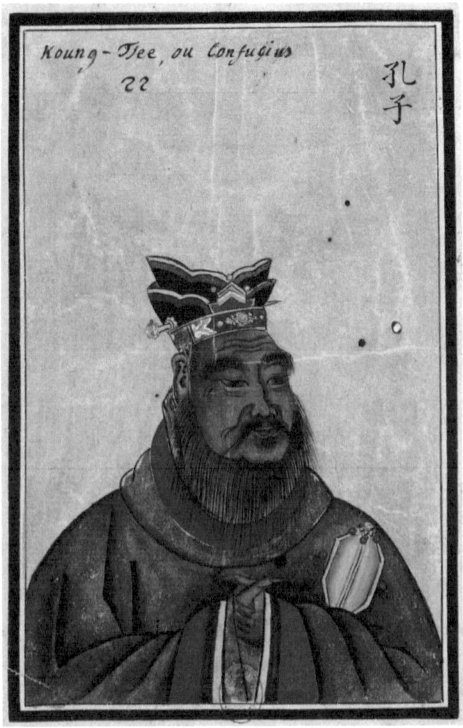

Plate 1 Anonymous, Chinese, "Koung-Tsee, ou Confucius, 22," ca. 1771, ink and color on paper, 21.0 × 14.5 cm. Paris, Bibliothèque nationale de France.

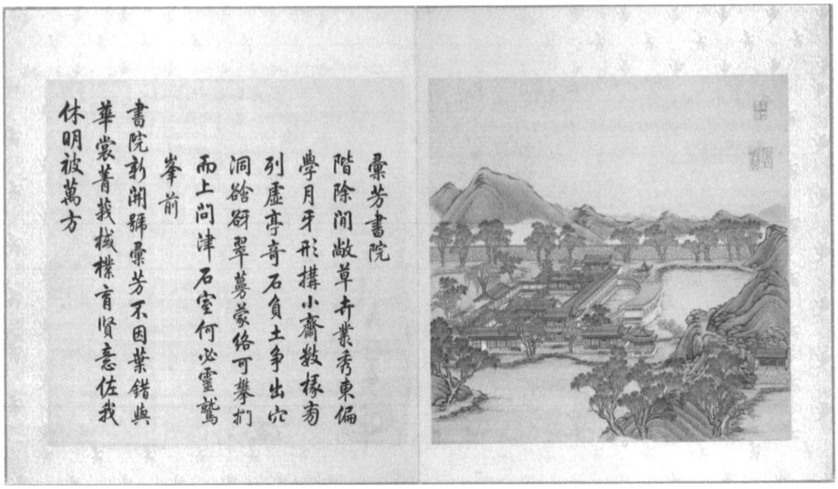

Plate 2 Tangdai, Shen Yuan, and Wang Youdun, *Forty Views of the Yuanming yuan*, no. 18, "Huifang shuyuan," 1738–1741, ink and color on paper, folio 82.7 × 148.8 cm. Paris, Bibliothèque nationale de France.

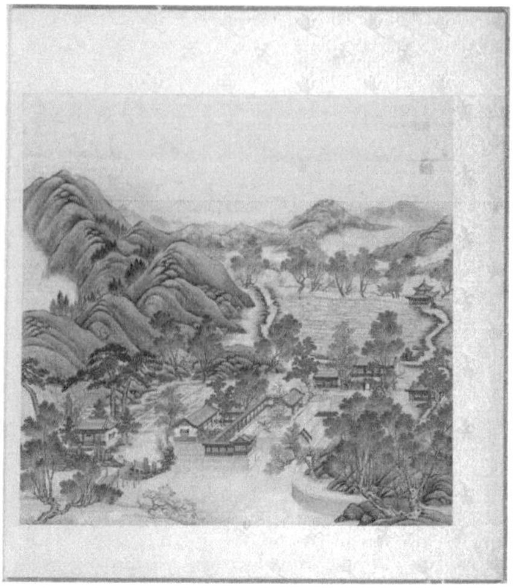

Plate 3 Tangdai and Shen Yuan, *Forty Views of the Yuanming yuan*, no. 22, "Shuimu mingse," 1738–1741, ink and color on paper, painting 61.7 × 64.1 cm. Paris, Bibliothèque nationale de France.

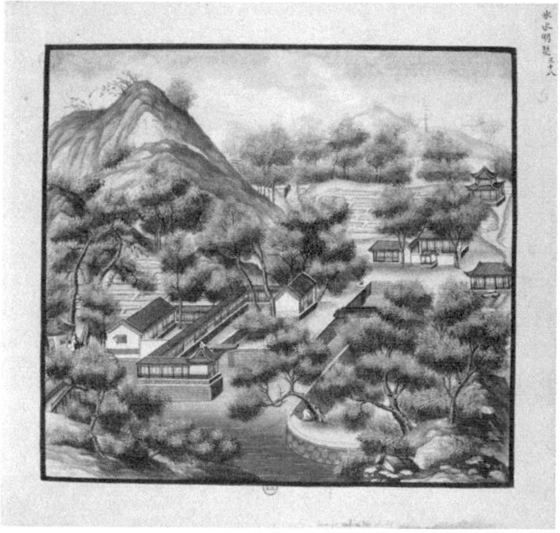

Plate 4 Anonymous, Chinese, *Haitien, Maison de plaisance, de l'Empereur de la Chine*, pl. 38, "Shuimu mingse," ink and color on paper, ca. 1750, 23.7 × 39 cm. Paris, Bibliothèque nationale de France.

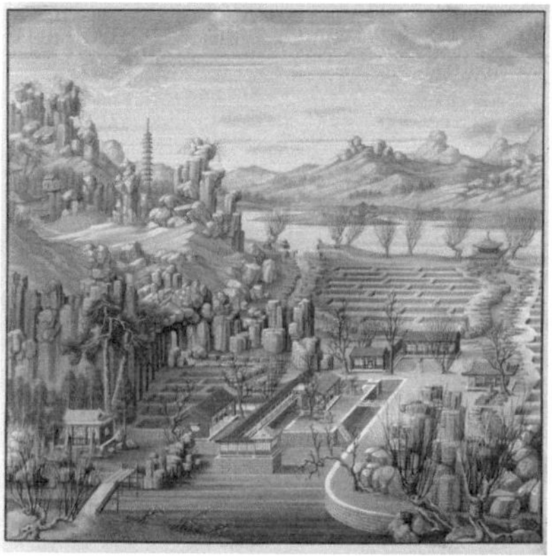

Plate 5 Anonymous, Chinese, *Recueil. Paysages Chinois*, composition based on "Shuimu mingse," ink and color on textile mounted on paper, 63 × 67 cm. Paris, Bibliothèque nationale de France.

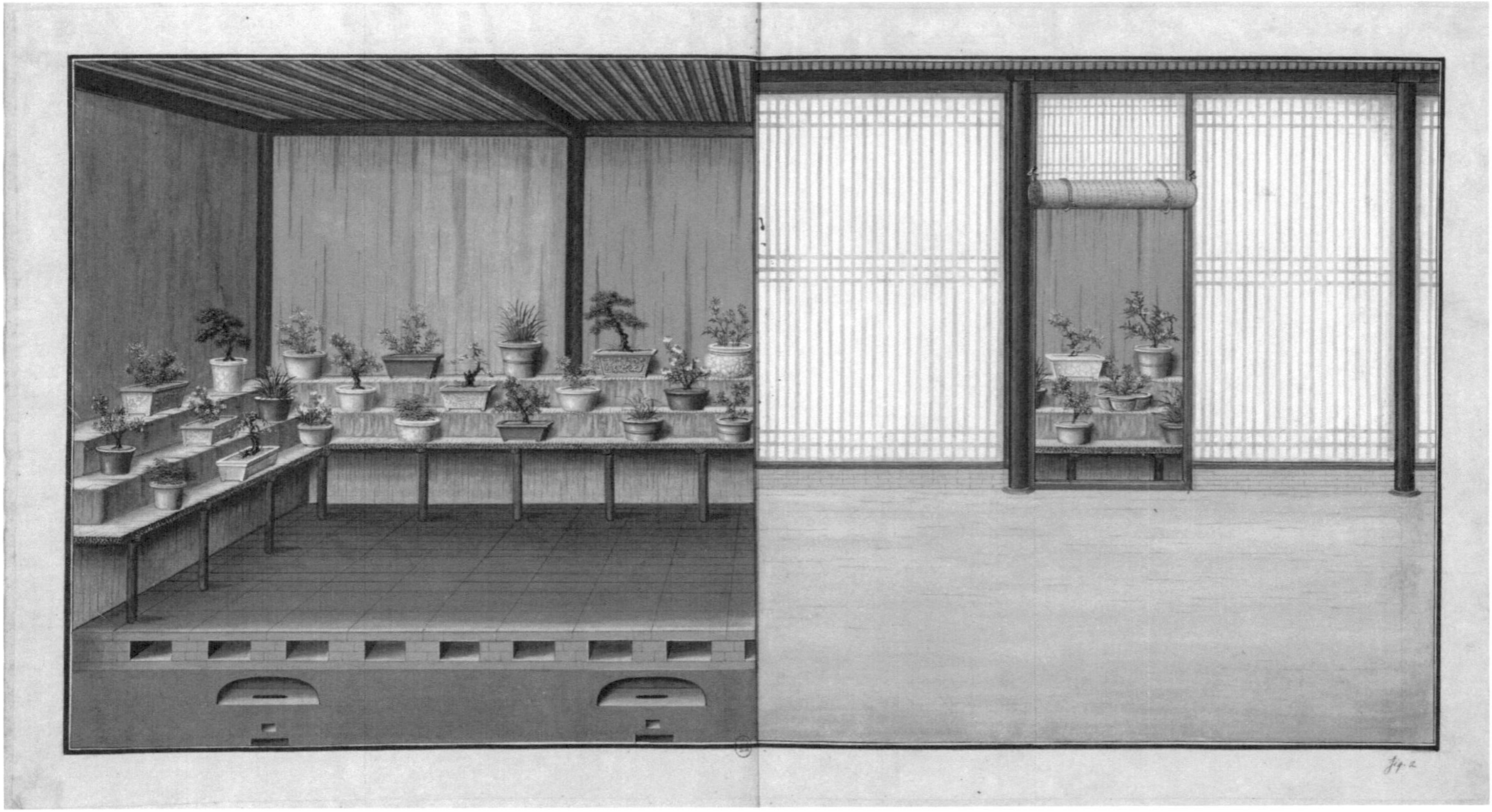

Plate 6 Anonymous, Chinese, *Serres chaudes des Chinois et fleurs qu'ils y conservent*, second painting, ink and color on paper, 40 × 48 cm, ca. 1777. Paris, Bibliothèque nationale de France.

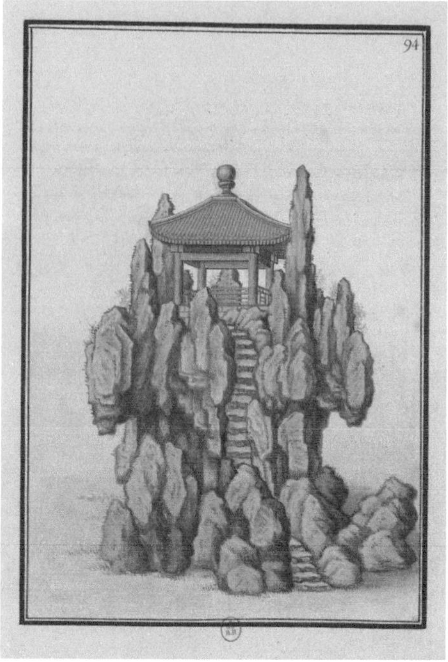

Plate 7 Anonymous, Chinese, *Essai sur l'architecture chinoise*, part I, pl. 94, "Cabinet sur un amas de Rochers," ink and color on paper, 36 × 27 cm, ca. 1773. Paris, Bibliothèque nationale de France.

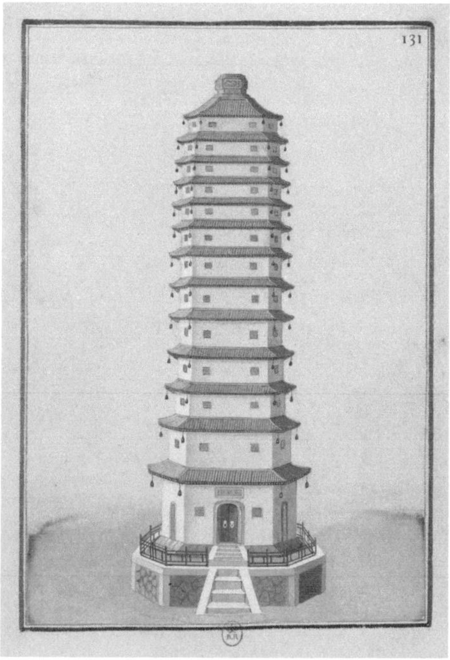

Plate 8 Anonymous, Chinese, *Essai sur l'architecture chinoise*, part I, pl. 131, "*Ta* dédié aux Esprits," ink and color on paper, 36 × 27 cm, ca. 1773. Paris, Bibliothèque nationale de France.

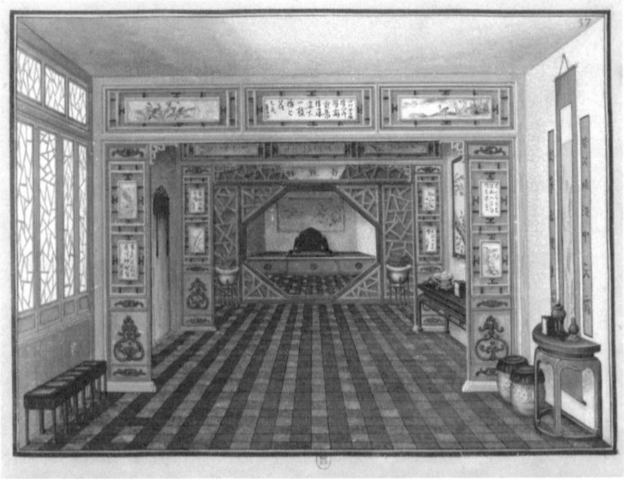

Plate 9 Anonymous, Chinese, *Essai sur l'architecture chinoise*, part II, pl. 37, "Salle de Cérémonie & d'Audience chez les Princes titrés," ink and color on paper, 35 × 45 cm, ca. 1773. Paris, Bibliothèque nationale de France.

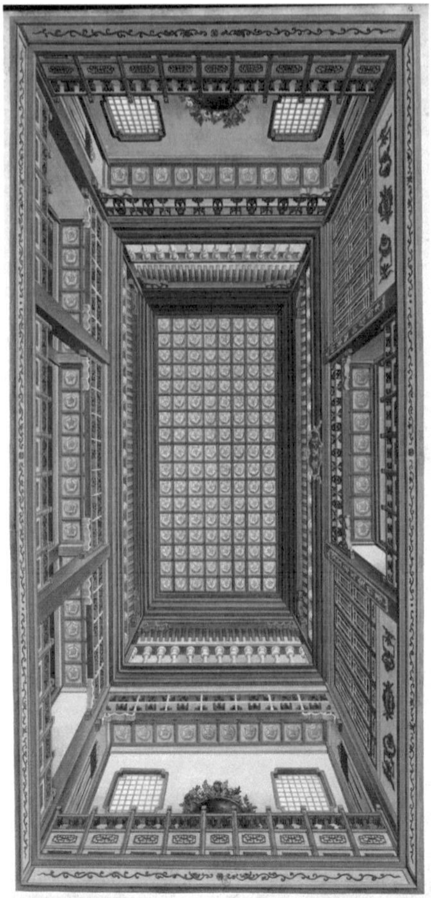

Plate 10 Anonymous, Chinese, *Plafonds chinois*, multistory ceiling, ink and color on paper, 96 × 62 cm, ca. 1773. Paris, Bibliothèque nationale de France.

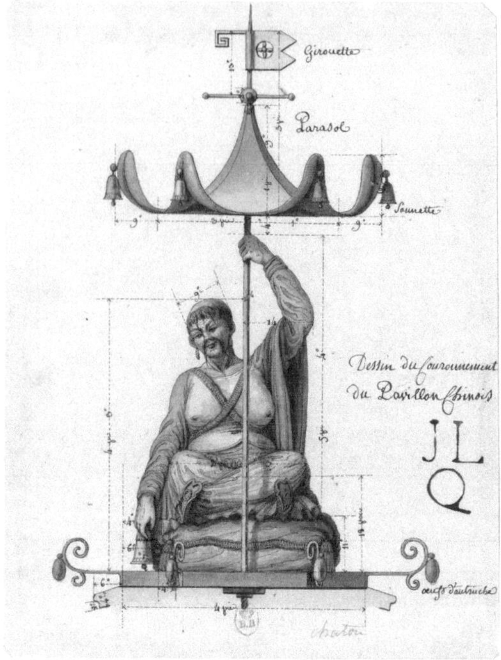

Plate 11 Jean-Jacques Lequeu, "Dessin du couronnement du pavillon chinois," ink and watercolor on paper, 21.2 × 16.6 cm, ca. 1780. Paris, Bibliothèque nationale de France.

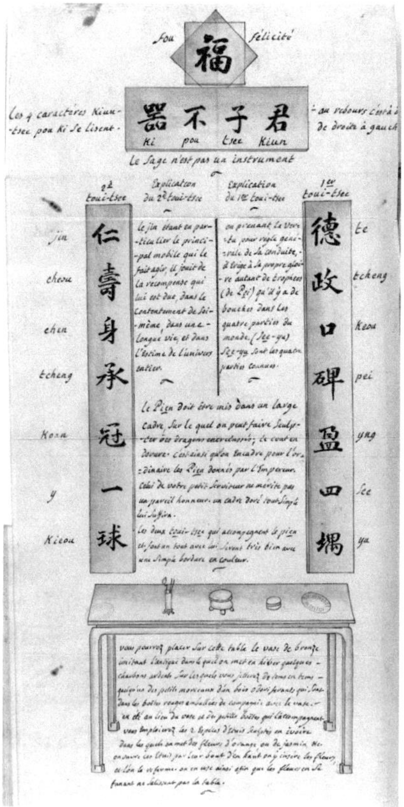

Plate 12 Joseph-Marie Amiot, "Junzi bu qi," ink on paper, 1790, Bibliothèque de l'Institut de France, Ms 1517, fol. 138.

Source: Photo ©RMN-Grand Palais (Institut de France)/Stéphane Maréchalle.

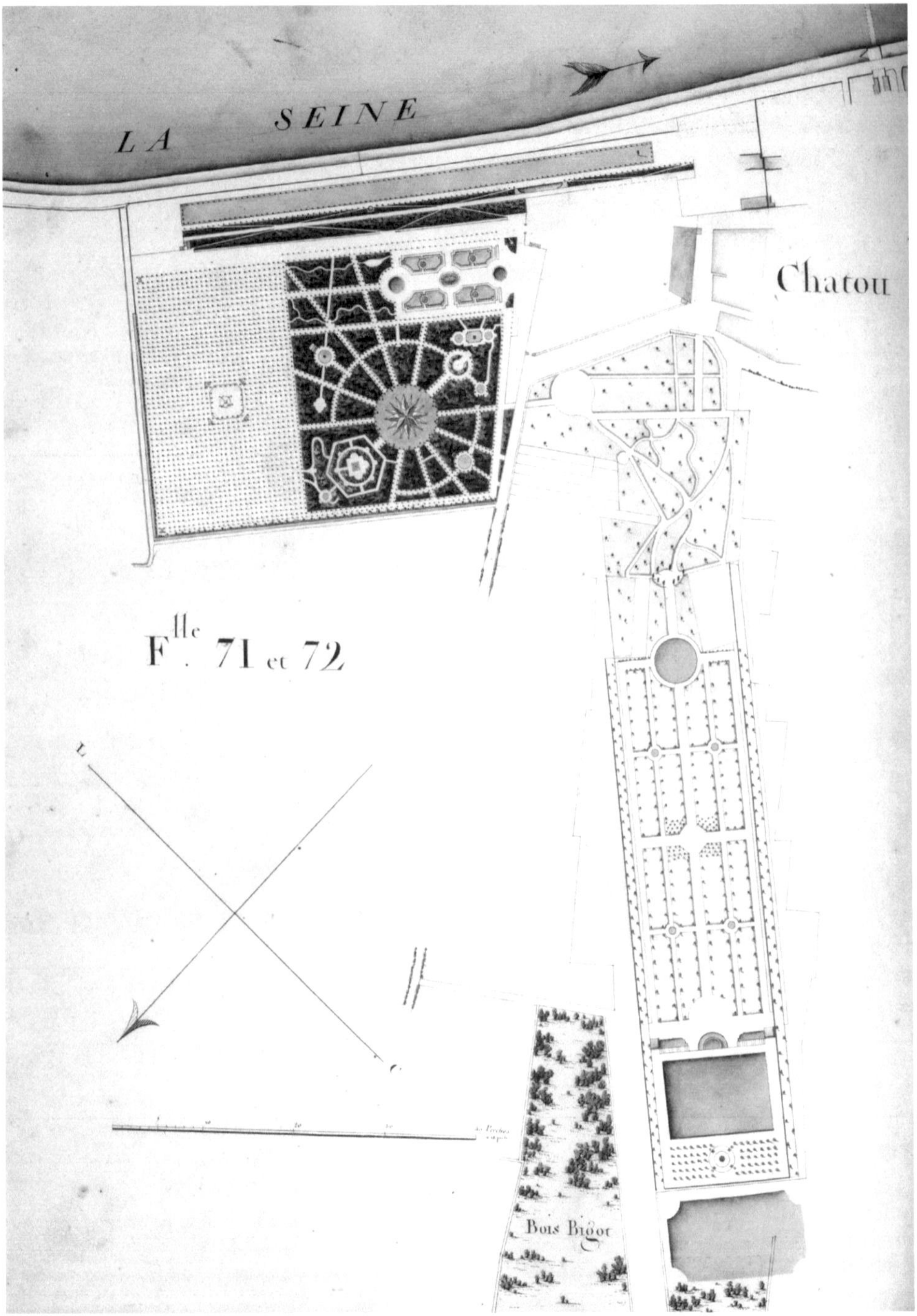

Plate 13 Anonymous, "Atlas de la Seigneurie de Chatou . . .," 1780, Feuille 71 et 72, ink and watercolor on paper, 63.5 × 45 cm. Archives Municipales de Chatou.

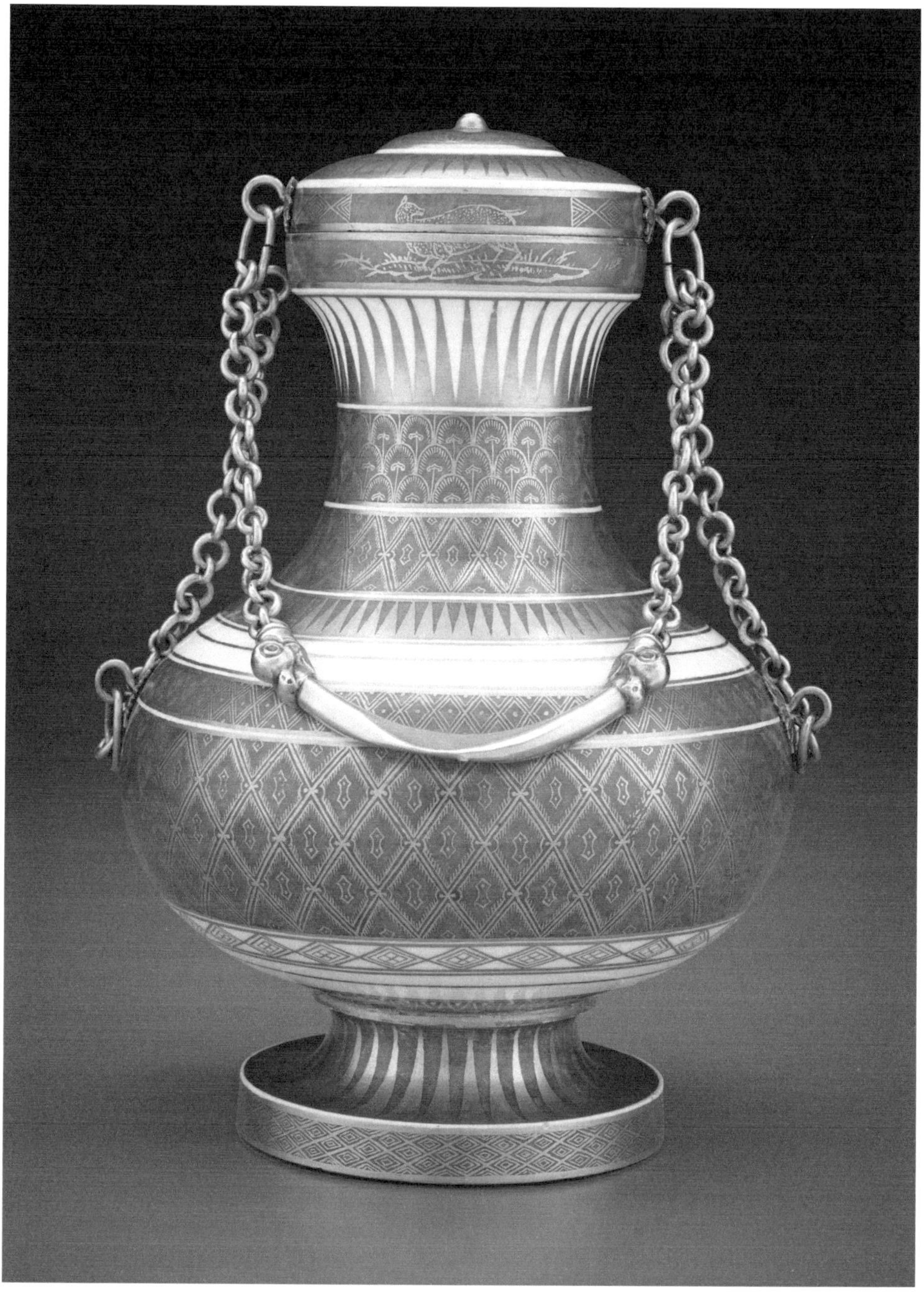

Plate 14 *Vase Japon*, Sèvres Porcelain Manufactory, 1774, hard-paste porcelain with silver-gilt mount, h.: 26.7, diam.: 20.3 cm. Purchase in Honor of Anne L. Poulet, 2011 (2011.9.01).

Source: ©The Frick Collection.

3 Constructing an Authentic China

For Henri Bertin, many widely varying aspects of China and Chinese civilization were the objects of his extraordinary curiosity, and he apparently made repeated requests for information about a number of them. Although few of Bertin's original letters to the French Jesuit missionaries in Beijing have survived, from their replies and the documents they sent to Paris, it is clear that Bertin returned a number of times to the question of Chinese architecture. What exactly first drew his attention to Chinese architecture—a subject that had until then received little attention as a serious field of inquiry—is not clear, although Bertin's interests in general seem to have focused very much on practical matters like architecture. Architecture as a concept was very much on the minds of educated Europeans of the period, and contemporary publications treated architecture in terms of history, practice, and theory—the last being an historically innovative approach to the field. Bertin was also acquainted with some of the most eminent architects of the period and, later in his life, spent a great deal of time and effort on the construction of his residence at Chatou, just outside Paris, which supposedly included a Chinese-style garden and studio of some sort. That construction project is considered in detail in the following chapter. Descriptions and images of Chinese constructions of various kinds had appeared in publications in the seventeenth century, notably in Johannes Nieuhof's account of the embassy of the Dutch East India Company to China from 1655 to 1657, an account first published in 1665, and in Athanasius Kircher's *China Illustrata* of 1667. Both titles were widely circulated, but the very real differences between their depictions of Chinese architecture and what Bertin possessed are discussed briefly later in the context of Nieuhof's illustrated account of the journey to China. Among the paintings in Bertin's collection and in the relevant archival documents, there is a remarkable amount of information about architecture. Some of it, such as the images and texts on Chinese greenhouses, reflects Bertin's very concrete goal of hoping to learn from China. And a group of superbly illustrated albums of paintings and their accompanying texts provides the first extended, serious examination of the subject of Chinese architecture to have reached Europe. Their formats and contents both resonate with European models and present new knowledge of eighteenth-century China unprecedented in its scope and detail.

Serres Chinoises

In 1777, Bertin received a set of paintings from the Jesuit missionaries in Beijing which were then bound into an album inscribed with the title *Serres chaudes des Chinois, et fleurs qu'ils y conservent*, literally "Hothouses of the Chinese, and the flowers that they keep there."[1] The album has the distinctive blue paste-paper cover that is typical of many albums of paintings from Bertin's collection. The date comes from an inscription along the top of the first painting, which reads "6 paintings of Chinese greenhouses. Received in 1777."[2] Beyond the title, the inscription on the first painting, and the numbers in the lower right-hand corners of each of the paintings (noted as *fig. 1*, *fig. 2*, etc.), there is no other text in French in the album, while there are Chinese labels on the first, third, and fourth paintings. And the paintings are wonderfully informative. The first painting shows a building that is ten bays (or inter-columnar units) wide. The relatively plain building faces a walled courtyard, which is empty except for three large baskets; bare trees indicate that the season is winter. The first four bays on the right have bamboo mats hanging from the beam just below the eaves; one mat is unrolled and hangs all the way to the ground. The next three bays are filled with lattice-work windows covered in white paper. The next bay apparently contains the doorway, but it and the last five bays seem to be blank, either unfinished or with minimal detail in the painting. The roof also seems incomplete, with tiles only over the first two and last two bays. The rest is covered with various layers of unidentified material, with wooden beams visible at the far end next to the section of tile-covered roof. It is likely that the painting thus reveals details from the actual construction of the hothouse.[3]

The second painting is visually the most complex (Plate 6). It shows two views of part of a building very similar to the one in the first painting, with, on the right, the courtyard, a door that can be covered with a rolled-up mat, and paper-covered lattices. On the left is a cut-away view of the interior with three shelves of flowering plants and miniature trees growing in ceramic containers. The most important detail of this half of the painting is the cross-section of the floor, which clearly shows the various channels and vents under the gray brick paving. These are detailed in an article on hothouses discussed immediately below. The third and fourth paintings in the album show two complete views of the interior of the hothouse filled with details, including the many different kinds of plants they contain and the daylight streaming through the white paper-covered lattice. The first, third, and fourth paintings are labeled in Chinese *hua'er jaozi* 花兒窖子 or *hua'er jiao* 花兒窖, a term that means literally "cellar" or "pit" for flowers but which was a contemporary term for greenhouse, hothouse, or conservatory.[4] These inscriptions, the only inscriptions in Chinese in this particular album, emphasize this special characteristic of Chinese greenhouses or hothouses: that they are excavated below ground level. The last painting, which is not labeled, shows a simpler method for protecting seedlings in cold weather. It is a bird's-eye view of a walled garden, where sunken beds of new plants can be protected from harsh weather either by unrolling a large bamboo mat to cover the shallow pits or by placing a bamboo mat on a rigid frame over a slightly sunken bed.

Although the 1777 album of "Chinese greenhouses" includes almost no text, Volume 3 of the *Mémoires concernant les Chinois*, published in 1778, contains a 15-page article entitled "Chinese Greenhouses."[5] Sent to Bertin by Father François Bourgeois (Chao Junxiu 晁俊秀, 1723–1792, arr. in China 1767), the administrator of the French mission in Beijing at the time and one of Bertin's frequent correspondents, the manuscript was dispatched from Beijing in November 1777 as one of 14 such articles on a wide variety subjects that were written by Father Pierre-Martial Cibot (Han Guoying 韓國英, 1727–1780, arr. in China 1758), himself one of Bertin's regular correspondents.[6] While it is not illustrated, the article contains information that corresponds exactly to what is depicted in the album of paintings of *serres chaudes*. Writing as "we," the way that the Jesuit missionaries conventionally referred to themselves in the texts sent to Bertin, Cibot mentions first what he understands to be the ancient history of greenhouses (or conservatories) in China, a subject, however, which he cannot explore in his text, but then he asks:

> Would our France recognize this wisdom of the Chinese, both in the manner in which greenhouses are built today, and in that which it has devised in order to supplement the vegetable gardens near cities and in the countryside? . . . We will only speak according to our observations and will only write of what we have seen.[7]

What Cibot has seen are specifically three different kinds of greenhouses—those in the palace of the emperor and his gardens, those of the flower merchants of Beijing, and those used by gardeners or farmers in the area around the capital—and all are built in the same style and according to the same basic forms. Here as elsewhere, the Jesuits remark on the relative modesty and uniformity of Chinese construction at all levels of society. Because of the extreme winter weather in the Beijing region, and indeed following the custom for most construction throughout China, greenhouses or conservatories are always aligned to face south. But, Cibot writes, what truly distinguishes Chinese greenhouses or conservatories is the way in which they are sunken down into the ground somewhat like a trench. This lowered floor level, clearly visible in the album paintings, provides some of the insulating effects of a cellar which, along with the south-facing façade composed of paper-covered windows as well as the rest of the building constructed of thick walls with no openings, takes full advantage of the light and warmth provided by the sun. Such design principles also mean that the distinctive northern Chinese heating system of hot-air ducts beneath the brick floor is most effective and uses the least amount of fuel.

In one section of his article, Cibot sums up seven critical elements of the construction of Chinese greenhouses, including the excavation of the greenhouse floor, the special qualities of the roof, the need for a *kang* 炕 or Chinese-style system of furnaces and flues below the brick floor or under a raised platform, and the provision of sturdy mats to roll down across the paper-covered windows at nighttime or when the weather is especially severe.[8] Cibot notes that French building techniques could be used to construct such greenhouses, and they would be improved by the incorporation of Chinese technical details. Then what follows is a comprehensive discussion in four numbered sections on exactly what Chinese greenhouses are used for and how they are managed. Here Cibot enters into much additional detail on how to maintain the proper atmosphere in a hothouse, noting especially how to maintain the proper humidity in an artificially heated environment. The preservation of plants and shrubs so that they might flower in winter is one particular goal—something again clearly illustrated in the paintings in the album of Chinese greenhouses—as is the propagation of seedlings and cuttings and even the provision of tender sprouts out-of-season.

The album of paintings of Chinese greenhouses or hothouses that Bertin received in 1777 illustrates the details discussed in the article that was sent to him from Beijing at the end of that same year and published almost immediately, in 1778. Surely the two—the paintings and the text—must be linked, and perhaps they respond to a request from Bertin himself. Nevertheless, the combination of a detailed written description with paintings that emphasize clear and practical information epitomizes Bertin's goal of France learning from China. Whether or not the information sent from Beijing to Paris and then disseminated in various publications had any long-lasting practical results is unclear.[9] Perhaps one indication of how knowledge of Chinese greenhouses may have spread appears in Émile Littré's classic later nineteenth-century *Dictionnaire de la langue française*, where the entry for the word *serre* (greenhouse or hothouse) includes the definition of a *serre chinoise* or "Chinese greenhouse, a greenhouse sunken in the ground."[10]

The *Essai sur l'Architecture Chinoise*

The album of paintings of Chinese greenhouses and the article on greenhouses in the *Mémoires concernant les Chinois* fulfilled one of Bertin's primary goals, to provide technical information from China on a specific type of building based on texts and images—information from which France could directly profit. However, sets of illustrations and extended texts that had been previously sent to Bertin provided more extensive information on Chinese architecture, much of which focused on types previously unknown in Europe, but these were never published. Evidence that the project for a broad study of Chinese architecture had been planned, or at least requested, for some time appears in an undated text entitled "Chinese Decorations, Etc."[11] For the writer, it seems curious that after some 200 years of commerce and shipping between France and China that there still was no treatise on Chinese architecture, and surprising, too, that the Jesuit missionaries had not yet written one. Despite all the difficulties involved in a comprehensive presentation of Chinese architecture, the missionaries have begun to respond to this need and feel that the best way to proceed is, first, to provide paintings of Chinese architecture, images which would "speak to the eyes,"[12] to show similarities and differences between European and Chinese architecture, a goal that would echo statements in subsequent writings on architecture. The text, however, is entitled "Décorations chinoises," and the reason for this soon becomes apparent. The images of Chinese architecture referred to here are paintings based on the temporary constructions lining the routes of imperial parades for the celebrations of the birthdays of the Qianlong emperor and of his mother, the Dowager Empress.[13] The reference to illustrations of one of the imperial celebrations, that of the Qianlong emperor's sixtieth birthday in the "winter just past," gives an approximate date for the text, 1771 or later, since the emperor celebrated his birthday as well as the eightieth birthday of the dowager empress in the winter of 1771–1772.[14] The images to which the text refers are surely the 11 paintings mounted in an album entitled *Arcs de triomphe et berceaux chinois* (Chinese triumphal arches and lattice pavilions).[15] *Arc de triomphe* is used in the eighteenth century to describe a particular type of Chinese gateway, permanent or temporary, called a *pailou* 牌樓, where the inscribed signboard (*pai*) that gives the structure its name is displayed on a decorative entablature supported on columns. Illustrations of these particular structures are chosen for the moment to demonstrate Chinese taste, given that a complete study of Chinese architecture would be an immense undertaking. And they are admittedly fantastic. The first illustration shows a gateway decorated as a mountain landscape inhabited by the Eight Daoist Immortals.[16] Several are described as being decorated with silk textiles or artificial flowers. Another, number nine, appears to be an arbor of pine trees filled with cranes. The most elaborate architecture is illustrated in number four, described as a "double arch in silk fabric and lanterns" (Figure 3.1).[17] Instead of a single row, two rows of columns support a set of miniature buildings surrounded by decorative draperies. Like the other illustrations, this *pailou* is rendered in a hybrid Chinese-European style, with a central vanishing point and subtle rendering in light and shadow. The signboard over the central opening is inscribed with an auspicious phrase: "An abundant harvest of all grains," and several of the gateways have similar inscriptions.[18] The missionary authors of "Décorations chinoises" provide a very abbreviated description of some of the principles of Chinese architecture, but they are careful to note that what is illustrated are fanciful, temporary constructions. These are profoundly different from what would be illustrated in the next set of paintings and texts to be sent to Bertin.

Much of what was promised in the text of "Décorations Chinoises" was provided in a truly remarkable, two-part album, which sought for the first time to present the totality of Chinese architecture. The album bears the title *Essai sur*

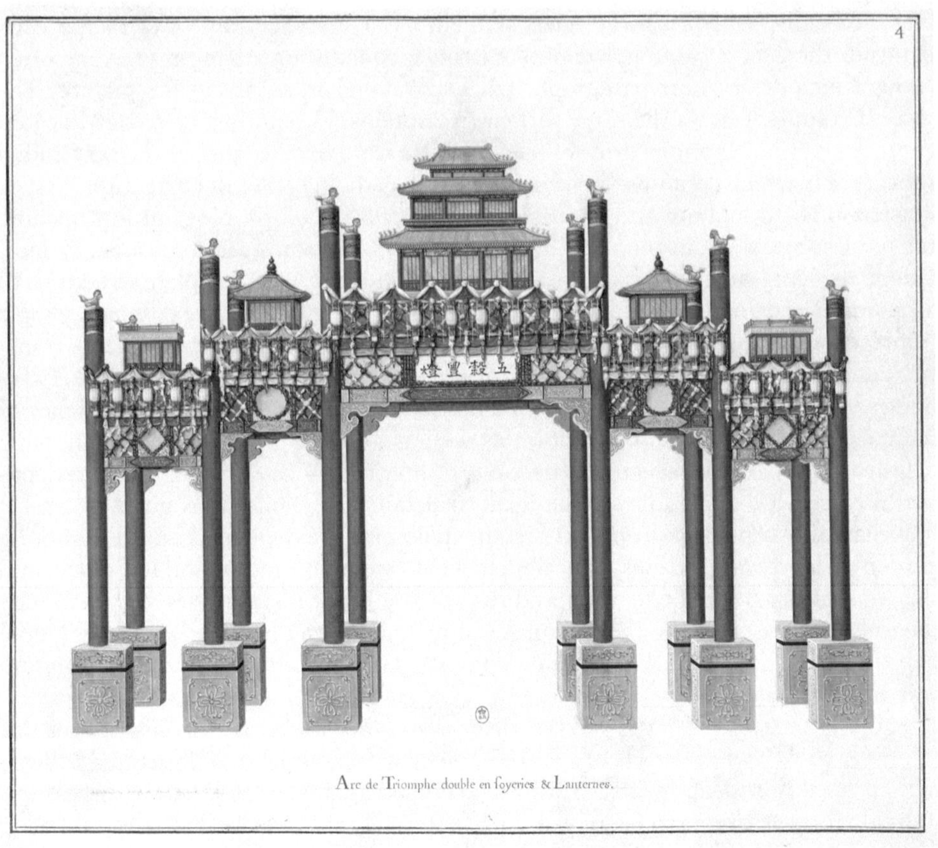

Figure 3.1 Anonymous, Chinese, *Recueil. Arcs de triomphe et berceaux chinois*, painting no. 4, "Arc de Triomphe double en soyeries & Lanternes," ink and color on paper, 64 × 75 cm, ca. 1772. Paris, Bibliothèque nationale de France.

l'architecture chinoise—Essay on Chinese architecture—and it combines dozens of highly detailed illustrations with captions and longer texts that set out to provide an overview of Chinese architecture.[19] Taking their cue from a European Enlightenment point of view that sought accurate knowledge of technology and the arts alongside historical traditions, the French Jesuits prepared detailed descriptions to accompany paintings commissioned especially for Bertin. Texts and pictures highlighted what was unknown and exotic in Chinese architecture in contrast with European practice. The two sumptuously bound albums—the first in a vertical format, the second in a horizontal format—have Bertin's coat of arms tooled in gold on the covers.[20] The title pages and detailed texts in both albums are written in calligraphy that is meant to imitate a printed page. For the moment, the specific author or authors of the text in the two volumes remain unknown, and no document has appeared that would indicate the circumstances under which Bertin requested this particular set of paintings and texts. Although the two albums themselves are undated, a manuscript that is the source for the texts copied into the albums provides an approximate date: The last page of the manuscript notes that it was completed in Beijing on 3 October 1773.[21]

The first album of the *Essai sur l'architecture chinoise* contains some 135 paintings. It begins with a short "Avertissement" (an Introduction), and facing each painting there is a caption, which sometimes consists of a simple title but often enough includes a short paragraph that explains what we see in the picture. The second volume follows the same format; it contains 53 paintings, a somewhat longer introduction, captions or brief texts facing each painting, and, at the very end, a short article which contains "several observations that deserve our attention."[22] The illustrations throughout the *Essai sur l'architecture chinoise* cover an astonishing range of subjects, from the tools and materials of carpenters and masons, to individual elements such as bricks, tiles, and walls, and of course complete structures of all kinds. These include buildings for all classes of society, from the common people (represented by only a few illustrations) to the literati and, most especially, imperial constructions, including constructions in the imperial garden-palace, the Yuanming yuan. Among the paintings is one remarkable sequence showing the stages of the construction of a simple pavilion as well as another group of images showing detailed views of furnished and decorated interiors. While the paintings emphasize the accurate depiction of architectural detail, each building is given at least a minimal landscape backdrop, and certain structures are depicted in more elaborate garden or landscape settings. The albums were assembled and bound in France, and this was surely Bertin's intention and that of the Jesuit missionaries who provided the illustrations, since the 1773 manuscript includes even the captions for individual paintings. The effort to describe and depict so many aspects of Chinese architecture was unprecedented.

The first part of the *Essai sur l'architecture chinoise* begins with illustrations of the basic tools and materials of Chinese construction, which are illustrated following a typical European format. They are arranged against a blank background, and individual tools or examples of building materials are numbered where the facing captions provide additional information keyed to those numbers. Among the first illustrations are carpenter's tools, which are close enough to European tools that the Jesuit missionaries did not supply detailed descriptions for many of them. A page of mason's tools (Figure 3.2), however, shows implements different enough from

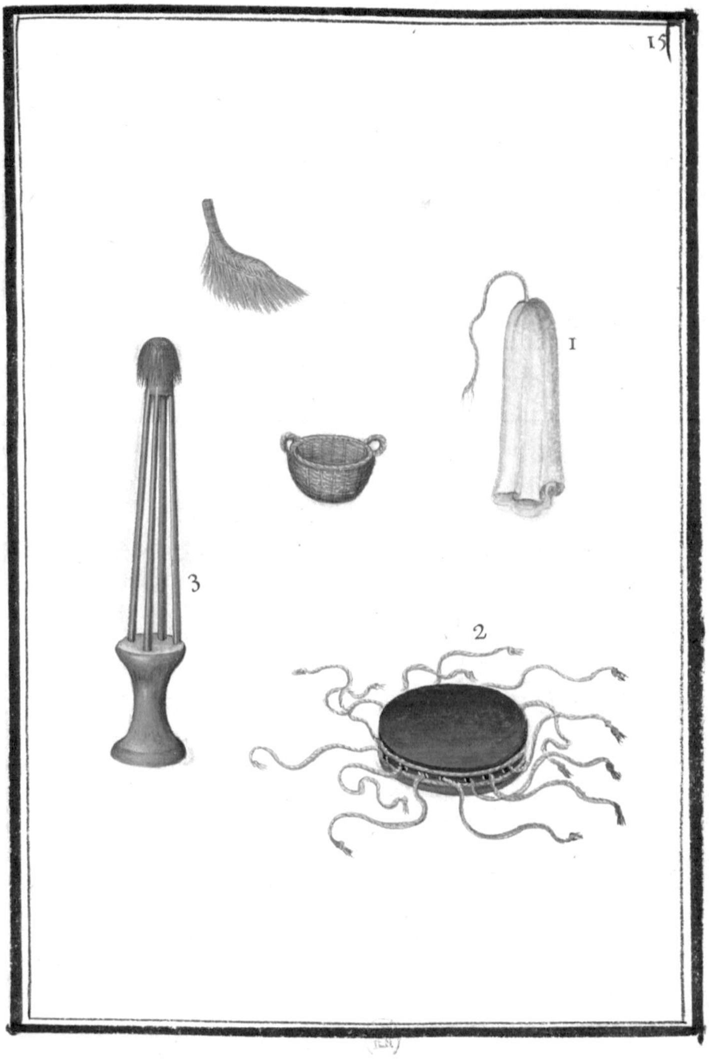

Figure 3.2 Anonymous, Chinese, *Essai sur l'architecture chinoise*, part I, pl. 15, "Instruments & outils du maçon," ink and color on paper, 36 × 27 cm, ca. 1773. Paris, Bibliothèque nationale de France.

European ones that the missionaries included a caption for the facing page with the following details:

> Instruments and tools of a mason. No. 1 is a sort of sack of heavy canvas which is filled with mortar and which one carries on his shoulders. No. 2 is a slab of lead for pounding foundations; 12 men lift it at the same time and let it fall flat. No. 3, a *demoiselle* for four for pounding pavements and foundations.[23]

A *demoiselle* or "maiden" is a tool roughly similar to ones still occasionally in use for pounding paving stones in place, even though in most modern construction this is accomplished with power tools.[24]

After the illustrations of tools, the album continues with pictures of building materials: lime and mortar, different kinds of bricks and tiles, both glazed and unglazed, and even roof ornaments. It then illustrates various types of walls, beginning with walls of constructions "of the people," and—following a model that we find in many of the groups of illustrations in these two volumes—ending with walls associated with the most elaborate or, in many cases, imperial constructions. The illustrations of walls are the first paintings to have Chinese titles written on them, and the first example is labeled *caiyuanzi tuqiang* 菜園子土墻, that is, "earthen wall of a vegetable garden." The French caption adds the basic details:

> Wall of earth mixed with lime, and pounded between two planks. Those which they make today sometimes collapse after the first year. One sees them in ancient tombs that are over a century [old]. [Later addition in pencil:] This type of Wall is used in Vegetable gardens.[25]

Pounded earth walls are an ancient Chinese construction practice still widely used in the countryside today. One of the "imperial walls," labeled *huangshang jia qiang* 皇上家墻, shows another practical and typical detail of Chinese construction, which is described in the French caption:

> Separation walls inside the Palace and the houses of the Emperor. The No. 1 on the part that is not yet plastered has been put there to show the way in which one leaves hemp hanging, which is put under the bricks in building the wall. The plastering sticks to the fibers & does not come loose that easily.[26]

The *Essai* then takes up a novel architectural element that was surely little known in Europe in the late eighteenth century, that of the screen-walls placed at the entrance to Chinese buildings or walled compounds. The 12 paintings in this section are described in the French texts as *Tchao Ping* (that is, *zhaoping* 照屏), *Tchao Pi* or *Tchao Pei* (*zhaobi* 照壁), and *Tchao Hiang* (*zhaoqiang* 照墻), all of which are conventional terms for screen-walls. These terms also appear in the Chinese labels on the paintings. One of the illustrations, for example, shows a screen-wall decorated with a painting of an official with his servant in a landscape (Figure 3.3). The illustration is labeled in Chinese *guanhuan ren jia zhaobi* 官宦人家照壁 or "screen-wall of the house of a government official," and the title in French on the facing page indeed says this is the screen-wall of a mandarin.[27] However, the two-page explanation that accompanies this and the previous painting in the album introduces an aspect of Chinese architecture to which the writer (or writers) return a number of times, that of the regulations governing official rank and its public display.

> It was surely not to enlighten our Architects on the great Architecture of the ancients nor on the manner in which we could improve new [constructions] that we have had painted the *Tchao Ping*, *Tchao Pi* and *Tchao Hiang* in the ten following paintings as well as this one; but to provide a view of how the Chinese Government deals with these, to make visible to all the difference in ranks, and to keep each within the Realm of his circumstances.[28]

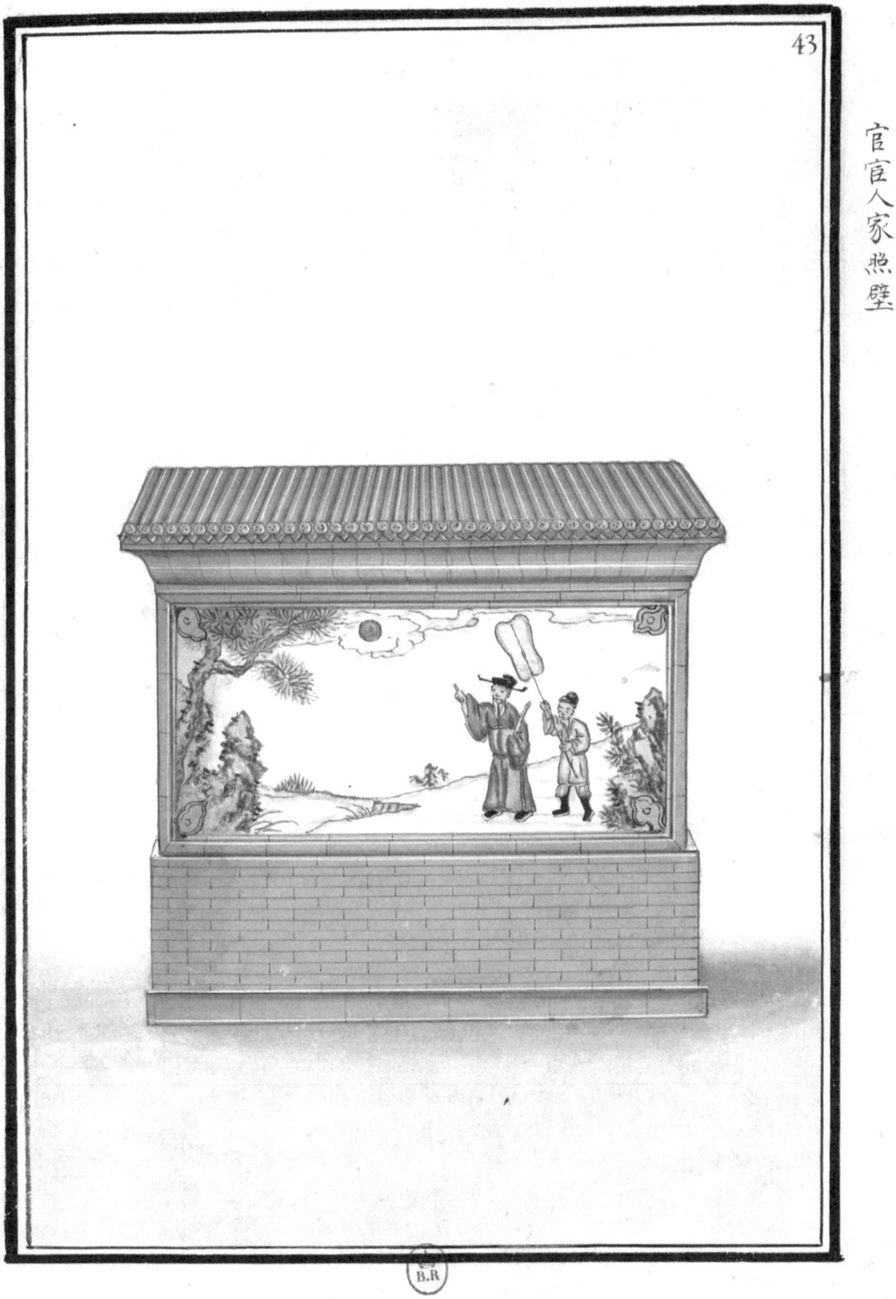

Figure 3.3 Anonymous, Chinese, *Essai sur l'architecture chinoise*, part I, pl. 43, "Tchao Pei de Mandarin," ink and color on paper, 36 × 27 cm, ca. 1773. Paris, Bibliothèque nationale de France.

That is, the various kinds of Chinese screen-walls, which would serve no purpose in a European context, are distinguished by styles and forms that directly reflect the official rank of the occupant of a building or the status of the building itself. That such architectural elements are governed by strict regulations that even imperial constructions must follow is repeated in the *Essai* in other contexts, for example, in descriptions of multistoried buildings or in the captions explaining buildings with colored tile roofs. Unknown in Europe, official regulation of architecture excited the curiosity of the Jesuit missionaries, but the intimate relationship between architecture and social or official status was in fact a question that was indeed discussed in eighteenth-century France.

In the first album of the *Essai sur l'architecture chinoise*, by far the largest group of paintings, a total of 57 images, depict buildings identified in their captions as *Cabinets Chinois*. In eighteenth-century French usage, this term can mean both a collector's private study or office and, in the specialized usage we see here, a garden pavilion.[29] These are, of course, typical and well-known constructions in Chinese gardens, and the text that introduces the paintings notes that they depict only a selection of the many types one could find in the gardens of high officials, princes and the emperor himself. The text, entitled "Plans and views of Chinese pavilions," states,

> We would have perhaps not had so many painted if we had not felt that one might be feel inclined to work in this style according to the designs of the Chinese or to refine them.[30]

As we shall see in the following chapter, Bertin himself hoped to build a "Chinese house" at his residence at Chatou, outside Paris, a project where the authenticity of the construction would be of primary importance.

At the beginning of this group of paintings is a set of ten remarkable images that show the steps in the construction of a simple garden pavilion. In the accompanying text we read:

> We have nothing to say on the manner of building these Pavilions; the Painter has described it better than we could have done, along with everything that one should be obliged to know of it.[31]

The paintings start with the digging of the foundations and the installation of the bases for the columns at the four corners. This is followed by an image of the stone and brick platform on which the pavilion stands, then the erection of the columns, and the placement of the wood structure that will support the roof. The following images continue with the all-important stages of the construction of the roof and the many steps necessary to support and secure the heavy roof tiles. One painting, the next-to-last, shows the plumb line used by the masons to keep the tiles properly aligned (Figure 3.4). At the end of the text describing garden pavilions, the missionaries again emphasize the accuracy of what one sees in the images:

> We have only three observations to make: first, that the painter has neither exaggerated nor embellished anything. We have seen in the Gardens of the Emperor many of the *Cabinets* that one finds here; they really are like that. The second is that the necessity of building in wood, the low price of paint and colors, and the

taste of the Chinese for that which is bright and shines from afar, has led [them] to ornament and paint these *Cabinets* as the Painter depicts them. The final observation is that the Emperor alone may have colored Tiles or *Lieou Li* [*liuli* 琉璃].[32]

In the remaining paintings of *cabinets* or garden pavilions, the images depict buildings that are more and more elaborate, passing from actual or possible constructions to pavilions that appear to be—despite the missionaries' statement "that the painter

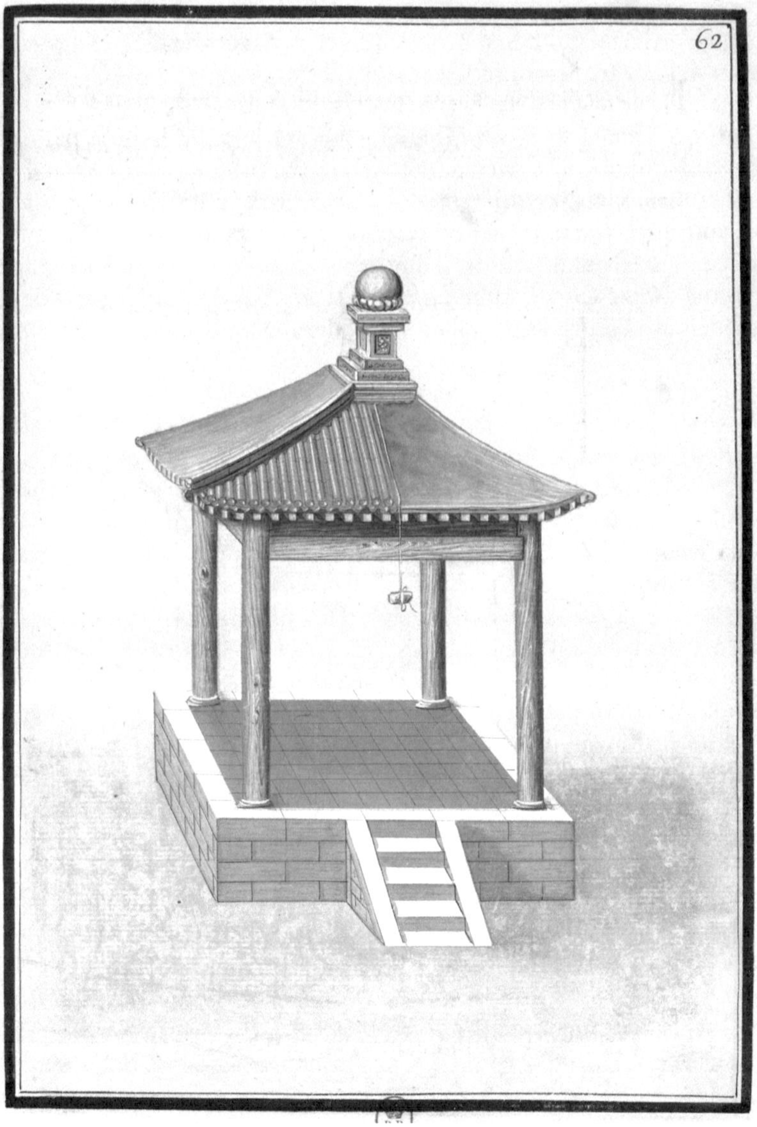

Figure 3.4 Anonymous, Chinese, *Essai sur l'architecture chinoise*, part I, pl. 62, "Plans & développements des Cabinets Chinois," ink and color on paper, 36 × 27 cm, ca. 1773. Paris, Bibliothèque nationale de France.

has neither exaggerated nor embellished anything"—more fantastic than actual contemporary pavilions. The paintings seem to illustrate all the possible variations and elaborations of pavilion forms and designs. It is not possible to say if this is the result of the painters' imaginations or the missionaries' instructions, but this kind of mixing of real and imaginary, fantastic forms appear in a number of Bertin's albums on other subjects as well.

Following the initial series of garden pavilions, some of which are indeed described as temporary or "decorative" constructions, are two pavilions situated on artificial, miniature mountains, another typical kind of Chinese garden construction that was already known in Europe of the eighteenth century (Plate 7). The description of the pavilion on an artificial mountain here returns to many of the themes described by the missionaries in their treatment of Chinese gardens:

> Pavilion on a mass of Rocks/The Chinese are admirable in their imitation of masses of natural Rocks which are found in the solitude of the Mountains. They transport them to their gardens in order to create a complete vision of Nature. . . . When you reach the top you find Pavilions, from which you can see the terraces, groves and canals that twist in a thousand ways in the plain. The Chinese call a Landscape *Chang Choui*, *Mountains and Waters*, and a garden according to them is a garden in as much as it is filled with hills and knolls interspersed with Canals and Ponds.[33]

The text accompanying these illustrations notes the Chinese term for landscape "*Chang Choui*" (*shanshui* 山水), literally "mountains and waters" or "mountains and rivers," describing these as an indispensable garden element, and the pavilions illustrated here are, like the artificial rocks, a key feature of gardens. The pavilion on the following page is depicted on top of an even more fantastic mountain, and it is further identified as a construction in the Yuanming yuan, the so-called Former Summer Palace, a subject to which we will return later. The pavilions in the rest of this group are depicted on small islands or, in a number of examples, surmounting bridges.

The next sequence of paintings shows various kinds of bridges that are also found in "Jardins de Plaisance" or "pleasure gardens," a term that is usually applied to gardens of the aristocracy or imperial gardens, both for European as well as Chinese gardens. To better illustrate the bridges, the 14 paintings in this group are turned sideways to take full advantage of the page. A short text describing these bridges, however, focuses on their practical rather than decorative aspects.

> If someday we should make a Complete Study of Chinese Architecture, the Bridges, Dikes, Levees, Causeways, and Locks would form a large chapter. We have preferred what was the easiest and have fixed upon Ornamental Bridges in Pleasure Gardens; but whoever might look at them with care will easily see that the knowledge that informs the particular construction of these purely decorative Bridges could build very solid and practical ones as these over Rivers and Streams.[34]

That is, the presentation of these details of Chinese architecture is meant to serve a practical purpose; France might again learn something useful from China.

The final series of images in the first album of the *Essai sur l'architecture chinoise* shows various forms of pagodas, identified by their Chinese name *Ta* (*ta* 塔). Here, however, there is less to be learned, and the Jesuit missionary author or authors state that "the Architects of Europe will not see here anything that merits their attention. . . ."[35] Pagodas are likened to pyramids, there is a clear disdain for Buddhism and other forms of idolatry and ignorance, and the only interest in these is whether they might reveal some connection between European antiquity and the history of China, since such constructions are not found in the first three dynasties. The first five illustrations show pagodas or towers that resemble in some form Tibetan Buddhist stupas (or *chorten*), recalling the massive stupa in the Qing imperial temple, the Baita 白塔 or White Dagoba, built by the Shunzhi emperor (順治, r. 1644–1661) in 1651 on Qionghua Island in the Western Park, northwest of the Forbidden City.[36] The illustration of another pagoda in the *Essai* shows a type that is less exaggerated and less fanciful than some of the other constructions, and the accompanying caption notes the great height—some 300 or 400 feet—as well as the numerous small bells suspended from the roofs, which produce a pleasant ringing sound when the wind blows (Plate 8).[37]

Images of Chinese pavilions, bridges, and pagodas, indeed, were not unknown in late eighteenth-century France, and these architectural elements formed part of the image of China that was transmitted by some of the first published descriptions of travel in the seventeenth century. Among the most widely circulated and influential is the account by Johannes Nieuhof (1618–1672) of the embassy of the Dutch East India Company to the court of the Shunzhi emperor, part of a journey that lasted from 1655 to 1657. Nieuhof's profusely illustrated book first appeared in Dutch and French editions (both in 1665), which were followed by German (1666), Latin (1668), and English editions (1669), as well as later reprints.[38] Among the most famous images in Nieuhof's account are the two views of the Porcelain Pagoda at the Bao'ensi 報恩寺 (Figure 3.5).[39] The pagoda was the principle feature of the Bao'ensi temple, located just to the south of the first Ming capital at Nanjing. The Ming Yongle emperor (永樂, r. 1402–1424) had ordered its construction, which lasted from about 1412 to 1431, and it was officially a monastery or temple that commemorated the emperor's filial gratitude to his parents, the Hongwu emperor and the Empress Ma, a sentiment he expressed in a stele inscription dated 1424.[40] The pagoda itself was an extraordinary construction, some 80–90 meters tall, with nine stories that were octagonal in plan, each decorated with elaborate, polychrome-glazed earthenware carved and molded blocks.[41] Dubbed the Porcelain Pagoda in European accounts, images and descriptions of the pagoda became key emblems of China. Along his travel route from the port of Canton (Guangzhou 廣州) to Beijing, Nieuhof stopped at Nanjing, where he produced several drawings that were later reproduced as engravings in his travel account. The illustrations of the pagoda and the text that describes it give the name as "Paolinxi," which is surely a misunderstanding of the Chinese name Bao'ensi. Nieuhof's drawing of 1658 showing the complete temple compound (Figure 3.6)[42] is simpler than the published prints, and, in the various editions of Nieuhof's account, the bird's-eye view of the Bao'ensi site is reproduced as a small print at the top of one page, followed by the larger, fold-out engraving with the detailed view of the Pagoda itself. The preface to the French edition of Nieuhof's account states that the first part of the book—the account of the journey from Canton to Beijing—is based on what he saw with his own eyes, supplemented by what "Mandarins and Lords"

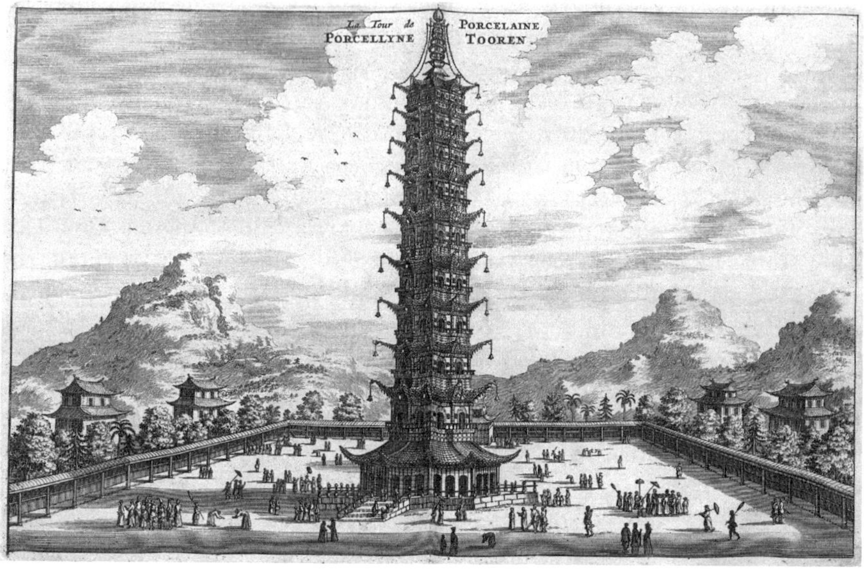

Figure 3.5 Joan Nieuhof, *Die Gesantschaft der Ost-Indischen Geselschaft in den Vereinigten Niederländern an den Tartarischen Cham. . .*, Amsterdam, 1666, "La Tour de Porcelaine," engraving, between pp. 124 and 125.

Source: ©Heidelberg University Library.

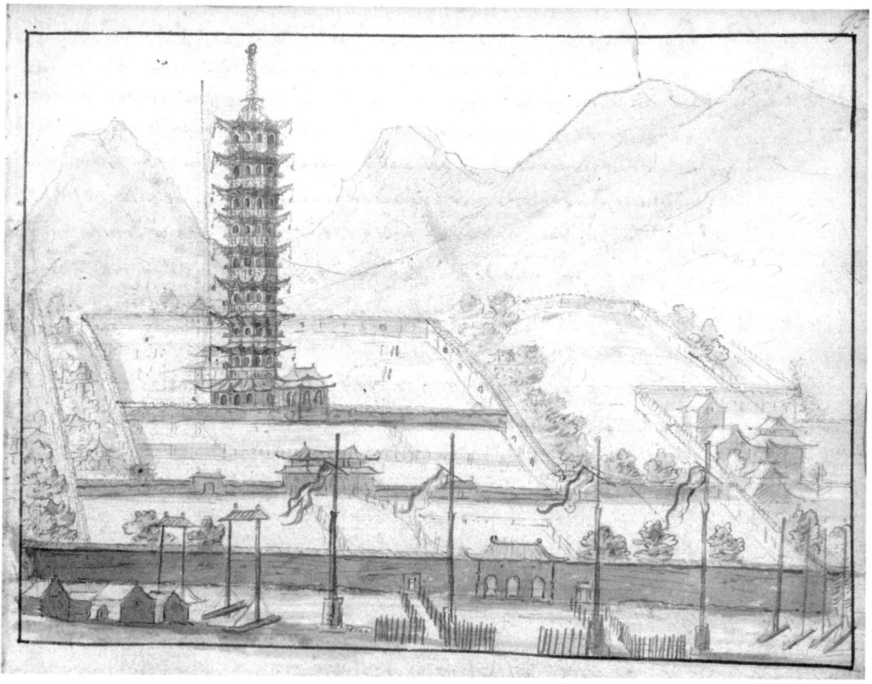

Figure 3.6 Johan Nieuhof, *Journaal van zommige voorvallen. . .*, fol. 95, View of the Porcelain Pagoda, Nanjing, ink and color on paper, ca. 1656–1659. Paris, Bibliothèque nationale de France, Société de Géographie.

who accompanied them had to say. And it states that the illustrations are based on Nieuhof's drawings, saying specifically that he had studied how to accurately represent landscapes and the principle places where the Embassy traveled.[43]

The second album of paintings and texts that make up the *Essai sur l'architecture chinoise* again begins with an introduction that seeks to clarify important elements of Chinese architecture that are distinctly different from European architecture.[44] The Jesuit missionary authors note that, although the forms of Chinese buildings are extraordinarily varied, once one moves beyond the constructions of the common people, it becomes clear, however, that this variety is essentially a series of progressions in size, elevation, and ornament or decoration. Here once again the feature that distinguishes Chinese from European practice is that in China all these features are supposedly determined by sumptuary laws that regulate the most minor details of construction according to the status of the owner of the building or the purpose of the building itself. The authors of the *Essai* write that the Chinese officials have even had a book printed that specifies the dimensions and costs of buildings down to the last detail.[45] Following the standard pattern of the two albums, just one illustration of a building typical of the "common people" is followed by buildings made for the literati, buildings for pleasure gardens, and various kinds of imperial buildings. These are followed by gates and an elaborate pavilion in the imperial palace, and then there begins a series of two-story buildings.

A number of these illustrations of typical constructions are followed by a second, related painting that shows what is labeled the "plan" of the building, that is, a painting showing the solid platform on which the building is constructed, with careful attention paid to the depiction and layout of the stone bases for pillars or columns. Given the general characteristics of Chinese architecture, it is these column bases that determine the actual floor plan. Two illustrations show a view and the "plan" of a hall of the imperial palace, where the rows of column bases on the foundation platform give an indication of the interior space (Figure 3.7).[46] The solid walls at the sides of the hall are not indicated, nor are any other architectural details. Such illustrations of the foundation platform are included for garden gates, free-standing pavilions, large halls and other imperial constructions, including a number of multistoried buildings.

The multistoried buildings in the second part of the *Essai* are often identified as belonging to the emperor; captions repeat that they are governed by sumptuary laws and that only the emperor has the right to use colored tile roofs. The text facing one illustration says such two-story structures are found in the Yuanming yuan or gardens in the city, presumably Beijing.[47] Another, similar hall has an elaborate geometric decoration worked into the colored roof tiles (Figure 3.8).[48] Colored roof tiles, briefly noted in the aforementioned discussion of garden pavilions, are again reserved for imperial constructions, and a short notice on *Lieou-Li* (*liuli*) or glazed tiles was published in the *Mémoires concernant les Chinois* in 1788.[49] The author is Father Cibot, and he described the splendor and brilliance of imperial structures with colored tile roofs among imperial residences as well as halls erected in honor of emperors, great men and heroes, and including temples.[50]

The last illustration in this section, a grand structure with three stories, is also described as located in the gardens of the emperor of China, and it is accompanied by a short notice that describes some of the environmental conditions that determine the forms of Chinese architecture.[51] Once again, the authors state that such multistory constructions are mostly forbidden by official regulations. Also, they would be

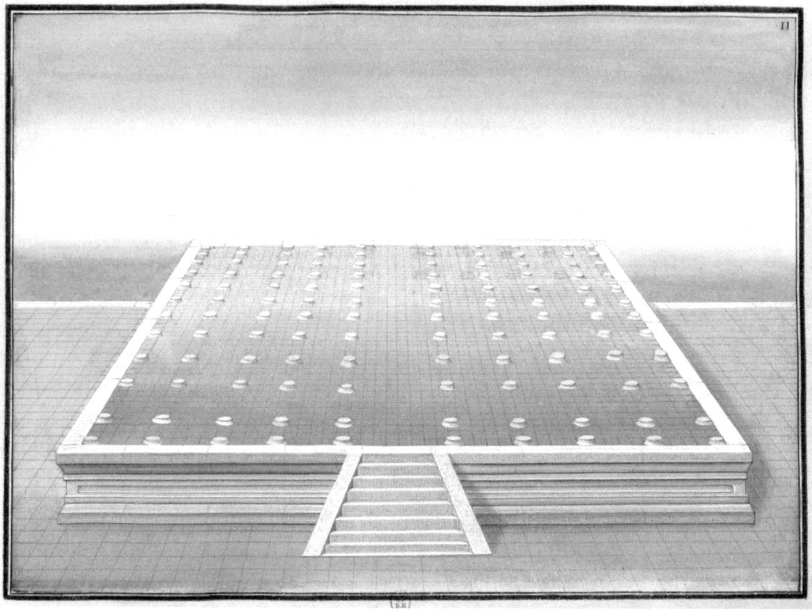

Figure 3.7 Anonymous, Chinese, *Essai sur l'architecture chinoise*, part II, pl. 11, "Plan de la Salle cy dessus," ink and color on paper, 35 × 45 cm, ca. 1773. Paris, Bibliothèque nationale de France.

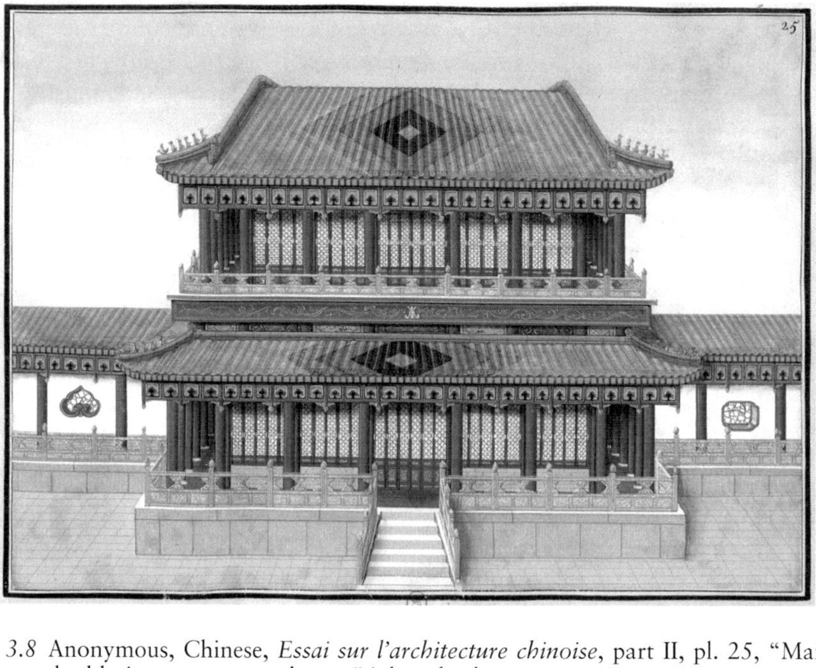

Figure 3.8 Anonymous, Chinese, *Essai sur l'architecture chinoise*, part II, pl. 25, "Maison à double étage comme cy dessus," ink and color on paper, 35 × 45 cm, ca. 1773. Paris, Bibliothèque nationale de France.

dangerous, given the frequent earthquakes which supposedly oblige the Chinese to build wooden structures. The climate, too, would discourage such buildings, since they would be too hot in summer and too exposed to the severe winters of the capital region. One-story buildings encourage more elaborate compounds, which means that there is space around them and a better circulation of fresh air, and buildings in China are generally oriented to the south, the most healthy direction in all seasons, a subject that was taken up in detail in the essay on Chinese greenhouses.

A final "note" appended here addresses the question of how Bertin, and perhaps others who see these albums of paintings, might obtain further information:

> Note. We might have had some intention to put forward ideas and conjectures on the different parts of Chinese Architecture, its dimensions, its proportions, and the different Plans that it produces in the distribution of Courtyards, Buildings, Galleries, Roofs, Columns, etc., but all things considered, it is better to wait for questions, all the more so given that they would as well speak to the eyes by more methodical Paintings, & to bring out details where it would be too difficult to enter into here.[52]

This type of comment is repeated in other contexts, where the Jesuit missionaries write that the pictures make the fullest presentation of what must surely be unknown in Europe, but that they can provide more detailed information if so requested.

A group of 11 paintings in the second part of the *Essai sur l'architecture chinoise* presents something truly novel—views of the interiors of Chinese houses or palaces. The Jesuit missionaries once again remark that these are quite different from what one finds in France, and no doubt a long text explaining the different customs and taste of the Chinese and even the effects of weather on the arrangement of interiors would be much appreciated, but for the moment one must rely on the pictures to tell the story.[53] The pictures are highly detailed, revealing much about the interiors of certain types of Chinese buildings, that is, upper-class or princely residences.[54] All of the paintings of interiors follow the same format, a strict single-point perspective view with the vanishing-point at the center. There are no people in these rooms, but the paintings are carefully rendered with a clear indication of light and shadow, and some of the paintings show views out into other rooms or elaborate gardens. Illustrations of Chinese interiors were not entirely unknown in eighteenth-century Europe, but what is striking here is the format of the paintings and the goal of providing details as accurate as possible of specific types of Chinese interior spaces.[55] What we now know about the culture of the Chinese literati elite, the social class referred to the album captions as *Gens aisés*, "those who are well-off," allows us to recognize and appreciate the rooms we see here and their contents. This is something that Bertin and his contemporaries surely would have perceived as a great novelty, and they likely would have posed a number of questions about such things as the paintings and calligraphy, the books, the furniture, the arrangement of the spaces, and the views into gardens through wide-open doorways.

Three of the interiors are given the same title, "Ceremonial and audience hall in the home of an imperial Prince."[56] The second painting of the three shows a reception room furnished with the accoutrements of a Chinese scholar (Plate 9). On the wall behind a dais set with cushions at the far end of the room is a framed painting imitating the manner of the Yuan dynasty scholar-painter Ni Zan (倪瓚, 1301–1374),

whose deliberately plain style in ink on paper was a key emblem of literati taste. The room is filled with paintings and calligraphy, including a name-plaque (*bian'e* 匾額) hanging over the octagonal entrance to the space where the cushioned throne sits. It reads *Jingmo xuan* (靜默軒), perhaps equivalent to "The Tranquil Study," which would be the name of the room.[57] One further detail is worth noting here: On the wall at the right is a landscape painting in ink flanked by a calligraphic couplet (*duizi* 對子), which hangs behind a table with a bundle of books, a bronze incense burner, and a red porcelain vase. These are all the accoutrements of a Chinese scholar, and we will see in the next chapter that Bertin received an illustration of just such an arrangement of calligraphy and objects to be recreated at his estate at Chatou.

A long text signals the subject of the last 14 paintings of buildings in the second album of the *Essai*, that of constructions built on a *Tai* (*tai* 臺) or raised platform. This distinctive feature of Chinese architecture especially impressed the Jesuit authors of the album texts because these platforms play an important role in both ancient and contemporary architecture. Here again the pages are turned sideways to accommodate the paintings of tall platforms and towers, taking full advantage of the page. One of the paintings shows what is clearly an imperial building with red lacquered columns and multi-colored tile roofs on top of a high platform or gateway that is covered with the red stucco that distinguished imperial constructions (Figure 3.9). The red earth that produces this special color is specifically illustrated among the building materials in the first part of the *Essai*.[58] For the Jesuit missionaries, such platforms were a source of curiosity and surprise, but that "surprise" is tempered by their rather severe judgment of Chinese imperial builders:

> Of surprise because all that we have wanted to teach so far about China does not lead one to imagine that it might have anything similar; of curiosity because the height, the beauty, and the vain magnificence of many of these *Tai* cannot be reconciled with the proclaimed Economies of their politics, and that the reason for this exception has much that would surprise.[59]

The "exception" is given a detailed explanation in the introductory text on platforms, although even this account is described as abbreviated. At the beginning of the Zhou dynasty, for which the missionaries accepted the traditional Chinese date at the end of the twelfth century BCE, the emperor had three great *tai* or buildings on platforms within his palace. The numerous feudal princes, who are compared to the noble houses of medieval France, vied with each other to erect such buildings as a demonstration of their wealth and power. The missionaries proposed an explanation that so many of these were built that they became the inspiration for pagodas (or *ta*, illustrated in the first part of the *Essai*). Having lost their original purpose, nevertheless such constructions were built in great numbers and at great expense, something the Jesuit missionaries felt was in direct contradiction to what they saw as the traditional "economies" represented in Chinese architecture. Having identified the uses of *tai* or elevated platforms, the authors leave the viewer to identify the specific examples in the following paintings.

Finally, one floor plan of a building compound is included at the end of the second album of the *Essai sur l'architecture chinoise*. Labeled "Plan of the House of a Colonel in the Imperial Barracks of the Manchu Banners,"[60] it copies the conventional, highly simplified style of contemporary eighteenth-century Chinese plans, showing

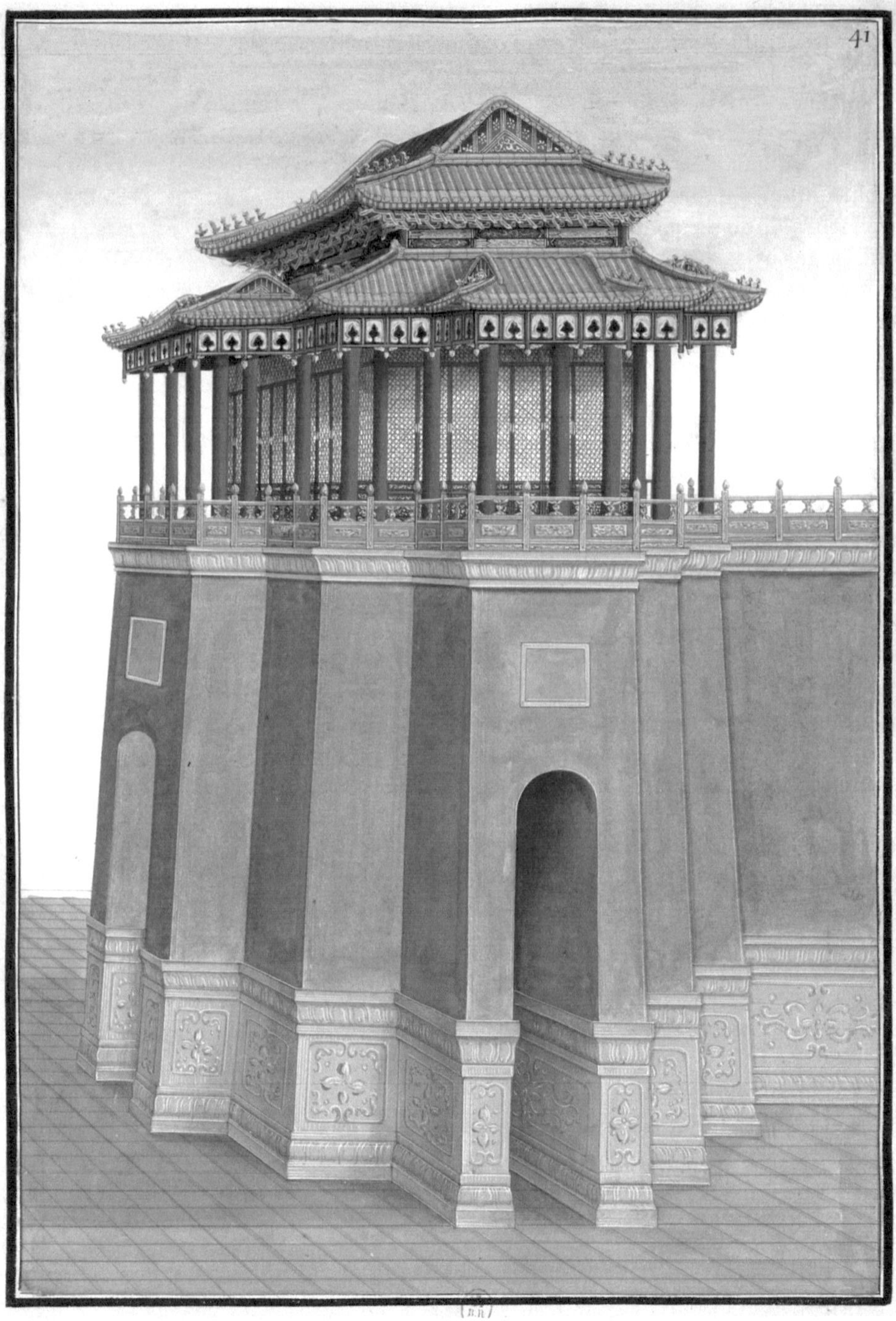

Figure 3.9 Anonymous, Chinese, *Essai sur l'architecture chinoise*, part II, pl. 41, "*Tai*. Voyez la note. . .," ink and color on paper, 45 × 35 cm, ca. 1773. Paris, Bibliothèque nationale de France.

the general outlines of buildings and the all-important placement of columns, which determine the possibilities for the internal layout. Such plans depict the interior layout of buildings through the convention of showing the bays, the spaces between columns (*jian* 間) as a kind of grid pattern. This concept of spacing based on the arrangement of the column bases is amply illustrated in the paintings described as "plans" in the *Essai sur l'architecture chinoise* (see Figure 3.7). The caption on the facing page includes a key that identifies the various types of buildings—both for public and private use—within the compound and, as an indication of the exterior spaces, also notes paved courtyards, walkways, and the location of trees. A separate, large-scale album, however, is directly related to the *Essai* and contains three highly detailed plans of the residential compounds associated with high officials of the Qing imperial government.[61] Entitled *Plans relatifs a l'essai sur l'architecture chinoise* (Plans related to the Essay on Chinese Architecture), it contains plans for the palace of the sixteenth son of the Kangxi emperor, for the residence of a high-ranking official or member of the Manchu nobility, and the palace of a prime minister.[62] The sixteenth son of the Kangxi emperor was Yunlu (允祿, 1695–1767), and the plan of his palace shows a vast urban complex that included spaces for guards and eunuchs, a grand hall for solemn audiences, a separate palace for one of his sons, the prince's private apartments and other structures.[63] The plan of the palace of the Prime Minister is equally complex in its detail, and the largest group of buildings along the central axis is labeled "Palace of the son of the Prime Minister, or rather that of the *Gongzhu*, his wife and daughter of the Emperor."[64] The most likely identification of this person is the Imperial Princess Hejia (和嘉公主 Hejia Gongzhu, 1745–1767),[65] who was married to Fulong'an (福隆安, 1743/46? –1784), the second son of Fuheng (傅恆, d. 1770).[66] Fuheng, an important official in the service of the Qianlong emperor, was named a Grand Councilor in 1768, and this is probably the title rendered here as Prime Minister.

The title of the plan of the residence of a high-ranking minister or member of the nobility (Figure 3.10) identifies the owner as a only *Ta-Gin*, a *daren* 大人, which is a standard reference to such a person, often a member of the extended imperial clan. Facing the plan is a key and a short note:

> As for the layout of the buildings, it is enough to say that everything that is in the front part are offices and housing for servants and officers, the middle is for the family, and what is in the gardens functions only for the magnificence [of the residence].[67]

The key identifies the front entrance, which includes a screen-wall of the type illustrated in the *Essai sur l'architecture chinoise* and discussed previously (see Figure 3.3), and it locates the hall for receiving visitors (labeled B in the plan). The various buildings of the family residence are not labeled, but the key distinguishes several of the features shown in the plan, including a pond in the rear garden, small mountains, rockworks or groups of rocks, shrubs with clumps of flowers, and a meandering raised path through the garden. The intimate links between an upper-class residence and its garden setting are amply illustrated here, and indeed the garden is presented in more detail than the buildings, which follow the conventions of architectural plans as simple outlines with the locations of columns defining the divisions of interior spaces.

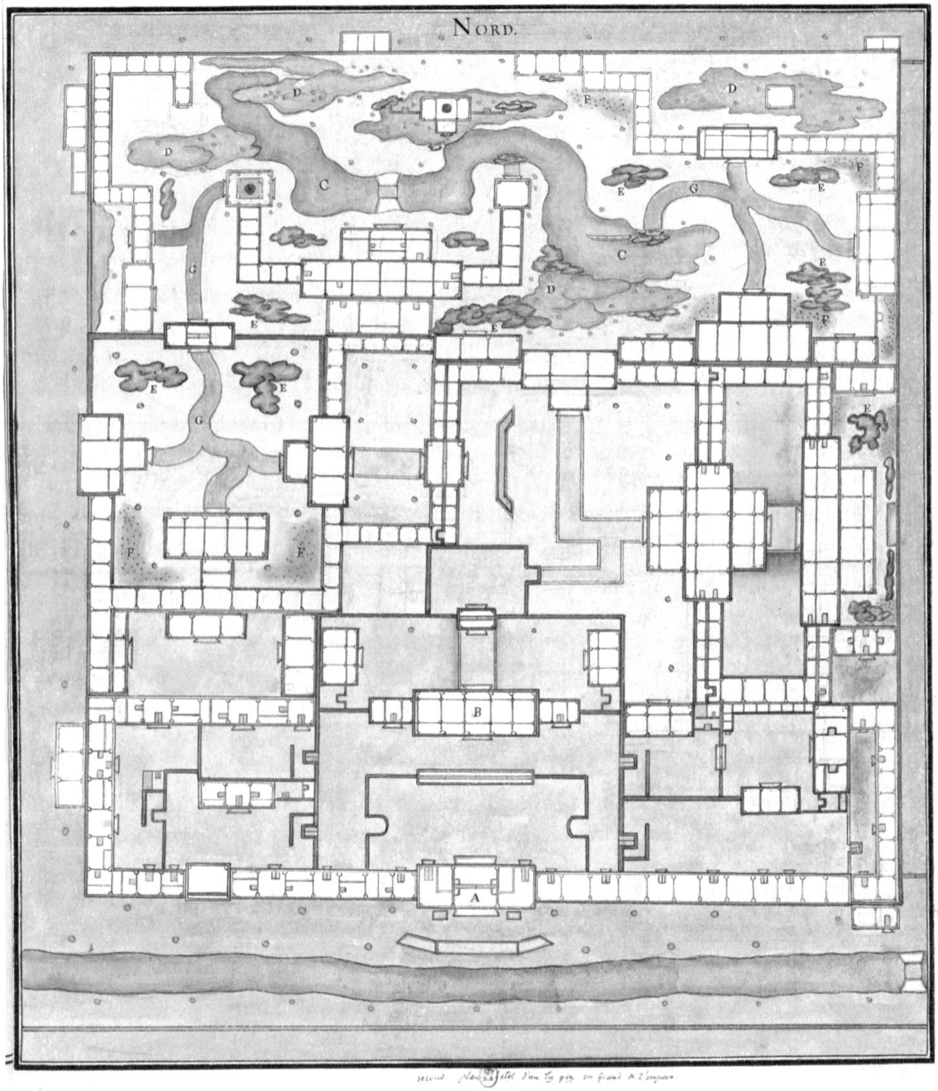

Figure 3.10 Anonymous, *Recueil. Plans relatifs à l'essai sur l'architecture chinoise*, no. 2, "Plans de l'Hôtel d'un *Ta-Gin* our Grand de l'Empire," ink and color on Chinese paper, 63 × 52 cm, ca. 1773. Paris, Bibliothèque nationale de France.

French Architecture and Chinese Architecture

Outside of Henri Bertin's insatiable appetite for knowledge of China, we have to consider other motives for the interest in and production of the two illustrated albums of the *Essai sur l'architecture chinoise*. Why would architecture appear as a focus of study at this time? Over a period beginning at the end of the seventeenth century and continuing throughout the eighteenth to the beginning of the nineteenth century, the field of architecture was the subject of a remarkable number of publications in France, many with detailed illustrations, which spread knowledge of both the theory and practice of architecture. Theory, however, had a different sense at the time from what the term might mean to modern writers on the critical theory (or theories) of architecture. For earlier writers the term pointed toward mathematics and its practical applications in building along with more general discussions of what was fitting in terms of historical models and their relevance to contemporary architectural design.[68]

One key indication of the role of publications in the theory and practice of architecture in France in the mid-eighteenth century can be found in the lengthy address given in 1754 by the eminent professor of architecture Jacques-François Blondel (1705–1774), a text which was published as the *Discours sur la nécessité de l'étude de l'architecture* or "Lecture on the necessity of studying architecture."[69] The *Discours* contains a list of books recommended for the education of architects, including "ancient" or early texts—the foundations of architectural theory and practice—followed by "modern" or contemporary publications, and it includes a further list of prints which might prove useful to "architects and other artists, who make their profession from works of [good] taste."[70] First on Blondel's list of publications is the *Ten Books on Architecture* by Vitruvius, the ultimate reference for almost all traditional writings on architecture, cited here in Claude Perrault's annotated French translation of 1684.[71] Perrault was himself an architect, among other learned vocations, who contributed to the transformation of the practice of architecture in France in the seventeenth century as well as a skillful draftsman who designed the illustrations for his edition of the *Ten Books*.[72] Vitruvius provides the basic format for treatises on architecture by including discussions of fundamental principles, building materials, symmetry and proportion in design, the origins of certain forms, comments on climate and siting of constructions, on tools and instruments necessary for building, and even notes on "how the rooms should be suited to the station of the owner."[73] Perrault's illustrated 1684 French translation and at least two other Latin editions of Vitruvius were held in the libraries of the Jesuits in Beijing in the eighteenth century, and surely these along with a significant number of other books on architecture, many of them also illustrated, helped serve as models for what the French missionaries sent to Bertin as the *Essai sur l'architecture chinoise*.[74] It is worth noting that the edition of Vitruvius in the Jesuit missionaries' possession included an illustration of masonry walls as they were constructed in Antiquity and also included illustrations combining plans and views of Greek temples, both of which are similar to the illustrations in the *Essai sur l'architecture chinoise*.[75] While *The Ten Books of Architecture* is essentially a written text that was frequently illustrated in later editions and the *Essai sur l'architecture chinoise* is effectively a set of illustrations with a brief but concise written text, the two treatises share common concerns in the description—the definitions—of what is architecture. The *Essai* does not include such things as weapons and machines, but the emphasis on Chinese imperial constructions echoes, consciously or not, Vitruvius's descriptions of specific temples, villas and other buildings, many of which were constructions of the Greek and Roman elite or rulers in ancient times.

If the long history of European writing on architecture had produced a considerable body of works on various theories of architecture, Chinese writings on the subject reflected very different, specifically Chinese concerns and traditions. In an article on the construction of the Qing imperial garden-palace Yuanming yuan, Cary Y. Liu briefly outlines the basic evolution of what a Chinese imperial architect might be. And it was a profession that effectively did not exist in any form comparable to historical European practice (combining the roles of designer, planner and builder) until the mid-Qing period in the eighteenth century. Construction, especially of imperial buildings, was the collective responsibility of craftsmen who did the actual labor, supervisors who administered and coordinated the craftsmen's work, and

> planners, usually well-educated ministers or imperial advisors, [who] were appointed to formulate the underlying ritual design of imperial buildings, palaces, gardens, and cities. Such planners, however, should not be viewed as "architects" in the modern sense; instead, their role was mainly limited to devising schematic or ideal plans that translated imperial demonstrations of political and dynastic legitimacy into building symbology, cosmology, numerology, and other ritual forms that often had roots in ancient models.[76]

A small number of Chinese texts are usually cited as the most significant traditional writings on architecture.[77] Among these are the *Yingzao fashi* 營造法式 (Treatise on architectural methods), compiled in the late eleventh to early twelfth century for the Southern Song imperial court.[78] The author or compiler, Li Jie (李誡, ca. 1065–1110 or 1035–1108), was the head of the imperial Department of Construction (Jiangzuo jian 將作監, also known as the Directorate for the Palace Buildings),[79] himself a practicing architect in the Chinese sense and widely knowledgeable in imperial constructions. The *Yingzao fashi* is the best-known and most comprehensive early Chinese work on architecture. Another often-reprinted traditional Chinese text, the *Lu Ban jing* 魯班經 (Classic of Lu Ban), is effectively a carpenter's manual compiled in the fifteenth century based on material dating back to the Song and Yuan dynasties (the tenth to fourteenth centuries).[80] It is named for the legendary craftsman Lu Ban of the fifth century BCE, and while some sections of the text are concerned with magic and ritual, other sections deal directly with the practical aspects of building houses, constructing furniture, and various implements. In the Qing dynasty, the imperially commissioned *Gongbu gongcheng zuofa* (工部工程做法, Building methods of the Board of Works) was completed 1734.[81] Compiled the supervision of Yinli (胤禮, Prince Guo 果親王), it codified existing regulations that guided imperial constructions. The emphasis in the *Gongbu gongcheng zuofa* is on economic concerns, and it is likely that this is the imperial publication referred to in the second album of the *Essai sur l'architecture chinoise*.[82] While the *Yingzao fashi* is generously illustrated, the *Gongbu gongcheng zuofa* contains only 27 illustrations, all of them cross-sections of various building types with little detail. None of these books is the equivalent of a Chinese Vitruvius, focusing as they do on extraordinarily different concepts of what building—or architecture—might be. And as Liu further notes:

> Although the Western-based Vitruvian categories of form, function, and structure are useful analytical tools, they are nevertheless inadequate for understanding Chinese architecture. Analysis of a building's symbology—including decoration, name, numerology, geomancy, calligraphy, ritual layout, and design models—is an additional lens through which to view Chinese architecture.[83]

Symbology, the system of symbols or elements of ritual design embodied in a Chinese structure, has no real equivalent in European architectural practice, at least in terms of the extent to which such elements determined the form, style and decoration of Chinese buildings. There is no formal European equivalent of the Chinese practice of *fengshui* 風水 in the siting and planning of construction, and no equivalent, either, of Chinese sumptuary laws. Nevertheless, Vitruvius' *Ten Books* includes discussions of climate in relation to the siting of a city (Book I, Chap. 4), the directions of the winds in the streets (Book I, Chap. 6), on climate in determining the style of a house (Book VI, Chap. 1), and how rooms should be suited to the status of the owner (Book VI, Chap. 5). In the *Essai sur l'architecture chinoise*, it was especially the regulations that supposedly determined the decoration, scale, and layout of buildings that caught the attention of the Jesuit authors of Bertin's albums. They seem to have been unaware of the traditional symbology, the underlying ritual requirements for any substantial Chinese construction, that determined Chinese architectural forms.

Plafonds Chinois

Among the albums and paintings in Bertin's collection that are related to the subject of Chinese architecture, one stands out for its remarkable size and quality and for its unprecedented subject. The album, entitled *Plafonds Chinois*, is truly monumental, the pages are almost one meter high, and it is bound in the blue paper typical of albums from Bertin's collection. The title *Plafonds Chinois* appears on the cover, and on separate title page is the inscription *Recueil Relatif à l'architecture chinoise* (Collection related to Chinese architecture).[84] The album contains just four paintings—two full-page illustrations of imperial buildings and what appear to be two highly detailed perspective views of Chinese ceilings—along with a two-page essay on Chinese ceilings that is written, like the articles and captions in the *Essai sur l'architecture chinoise*, in imitation of a printed text. In the manner of all the paintings produced for Bertin by Chinese artists in Beijing to illustrate Chinese architecture, the ceilings depicted in *Plafonds Chinois* are rendered in a hybrid Chinese-European style with linear perspective and modeling in light and shade. While the paintings of ceilings appear to show in clear and accurate detail the architecture of sumptuous Chinese interiors, the accompanying text identifies them as images of trompe-l'oeil paintings and not renderings of actual ceilings. In effect, a European decorative technique—a painting on a flat ceiling that creates the illusion of deep space—has supposedly been translated into a Chinese context, and then a representation of that adoption of European style in China has been sent back to Europe. The complexities of this unprecedented interchange are highlighted by the issues raised in the missionaries' text.

The story of the transfer of European linear perspective to China is a compelling one, and the subject has been studied in some detail. The best-known encounter between Chinese art and European perspective is the instruction of court painters in the mathematical principles and painterly effects of linear perspective by Jesuit missionary-artists serving in the imperial workshops of the Qing dynasty (1644–1911). Jesuit painters and Chinese court artists together created trompe-l'oeil murals, paintings designed to "fool the eye," for the interiors of imperial buildings.[85] The paintings in the album of *Plafonds Chinois* raise important questions of how European knowledge was transferred to eighteenth-century China, of who received such knowledge, and what the mathematics, the artistic, and even the theological implications of linear perspective might have meant there.[86]

The essay in the album *Plafonds Chinois* begins with a statement that it is generally believed in Europe that Chinese ceilings consist only of white paper or designs painted on paper, and that would make those who saw these illustrations believe that the images here exist only in the mind of the artist who painted them. To clarify this question, five detailed observations are offered. First, with the exception of imperial princes and certain great Manchu families, official status changes so often that no father would ever think to build on such a grand scale for the benefit of his sons, thus enforcing a kind of "universal equality" throughout Chinese society. Because men of high rank are almost all housed in buildings provided by the state and strictly regulated by sumptuary laws, they could not conceive of adding such opulent decoration. Since all such constructions are of one story only, a higher ceiling might display the wealth of the owner, but Chinese windows are covered with paper and thus the light they admit is not suitable for perspective views but favors instead painted and gilded paneling. Given that Chinese "eye" is prejudiced or ignorant in such matters, Chinese taste would be offended by different aspects of a trompe-l'oeil ceiling apparently meant to be seen from a single point-of-view only. And finally, Chinese painting, having flourished in the fourth and fifth centuries, had lost the relevant knowledge by the time Europeans arrived, and painters no longer had the skills to produce such a ceiling, where, in any case, the watercolors would have faded in a short time. The Jesuit author or authors then continue:

> Given these reasons, the result is that painted ceilings are rare in China, but it is not that there are none at all. Their rarity is one reason for us to have had two copied, so that one could see how the Chinese have finally come to appropriate the knowledge that has been brought to them from the Occident, and so that Artists in turn could see how they must prepare what they would intend for China. These two ceilings, which are in the Palace of the Prime Minister, have been painted so as to form a whole with the great rooms where they are, to complete one with a second floor, and the other with two. The illusion of perspective is all the better achieved in that everything corresponds, everything is linked, everything follows in order and is reproduced in color.[87]

Thus, what the Chinese artists working with the Jesuit missionaries have painted here for Bertin are not illustrations of Chinese ceilings in actual buildings but two images of trompe-l'oeil paintings pasted to the ceilings of a one-story room to give the illusion of a grand, multistory, Chinese interior space (Plate 10). We are asked to believe that in these admittedly rare examples the Chinese have adopted the European technique of an illusionistic painted decoration extending the perceived space of a room beyond its actual dimensions.

The text of the essay "Chinese Ceilings" goes on to note that the Jesuit missionaries have heard there are indeed actual ceilings in this style constructed in multistory interior spaces in the great halls of princes or nobles, referring to the carved and painted decoration we see represented in the album *Plafonds Chinois*. However, they have never heard of any decorated with figures, and they state that the European Palaces built by the emperor are the only place where there might ever be such representations of people or figural scenes. The European Palaces, created in a hybrid European style, occupied a small area of the Changchun yuan 長春園, the Garden of Lasting Springtime, which the Qianlong emperor added to the original Yuanming yuan beginning in 1747. The emperor had seen an image of a European fountain, and asked the Jesuits at court to design and build such constructions for him, a project overseen by Giuseppe Castiglione and Father Michel Benoist, who was responsible specifically for the fountains.[88] Construction of the first buildings began in 1751, and the emperor ordered a second group that was largely complete by 1759. One additional building was added in 1768.[89] Along with the rest of the Yuanming yuan garden-palace, the European Palaces were destroyed by British and French troops in the wake of the Second Opium War in 1860.

The reception and appropriation of European trompe-l'oeil painting techniques in late seventeenth and early eighteenth-century China is a fascinating subject that continues to attract significant scholarly interest.[90] It is not possible to outline all of the stages of this intercultural encounter here, but it is important, first, to note that the decoration of at least three of the Jesuit churches in Beijing included trompe-l'oeil mural paintings.[91] However, the two paintings of ceilings contained in the album of *Plafonds Chinois* are directly related to specific elements of the training in trompe-l'oeil painting techniques that was provided for Jesuit missionary-artists before they were sent to the imperial court in Beijing. This included practical instruction in the techniques of *quadratura*, the Italian term for the methods of using mathematical grids to transfer an image—often a trompe-l'oeil illusion—from a preparatory drawing to a wall or ceiling.[92] One of the masters of the technique of *quadratura*, the Jesuit brother Andrea Pozzo (1642–1709), did not himself travel to China, but he was the author of the highly successful and influential manual of perspective drawing and illustration entitled the *Perspectiva pictorum et architectorum*, which first appeared in Rome in 1693 but was soon translated into several European languages and reprinted many times.[93] All editions contained copies of Pozzo's highly detailed illustrations, which show how to compose various kinds of perspective views, both schematic outlines and highly detailed architectural renderings.

Like the illustrated edition of Vitruvius, Pozzo's textbook on perspective was also among the books held in the libraries of the Jesuit missionaries in Beijing in the early eighteenth century, and it was one of the principle sources, although by no means the only source, used in the compilation of a Chinese text on perspective, the *Shixue* 視學, the "Study of Appearances" or the "Science of Vision," as the title has been variously translated. The work of the court official Nian Xiyao 年希堯 (1671–1738),[94] the *Shixue* was first printed in 1729 and then reprinted in a second, expanded edition of 1735.[95] In the prefaces to both editions, Nian specifically acknowledged the Jesuit painter Giuseppe Castiglione for his continuing instruction in the art of European linear perspective.[96] Although it was not imitated in the *Shixue*, Plate 88 in Pozzo's *Perspective in Architecture and Painting* shows the stages of illustrating or painting the projection of a trompe-l'oeil balustrade on a flat ceiling (Figure 3.11).[97] As noted earlier, however, Pozzo's perspective manual was accessible in the Jesuits' libraries in Beijing, and this image is directly related to the two paintings of trompe-l'oeil ceilings in the album of *Plafonds Chinois*. Such an illustration provides a direct parallel to the two Chinese painted ceilings, which are of course rendered in illusionistic color with modeling in light and shade to produce a convincing three-dimensional effect.

The text in the "Essay" accompanying the *Plafonds Chinois* paintings notes that the Chinese might be offended, or at least uncomprehending, when they saw a painted ceiling whose illusionistic effect was meant to be seen only from one particular position, that is, with the viewer standing directly opposite (or under) the central vanishing

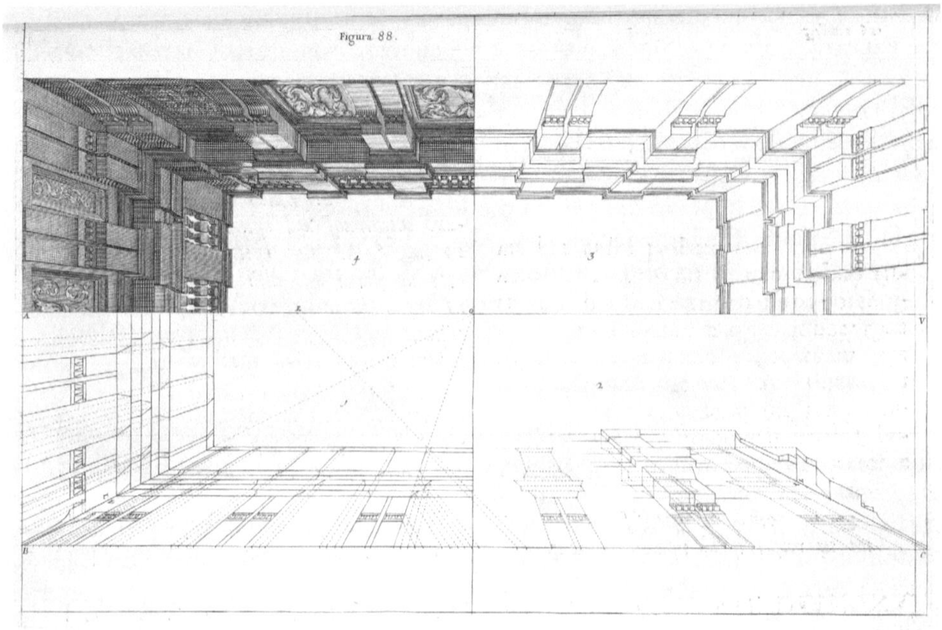

Figure 3.11 Andrea Pozzo and Vincenzo Mariotti, *Perspectiva Pictorum et Architectorum Andreae Putei*, Rome: Joannis Jacobi Komarek, 1693, fig. 88, "Horizontal projection of the balustrade. . .," engraving. Getty Research Institute, Los Angeles (317925).

point. The "Essay" noted, however, that such elaborately carved and painted multistory ceilings actually existed in some of the largest imperial buildings, and comparable examples are still extant in the Forbidden City. At the beginning of his textbook on perspective, Andrea Pozzo had admonished his students: "Therefore, Reader, my Advice is that you cheerfully begin your Work, and with Resolution to draw all the Points thereof to that true Point, the Glory of God; and I dare predict, and promise you good Success in so honorable an Undertaking."[98] For the missionary priests, the viewer's correct position in relation to the perspective illusion was analogous to his correct relation to the Christian religion.[99] This was a key element of the proselytizing role of perspective that the Jesuit missionary-artists had brought to China. Such an interpretation would not at first seem directly related to the two illusionistic ceilings of the Palace of the Prime Minister illustrated in *Plafonds Chinois*, but a closer look at the details of the painting of a multistory ceiling shows that the room contains a *bian'e*, a name plaque attached to a beam over the opening to a balcony, with a pair of verses or *duizi* framing the opening.[100] The plaque reads 信望愛 *Xin wang ai*, "Faith, hope, and love," a distinctly Christian motto, and the panels with the couplet are inscribed 仰承聖訓信為本 and 望受永恩愛作基, that is, "To revere holy teaching [or, holy scripture], faith is the source;/To hope for receiving eternal grace, love provides the foundation." I have not been able to find precisely the same lines in a Christian source, but several of the terms used here are again conventional translations of Christian terms. To add to the mystery of their interpretation, we cannot forget that the text accompanying the paintings says specifically that they are painted for the Palace of a Prime Minister, a title for which there is no exact Chinese equivalent, making it hard to identify any particular official for whom the ceilings were supposedly painted.[101] It is difficult to believe that a high court official in the Qianlong era would openly declare himself to be a Christian, and the texts in the representation of a Chinese ceiling—images that were intended for a European audience—might be an expression of the hope on the part of the Jesuit missionaries that such a conversion might take place. They provide, nevertheless, clear evidence of the missionaries' close collaboration with the Chinese artists who produced the illustrations for the album *Plafonds Chinois*, and they document a complex intercultural encounter.

The Lessons of Chinese Architecture

The text in the first album of the *Essai sur l'architecture chinoise* asks the questions: Is Chinese architecture worth being known in Europe, and would knowledge about it be of any use? The picture of Chinese architecture presented in the paintings and texts of the two parts of the *Essai* is in many ways an idealized and admiring one. The author or authors of the *Essai* repeat several times the supposed adherence of the Chinese to strict laws governing the size of buildings and other details of public display that would identify the rank of the person who lived in the building. But the Jesuit missionary authors admit on occasion that these complex rules are not always consistently followed. The realities of Chinese construction regulations were more complicated, and Bertin was made aware of this in a long letter from Father Amiot. In the letter dated 28 September 1777—the same year that the text on Chinese hothouses was sent to Bertin—Amiot remarks upon what is clearly the *Essai sur l'architecture chinoise*:

> I had no part in all the wonderful things that were said to Your Excellency on Chinese architecture, on the tools of the mason and carpenter, and on these admirable regulations which have been able to preserve for more than 4,000 years the hierarchy of different stations by the form and extent of buildings which serve to house each member of society. It seems that these regulations are hardly observed nowadays in Peking. I have been in the Palace and in private houses. I have seen the accommodations of people of all stations, and I admit, to my confusion, that I have never recognized this marvelous order which would have it so that an ordinary citizen could not live in a house decorated with columns, that a scholar could only have two columns in his gallery, that a mandarin of the third class has four columns and so on to the leading figures of the state.[102]

Amiot goes on to affirm that perhaps these regulations are more strictly observed in the provinces, but not in the capital, Beijing, where the Tartars—a term that generally refers to the Manchus but can also include Mongols and other non-Han Chinese—have taken up residence.

The direct connection between social status and its expression in architecture was a concern for European elites and for writers of eighteenth-century France. The noted architect Jacques-François Blondel, author of the "Lecture on the necessity of studying architecture" discussed previously, wrote the entries for "Architect" and "Architecture" in the first volume of the *Encyclopédie* of Diderot and D'Alembert, which appeared in 1751.[103] In the subsequent volumes of the "Plates" illustrating the *Encyclopédie*, which began to appear in 1762, Blondel is presumably the author of the section on "Architecture."[104] Part Five consists of "General Observations on Royal Houses & Palaces, applied in particular to a grand Residence."[105] While the discussion notes at the outset that royal palaces and other royal residences are buildings of the utmost importance whose noble character demands a magnificent and imposing style, the plates illustrating the discussion are actually restricted to the imposing urban dwelling of someone of the next lower rank. The text, however, describes in some detail the links between social rank and architectural styles.

> Hôtels [particuliers], the residences of great lords, are buildings constructed in capitals, & where they normally make their home. The character of their decoration demands a beauty that matches the birth & the rank of the persons who have them built; nevertheless, they must never proclaim that magnificence reserved only for the palaces of kings. It is this diversity of rank, from the monarch to the great princes, & from these to their subjects, which must necessarily give birth to the different qualities of constructions; indispensable knowledge that cannot be acquired except by the study of art, & particularly by the ways of the world; it is by this last, let us never doubt, that we arrive at propriety, that we observe decorum, that judgment is acquired, that order is born in ideas, that taste is refined, & that one learns to understand in a positive way the proper character one must give to each building. Certainly, the rank of the person who orders the construction is the source from which must be drawn the different types of expression of which we speak: otherwise, how could we reach this point without knowing the ways of the world, which teach us to distinguish all the needs & the style proper to such and such a dwelling erected for such and such an owner? [. . . Should those] persons who do not hold the same rank in society have residences of which the arrangement announces the superiority or inferiority of the different orders of status?[106]

Blondel defines the styles appropriate to a royal residence and to other kinds of buildings, insisting on the various levels of grandeur and style that must distinguish them. In the passage here, he argues that such distinctions should grow out of a shared expression of what is appropriate to various levels of society. What would have struck Europeans of the period, and what the Jesuit missionaries remark on several times, is that in China the customs of display are ostensibly codified in a complex set of official rules and regulations. In France, this is something that should grow out of a subtle and profound understanding of the prevailing social order.

The emphasis in the *Essai sur l'architecture chinoise* on imperial buildings and imperial gardens reflects, first, the French Jesuit missionaries' position within the Qing imperial court, where they served in many important and influential capacities. The long-term strategy of their mission was to convert the emperor of China to Christianity and thus to convert the entire nation. Their knowledge of and familiarity with imperial construction makes this prejudice understandable. Until the mid- to late eighteenth century, information and images of actual imperial construction—specifically the Forbidden City, the imperial palace at the heart of the capital, Beijing—was remarkably limited. Earlier travelers' accounts described this vast palace, but images tended to show schematic representations based on memory, second-hand accounts, and other observations that were effectively restricted by imperial protocol and court etiquette that limited Europeans from all but a small number of sites. Images of the garden-palace, the Yuanming yuan, had a certain circulation in late eighteenth-century Europe, which included both Qing imperial woodblock prints and painted copies of imperial paintings of the "40 Views of the Yuanming yuan."[107] Other Chinese sources of architectural images include so-called export paintings showing ports, views of riverside towns, broader landscapes, and so forth, and these had a wider popular circulation than the authentic imperial images that are documented in Europe, thus forming more of the general idea of what was Chinese architecture. But Bertin himself derided the quality of such paintings. In the preface to the first volume of the *Mémoires concernant les Chinois*, published in 1776, Bertin briefly discusses Chinese paintings, writing that what Europeans see are mostly the worst kinds of painting, those produced in the southern port city of Canton. He states, however, that he has superior works in his collection that come from Beijing, which might refer in part to the *Essai sur l'architecture chinoise*:

> We have before our eyes paintings in gouache from Peking: Some of them represent the magnificent interior of the palace of the Emperor and the houses of the Mandarins, cabinets of natural curiosities, etc.; others [show] charming landscapes, details of the countryside with figures of which the drawing is of an astonishing accuracy; perspective is well-observed in them, and the colors are of a brightness which we have not been able to attain up to the present.[108]

The highly detailed paintings contained in the *Essai sur l'architecture chinoise* along with the paintings in the album of *Serres chaudes des Chinois* and the *Plafonds Chinois* are unique in their rendering of buildings of all kinds and even princely interiors, but questions remain as to how widely Bertin's paintings were circulated and who actually viewed them.

The Jesuit missionary authors of the two albums of the *Essai sur l'architecture chinoise* pose the questions of what Europe might learn about Chinese architecture and what further information they might provide. In the Avertissement to the first part of the *Essai*, the authors state in response:

> Chinese architecture, does it deserve to be known in Europe? The knowledge that we could give about it, would it be of any use? What we thought was best to respond to these questions was to send a collection of various paintings which we could supplement with answers that we have not given here. Time has not permitted us to expound as much as we would have wished on the different parts of the little collection we have sent, and we limited ourselves to a simple listing. In the case where you might desire further clarifications, it would be necessary to attach a quick sketch of the piece on which you have questions because we have not been able to keep a copy of what we have sent. Since you have seemed to be well pleased to know a little of the arts and trades of China, we have begun this collection with the instruments and tools of Carpenters and Masons, who are not distinguished here from Roofers. It would be useless to enter into the details of what speaks to the eyes. We will identify only what would seem less easy to recognize.[109]

The authors specifically note Bertin's interest in many aspects of Chinese culture, including the "arts and trades" of China, and so they include images of the tools of carpenters, masons, and roofers, while noting, too, that these last are not separate trades. Interestingly, the volumes of annotated illustrations of the *Encyclopédie*, which are discussed briefly above, include tools and technology alongside the illustrations of building facades and plans. Among these are illustrations of the tools and techniques of stonecutting, masonry, tile work and roofing. While it is unlikely that there was a direct influence from the *Encyclopédie* on the *Essai sur l'architecture chinoise*, both clearly represent an eighteenth-century spirit of inquiry that seeks to be broadly inclusive. The Jesuit missionaries' main questions, however, are whether Chinese architecture deserves to be known in Europe and what would be the use of such knowledge. It is worth noting that the original text that was the source of the captions and articles in the *Essai sur l'architecture chinoise*, the text sent from China in 1773 discussed briefly above, was significantly edited when it was copied into the finished albums. After the question of whether Chinese architecture should be known in Europe, the manuscript versions adds, "A poor Missionary would fail in the face of such questions."[110] The rest of the text omitted from the formal inscription in the album concerns the difficulties of providing anything like a complete account of Chinese architecture, including the extraordinary time and expense necessary to describe everything that is strange and unknown in Europe about Chinese architecture. The answers, or at least the suggestions of what might be answers to these questions, are to be found in different texts in the *Essai* as well as other texts sent to Bertin from China.

The short article at the end of the second *Essai sur l'architecture chinoise* contains "several observations that deserve our attention,"[111] although ultimately it does not reply to the question whether Chinese architecture deserves to be known in Europe but instead concentrates on what might be characterized as the moral implications of architecture. First, it appeared to the Jesuit missionaries that the common people of China were for the most part badly housed, even in the capital Beijing, with much of the effort and expense of construction concentrated in certain grand public buildings. Those that need to be solidly constructed are assembled with care, and a remarkable number of well-built bridges, quays, towers, and other constructions have survived from earlier dynasties, but many buildings are really only brilliantly decorated constructions that will last just a short time. Why this should be so is due perhaps to two reasons: first, because of the limits on annual budgets and, second, that the maintenance of such buildings uses up quantities of material as well as the efforts of their builders. Funds and materials, too, are often requisitioned by the central government, leaving less for other constructions. Further answers to why this is so should be left to "wise men" to fathom, but the more the missionaries study the Chinese government, the more they realize that little is left to chance. One final paragraph remarks on the magnificence of religious architecture, of temples and pagodas—the products of the idolatry already condemned by the Jesuits in the first volume of the *Essai*. But among these, nothing can compare to the grandeur of the Temple of Heaven, the Tiantan 天壇, the great walled complex of imperial altars and ancestral halls just south of the walls of Beijing, which is built in a style that even the emperor himself is supposedly not permitted to imitate in other constructions. This brief text at the end of the *Essai sur l'architecture chinoise* focuses on a couple of very specific questions, moral issues that might indeed have concerned the Jesuit missionaries, but goes no farther in providing broader answers to the questions of whether Chinese architecture is worth knowing.

In his extended correspondence with the French Jesuit missionaries in Beijing and in the texts and images that he received from them, Henri Bertin pursued, first, a broadly based transfer of knowledge from China to France. Certainly the paintings in the album of the *Serres chaudes des Chinois et fleurs qu'ils y conservent* alongside the article on Chinese hothouses published in the *Mémoires concernant les Chinois* provided exactly the kind of illustrations and detailed technical information Bertin hoped he would receive from China. The paintings of trompe-l'oeil ceilings in the album of *Plafonds Chinois* document a particular type of European visual practice sent to China, where it was transformed and then sent back to Europe, documenting a remarkable, complex, and curious episode in eighteenth-century intercultural encounters. Bertin sought authentic and accurate knowledge of China, and this enthusiasm for China was linked both to his role as a minister of state and to his personal taste for all things related to China. The detailed plans that he conceived for a "Chinese pavilion" or a "Chinese house" at Chatou, the subject of the following chapter, testify to his enduring passion for China and specifically his keen interest in Chinese architecture. Like the savants and artists with whom he was in contact, Bertin sought knowledge from the objects, texts, and images that he possessed. In the realm of architecture, much of this knowledge was unknown to European audiences, and the French Jesuit missionaries in Beijing clearly realized this. Texts sent to Bertin, both unpublished documents and extended comments included in the *Mémoires concernant les Chinois*, highlighted the differences between Chinese and European architectural traditions.

Published remarks on Chinese architecture are scattered throughout the *Mémoires*,[112] and they touch on such subjects as the antiquity of Chinese architecture, the magnificence of imperial palaces, bricks and tiles, multistoried buildings, constructions on *tai* or platforms—many of the subjects illustrated and discussed in the two albums of the *Essai sur l'architecture chinoise*. The Jesuit missionaries who wrote on architecture highlighted especially such issues as the sumptuary laws that ostensibly governed most aspects of Chinese construction, something that was unprecedented in Europe. Pictures were key to an accurate and detailed understanding of Chinese architecture, and even those buildings in the two albums of the *Essai sur l'architecture chinoise* that seem most fantastic still contained important elements of genuine Chinese architectural practice. Whether or not Henri Bertin ever completed his own, authentic Chinese buildings at Chatou, still he remained true to his ultimate goal of acquiring accurate knowledge of the far-off Chinese empire.

Notes

1. *Serres chaudes des Chinois et fleurs qu'ils y conservent*, ca. 1777, BnF, Département des Estampes et de la photographie, Réserve OE-30-FOL.
2. "*6 planches de serres chinoises. Reçu en 1777.*" Exactly who wrote this is not clear, and there are only five paintings in the album.
3. See *Mémoires concernant les Chinois*, vol. 3 (1778), "Serres Chinoises," below; see esp. 427, where the description of the construction of a Chinese greenhouse describes roofs built with more than the usual care to keep out the winter cold. What we see are likely the additional layers needed for that purpose.
4. A modern glass greenhouse is sometimes called a *boli huajiao* 玻璃花窖 or, more commonly, a *boli wenshi* 玻璃温室.
5. *Mémoires concernant les Chinois*, vol. 3 (1778), "Serres Chinoises," 423–437.

6. See Bib. Inst. Ms 1524, fols. 164–165, for a list of 14 articles (*mémoires et notices*) authored by Cibot sent from Beijing on 18 November 1777, including one "sur les serres chinoises."
7. *Mémoires concernant les Chinois*, vol. 3 (1778), "Serres Chinoises," 423: "Notre France, reconnoîtra-t-elle cette sagesse des Chinois, & dans la manière dont sont construites les serres d'aujourd'hui, & dans ce qu'elle a imaginé pour y suppléer dans les jardins potagers des environs des villes & des campagnes? . . . Nous ne parlons que d'après nos yeux, & nous ne faisons qu'écrire ce que nous avons vu."
8. Ibid., 427–428. For additional details on the heating system and the construction of the roof, the text refers the reader to the article (*mémoire*) on public granaries in another volume of the *Mémoires*, but I have not been able to locate a published text or a manuscript on this subject. The subject of *greniers publics*, however, is mentioned in a few other contexts.
9. An abbreviated version of Cibot's article appeared in the later edition of *De la Chine, ou description générale de cet empire. . .*, 7 vols. (Paris: Pillet Ainé, 1818–1820). The article on greenhouses appears in vol. 3, book VII, chap. XXII, 374–383, and the various editions of this series were widely circulated.
10. See Émile Littré (1801–1881), *Dictionnaire de la langue française*, 4 vols. (Paris: L. Hachette, 1863–1872); vol. 4, p. 1915: "Serre chinoise, serre enfoncée dans la terre." See also the online edition, Dictionnaire de français "Littré," http://littre.reverso.net/dictionnaire-francais/definition/serre, accessed 5 May 2013.
11. The text, copied in a fine, calligraphic hand with very few corrections, is in BnF Fonds Bréquigny 123, fols. 189–194: "Décorations chinoises &c." One note at the top of the first page asks: "où sont les figures?" and a note in another hand reads: "voyez les arcs de triomphes." For the "arcs de triomphes [*sic*]," see immediately below.
12. Ibid., fol. 191 verso: "Ce qui nous y a déterminé surtout c'est que ces peintures parlent aux yeux. . . ."
13. On the constructions lining the imperial parade routes, see Ellen Uitzinger, "For the Man Who Has Everything: Western-Style Exotica in Birthday Celebrations at the Court of Ch'ien-lung," in Leonard Blussé and Harriet T. Zurndorfer, eds., *Conflict and Accommodation in Early Modern East Asia: Essays in Honour of Erik Zurcher*, Sinica Leidensia XXIX (Leiden, New York and Köln: E.J. Brill, 1993), 206–239. For a reproduction of one handscroll, see J.R. ter Molen, and others, *De Verboden Stad / The Forbidden City* (Rotterdam: Museum Boymans—van Beuningen, 1990), cat. 9, "Festivities to Celebrate the Birthday of the Dowager Empress Chongqing" (part 4), which clearly shows the temporary constructions in 1751.
14. The ages given for the Qianlong emperor and his mother, the Dowager Empress Chongqing (崇慶皇太后, 1693–1777), follow the Chinese practice where age is given as 1 *sui* 歲 at birth. The text also mentions a description of the Dowager Empress's own sixtieth birthday celebrations in 1751 with its parade route and extraordinary, temporary constructions; see the letter by Father Amiot, dated 20 October 1752, in the *Lettres édifiantes et curieuses*, vol. 23 (1781), 154–181, esp. 164ff.
15. The full title is *Recueil. Arcs de triomphe et berceaux chinois*, BnF, Département des Estampes et de la photographie, Réserve OE-24-FT 4. See Henri Cordier (1849–1925), *Catalogue des albums chinois et ouvrages relatifs à la Chine conservés au Cabinet des estampes de la Bibliothèque nationale*; extrait du *Journal asiatique*, Septembre–Octobre 1909 (Paris: Impr. nationale, 1909), 209–262, see esp. p. 12, noting the large scale of the album, the blue paper cover, and listing the 11 French captions that accompany the Chinese inscriptions on the paintings. See also Anne Gall, *Inventaire avec indication de provenance des collections d'albums, d'estampes et de peintures chinoises du Département des Estampes* (Paris: Bibliothèque nationale de France, 1990; available only as a photocopy in the BnF), which lists the album as part of Bertin's library seized in Year 2 of the French Republic (1793–1794).
16. All eleven paintings are numbered, with titles in French and, on some, titles in Chinese.
17. "Arc de Triomphe double en soyeries & Lanternes."
18. The inscription here, however, contains a curious mistake or perhaps uses variant characters. As written it reads 五穀豊燈 (*wugu lideng* [*sic*]), which should be 五穀豐登 (*wugu fengdeng*, An abundant harvest of all grains). See *Mathews' Chinese-English*

Dictionary, Revised American Edition (Cambridge, MA: Harvard University Press, 1943), no. 7187.59.

19. A portion of the discussion here appears in my essay "Constructing an Authentic China: Henri Bertin and Chinese Architecture in 18th-Century France," in Stephen Whiteman, ed., *Rhetorics of Landscape: Articulating Authority in the Early Modern World* (Forthcoming, 2020).
20. *Recueil. Essai sur l'architecture chinoise*, BnF, Département des Estampes et de la photographie, Réserve OE-13-PET FOL and Réserve OE-13 (A)-PET FOL. The title page of the first album reads *Premiére* [*sic*] *Partie de l'Essai sur l'Architecture Chinoise*. The second reads *Seconde Partie*. . . . The illustrations have been published in Li Weiwen, *Lun Zhongguo jianzhu: 18 shiji Faguo chuanjiaoshi bixia de Zhongguo jianzhu*, preface by Antoine Gournay (Beijing: Publishing House of Electronics Industry, 2016); the volume includes translations of the French texts and additional research by the author.
21. The manuscript is BnF Fonds Bréquigny, vol. 126, which is described on fol. 2 as "Manuscrits concernant la Chine non employés dans les *Mémoires chinois*. Architecture, Jardins, Vases, Ornemens." The text in question appears on fols. 4–17, with the title "Notices Relatives à l'Architecture Chinoise"; the date "a pe-king ce 3. oct. 1773" appears on fol. 17. This would then be the approximate date when Bertin received the paintings and text of the *Essai sur l'architecture chinoise*, approximately two or three years after the "Décorations Chinoises."
22. The article, on two unnumbered folios, begins with the sentence "On finira par quelques observations qui méritent attention." See the following discussion of this text.
23. *Essai sur l'architecture chinoise*, part I, facing p. 15: "Instruments & outils de maçon. Le No. 1. est une espèce de sac de grosse toile qui se remplit de mortier & qu'on porte sur les épaules. Le No. 2. est une plaque de plomb pour battre les fondements, douze hommes l'enlèvent à la fois & la laissent tomber à plat. No. 3. Demoiselle à quatre pour battre les pavés & fondements." The French texts here are transcribed with the spelling and punctuation as they appear in the *Essai sur l'architecture chinoise*.
24. For the historical sense of *demoiselle*, see the online Dictionnaire de français "Littré," *demoiselle*, http://littre.reverso.net/dictionnaire-francais/definition/demoiselle, accessed 25 May 2013.
25. *Essai sur l'architecture chinoise*, part I, facing p. 26: "Muraille de terre meslée de chaux, & batie entre deux planches. Celles qu'on fait aujourd'hui déboulent quelque fois dès la premiére année. On en voit dans d'anciennes sépultures qui ont plus d'un siécle. [Later addition in pencil:] Ce genre de Murailles sont utilisées dans les Potagers."
26. Ibid., part I, facing p. 33: "Murs de séparation dans l'intérieur du Palais et des maisons de l'Empereur. Le No. 1. sur la partie qui n'est pas encore crépie a été mis pour faire observer la manière dont on laisse pendre le chanvre qu'on met sous les briques en bâtissant la muraille. Le crépissage s'attache à des chevelures & ne se détache pas si aisément."
27. Ibid., part I, facing p. 43: "Tchao Pei de Mandarin." Interestingly, the man seems to be wearing court robes in Ming-dynasty style, not Qing.
28. Ibid., part I, facing pp. 42–43: "Ce n'est surement point pour éclairer nos Architectes sur la grand Architecture des anciens, ni sur la manière dont on pourroit perfectionner la nouvelle que l'on a fait peindre ces Tchao Ping, Tchao Pi & Tchao Hiang des dix peintures suivant ainsi que celle cy; mais pour faire entrevoir comment le Gouvernement Chinois s'y prend, pour montrer aux yeux la différence des rangs, & contenir chacun dans la Sphère de son état."
29. See the Dictionnaire de français "Littré" online, *cabinet*, no. 7: Petit lieu couvert dans un jardin, http://littre.reverso.net/dictionnaire-francais/definition/cabinet, accessed 25 February 2014.
30. The title of the section appears in *Essai sur l'architecture chinoise*, part I, facing p. 54: "Plans et développements des Cabinets Chinois. / On n'en auroit peut-être pas tant fait peindre si l'on n'avoit songé que l'on seroit bien ais[é] d'avoir à travailler en ce genre sur les desseins des Chinois, ou a les perfectionner."
31. Ibid.: "On n'a rien a dire sur la manière de bâtir ces Cabinets: le Peintre l'a racontée mieux que l'on n'auroit sçu le faire, ainsi que tout ce qu'on sera bien aise d'en sçavoir."
32. Ibid.: "L'on n'a que trois observations à faire; la premiére, que le peintre n'a rien ni exagéré ni orné. L'on a vu en réalité dans les Jardins de l'Empereur plusieurs des Cabinets

qu'on trouve ici; ils sont réellement comme cela. La seconde est que la nécessité de bâtir en bois, le bon marché du Vernis & des couleurs, & le gout des Chinois pour ce qui est voyant & brille de loin, à conduit a orner & peindre ces Cabinets comme la Peinture les représente. La derniére observation c'est que l'Empereur seul peut avoir des Tuiles colorées, ou de *Lieou Li*." The imperial character of colored tiles is discussed briefly in the following.

33. *Essai sur l'architecture chinoise*, part I, facing p. 94: "Cabinet sur un amas de Rochers. / Les Chinois sont admirables pour imiter les amas de Rochers sauvages qu'on trouve dans la solitude des Montagnes. Ils les transportent dans leurs Jardins, pour y réunir le spectacle entier de la Nature. . . . Quand on est parvenu au haut, on y trouve des Cabinets, d'où l'on voit des parterres, des bosquets & des Canaux qui serpentent en mille maniéres dans la plaine. / Les Chinois nomment un Païsage *Chang Choui, Montagnes & Eaux*, & un Jardin selon eux, n'est Jardin qu'autant qu'il est semé de Collines & Monticules entrecoupés de Canaux & Bassins."
34. Ibid., part I, facing p. 111: "Si l'on donne un jour l'Architecture Chinoise en Grand, les Ponts, les Digues, les Levées, les Chaussées, & les Écluses y feront un grand article. L'on a préféré ce qui étoit le plus facile & on s'est attaché aux Ponts de Parade des Jardins de plaisance; mais qui les regardera avec soin verra bien que les connoissances qui ont dirigé la construction singuliére de ces Ponts de pure décoration, peuvent en bâtir sur les Fleuves & les Riviéres de trés solides & de trés commodes."
35. Ibid., part I, facing p. 125: "Les Architectes de l'Europe n'y verront rien qui méritte [*sic*] attention. . . ." For a broad selection of photographs of historical pagodas, recording their many variant forms, see Liang Ssu-ch'eng, *A Pictorial History of Chinese Architecture: A Study of the Development of Its Structural System and the Evolution of its Types*, Wilma Fairbank, ed. (Cambridge, MA and London: MIT Press, 1984); reprint (Dover Publications, 2005), "Buddhist Pagodas," 123–165.
36. See Susan Naquin, *Peking: Temples and City Life, 1400–1900* (Berkeley: University of California Press, 2000), esp. 309.
37. *Essai sur l'architecture chinoise*, part I, p. 131; the text on the facing page gives the title "*Ta* dédié aux Esprits" and cites the great height (300–400 *pieds*) and the bells.
38. Joan Nieuhof, *Het gezantschap der Neêrlandtsche Oost-Indische Compagnie, aan den grooten Tartarischen Cham* . . . (Amstedam: Jacob van Meurs, 1665). For bibliographic information on the various editions, see Bibliotheca Sinica 2.0, www.univie.ac.at/Geschichte/China-Bibliographie/blog/2010/04/22/neuhof/, accessed 23 March 2018. Nieuhof's name has various spellings; the first English edition of 1669 gives his name as John Nieuhoff. The dates of the mission appear on the title page.
39. The discussion here is based on the French edition, Jean Nieuhoff, *L'Ambassade de la Compagnie orientale des Provinces unies vers l'empereur de la Chine. . .*, Jean Le Carpentier, trans. (Leiden: Pour Jacob de Meurs, Amsterdam, 1665). The illustrations are the same plates in the first Dutch edition; the overall view of the site appears on p. 136, and fold-out view of the Porcelain Pagoda is bound between pp. 138 and 139. In the Dutch edition, the overall view appears on p. 108 with the fold-out view between pp. 124 and 125.
40. The history of the temple is complex; see *The Cambridge History of China*, vol. 8, Ming dynasty, part 2, Chapter 14, "Ming Buddhism," Pao-en 報恩 temple, 905, 908, 937 passim.
41. Tiles, roof finials, and carved and/or molded blocks produced for the pagoda appear in two recent exhibition catalogues: Li He and Michael Knight, *Power and Glory: Court Arts of China's Ming Dynasty* (San Francisco: Asian Art Museum, 2008); and Craig Clunas and Jessica Harrison-Hall, *Ming: 50 Years That Changed China* (London: British Museum Press, 2014). Clarence Eng, *Colours and Contrast: Ceramic Traditions in Chinese Architecture* (Leiden: Brill, 2014) discusses many of the unique features of the colored tile elements of the pagoda; see Chapter 8, "Conflicting Requirements, Problems and Solutions," esp. 238–251, for the discussion of the Dabao'ensita 大報恩寺塔, the pagoda of the Bao'ensi.
42. The handwritten journal is entitled *Journaal van zommige voorvallen, inde voyagie vande E. Heeren Pieter de Goyer en Jacob Keyser, ambassadeurs, aande grootmachtige keizer van Chyna en Tartaryen, inde jaaren 1655, 56 & 1657*, including 229 pp. and

81 drawings, dated 1659, Société de Géographie, kept in the Bibliothèque nationale de France, call no. SG MS8–17 (1271). The ambassadors Pieter de Goyer and Jacob Keyser are credited with parts of the text. The ink and wash drawing of the Porcelain Pagoda is on a folio numbered 95 in pencil; the account of the visit to the site on the adjacent pages is dated May 1656.

43. *L'Ambassade de la Compagnie orientale. . .*, Préface, n.p. The title page to the first Dutch edition includes the information that the book contains over 150 illustrations sketched from life in China.
44. *Essai sur l'architecture chinoise*, part II, Avertissement, 2 unnumbered pages.
45. Ibid.: "[L]a politique Chinoise tient bon à cela au point d'avoir fait Imprimer un Livre où toutes les dimentions & dépenses sont articulées avec la derniére précision." See the following brief discussion of the 1734 imperial compilation, the *Gongbu gongcheng zuofa*.
46. Ibid., part II, p. 10 (the exterior) and p. 11 (the platform). The illustration of the hall is labeled on the facing page "Grande Salle extérieure du Palais de l'Empereur. Les toits de celles de l'intérieur sont jaunes." "Large outer hall of the Emperor's palace. The roofs of those on the interior are yellow." This probably refers to the Outer Court, the ceremonial halls, and the Inner Court, the imperial residences, of the Forbidden City, but the depiction of a green roof on p. 10 is not technically accurate.
47. Ibid., part II, facing p. 24.
48. Ibid., part II, p. 25. The painting, along with others from the *Essai sur l'architecture chinoise*, is reproduced as a drawing in Maurice Paléologue, *L'Art Chinois* (Paris: Alcide Picard & Kaan, 1887), in a long chapter on Chinese architecture, 82–130; each is credited simply as "D'après une peinture chinoise."
49. *Mémoires*, vol. 13 (1788), 396–397, "Notice sur le *Lieu-Li*, ou tuiles chinoises vernisées."
50. Published in 1788, the text was one of at least 14 articles set from Beijing on 18 November 1777; see Bib. Inst. Ms 1524, fols. 164–165; and see n. 6 above.
51. *Essai sur l'architecture chinoise*, part II, facing p. 27; the text is entitled "Bâtiment à trois étages dans les Jardins de l'Empereur."
52. Ibid.: "N[ot]a. *On avoit eû quelque envie de hazarder des idées & conjectures sur les différentes parties de l'architecture chinoise, ses dimensions, ses proportions, & les différents Plans qu'elle fait dans la distribution des Cours, des Bâtiments, des Galleries, des Toits, des Colonnes &c. mais tout bien considéré, il vaut mieux attendre des questions, d'autant plus qu'elles mettront à même de parler aux yeux par des Peintures plus méthodiques, & d'entamer des détails où il seroit trop difficile d'entrer icy*" (italics in the original text).
53. The text faces the first image of the series, p. 28, with the title "Salle bourgeoise des Tartares avec une estrade échauffée par un Fourneau" (Ordinary city room of a Tartar [Manchu] with a platform heated by a furnace). See the aforementioned discussion of heating in greenhouses.
54. See the brief discussion of these paintings in Gustave Ecke, "A Group of Eighteenth-Century Paintings of Beijing Interiors," *Journal of the Chinese Classical Furniture Society* 4, no. 3 (Summer 1994), 60–70. Ecke's article was originally published as "Sechs Schaubilder Pekinger Innenräume des achtzehnten Jahrhunderts," *Bulletin of the Catholic University of Peking*, no. 9 (November 1934), 155–169. My thanks to Nicholas Grindley for bringing the article to my attention.
55. China export watercolors gave some sense of the interiors of shops or residences. For an illustration similar to the interiors in part II of the *Essai*, see Chambers, *Designs of Chinese Buildings*, pl. IX, which shows a "section . . . thrown into perspective," that is, view of the interior of a two-story Chinese residence; see both the English and French editions of 1757, pls. VIII and IX, and pp. 8, 10–11.
56. *Essai sur l'architecture chinoise,* part II, facing pp. 36, 37, 38: "Salle de Cérémonie & d'Audience chez les Princes Titrés."
57. The longest inscription is a four-line poem at the top center of the partition between the outer spaces. I have not been able to identify the poem, but the calligraphy ends with a date: "in the *yihai* year [1755] written on a summer's day" (乙亥夏日書).
58. *Essai sur l'architecture chinoise*, part I, facing p. 18: "No. 2. terre rouge qu'on mêle à la chaux pour crêpir les murailles du Palais des *Miao* &c." (No. 2. red earth one mixes with lime to stucco the walls of Palaces and *Miao* [*miao* 廟, temple or shrine], etc.)

59. Ibid., part II, the introductory text on *Tai* facing pp. 39–40: "De surprise parceque tout ce qu'on a voulu apprendre jusqu'icy sur la Chine, ne mene pas à imaginer quelle puisse avoir chez elle rien de pareil; de curiosité, parceque la hauteur, la beauté, & la vaine magnificence de plusieurs de ces *Tai* ne se concilie pas avec les tant vantées Economies de sa politique, & que le motif de cette éxception a de quoi surprendre." The labels identifying the various *Tai* all refer back to the notes on p. 39.
60. "Plan de la Maison d'un Colonel dans les Cazernes Impériales des Baniéres Tartares." The folios in this final section of the second part of the *Essai sur l'architecture chinoise* are not numbered.
61. Maurice Courant, *Catalogue des livres chinois, coréens, japonais*, 3 vols. (Paris: Ernest Leroux, 1902, 1910, 1912), vol. 2, lists four albums that are linked as one group—the two albums of *Essai sur l'architecture chinoise* (nos. 5543–5544), the album *Plans relatifs a l'essai sur l'architecture chinoise* (no. 5545), and *Plafonds Chinois* (no. 5546), which is discussed later. The album of *Plafonds Chinois* includes a page that notes it is a "Recueil Relatif à l'Architecture Chinoise."
62. *Recueil. Plans relatifs à l'essai sur l'architecture chinoise*, BnF, Département des Estampes et de la photographie, Réserve OE-15-FT 4. The plans are entitled: "1. Plan du Palais du Seixieme [*sic*] Fils de l'Empereur *Kang-Hi*; 2. Plan de l'Hôtel d'un *Ta-Gin* ou Grand de l'Empire; and 3. Plan du Palais d'un Premier Ministre." The album also contains two paintings of stone basins with miniature trees, rocks, and flowers in garden settings.
63. Yunlu was in charge of the compilation of the Qing imperial catalogue of court and ritual paraphernalia, the *Huangchao liqi tushi* 皇朝禮器圖式, in 16 volumes, completed in 1759; the copy in the BnF, Manuscrits Chinois 2289–2304, was seized from Bertin's collection in 1796. See *1789, le patrimoine libéré: 200 trésors entrés à la Bibliothèque nationale de 1789 à 1799*, exhibition catalogue, edited by Marie-Pierre Laffitte (Paris: Bibliothèque nationale, 1989), cat. 190; see also Marie-Laure de Rochebrune, *La Chine à Versailles*, cat. 62, entry by Nathalie Monnet. I have not been able to identify the location of this palace or the other residences in the three plans.
64. "Palais du fils du premier Ministre ou plustôt de la *Kong Tchou* son Epouse fille de l'Empereur."
65. For the title *Gongzhu*, see Hucker, *Official Titles*, 3408, *kung-zhu*, Princess or Imperial Princess.
66. See Arthur W. Hummel, ed., *Eminent Chinese of the Ch'ing Period (1644–1912)*, 2 vols. (Washington, DC: U.S. Government Printing Office, 1943), vol. 1, 372–373 for the imperial princesses, daughters of the Qianlong emperor; 259–260 for Fulong'an; and 252–253 for Fuheng.
67. "N[ot]a. Quand à la distribution des bâtiments, il suffit de dire que tout ce qui est sur le devant sont des Offices & logements des Domestiques & des Officiers, le milieu est pour la Famille, & ce qui est sur les Jardins ne sert qu'à la magnificence."
68. See Werner Szambien, *Symétrie, goût, caractère: Théorie et terminologie de l'architecture à l'âge classique 1550–1800* (Paris: Picard, 1986); esp. the Preface and Avant-propos, 11–14.
69. Jacques-François Blondel (1705–1774), *Discours sur la nécessité de l'étude de l'architecture: Prononcé à l'ouverture du cinquième cours public . . .* (Paris: C.-A. Jombert, 1754); see esp. 83–89.
70. Ibid., 88: "Oeuvres d'Estampes utiles aux Architectes & autres Artistes, qui font leur profession des ouvrages de goût"; the citation is part of Blondel's brief note on the prints to be consulted.
71. The *De Architectura* of Marcus Vitruvius Pollio (ca. 70 BCE–after 15 CE) has been translated numerous times into many languages. See Claude Perrault's first edition, *Les dix Livres d'architecture de Vitruve, corrigez et nouvellement traduits en françois, avec des notes et des figures* (Paris: J.-B. Coignard, 1673); see also the second, expanded edition, *Les dix Livres d'architecture de Vitruve, . . .*, Seconde édition, reveuë, corrigée, et augmentée, par M. Perrault de l'Académie Royale des Sciences, . . . (Paris: J.-B. Coignard, 1684). This edition is available online, www.e-rara.ch/doi/10.3931/e-rara-19628, accessed 13 November 2015.
72. For Claude Perrault (1613–1688), see Alexandre Cojannot and Alexandre Gady, *Dessiner pour bâtir: le métier d'architecte au XVIIe siècle* (Paris: Archives Nationales; Paris:

Le Passage, 2017); cats. 3, 93–95; see esp. 209–210 for the citation from Claude Perrault's brother, Charles Perrault, attributing to Claude Perrault the drawings reproduced as engravings in the translation of Vitruvius.

73. See *Vitruvius: The Ten Books on Architecture*, Morris Hicky Morgan, trans. (Cambridge, Mass.: Harvard University Press, 1914; reprint, New York: Dover Books 1960). For the suitability of rooms, see Book VI, chap. V, "How the Rooms Should be Suited to the Station of the Owner."
74. On the contents of the Jesuit libraries in Beijing, see Hubert Germain Verhaeren; Mission catholique des Lazaristes à Pékin, *Catalogue de la Bibliothèque du Pé-T'ang* (Beijing, 1949). See also the Appendix to Hui Zou, "The *jing* of a perspective garden," *Studies in the History of Gardens and Designed Landscapes* 22, no. 4 (Oct.–Dec. 2002), 293–326; esp. 317–318. See also Noël Golvers, *Libraries of Western Learning for China: Circulation of Western Books between Europe and China in the Jesuit Mission (ca. 1650–ca. 1750)*, Part 3, Chap. 5, "Civil Architecture"; see esp. 198–203.
75. See *Les dix Livres d'architecture de Vitruve,* Book II, 43, for an illustration of walls; and see Book III, esp. 60–73 for plans and elevations of famous temples.
76. Cary Y. Liu, "Architects and Builders of the Qing Dynasty Yuanming Yuan Imperial Garden-Palace," *The University of Hong Kong Museum Journal* 1 (September 2002), in English and Chinese, pp. 38–59, 151–161; see esp. pp. 38–39.
77. See Klaas Ruitenbeek, *Carpentry and Building in Late Imperial China: A Study of the Fifteenth-century Carpenter's Manual* Lu Ban jing (Leiden; New York; and Cologne: E.J. Brill, 1993); see esp. 24–32 for "Technical Works" among "Chinese Sources on Building."
78. For the *Yingzao fashi*, see Liang Ssu-ch'eng, *A Pictorial History of Chinese Architecture*, 14–18.
79. See Hucker, *Official Titles*, 708, *chiang-tso chien*.
80. Ruitenbeek, *Carpentry and Building*, focuses on this text.
81. See the brief description of the *Gongbu gongcheng zuofa* in Liang, *A Pictorial History of Chinese Architecture*, 18–21. Liang cites the title as the *Kung-ch'eng tso-fa tse-li* (*Structural Regulations*). For *Gongbu*, see Hucker, *Official Titles*, 3462, *kung-pu*.
82. See n. 45 above.
83. Liu, "Architects and Builders," 48, n. 7.
84. The BnF catalogue information lists the album as *Recueil. Plafonds Chinois*, Département des Estampes et de la photographie, Réserve OE-25-FT 5. The size is some 63 × 96 cm. See Courant, *Catalogue des livres chinois*, vol. 2, no. 5546; and for additional information, see Cordier, *Catalogue des albums chinois*, 221. Cordier lists the individual paintings and quotes part of the text as it appears in the album.
85. For a detailed study of Qing imperial trompe-l'oeil murals, see Kleutghen, *Imperial Illusions: Crossing Pictorial Boundaries in the Qing Palaces*.
86. On perspectival illusions in Qing imperial constructions, see John Finlay, "The Qianlong Emperor's Western Vistas: Linear Perspective and Trompe l'Oeil Illusion in the European Palaces of the Yuanming yuan," *Bulletin de l'École française d'Extrême-Orient*, 94 (2007), 159–193.
87. *Plafonds Chinois*, n.p.: "Toutes ces raisons rapprochées, il en résulte que les plafonds peints sont rares en Chine, mais non pas qu'il n'y en ait point. Leur rareté a été pour nous une raison d'en faire copier deux, afin qu'on vit comment les Chinois viennent à bout de s'approprier les connoissances qu'on leur a portées d'Occident, & que les Artistes voyent à leur tour comment ils doivent travailler ce qu'ils déstineroient pour la Chine. Ces deux plafonds qui sont dans le Palais du premier Ministre, ont été peints pour faire un tout avec les grandes Salles où ils sont, en exhausser une d'un second étage, l'autre de deux. L'illusion de la perspective est d'autant mieux ménagée que tout se correspond, tout est lié, tout se suit & se ressemble dans les couleurs." The text in the album is selected from a much longer version in the BnF Fonds Bréquigny 123, fols. 221–223. See also BnF Fonds Bréquigny 126, fols. 19–22, for what is essentially the same text, which here follows immediately a manuscript version of the text in the first album of the *Essai sur l'architecture chinoise*.
88. On the basic history of the European Palaces, see Pirazzoli, *Le Yuanmingyuan: jeux d'eau et palais européens*. See also Finlay, "The Qianlong Emperor's Western Vistas," esp. 160–162.

89. This was the Yuanyingguan 遠瀛觀, the View of Distant Seas, which was constructed to house a set of Beauvais tapestries sent to China by Louis XV and ultimately presented to the emperor by the Jesuit missionaries. For the story of the tapestries, see Finlay, "Henri Bertin and Louis XV's Gifts to the Qianlong Emperor."
90. See, among others, Kleutghen, *Imperial Illusions*.
91. Trompe-l'oeil decoration of Jesuit churches in Beijing include the dome and walls of the Nantang 南堂, the South Church, officially Nossa Senhora da Assunção, rebuilt in 1703; the ceiling of the nave of the Church of Our Savior, known in Chinese as the Beitang 北堂 or North Church, dedicated in 1703, painted by Giovanni Gherardini, see p. 31, n. 17 and a trompe-l'oeil dome painted in the Church of St. Joseph, the Dongtang 東堂 or East Church, by Castiglione himself 1728 or 1729. See Finlay, "The Qianlong Emperor's Western Vistas," 172–174.
92. On the origins of *quadratura*, see Musillo, *The Shining Inheritance*, 78–79 on *quadraturismo*, originating in the expression "*far di quadro*" used by Italian architects to describe tasks that required measuring tools, a square, and so forth.
93. The first French edition, *La Perspective propre des peintres et des architects*, appeared in 1700, and the first English-language edition, *Rules and Examples of Perspective for Painters and Architects, etc.*, was published in London around 1707; reprint, *Perspective in Architecture and Painting* (New York: Dover Books, 1989).
94. See the brief mention of Nian Xiyao in Hummel, ed., *Eminent Chinese of the Ch'ing Period (1644–1912)*, vol. I, p. 588, in the biography of his younger brother, Nian Gengyao 年羹堯. See also Elisabetta Corsi, "Envisioning Perspective: Nian Xiyao's (1671–1738) Rendering of Western Perspective in the Prologues to 'The Science of Vision'," in *A Life Journey to the East: Sinological Studies in Memory of Giuliano Certuccioli (1923–2001)* (Kyoto: Italian School of East Asian Studies, 2002).
95. See the reprint of the 1735 edition in the series *Zhongguo kexue jishu dianji tonghui: Shuxue juan* 中國科學技術典籍通彙, 數學卷四 (Zhengzhou: Henan jiaoyu chubanshe, 1993), vol. 4, 709–858.
96. For the most recent translation of the two prefaces, see Jacques Giès, "*Perspectiva* ou *Science de la vision* de Nian Xiyao (?-1739): Le paradoxe récurrent de la rencontre Chine-Occident," in Marie-Catherine Rey, *Les Très Riches Heures de la Cour de Chine: Chefs-d'oeuvre de la peinture impériale des Qing, 1662–1796* (Paris: Éditions de la Réunion des musées nationaux, 2006), pp. 13–43. Giès is mistaken in asserting that his is the first complete translation into a European language. See Elisabetta Corsi, *La fábrica de las ilusiones: los Jesuitas y la difusión de la perspectiva lineal en China (1698–1766)* (Mexico City: El Colegio de México, 2004); and see Hui Zou, "Jesuit Perspective in China," *Architectura*, vol. 31 (2001), 145–168; see esp. 157–158.
97. See Pozzo, *Perspective in Architecture and Painting*, reprint, p. 190.
98. See Chap. 1, n. 20.
99. See the discussion of Pozzo and the liturgical implications of perspective in Chap. 1.
100. See the aforementioned discussion of such plaques and inscriptions.
101. See the aforementioned discussion of the *Plans relatifs*, especially the plan of the residence of the son of a Prime Minister married to an imperial princess, but a positive identification of the official referred to here is not possible.
102. Bib. Inst. Ms 1515, letters from Amiot to Bertin, fols. 108–195; the date appears on the first page, and the text here is on fol. 172. "Je n'ay aucune part à toutes les belles choses qu'on a dites à votre grandeur sur l'architecture chinoise, sur les instruments du maçon et du charpentier, et sur cette police admirable qui a sû conserver depuis plus de 4000 ans la hiérarchie des états différents par la forme et l'étendue des bâtiments qui servent à loger chaque membre de la société. Il paroît que cette police n'est guère observée aujourd'huy à Péking. J'ay été dans des Palais et dans des maisons particulières. J'ay vû les logements des personnes de tous états, et j'avoue, à ma confusion, que je n'y ay point reconnu cet ordre merveilleux qui veut qu'un simple bourgeois ne puisse pas habiter dans une maison décorée avec des colonnes, que le lettré ne puisse avoir que deux colonnes à sa gallérie, le mandarin du troisième ordre, quatre colonnes et ainsi jusqu'aux premiers personnages de l'état."
103. *Encyclopédie, ou Dictionnaire raisonné des sciences, des arts et des métiers, par une Société de gens de lettres. Mis en ordre et publié par M. Diderot, et, quant à la partie*

mathématique, par M. d'Alembert, 35 vols. in fol. (Paris: Briasson, 1751–1780); see vol. 1, 616–618. The author is indicated by the initial (P) at the end of the entries; the Avertissement, xlvi, identifies (P) as Blondel.

104. *Recueil de planches, sur les sciences, les arts libéraux et les arts méchaniques: avec leur explication. . .* (Paris: Briasson, David, Le Breton, Durand; 1762); the contents of the volume are not numbered consecutively. Illustrations are accompanied by notices on the various sections (*parties*) and detailed entries on each of the engraved plates.
105. Observations générales sur les Maisons royales & les Palais, appliquées en particulier à un grand Hôtel.
106. *Recueil de planches*, vol. 1 (1762), "Architecture," section 5: "Les hôtels, demeures des grands seigneurs, sont des bâtimens élevés dans les capitales, & où ils font habituellement leur résidence. Le caractere de leur décoration exige une beauté assortie à la naissance & au rang des personnes qui les font bâtir; néanmoins ils ne doivent jamais annoncer cette magnificence réservée seulement pour les palais des rois. C'est de cette diversité de rang, du monarque aux grands princes, & de ceux-ci aux sujets, que doivent naître nécessairement les différens caracteres d'édifices; connoissances indispensables qui ne peuvent s'acquérir que par l'étude de l'art, & particulierement par l'usage du monde; c'est par ce dernier, n'en doutons point, qu'on arrive à la convenance, qu'on observe les bienséances, que le jugement s'acquiert, que l'ordre naît dans les idées, que le goût s'épure, & qu'on apprend à connoître positivement le caractere propre qu'il faut donner à chaque bâtiment. Certainement le rang du personnage qui fait bâtir, est la source où doivent se puiser les différens genres d'expressions dont nous voulons parler: or comment y arriver sans l'usage du monde, qui nous apprend à distinguer tous les besoins & le style convenable à telle ou telle habitation érigée pour tel ou tel propriétaire? [. . . Should those] personnages qui ne tenant pas le même rang dans la société, doivent avoir des habitations dont l'ordonnance annonce la supériorité ou l'infériorité des différens ordres de l'état ?"
107. See my essay, "Between France and China in the Late 18th Century: Henri Bertin and the Commerce in Images," in Petra Chu and Ning Ding, eds., *Qing Encounters*, 79–94; the paper was first presented at a symposium organized by Peking University and Seton Hall University in Beijing, 10–13 October 2012. See also the discussion above of Bertin's copies of the "40 Views" in Chapter 2.
108. *Mémoires concernant les Chinois*, vol. 1 (1776), *Préface*, xi-xii: "Nous avons sous les yeux des peintures à la gouache de Peking: elles représentent les unes, l'intérieur magnifique des palais de l'Empereur & des maisons des Mandarins, des cabinets de curiosités naturelles, &c. d'autres, des paysages charmants, des détails champêtres avec des figures dont le dessein est d'une correction étonnante; la perspective y est bien observée, & les couleurs sont d'une vivacité à laquelle nous n'avons pu atteindre jusqu'à présent."
109. *Essai sur l'architecture chinoise*, part I, Avertissement, n.p.: "L'Architecture Chinoise mérite t'elle d'être connüe en Europe? les connaissances qu'on pourroit en donner y seroient-elles de quelque utilité? Ce qu'on a imaginé de mieux pour répondre à ces questions a été d'envoyer un Recueil de différentes Peintures sur lesquelles on pourra suppléer à des réponses qu'on n'est pas en état de donner. Le tems n'as pas permis de s'étendre autant qu'on auroit voulu sur les différentes parties du petit Recueil qu'on envoye, & on se bornera à une simple nomenclature; dans le cas où l'on désiraît quelques Eclaircissements, il seroit nécessaire de joindre un petit croquis de la Piéce [*sic*] sur laquelle on fera des questions parcequ'on n'a pas été en état de garder une Copie de ce qu'on a envoyé. Comme on a paru bien aise de connoître un peu les Arts & metiers de la Chine, on a commencé ce Recueil par les instruments & outils du Charpentier & du Maçon qui n'est pas ici distingué du Couvreur. Il seroit inutile d'entrer dans les détails sur ce qui parle aux yeux. On ne nommera que ce qui seroit moins aisé a reconnoître."
110. BnF Fonds Bréquigny 126, fol. 4: "Un pauvre Missionnaire est en Echec vis-à-vis de ces sortes de questions." recto-verso. See also n. 21 above.
111. See nn. 21 and 22 above.
112. The cumulative index, the *Table Générale des Matières* in vol. 10 (1784), lists architectural subjects in detail. Much of this discussion figures in an article in vol. 2 (1777) entitled "Remarques sur un Écrit de M. P**. . .," a text sent from Beijing in 1775. This refutation of the *Recherches philosophiques sur les Egyptiens et les Chinois* by Cornelius de Pauw is discussed in Chap. 2 in relation to gardens.

4 The Confucian Scholar of Enlightenment France

Consciously or not, throughout his official career, Bertin in many ways embodied the ideal image of a Chinese scholar. He sought accurate knowledge of China through the texts and pictures that the Jesuit missionaries in Beijing sent to him, and he published a substantial part of this material in the *Mémoires concernant les Chinois*. Bertin consistently believed that France had much to learn from China, and indeed that both nations could directly benefit from an active, purposeful exchange. After his retirement as a minister of state, he maintained his "Correspondance littéraire" with the French missionaries and continued the publication of the *Mémoires* until the Revolution drove him from France. The *Mémoires concernant les Chinois*, along with Isidore-Stanislas Helman's more popular publications, would spread knowledge of Confucius alongside Confucian thought and morality. The European fascination with Confucius that had begun in the late seventeenth century with the appearance of the *Confucius sinarum philosophus*, the selection of Confucian classics first published in 1687, would continue through the end of the eighteenth century in a number of publications.[1] Writings on Confucius extend from the works of Gottfried Wilhelm Leibniz (1646–1716), whose *Novissima sinica* (Recent news of China) first appeared in 1697,[2] to the works of Voltaire, who often returned to the subject of China and Confucius. Bertin's personal project for Chatou remained incomplete, but his efforts were still crucial for the dissemination of an image of Confucius that served the goals and aspirations of the late eighteenth century.

On 11 March 1762, Bertin formally acquired the domains of Montesson and Chatou along with the noble titles attached to them.[3] For the new chateau that he would construct at Chatou, Bertin sought to put into practice his knowledge of China, the materials in his collections—both paintings and texts—and the collaboration of his Jesuit correspondents in Beijing in the creation what he envisioned as an authentic Chinese construction in an authentic Chinese garden setting. His plans for Chatou, which would include a *Cabinet chinois* for his Chinese collections, were ostensibly in contradiction to the prevailing European taste for chinoiserie garden follies—decorative structures in a fanciful "oriental" style—and his vision for what he would build was informed by a knowledge of the historical figure of Confucius and certain crucial Confucian texts. What he planned to build at Chatou manifested in many ways a self-styling as a Confucian scholar in Enlightenment France.

The Chinese Constructions at Chatou

The Chinese constructions that Bertin planned at Chatou, ideally to have included a building described variously as a *résidence chinoise, maison chinoise*, or an independent *cabinet chinois* which would be set in a Chinese-style garden, represent many of the aspects of a traditional Chinese scholar's garden or country retreat. Bertin began living at Chatou as his primary residence beginning in April 1781, although he still had an apartment at Versailles and a residence in Paris, 24 rue des Capucines.[4] At Chatou he dedicated himself to his collections, to the Correspondance littéraire with the Jesuit missionaries who still remained in China, and to the publication of the *Mémoires concernant les Chinois*, the last volume of which would appear after his death.[5] One phase of Bertin's early, tentative plans for a Chinese construction at Chatou is revealed in a letter he received from Father Amiot. Dated 15 September 1778, the very long letter ends with Amiot informing Bertin that Étienne Yang, one of the two Chinese Christian clerics who had obtained their return voyage from France at Bertin's behest, had written from Canton that he would not be able to furnish "an assortment of small bells to decorate an octagonal pavilion of six levels or stories."[6] Amiot suggests that Bertin could have such bells cast in Paris, and he gives details on their size, which diminishes from the lower to the upper levels, as well as their form and decoration. The image of a multistoried pagoda (Bertin's "pavilion") with bells hanging from the eaves is an emblematic image of Chinese architecture since the circulation of detailed illustrations of the Porcelain Pagoda at Nanjing in the mid-seventeenth century.[7] A multistoried pagoda with bells hanging from the eaves is illustrated in the first volume of the album *Essai sur l'Architecture Chinoise* in Bertin's collection, where the caption describes the sound of the bells.[8]

Bertin's later, far more elaborate plans for an authentic Chinese construction, however, are recorded in two separate texts, neither of which is specifically dated, although their composition can be dated to approximately the mid- to late 1780s through references to them made in letters, which are discussed later, replying to or referring to Bertin's requests sent by the missionaries in Beijing. One of the texts consists of a series of "Questions to be sent to Monsieur Bourgeois . . .," and it contains a number of comprehensive and well-informed questions about details of Chinese architecture.[9] The other is recorded in two essentially identical documents that are labeled as a *Mémoire* to Father Bourgeois.[10]

In the documents labeled as a *Mémoire* to Father Bourgeois, Bertin—who is ostensibly the author—describes in detail his very elaborate plans, which were accompanied by a drawing of the project. He begins:

> Attached here is the sketch of a house situated at the end and closing off a terrace of a French garden, on the banks of a beautiful river and a very beautiful and immense landscape, with its small square terrace along the length of its small building, facing the river, with two terraces leading down.[11]

Bertin also included a map of the site of the proposed construction, which he summarized in some detail to give Bourgeois a sense of the setting of his planned constructions. (The sketch and the map noted here are possibly those described in a document sent to China in January 1786, which is discussed below.) According to the *Mémoire*, the site is bordered along the east by the terraces and a towpath along the river Seine and on the north by what Bertin refers to as his "French garden," a garden in formal eighteenth-century style. To the west are additional gardens attached to Bertin's chateau, and to the south are the houses and gardens of the village of Chatou itself, directly adjacent to the space for the proposed construction. It its current state the site was considered unsatisfactory as the final feature of the gardens. Nevertheless, it could be transformed into a charming addition to Bertin's gardens:

> We envision using it along with the house to make a Chinese dwelling [emphasis in the original]. It would provide an end point to the garden from these two sides in a novel and pleasing way; and as for the two others, they are of no consequence, not being visible from the garden.[12]

After outlining the site he has chosen in the *Mémoire* to Bourgeois, Bertin goes on to describe his intentions for his Chinese house or Chinese residence (*habitation chinoise*) and surrounding gardens in great detail, referring to what he envisions in their construction. The main façade would face east, toward the Seine, it would have a roof in Chinese style decorated at the ends with dragons, and a parallel gallery along the riverside terraces would have the same style roof. To add to the Chinese style, the windows of the two floors would be decorated with frames or small panes (the text is not clear) of mother-of-pearl brought from Canton.[13] Throughout his description, Bertin is concerned about the potential conflict between what he sees as Chinese taste and what he specifically refers to as European taste. Would all the galleries and roofs in Chinese style not be too much for European eyes, especially for a small house that can be seen, too, as part of the larger garden complex for which it is a kind of end-point? In this, as for additional questions, Bertin requests that Bourgeois should consult a Chinese architect—assuming that such a person exists in a role comparable to an architect in Europe.[14] He asks what a good Chinese architect might remove from these plans after having reviewed them:

> On the other hand, in as much as Chinese taste would allow all four of them [i.e., the planned galleries], we shall opt not to eliminate any of them, since it is a question here of making something following Chinese taste and not just with no respect for European taste. But the more that this last [i.e., European taste] should find itself opposed, the better that would be. I would ask my correspondent, then, to be sure to have this determined by Chinese architects, that if this quadrangle of four galleries seems good to them and to their taste, and to indicate this [on the plan], and in the opposite case what they would eliminate.[15]

Bertin asks, too, that a Chinese architect should provide him with drawings of Chinese flowerbeds to be incorporated into the project at Chatou. He inquires what kinds of shrubs or plants the Chinese use, specifically mentioning boxwood, yews, hollyhocks and chamomile as well as actual lawns—all of which seems to be very much a French selection of garden plantings.[16] The plantings, all supposedly indicated on Bertin's sketch map, continue around to the west and north of the Chinese house, the side facing the terraces of the formal French garden. Here there would be paths set among various plantings of trees or shrubs, again following what a Chinese architect or Bourgeois himself might suggest. Extending to the west, Bertin envisioned a single-story gallery connecting to a building in the same Chinese style as the façade facing the river, which would give the impression of two connected pavilions. And a detached Chinese pavilion would be built on the end of the terrace at the bottom of the garden along the river, in a place where the various paths from the Chinese residence would converge. In all of this, Bourgeois is again instructed to consult with "amateurs or

Chinese architects," and to help with this process another sketch of the space and the house "disguised" as a Chinese residence as Bertin imagines it is included (i.e., altogether one map and two designs accompany the letter to Bourgeois).[17] In addition to the plans and sketches drawn up for Bourgeois, Bertin has other resources at hand for his project:

> We have in addition many drawings of Chinese pavilions of all kinds, but if some architect in Peking provided us another of these, we could of course prefer to execute that. In that case, as in so many others, we would depend upon the kindness of M. Panzi, who would do us the favor of lending his pencil to render for us the ideas and projects that you would wish to send us.[18]

The other relevant document, the "Questions" addressed to Bourgeois, begins with a request for information: "Drawings of Chinese buildings and gardens cannot explain many small details, on which we would like to be informed."[19] As in the reference to drawings in the *Mémoire* to Bourgeois, those referred to here are surely drawings or paintings in Bertin's collection, including the illustrations of the two volumes of the *Essai sur l'Architecture Chinoise* as well as other visual documents. The "Questions" are divided into two sections, and the main subject of both is the specific information necessary for the construction of an authentic Chinese *galerie*—a gallery or covered porch—first as a construction attached to a building and then as free-standing arcade in a garden setting. Each section contains precise questions numbered for reference. The relevant details of Chinese galleries attached to buildings include the shape of the roof, the composition of pavements of brick or stone, the various kinds of columns that are appropriate, the finishing details of walls and wall coverings, and the placement of windows and wall paintings. These questions are followed by requests for instruction on roof tiles, colors appropriate for imperial constructions and other buildings, ceilings and hanging lanterns, furniture of various kinds, as well as additional questions on columns, tiles, and even small bells hanging from the eaves. One section on the galleries attached to a building asks if it is the custom to mount quotations from Confucius over the door or elsewhere in the construction and if there are also such quotations mounted between the windows.[20] And the text asks if they are to be written on marble or brass, and are they to be framed. The writer suggests that perhaps the Jesuit brother Giuseppe Panzi, who served the French mission as an artist, might paint these. This particular question is addressed in a crucial letter to Bertin from Father Amiot accompanying the gift of just such a set of calligraphic inscriptions along with a detailed description of what Bertin's *Cabinet chinois* should be. That letter is discussed in detail later.

The questions on galleries attached to buildings end with a brief note on how the replies sent from China are to be numbered in accordance with the list of questions, and the beginning of the following section—on galleries or arcades as free-standing garden constructions—begins with even more detailed instructions on how to organize and identify both the written replies and accompanying drawings. For garden arcades, the text notes that they may be built on piles over water, that they may be zig-zag in form, and that they may be attached to buildings or completely independent structures. For galleries constructed separately in a garden setting, the text refers to examples illustrated in "prints of the Versailles of Peking." The expression *le Versailles de Pékin* is a relatively frequent reference to the Yuanming yuan, and the prints cited here are no doubt the imperial woodcut edition of the "40 Views of the Yuanming yuan."[21] Questions about such independent structures are tied to questions about trellises and stands of pruned flowering trees. Galleries are seen as frequently concealing walls and terraces, as is the case in European practice, and the question of terraces and walls along a riverbank was an issue in the designs for Bertin's gardens at Chatou. The text ends with questions about stairways, reflecting more closely European than Chinese practice, and the final note is a request for details on the scale and proportions of gardens, that is, instructions that would permit a more accurate consideration of the drawings and paintings already available.

The Role of Jean-Jacques Lequeu, Architect and Draughtsman

The name of the author of the "Questions to be sent to Monsieur Bourgeois . . ." is not indicated on the document itself, and the later replies from the missionaries in Beijing, which are discussed later, are simply addressed to Bertin, but the detail and the knowledge of Chinese architecture—and architecture in general—would indicate that the writer is someone other than Bertin. The architectural historian Philippe Duboÿ has suggested that the author was Jean-Jacques Lequeu (1757–1826), who has been identified as one of the architects of Bertin's constructions at Chatou.[22] Lequeu is a mysterious figure for whom there is relatively little documentary evidence outside of his drawings and texts now in the Bibliothèque nationale de France.[23] Trained in Rouen as an architectural draughtsman, Lequeu went to Paris in 1779 with letters of introduction to Jacques-Germain Soufflot (1713–1780), one of the most important and influential architects of the day, and on Soufflot's recommendation Lequeu was accepted as a student at the Académie Royale d'Architecture.[24] Lequeu held a position as a draughtsman in Soufflot's studio, but when Soufflot died on 29 August 1780 Lequeu no longer had the architect's support to study at the Royal Academy, and his name disappeared from the registers in 1781. He also lost his position as draughtsman in Soufflot's studio.[25] Bertin had known Soufflot in Lyon and requested that he design the residence Bertin intended to construct at Chatou, a project on which Lequeu apparently collaborated.[26] The project for Chatou may have been begun as early as 1774, although the dates are not clearly documented. However, at this time Bertin was actively securing sources for the stone that could be used in the construction of the Nympheum, the Nymphée or grotto along the banks of the Seine that Soufflot designed for his garden.[27] Soufflot, however, passed away in 1780, before the project had been completed, and according to most accounts Lequeu took over his responsibilities as the architect.[28] Bertin apparently took up official residence in the chateau designed for him by Soufflot at Chatou on 23 April 1781.[29]

In 1825, just before he death in 1826, Lequeu made a gift of some 770 of his drawings of architecture and a number of other subjects to the Bibliothèque royale—the modern Bibliothèque nationale de France.[30] Among the most remarkable in terms of content and quality are the 104 drawings in the two albums referred to as *Architecture civile*. The first volume is entitled *Architecture civile de Jean Jacques Le Queu: Contenant nombre d'Édifices de diférents Peuples disséminés sur la terre. . .*, and the two volumes imitate the format of a book of instructions in the rendering of various constructions around the world.[31] The buildings illustrated are more or less fantastic, and two of them in the first volume purportedly represent Chinese buildings. One of these is described as a "Kiosque" in the style of a Chinese pagoda, but there is relatively little that is ostensibly Chinese about the design, outside of the form of the roof and the grille-work on the windows.[32] The following design, labeled as a Chinese house or the residence of a gardener, is also essentially a chinoiserie design incorporating certain Chinese elements in the rooflines as well as two inscriptions in Chinese characters (Figure 4.1).[33] The two designs reflect little of the authentic details in the paintings from Bertin's collection that might have been available to Lequeu, but they are directly related to the illustrations in William Chambers' *Designs of Chinese Buildings*, first published in English and French editions in 1757 and reprinted in a second French edition, entitled *Traité des édifices, meubles, habits . . .* in 1776.[34] The French re-edition, which includes adaptations to Chambers' text and revisions or combinations of the original plates, appeared as Volume 5 in George-Louis Le Rouge's widely circulated and influential series *Jardins anglo-chinois*.[35] Lequeu himself owned a copy of the 1776 edition, which he donated to the Bibliothèque royale along with his drawings in 1825.[36] Lequeu's "Kiosque" generally resembles the pavilions in Chambers' plate 4, but Lequeu's Chinese house or residence of a gardener is based directly on Chambers' plate 10, mimicking the two-story construction with an open-sided upper pavilion, a central doorway, and side wings with a curved roofline facing toward the front (Figure 4.2). For his Chinese house, Lequeu also copied the Chinese characters in Chambers' plates 4, 6, and 10.[37]

Among Lequeu's drawings, however, are four others that are directly linked to his project for Bertin at Chatou. The first is the very precise design entitled "Détails du jeu de bague chinois. . ." executed for the Chinese garden designed by Louis Carrogis (1717–1806), known by his pseudonym Carmontelle, for the Parc Monceau on the outskirts of Paris between 1773 and 1778, plans and illustrations of which were published in 1779.[38] Lequeu wrote on the original drawing, which shows three figures in Chinese-style costumes standing under a broad parasol decorated with tiny bells, that there were changes for the *jeu de bague* at Chateou [*sic*] (Figure 4.3).[39] Two other drawings are also designs for the *jeu de bague*, a genteel game played on a small merry-go-round, a garden element often constructed in a Chinese or chinoiserie style. One rough sketch shows two figures of women, and the drawing is simply inscribed: "Pour le jeu de Bague de Chatou."[40] A more highly finished drawing shows a young African man in eighteenth-century European costume holding what appears to be a quiver full of arrows, which would have held the ring that those riding on the *jeu de bague* reach out for.[41] The drawing is signed "Le Queu, fondé du pouvoir de Soufflot," which signals his role as Soufflot's successor as designer. One final drawing is the design for the decorative sculpture crowning a "Chinese pavilion" (Plate 11).[42] Carefully rendered, with indications of the final measurements, the design shows a figure seated cross-legged on a cushion and holding a parasol with up-turned corners decorated with bells. The figure itself seems to be a heavy-set woman with large breasts clearly visible under her elaborate robes—but also with a long, drooping moustache—combining in pure chinoiserie style vague and fantastic images of Buddhist figures with an erotically sensual, Oriental "other."[43]

Although documents were sent to the missionaries in China requesting detailed, accurate information on Chinese architecture, the decorative elements Lequeu designed for Bertin at Chatou are clearly part of an exoticizing chinoiserie aesthetic. This discrepancy may be explicable in relation to the dates of various documents and the very real delays in communications between France and China. Lequeu as the successor to Soufflot would have begun his subsequent designs for Chatou in 1779 at the

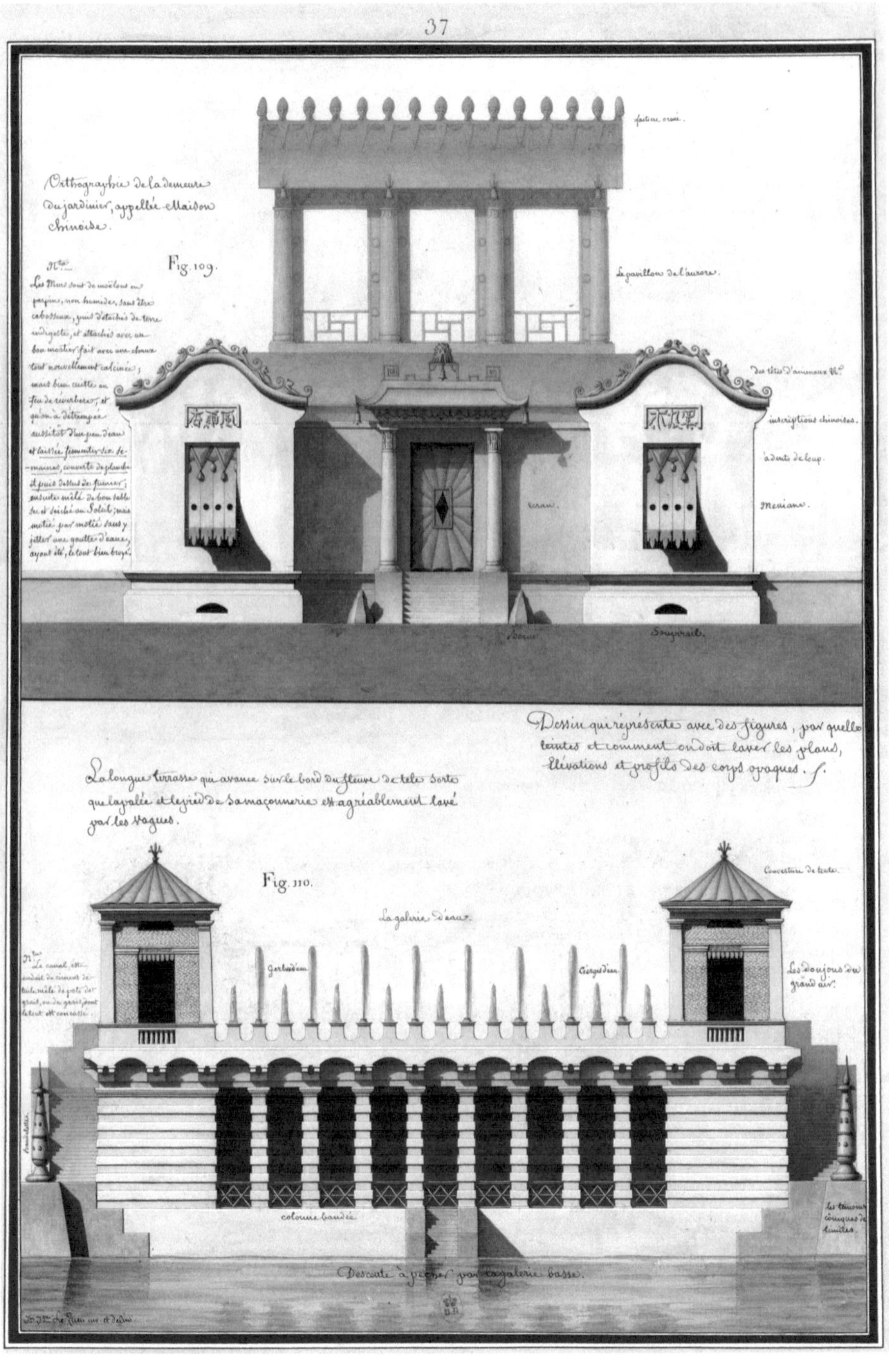

Figure 4.1 Jean-Jacques Lequeu, *Architecture civile de Jean-Jacques Lequeu*, Plate 37, Fig. 109, "Orthographie de la demeure du jardinier, appellée Maison chinoise," ink and color on paper, 51.7 × 34.7 cm, ca. 1777–1825. Paris, Bibliothèque nationale de France.

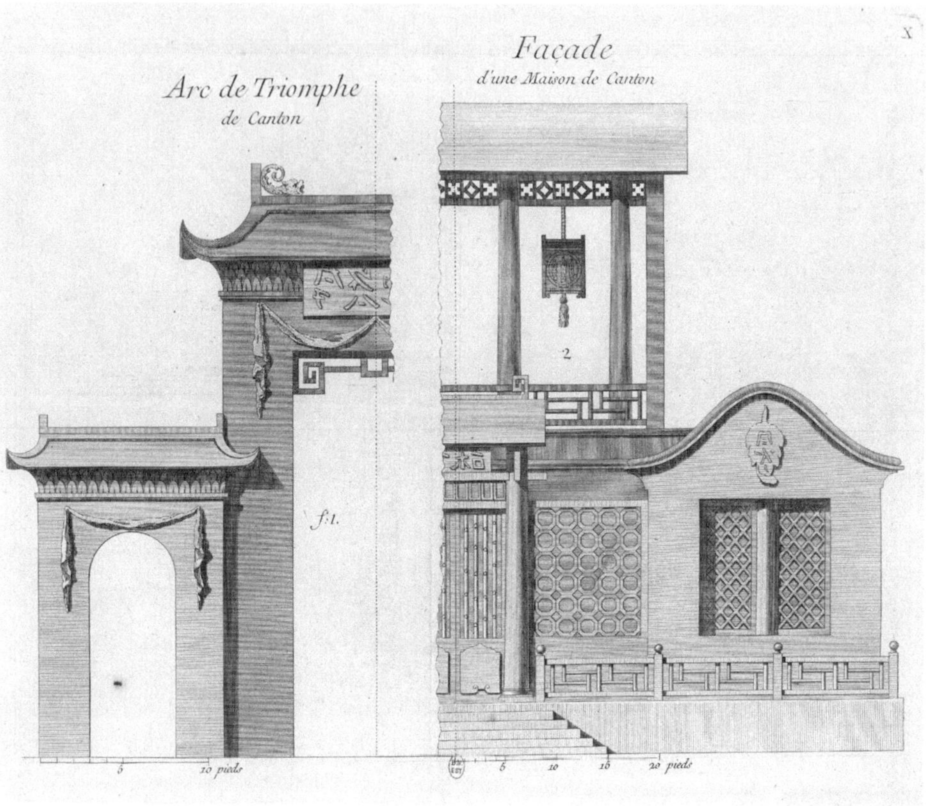

Figure 4.2 After William Chambers, *Traité des édifices*, . . ., "Arc de Triomphe de Canton; Façade d'une Maison de Canton," etching, 29 × 23.1 cm, 1776, in George-Louis Le Rouge, *Jardins anglo-chinois*, vol. V, pl. 10. Paris, Bibliothèque nationale de France.

earliest, when he first served in Soufflot's studio, but more likely no earlier than 1780, when he took on responsibility for the Chatou project at Soufflot's death. However, neither of the two extended documents discussed previously detailing the plans for Chinese constructions at Chatou are dated. A separate document—noted as having been sent to China in 1786 to accompany a plan and view of a building with Chinese elements—provides an outline of the site of the proposed construction, and the plan and view may possibly be the designs referred to in the *Mémoire* to Bourgeois.[44] While many of the relationships between the buildings and the site are not clear from the description in this document, it seems to echo the documents discussed previously and refers to galleries attached to a building described as a house with an entry on a courtyard on one side and terraces descending to a river on the other. It also notes galleries attached to garden walls which connect to a riverside terrace, a free-standing Chinese pavilion, and additional details of extant constructions and a neighboring building. Although it is not labeled as such, the text here clearly describes the layout of Bertin's estate on the banks of the Seine at Chatou.

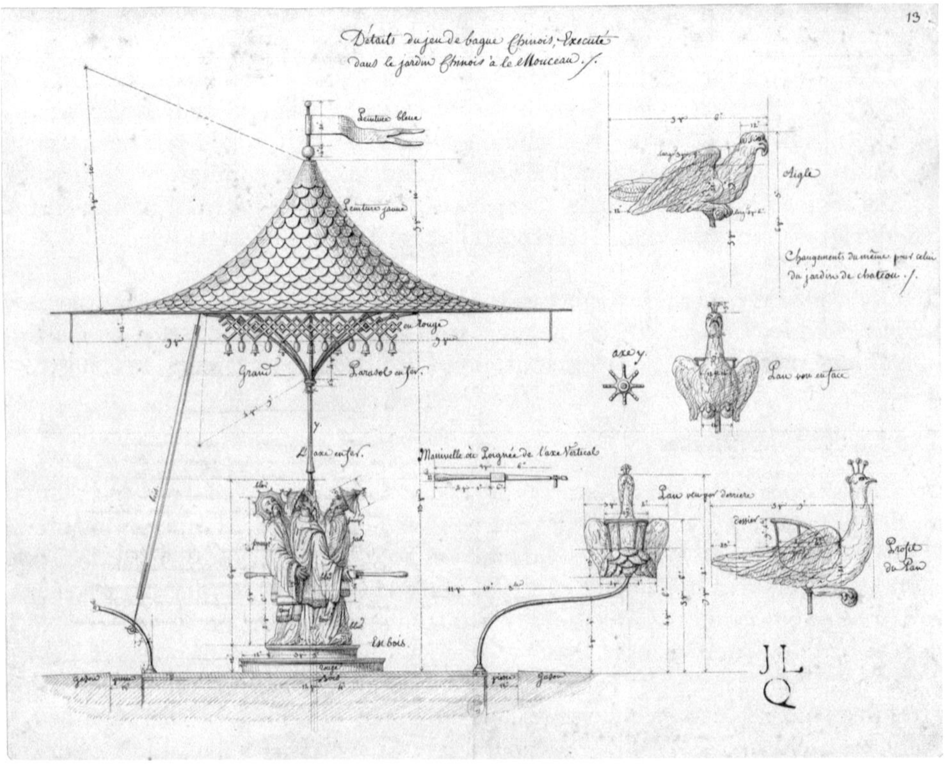

Figure 4.3 Jean-Jacques Lequeu, "Détails du jeu de bague chinois. . .," ink and color on paper, 34.9 × 44.8 cm, ca. 1780. Paris, Bibliothèque nationale de France.

Both of the requests for detailed information for Bertin's constructions were addressed to Father Bourgeois. Three related documents describe Bourgeois' efforts and give at least one direct reply—and they provide dates that help to establish when the original requests were first sent. A letter from Bourgeois himself, dated 10 October 1788, expresses his regrets that he has not been able to succeed in that which was closest to his heart, which was to provide assistance from a Chinese architect in the embellishment of Bertin's project.[45] Chinese architects have their own procedures, and Bourgeois recommends Bertin put plans for Chinese buildings or gardens in the hands of a European architect, who would know better than Chinese professionals how to create what Bertin wants. A very long letter from Father Amiot, dated 10 October 1789, acknowledges the receipt of letters from France dated 1787 to 1788, and in his reply Amiot explains that restrictions imposed on the Jesuit missionaries meant that these letters had been held at Canton and he could not reply until 1789.[46] He also notes that Father Bourgeois had ". . .taken on having the Chinese-style designs made for the embellishment of your gardens at Chatou," and that he had received the funds necessary to acquire such drawings.[47] But, he adds, he does not know how successful Bourgeois has been so far. Later in the same letter Amiot returns to the Chinese house that Bertin has proposed for his garden at Chatou:

> I had proposed to send you a *bian* with its *duizi*, that is an inscription of an auspicious expression to be placed at the back of your Chinese study along with its two pendants, one to the right and the other to the left, to indicate its meaning. But, since M. Bourgeois has not yet obtained from his painters the designs for the arrangement of the rooms that should embellish the garden, I thought that I should wait in order that you receive all these together.[48]

Amiot did indeed send the inscriptions that he promised for Bertin's Chinese study, his *cabinet d'étude chinoise*, at Chatou along with detailed instructions and an illustration of how these should be properly arranged in a thoroughly Confucian context.

The Lives of Confucius

Confucius is present in the *Mémoires concernant les Chinois* from the publication of the first volume in 1776, where he is referred to as a "philosopher" and, several times, as the "Socrates of our China."[49] Two different accounts of the life of Confucius, one short biography and one unprecedented, detailed account of his life and teachings, would be published in the *Mémoires*. Bertin announced in the preface to Volume 1 that he had "portraits or brief lives" of famous Chinese figures throughout history which had been prepared by Father Joseph-Marie Amiot. The first selection of some 52 of these biographies, including the short biography of Confucius, was published in Volume 3 of the *Mémoires* in 1778, and they are discussed in Chapter 1 in the present volume. However, the biography itself is very brief, just two pages long, and contains only the bare outline of Confucius' life and career, but it ends with a statement from Amiot that he will provide a biography of this Sage in greater detail.[50] In a letter dated 26 July 1780, Amiot repeated his promise that he would send a complete life of Confucius, but he admits that such a history has required a great deal of time, since the information is scattered across many different books and thus hard to assemble.[51] The biography, however, will show Confucius not as Europeans have portrayed him but as he is seen in China and depicted in his own writings, an assertion Amiot also makes a number of times in the final text. In addition, Amiot has put together more than 100 "plates" drawn by one of the most skillful artists in Beijing based on illustrations from the most authentic sources.[52] Convinced that such an album will find a place of honor in Bertin's collection, Amiot also says that he is sending all the authentic portraits of Confucius at the head of the prints that will accompany his history.[53] These will represent the principal events of the philosopher's life. A portrait of Confucius (Figure 4.4) faces the title page of Amiot's "Vie de Koung-tsée," which was finally published in Volume 12 of the *Mémoires* in 1786. In addition to the biography itself, the volume contains a chronological table of the events of Confucius' life, a detailed explanation of the 18 engraved plates illustrating the text, and a series of genealogical tables of Confucius' family down through the seventy-first generation in 1784.

The portrait of Confucius at the beginning of his biography is engraved in a thoroughly European style, but the composition and details of the costume and throne carefully reproduce a woodcut image that ultimately dates to the early sixteenth century, a copy of which was presumably among the prints sent by Amiot.[54] In his explanation

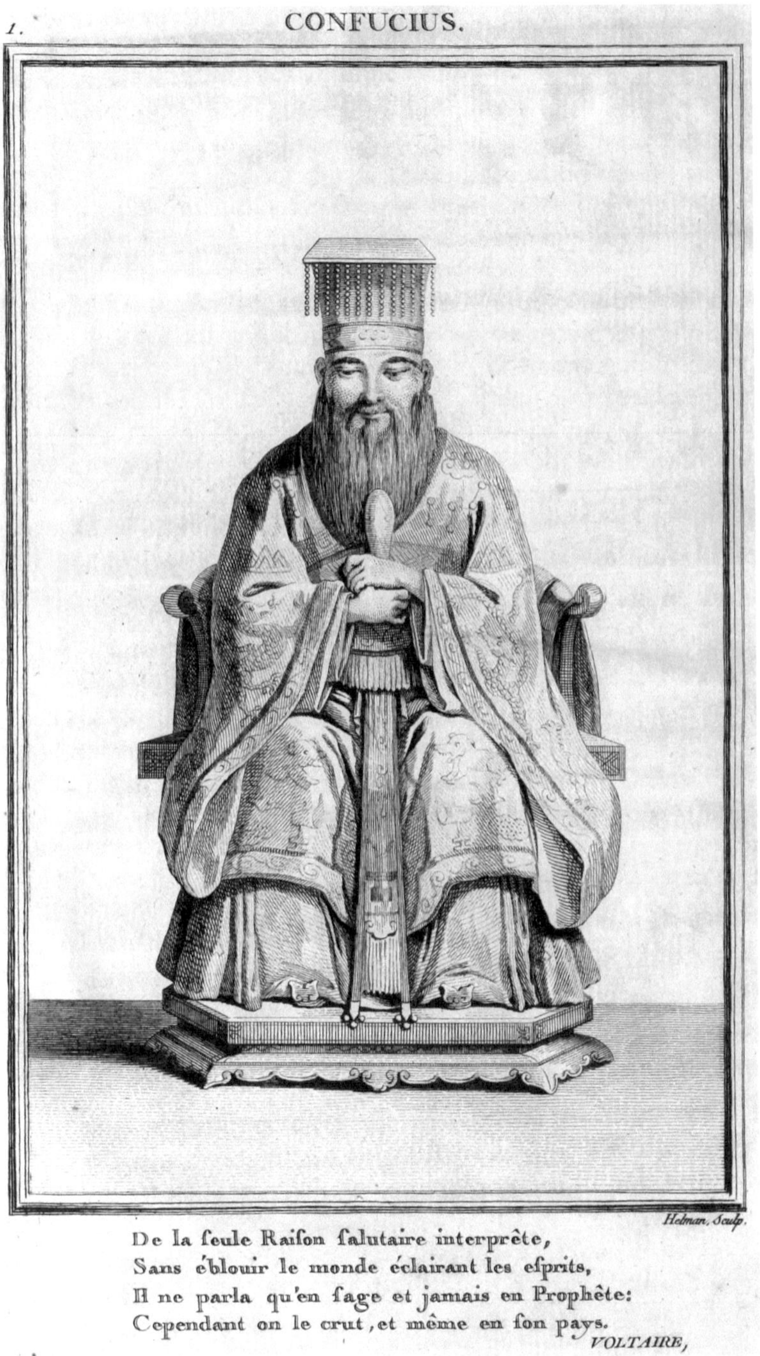

Figure 4.4 Isidore-Stanislas Helman (1743–1806?), "Confucius," *Mémoires concernant les Chinois*, vol. 12, (1786), Pl. 1, engraving, overall 25 × 20 cm, facing p. 1, "Vie de *Koung-tsée*, Appellé vulgairement Confucius, . . ." Getty Research Institute, Los Angeles (41–499).

of this portrait, Amiot noted that it represents Confucius as he was displayed for the veneration of Chinese scholars. It seems that one of Confucius' descendants—of the 47th generation—had described how the Confucius temple in Qufu, in Shandong province, possessed a small portrait known to show him as he actually appeared.[55] Amiot stated that portraits of Confucius were only hung in academies beginning in the Eastern Han, in the second century BC, and then goes on to narrate a history of the uses of the various portraits of the sage and those of his disciples, both as paintings and statues. Amiot's short history of portraits ends with a detailed description of how, in 1530, the Ming Jiajing emperor (嘉靖, r. 1521–67) ordered the removal of all statues and paintings of Confucius from official temples—the images of his disciples having already been replaced by inscribed tablets.[56] Although Amiot repeated here his claim that he was presenting the life of Confucius as the Chinese saw it, with no criticism on his part and only for the judgment of others, it is clear that the story of images being replaced with inscribed tablets reflects the very strong prejudice against idols by the Jesuit missionaries in China.

All of the other illustrations inserted in the text, however, translate their Chinese sources into a completely European style, transforming and restructuring the landscape settings and the pictorial space. For just one example, Plate 15 shows Confucius receiving the blessings of Heaven for having compiled the Six Classics (Figure 4.5).[57] Amiot's biography narrates the episode, and the commentary on the plates at the end of the volume gives a concise description of the scene. Confucius, kneeling before an altar with six books on it, thanks Shangdi 上帝, the supreme deity, for letting him live long enough to have completed the Six Classics.[58] Heaven, as a sign of approval, sends down a ray of light, shining on the books themselves, a scene witnessed by six of Confucius' disciples.[59] In the "Avertissement," the introduction to Volume 12 of the *Mémoires*, Bertin noted that the illustrations of the life of Confucius were engraved by an artist who was skillful enough to understand and render what is characteristic of them. This was because the artist had already worked for several years on drawings from China of which he has successfully published several series.[60] The illustrations that Bertin published were engraved by Isidore-Stanislas Helman (1743–1806?), who was indeed a skilled artist and successful publisher.[61] Helman himself published a version of the life of Confucius in which he re-used and added to the engravings originally produced for Bertin. Helman included the portrait of Confucius in his independent edition, entitled the *Abrégé historique des principaux traits de la vie de Confucius, Célèbre Philosophe Chinois* (the Historical synopsis of the principal events of the life of Confucius, the celebrated Chinese philosopher), which appeared soon after the publication of Amiot's biography in the *Mémoires*.[62] To the portrait Helman added a citation from a poem by Voltaire, which appears in a short passage on Confucius in which the French writer praises the sage's integrity:[63]

> I knew a philosopher who had only the portrait of Confucius on the wall of his private study; below he had put these four lines:
>
> Interpreter of the sole abiding wisdom,
>
> Enlightening the spirit without dazzling the world,
> He spoke only as a sage, never as a prophet;
>
> And still he was believed, and even in his own country.
>
> I have carefully read his books, and I have taken quotations from them; I have found there only the purest ethics with no trace of fraud.[64]

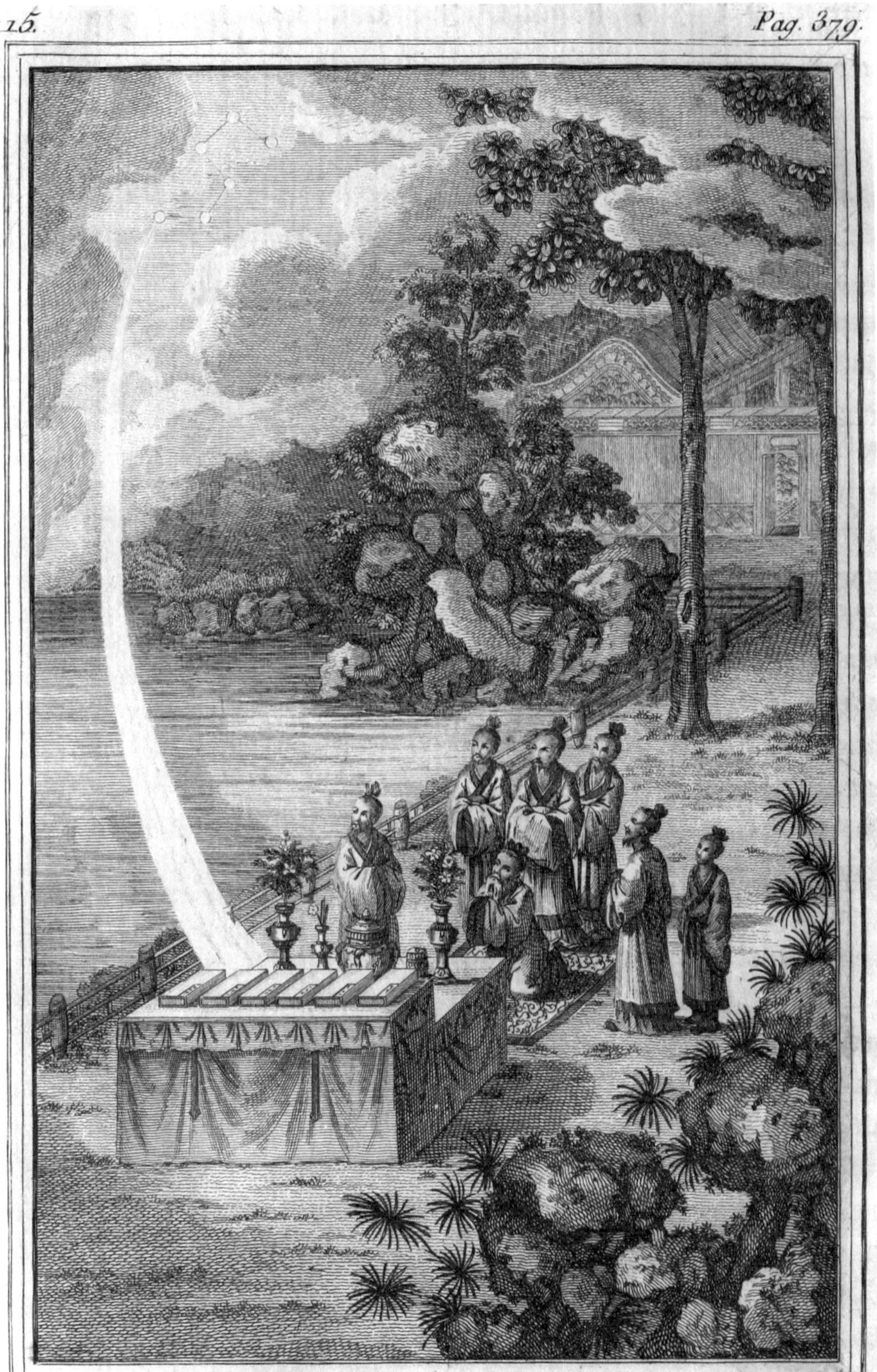

Figure 4.5 Isidore-Stanislas Helman, Confucius receiving the blessings of Heaven for having compiled the Six Classics, *Mémoires concernant les Chinois*, vol. 12 (1786), engraving, overall 25 × 20 cm, Pl. 15, facing p. 379. Getty Research Institute, Los Angeles (41–499).

The evocation of Voltaire surely added to the popular appeal of Helman's publication, which featured descriptions of the 24 engraved illustrations, descriptions which were taken from the text of a small volume on Confucius that had first appeared in 1782.[65] Helman's prints based on Chinese sources are a kind of cultural translation—very much a transformation—of the Chinese images, which are recreated in European visual terms for the edification of a European audience.[66] Bertin's life of Confucius in the *Mémoires concernant les Chinois* and Helman's *Abrégé historique* were surely among the more visible and widely circulated texts and images of Confucius in the late eighteenth century. At the time that he was looking outward, with the dissemination of information to an educated European public, Bertin was also turning inward toward a much more personal project, the construction of his new chateau and gardens at Chatou, just west of Paris.

"A Sage Is Not an Instrument"

Given the disparity between Bertin's written declarations on the authenticity of what he planned to build in the Chinese style at Chatou and the complete chinoiserie fantasy image of the Chinese figures in Lequeu's designs, it is not easy to make a definitive statement on what Bertin actually succeeded in creating. To the end of his life, however, Bertin was still engaged in creating—or imagining—something authentically Chinese for Chatou. On 16 October 1790, Amiot wrote to Bertin wrote that while he had promised to help with the arrangement of Bertin's *cabinet chinois*, here meaning his Chinese-style study, he regrets that he cannot be there in reality but only travel there in his imagination.[67] He envisioned Bertin as a Confucian sage, reading one of the Chinese Classics (*jing* 經) or the "Life of Confucius,"[68] and meditating on the principles of the things of this world. Amiot himself was keenly aware of the persona of a Chinese literatus, a Confucian ideal embodied by many of the scholar-officials of the Qing court, and in this, too, it appears he wanted Bertin to be authentically Chinese.

For Bertin's study, Amiot imagined an elaborate structure with the central building facing south flanked by two identical wings—where everything so far is "completely Chinese." Here Bertin could install a *ting* (亭, a small pavilion), a private office or *shufang* (書房, a library), and a *zuofang* (作房, a workshop) where he could amuse himself with some work with his own hands.[69] Amiot's letter accompanied several crates containing decorative objects, some of which were clearly intended for Bertin's Chinese study. The most important for Amiot's image of Bertin as a Confucian scholar were a sign-board (*bian'e* 匾額), a pair of couplets (*duizi* 對子), and three different examples of the character *fu* 福, meaning "good fortune." For the arrangement of Bertin's study in an authentic Chinese manner Amiot sent a detailed drawing with extensive notes showing the character *fu*, the sign-board, the couplets, and a Chinese table set with objects for burning incense (Plate 12).[70] The layout of typical elements from a Chinese scholar's studio clearly echoes images of Chinese interiors presented in the *Essai sur l'architecture chinoise* (e.g., Figure 3.12). To help Bertin understand what he has been sent, Amiot gives the meanings of all the Chinese inscriptions, beginning with the four characters the sign-board, "Kiun-tsee pou Ki" (*Junzi bu qi* 君子不器), which he translates as "A Sage is not an instrument."[71] The citation is from the *Analects* of Confucius, and it means that a true scholar is not a simple tool but rather someone ready for all things.[72] Amiot also explains the sense of the couplet for Bertin: Beginning with the first line, at the right, he writes that in taking virtue as the guiding principle of his actions, the sage (by implication) effectively erects as many monuments to his own glory as there are "mouths in the four corners of the world."[73] Amiot notes that the second line, on the left, implies that if *ren* 仁, or benevolence, is the moving force behind a sage's actions, he will enjoy the rewards that he is due in personal contentment, a long life and the esteem of the whole world.[74] After much additional detail on how to enjoy the studio and gardens as a true Chinese scholar, Amiot ends by saying that he has mentioned Bertin to the Qianlong emperor, noting the esteem Bertin feels for the Chinese nation, and how the emperor was grateful for this. The emperor, too, apparently had his own studio decorated as best as possible in the French style, where he even practiced a little of the French language.[75] Through the choice of the Chinese texts Amiot sought to position Bertin himself as an equivalent of a Confucian sage or superior man. Bertin surely envisioned his chateau and gardens at Chatou, complete with authentic Chinese constructions, as somehow a replica of a Chinese garden, perhaps even the Yuanming yuan. Father Amiot provided him with the genuine accoutrements of a Chinese scholar, including auspicious texts that proclaimed the Confucian virtues Bertin might adopt as his own.

The Actual Constructions at Chatou

A document entitled "Atlas de la Seigneurie de Chatou . . ." was compiled on Bertin's orders in 1780.[76] Referred to as the "Atlas Censier," it contains detailed maps, carefully rendered in color, and relevant documents on the taxes or duties due to Bertin as the seigneur of Chatou according to the size of each owner's holdings.[77] One map shows Bertin's personal properties at Chatou, and while the map does not show Bertin's chateau itself, the residence designed by Soufflot was located in the space adjacent to the village of Chatou (Plate 13).[78] It includes the layout of the gardens that extended to the northwest as a long rectangle laid out with formal paths, plantings, and bodies of water. The map also shows the Nympheum—a crucial element of Bertin's gardens—which is clearly indicated facing the Seine. Terraces extend along the river, and what is most important to the discussion here is the area that appears to be a less formal garden in the Anglo-Chinese style set above the terraces along the Seine.[79] Here geometrically laid-out lanes alternate with more meandering paths among various garden constructions through what appears to be woods or shrubbery.[80] These are not labeled, and it is difficult to accurately identify them from the "Atlas Censier" map. One element in this part of the garden, adjacent to a hexagonal site with a small structure in the center, appears to be an elaborate rockwork or possibly a grotto, which would be a typical feature of a late eighteenth-century garden. Beyond these is a wide area of regular plantings in the center of which is a square construction around a circular center. This element is identical to the *jeu de bague* in the plan of Carmontelle's publication of the *Jardin de Monceau*—the *jeu de bague* in Lequeu's design for Monceau that was supposedly adapted for Bertin's garden at Chatou.[81] There is no evidence on this map, however, of the elaborate Chinese-style constructions that were so carefully described in the documents sent to Father Bourgeois in Beijing.

Bertin sold the chateau to the Marquise de Feuquières in 1790 and departed France, first to Aix-la-Chapelle, and then Spa, in Belgium, where he died on 16 September 1792.[82] The Marquise herself was executed in 1794, and the chateau passed through various owners until it was acquired in 1810 by Charles-Alexis Travault, who would

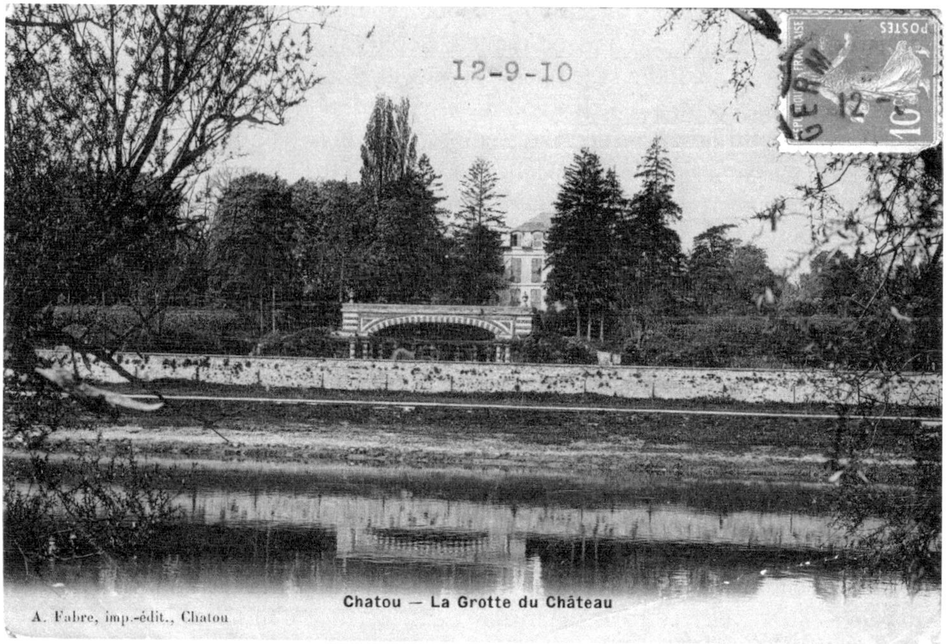

Figure 4.6 "Chatou—La Grotte du Château," postcard, postmarked 12 September 1910, photo: A. Berger frères, publ.: A. Fabre, Chatou. Private collection, Paris.

become the mayor of Chatou.[83] Sometime before 1824 Travault added a new wing to the chateau, comprising a new entrance in neo-Classical style, and this is the view that appears in most photographs—many of them reproduced as postcards—before the final demolition of the chateau in 1910. Soufflot's original construction is only partly visible in these photographs, when it was already in a dilapidated condition. A photograph reproduced on a card postmarked 1910, entitled "La Grotte du Château," shows the Nympheum from the island in the Seine opposite Bertin's estate (Figure 4.6).[84] Part of the façade of the chateau, with the shutters closed or half-open, appears among the trees behind the Nympheum, which is itself the only part of the estate still extant. Bertin's gardens as laid out in the "Atlas Censier" map would have been to the right of the chateau in this photograph.

One document from Bertin's lifetime appears to describe a Chinese-style garden feature, possibly the rockworks that appear on the "Atlas Censier" map. On 26 May 1778, John Adams (1735–1826), who would serve as the second President of the United States (1797–1801), spent the day with Benjamin Franklin and Franklin's grandson, William Temple Franklin, on a visit to Bertin's chateau and gardens at Chatou. Adams' diary entry for the day briefly describes his pleasant carriage ride through the countryside from Paris to Chatou, but his description of the gardens is frankly dismissive:

> The Gardens, Walks and Waterworks of Mr. Bertin were in a Style of magnificence, like all other Seats of the Gentlemen in this Country. He was a Batchelor.

His House and Gardens were situated upon the River Seine. He shewed his Luxury, as he called it, which was a collection of misshapen Rocks, at the End of his Garden, drawn together, from great distances, at an Expence of several Thousands of Guineas. I told him I would sell him a thousand times as many for half a Guinea.[85]

The late dates that can be associated with the construction of Bertin's *cabinet chinois* at Chatou, generally in the decade after Soufflot's death in 1780, raise significant questions about what was actually built, but surely some part of Bertin's Paris collections was kept at Chatou. Georges Bussière, writing in 1909, believed Bertin had installed his Chinese collections at Chatou. An inventory from 1810 contains a description of some of the works of art remaining at Chatou, nothing Chinese is recorded here, although Bertin's personal library had apparently been transferred to Chatou, along with his "cabinet d'histoire naturelle."[86] However, Bussière described Bertin's new chateau both as a place to bring together his extended family as well as a "pagoda in miniature for his collections and his Chinese curiosities."[87] In the face of the images of Chinese architecture already in Bertin's collection, Lequeu's designs—of which the *jeu de bague* was most likely the only part actually built—are a chinoiserie fantasy. The sketches and plans sent to China are no longer extant and cannot be compared to what appears in the 1780 "Atlas Censier," where specific details strongly suggest Anglo-Chinese style garden constructions in some form. The "Atlas Censier," however, was prepared in the same year that Soufflot died, at a time when the project for the chateau at Chatou was in its early stages. For the installation of a *cabinet chinois*, Amiot's letter and the diagram on how to arrange a Chinese studio point to the inspiration of Confucian ideals on Bertin's constructions, echoing the many texts published in the *Mémoires concernant les Chinois*, constructions which, we are left to assume, perhaps only existed in Bertin's—as in Amiot's—imagination.

Notes

1. See Meynard, *Confucius Sinarum Philosophus (1687): The First Translation of the Confucian Classics.*
2. Among many other studies, see Donald Lach, "Leibniz and China," *Journal of the History of Ideas* 6, no. 4 (1945), 436–455; idem, *The Preface to Leibniz' Novissima Sinica: Commentary, Translation, Text* (Honolulu: University of Hawai'i press, 1957; and see David Mungello, *Leibniz and Confucianism: The Search for Accord* (Honolulu: University of Hawai'i Press, 1977).
3. Albert Curmer, *Les Seigneurs de Chatou* (Versailles: Impr. de J. Aubert, 1919), 114, n. 1. Curmer's research on Bertin, reprinted here, was first published in the *Revue de l'histoire de Versailles et de Seine-et-Oise*, January-June 1918, and July-Dec. 1918.
4. *Bulletin de la Société historique et archéologique du Périgord*, vol. 36 (1909), 278.
5. On the publication of the *Mémoires concernant les Chinois*, see the discussion in Chap. 1.
6. Bib. Inst. Ms 1515, fols. 212–219; see fol. 219: "Le P. Yang m'écrit de Canton que votre grandeur lui avoit donné la commission de faire fondre, ou de se procurer à Canton un assortiment de clochettes pour en garnir un pavillon octogone à six rangs ou étages. . . ."
7. See the discussion and illustration of the Porcelain Pagoda at the Bao'ensi in Chap. 3; Figs. 3.8 and 3.9.
8. *Essai sur l'Architecture Chinoise*, part I, pl. 131; see also Plate 8.
9. Bib. Inst. Ms 1526, fols. 40–46: "Questions à Envoyer à Monsieur Bourgeois en le priant d'y satisfaire, si'il le peut, à Son Loisir."
10. See Bib. Inst. Ms 1524, fols. 104–107, which appears to be a draft document with corrections in Bertin's own hand. The second manuscript addressed to Father Bourgeois is in

the Institut National d'Histoire de l'Art (INHA), Ms 131, entitled "Bertin et la Mission de Chine, 1764–1792," on fols. 91–96. This document incorporates many of Bertin's corrections, details that help to identify it as a copy of the Bib. Inst. Ms 1524 text, although it contains a few additional changes as well.

11. Bib. Inst. Ms 1524, fol. 104 recto: "Memoire / On joint ici l'esquisse d'une Maison située au bout et terminant une Terrasse d'un Jardin François, sur le bord d'une belle rivière et d'un très beau et immense paysage, ayant sa petite Terrasse quarrée dans la longueur de son petit Bâtiment, donnant sur cette Rivière, avec deux autres Terrasses descendants."
12. Ibid., fol. 104 verso: "On a imaginé de l'employer, ainsi que la Maison, à faire Une habitation Chinoise. Elle terminera d'une façon nouvelle et agréable ce jardin de ces deux côtés; et à l'égard des deux autres, ils sont absolument indifférents, n'étant point aperçus du Jardin."
13. Ibid., fol. 105 recto: "Par là on croit imiter le Chinois, et d'autant plus qu'on se procure de Canton les vitrages en Nacre de la Chine, dont les fenêtres de la Maison, soit au premier, soit au Rès de Chaussée, seront garnies. . . ."
14. The lack of a Chinese equivalent to the profession of an architect is discussed in Chap. 3.
15. Bib. Inst. Ms 1524, fol. 106 recto: "Pour peu, au contraire, que le gout chinois les admette toutes les quatre, on prendra le parti de n'en diminuer aucune, s'agissant ici de faire une chose suivant le gout chinois, et non seulement sans aucun égard au gout de l'Europe; Mais plus ce dernier se trouveroit contredit, mieux cela vaudroit. On prie donc le Correspondant de faire bien le décider par les architectes de Chine, si ce quarré de quatre Galeries, leur paroit bien, et de leur goût, et de le marquer, et dans le cas contraire, la partie qu'ils en retrancheroient."
16. A good portion of the text in Bib. Inst. Ms 1524 is quoted and discussed in Janine Barrier, Monique Mosser and Che Bing Chiu, comp., *Aux Jardins de Cathay: l'imaginaire anglo-chinois en Occident, William Chambers* (Besançon: Éditions de l'Imprimeur, 2004), 117–121; nn. 225 and 226 cite sources that deal with the questions of plants and plantings: see Marie-Pierre Dumoulin-Genest, "L'Introduction et l'acclimatation des plantes chinoises en France au XVIIIe siècle," PhD diss., EHESS, Paris, October 1994; and Jacques Roi, "Les Missionnaires de Chine et la botanique," *Collectanea Commissionis Synodalis in Sinis*, vol. VI, nos. 7–8 (July-August 1938).
17. Bib. Inst. Ms 1524, fol. 107 recto-verso.
18. Ibid., fol. 107 verso, the last paragraph of the document: "Nous avons au surplus beaucoup de Desseins de Pavillons chinois, et de toute espèce, mais si quelque architecte de PeKin nous en donnoit un, nous pourrions volontiers l'exécuter de préférence: dans ce cas, comme dans plusieurs d'autres, on se recommande à l'amitié de M. Panzy, qui nous feroit bien le plaisir de prêter son Crayon, pour nous rendre les idées et projets qu'on voudra bien nous envoyer."
19. Bib. Inst. Ms 1526, fol. 104: "Les desseins des bâtiments et jardins chinois, ne peuvent expliquer bien de petits détails, sur les quels on désire être instruit."
20. Ibid., fol. 41 verso.
21. See the discussion of the "40 Views of the Yuanming yuan" in Chap. 2.
22. Philippe Duboÿ, *Jean Jacques Lequeu: dessinateur en architecture* (Paris: Gallimard, 2018), 21. Duboÿ offers no support here for his assertion, which is included in the chapter "Lequeu, Bertin ou 'le véritable bonheur est dans les campagnes'" of his PhD dissertation, "Jean Jacques Lequeu Architecte?", for the Istituto Universitario di Architettura di Venezia (IUAV), Venice, 1972. In *Jean Jacques Lequeu: dessinateur en architecture*, 22–23, Duboÿ states that his dissertation contains the "Questions" to Bourgeois along with the replies but provides no further details.
23. See the recent exhibition catalogue *Jean-Jacques Lequeu: bâtisseur de fantasmes*, under the direction of Laurent Baridon, Jean-Philippe Garric, and Martial Guédron (Paris: Bibliothèque nationale de France; Éditions Norma, 2018). See also Frédéric Morvan, "Jean Jacques Lequeu," Appendix, pp. 233–261, in Duboÿ, *Lequeu: dessinateur en architecture*; see esp. 235–236. Morvan provides the most thorough documentary evidence for Lequeu's biography and career.

24. Emil Kaufmann, "Three Revolutionary Architects, Boullée, Ledoux and Lequeu" *Transactions of the American Philosophical Society*, New series, vol. 42, part 3 (1952), 431–564; see Part III, Jean-Jacques Lequeu, 538–558.
25. *Lequeu: bâtisseur des fantasmes*, 154–157.
26. Ibid., 155, n. 33, citing Jean Monval, *Soufflot, sa vie, son oeuvre, son esthétique (1713–1780)* (Paris: A. Lemerre, 1918), 420, n. 3.
27. Catinat, *Les Châteaux de Chatou*, 64–66; the text includes additional documentation on the stone needed for construction in 1775. While citing numerous sources, Catinat does not give a date for the beginning of the design and construction of Bertin's so-called new chateau, the "Chateau neuf"; see also Curmer, *Les Seigneurs de Chatou*, 140 ff.
28. Curmer, *Les Seigneurs de Chatou*, 141, asserts that it was probably Lequeu, as Soufflot's *secrétaire*, who completed the construction. Philippe Duboÿ, in *Jean Jacques Lequeu: une énigme* (Paris: Hazan, 1987), 353, refers to Lequeu as a "fondé de pouvoir de Soufflot," that is, as a proxy-holder or representative. See the drawing "Noir qui présente l'anneau. . ." below, where Lequeu signs his name with this designation; see also n. 41 below.
29. Catinat, *Les Châteaux de Chatou*, 101; the author, however, does not provide documentation for the date. See also n. 4 above for the same date.
30. Lequeu's architectural illustrations, along with portraits and figure studies that are truly fantastic and often highly erotic, were the subject of the exhibition "Jean-Jacques Lequeu (1757–1826): Bâtisseur de fantasmes" at the Petit Palais, Paris, 11 December 2018–31 March 2019. On the donation of his drawings to the Bibliothèque du roi (the Bibliothèque royale), see Corinne Le Bitouzé, "'Un très curieux recueil': Les dessins de Jean-Jacques Lequeu dans les collections du Département des estampes et de la photographie de la BnF," in Baridon, *Jean-Jacques Lequeu: bâtisseur de fantasmes*, 173–177.
31. Jean-Jacques Lequeu, *Architecture civile de Jean Jacques Le Queu contenant nombre d'édifices de diférents peuples disséminés sur la terre. . .*, 2 vols., 1777–1825), BnF, Département des Estampes et de la photographie, Réserve HA-80 (1)-FOL and HA-80 (2)-FOL.
32. *Architecture civile*, vol. 1, plate 36, fig. 108, "Kiosque dans le goût des pagodes des Chinois, élevé dans l'isle du levant à la tête du grand canal; il sert de repos de chasse."
33. Ibid., Plate 37, Fig. 109, "Orthographie de la demeure du jardinier, appellée Maison chinoise." Fig. 110, on the same plate, shows a long, colonnaded terrace with two pavilions set along a riverbank, a distant echo, perhaps, of Soufflot's Nympheum.
34. Chambers, *Designs of Chinese Buildings*; *Desseins des édifices, meubles, habits, machines, et ustenciles* [*sic*] *des Chinois . . .*, 1757; and *Traité des édifices, meubles, habits, machines et ustensiles des Chinois . . .* (Paris: Chez le Sieur Le Rouge, 1776). For an extended study of Chambers and Chinese gardens with reprints of Chambers' texts published in French, see Barrier and others, *Aux jardins de Cathay*.
35. Georges-Louis Le Rouge, *Jardins anglo-chinois ou Détails de nouveaux jardins à la mode*; see Véronique Royet and others, *Georges-Louis Le Rouge: Jardins anglo-chinois*; esp. Cahier V, 124–129.
36. Royet, *Georges-Louis Le Rouge: Jardins anglo-chinois*, 124; the title page is inscribed at the bottom: "vendu à M. Lequeu Archit.te"; and the entry in the inventory of his gifts, no. 7131, notes: "donné par M. Lequeu en 1825"; *Traité des édifices*, BnF Département des Estampes et de la photographie, call no. HD-89 (5)-Pet Fol.
37. Chambers, *Traité des édifices*, Pl. IV (Pavillons dans une Pagode des Faubourg [*sic*] de Canton), Pl. VI (Pont dans un jardin de Canton), and Pl. X (Façade d'une Maison de Canton).
38. For the published illustrations, see Carmontelle (Louis Carrogis, 1717–1806), *Jardin de Monceau, près de Paris, appartenant à S.A.S. Mgr. le duc de Chartres* (Paris: Delafosse, 1779); see esp. Pl. XVI, "Vüe du principal Pavillon et du jeu de Bague, Prise du Point P." See also *Grandes et petites heures du parc Monceau*, exhibition catalogue (Paris: Musée Cernuschi, 1981), 100, and cats. 30, 43.
39. Jean-Jacques Lequeu, "Détails du jeu de bague chinois, exécuté dans le jardin chinois à le Monceau; Changements du même pour celui du jardin de Chateou," red and black ink; 44.8 × 34.9 cm, BnF, Département des Estampes et de la photographie, Réserve HA-80 (D)-FOL.

40. "Pour le jeu de bague de Chatou," pencil, 20.4 × 12.4 cm, BnF, Département des Estampes et de la photographie, Réserve HA-80 (D)-FOL. Kee Il Choi has demonstrated that the two figures are based on detailed paintings in an album now in a private collection entitled *Recueil de Vases Antiques, et Piéces, tires des Cabinets Chinois de l'Empereur Kien-Long*. See the presentation, "Ornament from China: Henri-Léonard Bertin's drawings of the Qianlong emperor's vases Chinois," IFA China Project Workshop, New York, 29 March 2019. My thanks to Kee Il Choi for bringing this link to my attention.
41. "Noir qui présente l'anneau à celui qui court la bague." The drawing is inscribed: "Pour le jeu de bague de Mr. Bertin à Chatou / Le Queu / fondé du pouvoir de Soufflot," ink and watercolor, 29.1 × 18.2 cm, BnF, Département des Estampes et de la photographie, Réserve HA-80 (D)-FOL.
42. "Dessin du couronnement du pavillon chinois," ink and watercolor on paper, 21.2 × 16.6 cm, BnF, Département des Estampes et de la photographie, Réserve VA-78 (2)-FOL; the image is discussed in Duboÿ, *Jean-Jacques Lequeu: une énigme*, p. 339. The drawing bears Lequeu's monogram JLQ, and the word "Chatou" is written in pencil below the design, bottom right. Lequeu's designs are briefly discussed in Curmer, *Les Seigneurs de Chatou*, 143–144.
43. Bizarre sexual elements figure in many of Lequeu's drawings; see Baridon, *Lequeu: bâtisseur de fantasmes*.
44. Bib. Inst. Ms 1524, fol. 191 recto-verso: "Envoyé En janvier 1786. vu profil et vu Élévation d'une maison pour consulté [*sic*]."
45. Barrier and others, *Aux jardins de Cathay*, 119–120; the authors, however, do not provide a specific source for the citation from Bourgeois' letter.
46. Bib. Inst. Ms 1517, fols. 65–86; the letter dated on the last page: Peking le 10e 8bre 1789 (8bre orig. written 9bre, i.e., novembre, then corrected).
47. Ibid., fol. 66: "Il [Bourgeois] s'est chargé pareillement de faire des dessins à la chinoise pour l'embellissement de vos jardins de Chatou."
48. Ibid., fol. 77 verso: "Je m'étois proposé de vous envoyer un Pien et ses toui-tsee, c'est à dire une inscription sentencieuse pour être placée au fond de votre cabinet d'étude chinoise, et ses deux pendentifs, l'un à droite et l'autre à gauche, pour en indiquer l'explication. Mais comme M. Bourgeois n'a pas encore obtenu de ses Peintres les dessins pour l'arrangement des pièces qui doivent orner le jardin, j'ay cru pouvoir différer, à fin que vous receviez le tout ensemble."
49. See the *Mémoires concernant les Chinois*, vol. 1 (1776), "Essai sur l'Antiquité des chinois," 1–271; see esp. 33–63. The article is based on Amiot's text "L'antiquité des chinois prouvée par les monuments"; for the document, see BnF Fonds Bréquigny, vol. 107, fols. 9–74; Amiot's signature and the date, 15 September 1775 (15e 7bre 1775), appear on fol. 73.
50. *Mémoires concernant les Chinois*, vol. 3 (1778), 43–45; Confucius' biography is numbered XXI.
51. *Mémoires concernant les Chinois*, vol. 9 (1783), extract from Amiot's letter, 1–5.
52. Amiot specifically says *planches*, the term for printed plates or illustrations, and it is not entirely clear if he means prints here or images drawn after various other illustrations; see ibid., 4. On the images accompanying the life of Confucius, see Paola Demattè, "A Confucian Education for Europeans," *The Art Bulletin* 98, no. 1 (March 2016), 43–71; see esp. 48–57.
53. *Mémoires*, vol. 9 (1783), Amiot's letter, 5.
54. See Demattè, "A Confucian Education," 49, figs. 5, 6; citing in the text the original 1505 edition, of the *Queli zhi*, the ritual text by Chen Hao (陳鎬, *jinshi* 1487). Demattè reproduces a later version of the "Portrait of the Great Sage, Disseminator and King" in Kong Zhencong 孔貞叢 and others, *Queli zhi* (Records of Queli 闕里誌) in 12 *juan* (Qufu: Kongshi, dated to the Ming Wanli *jiyou* year, 1609). See also Reed and Demattè, *China on Paper*, cat. 21.
55. Another version of the same portrait had been recorded, too, in a different temple during the Tang dynasty (618–907).
56. *Mémoires concernant les Chinois*, vol. 9, 431–437, the "Explication des Planches." Amiot translates at length a text written by Zhang Fujing (張孚敬, 1475–1539), describing him as the head of the Board of Rites. Other sources describe him as the Chief Grand Secretary; see also John W. Dardess, *A Political Life in Ming China* (Lanham, MD: Rowman &

Littlefield, 2013), 5, 7, 14, passim. And see Murray, "'Idols' in the Temple," for details on the various prohibitions—all paintings and statues to be suppressed in official Confucius temples; paintings and other images still extant, however, in schools or academies; and images of all kinds permitted in the Confucius Temple complex in Qufu.

57. *Mémoires concernant les Chinois*, vol. 12; the episode illustrated here appears on 379–383; the short explanation of the plate is on 444–445. See also Reed and Demattè, *China on Paper*, cat. 21, fig. 74, for this engraving.
58. The "Six Classics" (*Liujing* 六經 or *Liuyi* 六藝) cited by Confucius include the *Yijing* 易經 (Book of Changes), the *Shangshu* 尚書 (also known as *Shujing* 書經, the Book of Documents), the *Shijing* 詩經 (or *Maoshi* 毛詩, the Book of Poetry), the *Liji* 禮記 (Records of Rites), and the *Chunqiu* 春秋 (Spring and Autumn Annals), along with the now-lost book about music, *Yueji* 樂記 (Records of Music). See Endymion Wilkinson, *Chinese History: A Manual*, Harvard-Yenching Institute Monograph Series 52 (Cambridge, MA: Harvard University Asia Center, Harvard-Yenching Institute; Harvard University Press, 2000), 475; see also the website ChinaKnowledge, www.chinaknowledge.de/Literature/Classics/classics.html, accessed 27 June 2016.
59. The explanation of the plate even mentions the railing which leads back to the entrance of a pavilion or *ting* 亭 where the memory of the compilation of the Classics would be preserved.
60. *Mémoires concernant les Chinois*, vol. 12 (1786), Avertissement, iii.
61. In addition to the *Abrégé historique*, discussed immediately below, Helman also published the *Faits mémorables des empereurs de la Chine, Tirés des Annales Chinoises, Dédiés à Madame, Ornés de 24 Estampes en 4o.* Gravées par Hellman, d'après les Desseins Originaux de la Chine, tirés du Cabinet de Mr. Bertin, Mtre. et ancien Sre. d'Etat (A Paris: Chez l'Auteur . . ., 1788); that is, a volume of 24 "Memorable events of the emperors of China, taken from Chinese annals . . ." illustrated by engravings of important historical episodes based on original in Bertin's collection. The source is a two-album set of Chinese paintings entitled *Recueil Historique des Principaux Traits de la Vie des Empereurs Chinois*, now in the Département des Estampes et de la photographie, Réserve OE-5-BOITE FOL and Réserve OE-5 (A)-BOITE FOL. See also the various editions of the *Suite des seize estampes représentant les conquêtes de l'empereur de la Chine* (Paris, 1785–1786), adding four more views, of which three form a panorama, with the central image inscribed "tiré du cabinet de Mr. Bertin."
62. Various dates are given for Helman's *Abrégé historique*, including 1786, the same year as vol. 12 of the *Mémoires concernant les Chinois*, and 1788.
63. Voltaire's poem first appears in the entry "De la Chine," in the *Questions sur l'Encyclopédie*, vol. III (Paris: 1770), 333–334; it was later included in the section "De la Chine" in the *Dictionnaire Philosophique*.
64. "J'ai connu un philosophe qui n'avait que le portrait de Confucius dans son arrière-cabinet: il mit au bas ces quatre vers: / De la seule raison salutaire interprète, / Sans éblouir le monde, éclairant les esprits, / Il ne parla qu'en sage, et jamais en prophète; / Cependant on le crut, et même en son pays. / J'ai lu ses livres avec attention; j'en ai fait des extraits; je n'y ai trouvé que la morale la plus pure, sans aucune teinture de charlatanisme." Demattè, "A Confucian Education," 49, includes a more literal translation of the poem.
65. *Pensées morales de Confucius, recueillies et traduites du latin par M. Levesque*, Pierre-Charles Levesque, ed. (Paris: chez Didot l'aîné et De Bure l'aîné, 1782). The text is 166 pages long, but the source or sources in Latin are apparently unidentified. The reference to the *Pensées morales* appears on the last page of Helman's *Abrégé historique*.
66. Paola Demattè, writing in English, and Chao-Ying Lee, writing in French, have both published important research on the meanings and implications of Helman's illustrations and other Chinese images published for Bertin. See Demattè, "Chinese History and Philosophy for European Scholars," and the entries in *China on Paper*. For Chao-Ying Lee, see "L'enjeu politique et religieux des modes de représentation dans les *Mémoires concernant les Chinois* (1776–1791)," *Histoire de l'Art* no. 51, November 2002, 87–99; see also "L'enjeu politique dans les *Mémoires concernant les Chinois* (1776–1791)," *Croisements* 4 (2014), Atelier des cahiers voyages/voisinages, 190–208; and see *Visions de l'Empire du Milieu au 18e siècle en France*.

67. See Georges Bussière, "Henri Bertin et sa famille. Troisième partie. Les Ministères de Bertin, Bertin à la Cour, Bertin chez lui . . .," in *Bulletin du Périgord*, 36 (1909), 159–160. Bussière transcribes the opening paragraphs of the letter, citing the *Fonds Nepveu*, vol. III of Amiot's letters to Bertin. This document is Bib. Inst. Ms 1517, fol. 139 recto: "Ne pouvant le faire en réalité, je le fais en idée et je me trouve déjà dans votre agréable séjour de Chatou." See Constance Bienaimé and Patrick Michel, "Portrait du singulier monsieur Bertin, ministre investi dans les affaires de la Chine," in Rochebrune, *La Chine à Versailles*, 150–177; see esp. 156–157, fig. 6.
68. See the discussion above of the life of Confucius in vol. 12 of the *Mémoires*, published in 1786; it is likely that this is the text to which Amiot refers here.
69. See Bussière, loc. cit.: ". . . dans la partie du milieu ce que nous appelons un *ting*; dans la partie de l'est, votre cabinet particulier ou votre *chou-fang* chinois; et, dans la partie de l'ouest, vous aurez un petit *tso-fang* ou laboratoire, où vous irez, de tems en tems, vous amuser ou vous délasser par quelque travail des mains."
70. The notes on the drawing are a condensed version of the instructions and comments in Amiot's letter.
71. "Le Sage n'est pas un instrument." The citations here and immediately below follow what Amiot wrote on the drawing.
72. See James Legge, trans., *Confucius: Confucian Analects, the Great Learning & the Doctrine of the Mean*, The Chinese Classics, vol. 1 (Oxford: Clarendon Press; reprint, New York: Dover Publications, 1971), 150, *Analects*, Book II, Chap. XII. Legge's comments clarify the broader role of a superior man, that is, a *junzi*.
73. 德政口碑盈四堣. "En prenant la vertu pour règle générale de sa conduite, il érige à sa propre gloire autant de trophées (de Pei) qu'il y a de bouches dans les quatre parties du monde." Amiot, however, mistakes the sense of the characters *koubei* 口碑, which is an expression meaning public sentiment or public praise, since what people say can substitue for the commemorative tablets called *bei*. See *Mathews' Chinese-English Dictionary* 3434.38, p. 511, *k'ou-pei*.
74. 仁壽身承冠一球. "Le *jin* étant en particulier le principal mobile qui le fait agir, il jouit de la récompense qui lui est due, dans le contentement de soi-même, dans une longue vie, et dans l'estime de l'univers entier."
75. Amiot's remarks on the Qianlong emperor appear at the end of his letter, Bib. Inst. Ms 1517, fol. 142 verso.
76. The document, bound in leather with Bertin's arms on the cover, is preserved in the Municipal Archives of the city of Chatou; see www.chatou.fr/La-mairie/Les-archives-municipales, accessed 28 February 2019. A parallel "Atlas de la Seig[nu]rie de Montesson. . .," Bertin's other domain, was also prepared at his orders in 1780. Of approximately the same size as the Chatou volume, it is also bound with Bertin's arms on the cover and is preserved in the Archives Départementales des Yvelines. See www.montesson-histoire.com/montesson_magazine_7.html, accessed 7 March 2019.
77. The title page includes all of Bertin's official titles as well the date of the compilation. See Curmer, *Les Seigneurs de Chatou*, 140–141.
78. Bertin's holdings are listed as "F[eui]lle 71 et 72," that is, sections (or pages) 71 and 72. The Cadastre of 1780, the land registry for Chatou, shows the outline of Bertin's chateau and the Nympheum, although it contains no details of the adjacent gardens; see www.chatou.fr/chatou/ch06-cadastre-C1.asp, accessed 10 September 2015 but no longer accessible; see also Jacques Catinat, *Les Châteaux de Chatou et le nymphée de Soufflot* (Chartres: S.O.S.P., 1974), 106, for a redrawn version of the map.
79. The publications of Le Rouge on Anglo-Chinese gardens are discussed above; note that many of the garden plans illustrated by Le Rouge closely resemble what appears in Bertin's "Atlas Censier."
80. Catinat, *Les Châteaux de Chatou*, 93, reproduces a detail of the plan from the "Atlas Censier," which he labels as the Chinese garden with the *jeu de bague*, and refers to Bertin's, "pavillon chinois," 94–95, without providing any further documentation.
81. See the citation above of Carmontelle's garden at Monceau, n. 38.
82. Bussière, *Bulletin du Périgord*, vol. 36 (1909), 238–239.
83. Catinat, *Les Châteaux de Chatou*, 116–117.

84. The card was published in Chatou by A. Fabre; the postmark reads 12–9–10.
85. John Adams autobiography, part 2, "Travels, and Negotiations," 1777–1778, sheet 26 of 37 [electronic edition]. *Adams Family Papers: An Electronic Archive.* Massachusetts Historical Society. www.masshist.org/digitaladams/, accessed 1 August 2014.
86. Bussière, *Bulletin du Périgord*, vol. 36 (1909), 238–240; see 239, n. 1: (1) *Inventaire partiel imprimé*, in-4° de 8 pages, dated 1907; for Bertin's library, see 240, n. 1, citing a letter of 1826.
87. Ibid., 240: ". . . comme une pagode en miniature à ses collections et ses curiosités chinoises."

Conclusion

After the death of Louis XV on 10 May 1774, Bertin retained his position as a minister of state and served under Louis XVI until circumstances at court and the effective dismantling of his Secretariat led him to offer his resignation on 26 May 1780.[1] To the end of his own life in 1792, Bertin maintained his "Correspondance littéraire" with the French mission in Beijing, and it was clearly his purpose to assemble a collection for the benefit of those who would examine it and learn from what it contained. In his Paris residence he had established a "Cabinet de curiosités chinoises," his unparalleled library and assembly of Chinese objects, texts, and paintings, and these rooms were open to those who were curious to see them. A guidebook published in 1787, intended for "amateurs and foreigners traveling to Paris," described Bertin's holdings:

> Monsieur Bertin's Study . . . is especially rich in rarities from the Indies, and in particular from China. An extensive correspondence which Bertin has maintained for over 20 years with the French [Jesuits] resident in Beijing has provided him the means to acquire that which this country produces that is most curious either in the Arts, or for natural History. . . . But what makes this Study all the more interesting is the considerable collection of Paintings that Bertin has received from China, and which put before our eyes the manners, the customs, the products and the arts of this great Empire which has been up to now so little known to us. Monsieur Bertin takes pleasure not only in allowing his study to be seen but even in making available the different objects to the Savants and Artists who hope to take away some practical value from examining them.[2]

It had been Bertin's intention from the beginning of his contacts with Ko and Yang and the inception of his "Correspondance littéraire" to make the results—both texts and objects—available for study. In a letter to Ko and Yang, dated 18 January 1774, he described in detail what he had already received, including texts and illustrations, and how he hoped that they, and the French Jesuit missionaries, would continue in their efforts to reply to his requests

> because, first, I am determined to have printed every year everything that you send us, so that the public can immediately enjoy the literary resources from which the sciences and the arts could not profit too soon. And second, I have created a study where everything that you send me from China is carefully preserved in order to present them to all those who, having obtained your articles and would be curious to see, compare, and even analyze the originals.[3]

The letter included a list of articles (some referred to as *notices*), translations (such as the *Daxue* and the *Zhongyong*), images, and even albums that had already been received which Bertin hoped to publish in the course of that year.[4] The first volume of the *Mémoires concernant les Chinois*, however, would be published in 1776, and it did not contain all of the material already received. Many documents remained unpublished, while others would be published in later volumes. And all of these texts, however, along with the paintings and other objects that had been sent from China would be accessible to an interested public in Bertin's study—his *cabinet*.

The texts and images that formed the basis of Bertin's "Correspondance littéraire," the exchange of letters and documents with the French Jesuit missionaries in Beijing, and what was published from the very first volumes of the *Mémoires concernant les Chinois* represented the most public aspect of Bertin's goal of presenting an authentic image of China. The Préface to Volume 1 outlined what Bertin hoped France might learn from China and depicted China as an ideal nation ruled by an emperor who himself brought together the most learned men in the sciences and the arts for the benefit of the Chinese people. As testimony of the esteem in which the Qianlong emperor was held, the frontispiece to the volume was his portrait accompanied by a laudatory poem (Figure 5.1). The original design for the portrait, now lost, was painted by the Jesuit Brother Giuseppe Panzi (1734–ca. 1812, arrived in Beijing 1773),[5] who had been sent by the Jesuits specifically to replace Giuseppe Castiglione, the most important of the missionary-artists discussed in Chapter 1, who had died in 1766, and Jean-Denis Attiret, himself also an accomplished artist, who died in 1768. The story of Panzi's portrait of the Qianlong emperor was reported to Bertin by Father Amiot in a letter dated 7 October 1773.[6] The emperor wanted to see a demonstration of Panzi's skills as a painter, and Panzi was given all the time he needed to paint the emperor's portrait. He then made the smaller-scale copy that Amiot sent to Bertin along with four lines of poetry to be included below the painting.[7] This is indeed the poem that appears on the portrait of the emperor in the first volume of the *Mémoires* in 1776:

> Tirelessly engaged in all the various tasks
> Of a Government we admire
> The grandest Potentate there is in the Universe
> Is the greatest Scholar there is in his Empire.[8]

As discussed in Chapter 1, the role of visual images is crucial to the communication of the knowledge sent from China in the publication of the *Mémoires*. Volume 1 included a series of plates illustrating Chinese characters and their presumed connections with Egyptian hieroglyphs, which were also illustrated in engraved plates (*Planches*), and Volume 2 contained some 36 plates that included tables, charts, diagrams, maps, and illustrations—many adapted from Chinese sources. Illustrations of the benevolent imperial response to the flooding of Yanzhou fu accompanying the account of the natural disaster are prominently featured in Volume 9 of the *Mémoires* (1783), and they constitute one of the rare examples of Chinese paintings considered as works of art, a judgment which is discussed later, implying their equivalence to European works of art.[9] Illustrations in subsequent volumes would be more and more sophisticated, evolving toward an increasingly European visual idiom and culminating in the illustrations of the "Life of Confucius" published in Volume 12 in 1786.

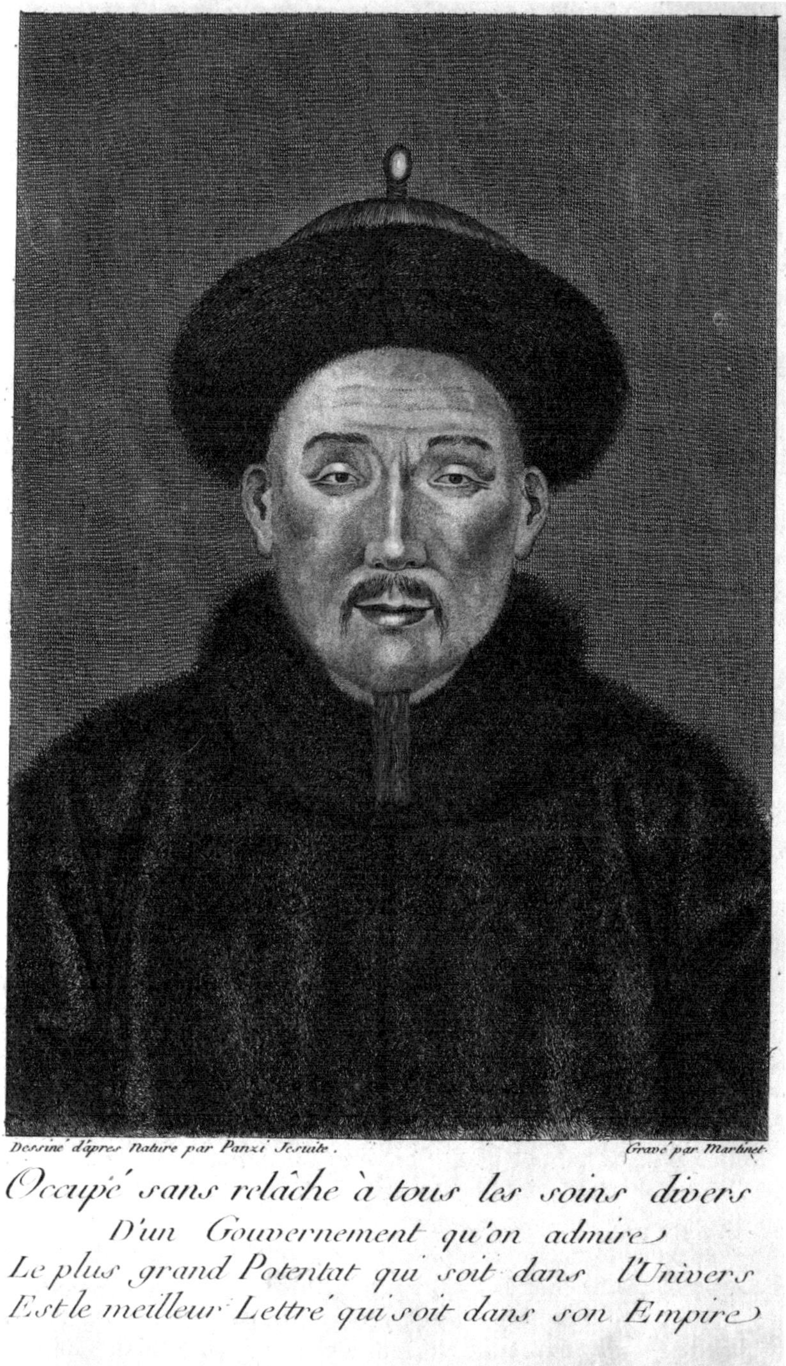

Figure 5.1 Portrait of the Qianlong Emperor, engraved by François Nicolas Martinet (1731–1804), after Giuseppe Panzi, *Mémoires concernant les Chinois*, vol. 1 (1776), frontispiece, engraving, 20 × 12 cm. Getty Research Institute, Los Angeles (41–499).

The Translation of Images

Indeed, the differences between the engravings published in the *Mémoires* depicting the flooding of Yanzhou fu and the images illustrating the life of Confucius, which is discussed in detail in Chapter 4, exemplify the transformation of the style in the illustrations from relatively straightforward copies of the original Chinese sources to transformations of the images—what has been constructively called their "translation" into European visual style.[10] The 18 plates illustrating the life of Confucius were engraved by Isidore-Stanislas Helman, who, in the brief period between 1783 to 1788, would produce an astonishing total of some 72 prints based on Chinese sources or with Chinese themes.[11] Helman added six plates to the 18 published in the *Mémoires*, Volume 12, and published them himself in 1786 in a volume of engravings entitled *Abrégé historique des principaux traits de la Vie de Confucius*, as discussed in Chapter 4. In the *Avertissement* to Volume 12, one section specifically noted Helman's fitness for reproducing the Chinese source:

> II. He [Amiot] has had sent to us more than one hundred Drawings relative to the various circumstances of the life of Confucius; we have used only the most inţeresting, & and we have had them engraved by an Artist who is all the more qualified to grasp & render what characterizes them in that he has worked now for several years on Drawings from China, of which he has successfully published various series.[12]

Helman was a prodigious print-maker and successful publisher who reproduced other Chinese images from Bertin's collection in addition to the life of Confucius. His commercial success in the production and circulation of prints based on Chinese sources is surely relevant to the circulation of the *Mémoires* as illustrated texts, and likewise must have had an influence on the choice of an artist who could reproduce the original Chinese images in a style that would be visually comprehensible to a European audience. Indeed, the choice of Helman as an illustrator and, especially, the cost of the number of figures and the care taken in their engraving forced the publishers to raise the price of this volume of the *Mémoires*, as is indicated in a notice facing the title page.[13]

The French royal porcelain manufacture at Sèvres was part of Bertin's official responsibilities, and a number of the questions he posed to Ko and Yang dealt with details of the Chinese techniques of porcelain production. Characteristically, the search for knowledge of Chinese porcelain was coupled with successful attempts in France to make true hard-paste porcelain (*pâte dure*) with the addition of kaolin, which had recently been discovered in France. Bertin's emulation of Chinese models is perhaps most clearly expressed in the creation of the so-called Vase Japon (the Japan[ese] Vase), a remarkable vessel based directly on the woodblock illustration of an ancient Chinese bronze in the *Xiqing gujian*, the catalogue of the Qing imperial collection of ancient bronzes. The Jesuit missionaries in Beijing had sent Bertin a copy of this superbly illustrated imperial publication, one of a surprising number of such illustrated books that reached eighteenth-century Paris, and we will return to the Vase Japon immediately below.

At least five albums from Bertin's collection either contain the term "Chinese vases" in their titles or illustrate so-called *vases chinois*.[14] An album to which Bertin gave the

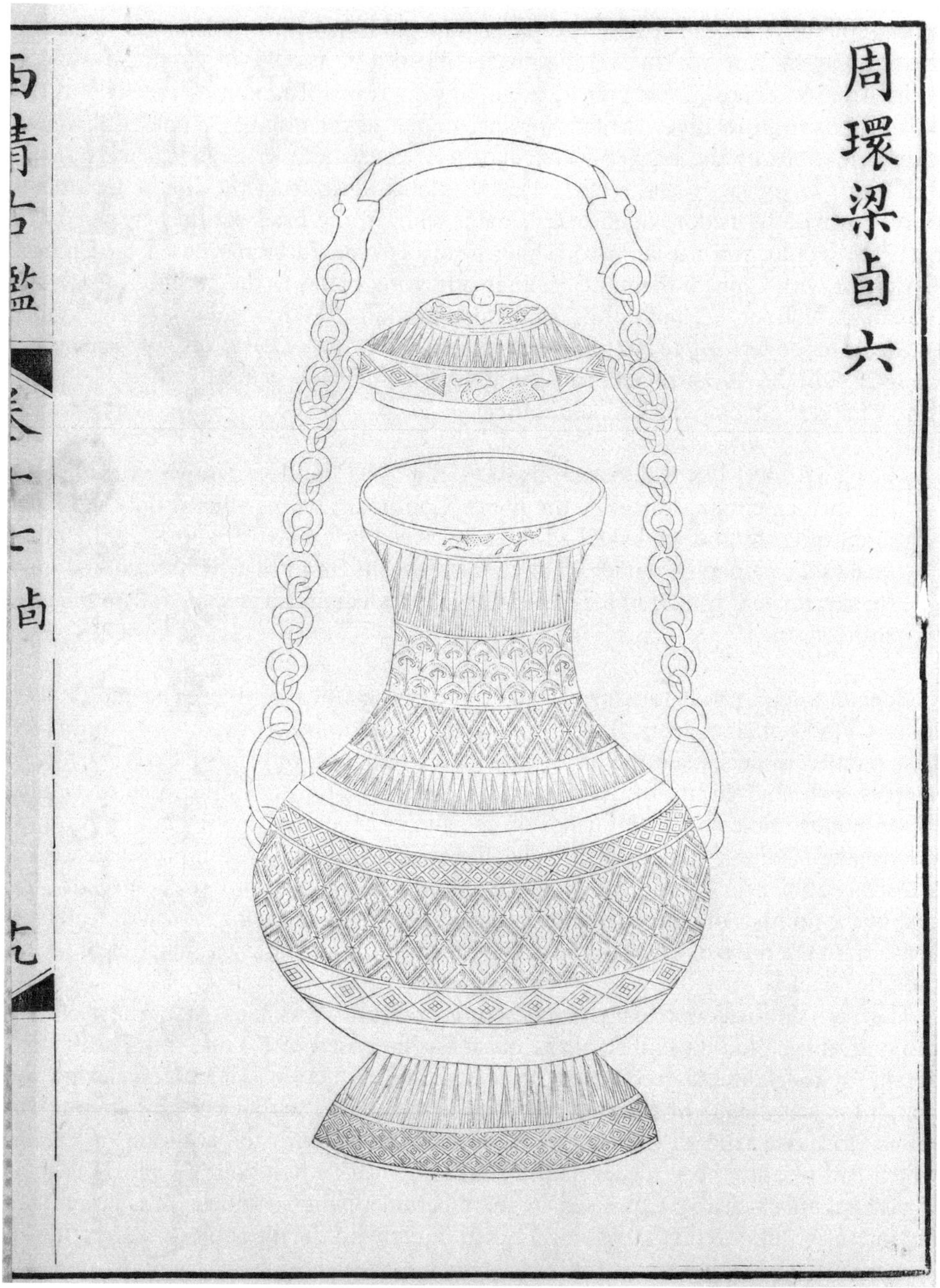

Figure 5.2 *Qinding Xiqing gujian, juan* 17, p. 19, Zhou *huanliang you* no. 6, woodcut, 28.7 × 43.6 cm, 1755. Paris, Bibliothèque nationale de France.

name "Ancient vases and various porcelains from China" (*Vases anciens et diverses porcelaines de Chine*)[15] was accompanied by a text which notes that the paintings were received in 1777, and there is an additional note on the document reading "See the paintings."[16] In speaking of porcelain imitations of ancient bronzes, the Jesuit author, writing about the "Ancient vases" in 1777, made reference to the imitations in porcelain based on ancient Chinese models that Bertin had already ordered to be made in France and how these had pleased the French court. It would be to the advantage of the French porcelain industry to continue in this way, and the writer further states that the Qianlong emperor has also had many porcelains produced in imitation of ancient vessel shapes. The missionary is referring here to a particular episode. In a letter dated January 1774, Bertin wrote to the missionaries in Beijing that there was some confusion in acknowledging the fact that among the books that had previously been sent by Father Amiot were "four magnificent volumes which contain engravings or prints of Chinese vases of the greatest antiquity,"[17] which had probably been received in 1767.[18] The books in question are the volumes of the *Qinding Xiqing gujian* 欽定西清古鑑 (Imperially commissioned investigation of antiquities in the Inner Palace), which is the illustrated catalogue of the Qing imperial collection of ancient bronzes.[19] Commissioned by the Qianlong emperor in 1749 and completed in 1755, the *Xiqing gujian* contains woodblock illustrations of the bronzes in the imperial collections; these are followed by texts describing them. One of the illustrations from the *Xiqing gujian* depicts a vessel entitled "Zhou[-dynasty] ring-handled vessel *you*, no. 6" (Zhou huanliang you 周環梁卣 六) (Figure 5.2).[20] Bertin's letter of 1774 notes his regrets there is no one to interpret the uses of such vases, which he assumes is contained in the text that accompanies each illustration. Then he continues, "I have had produced this year two of these vases in the Royal manufactory; they were very much appreciated by the court, and the King made a present to one of his grandchildren."[21] The two vases which Bertin describes were given the name Vase Japon—a French porcelain based directly on the woodcut in the *Xiqing gujian* (Plate 14). In 1774, Bertin had just been appointed the Commissaire du roi, effectively the director or supervisor of the Royal porcelain manufactory of Sèvres, and he held this administrative position until 1780. The Vase Japon is exceptional in that it differs markedly from the royal manufactory's chinoiserie productions, the form and decorations of which evoke a fanciful vision of China. The Vase Japon represents an attempt by the Sèvres manufactory to produce something that appears authentically Chinese, including even the chain-link handle illustrated in the Qing imperial woodcut, but such direct imitations of ancient vessels were not common practice until the nineteenth century.[22] Bertin's commission for the Vase Japon is truly an extraordinary example of the translation of a Chinese image into a European form.

The Missionaries' Views on Chinese Painting

The reliance of the Jesuit missionaries on visual images—paintings, prints, and drawings—in the transmission of knowledge raises the question of the missionaries' understanding of the long history of Chinese painting and the status of this art form in Chinese culture at large. The subject is discussed in a number of the texts sent to Bertin and in several of the articles published in the *Mémoires concernant les Chinois*, although there is no one specific essay dedicated to this particular aspect of Chinese history. Instead, information on Chinese painting appears in other, related contexts, frequently accompanied by the missionaries' comments on the moral content—or the lack of proper moral content—in the paintings in question.

Paintings produced in Canton for the European market—no doubt the best known, and most frequently the only known examples of Chinese painting in eighteenth-century Europe—are referenced in documents sent to Bertin, which directly link China export paintings from Canton to remarks on the long history of Chinese painting. One especially detailed expression of such connections appears in the text copied into the album of *Plafonds Chinois*, which was discussed in Chapter 3 in the context of Chinese architecture, European trompe-l'oeil painting, and the introduction of European linear perspective in China. This is no doubt one of the earliest documents dealing with Chinese painting sent to Bertin, although a precise date is difficult to determine. The album of *Plafonds Chinois* is part of a group of four volumes illustrating Chinese architecture.[23] A letter from Father Amiot, dated 28 September 1777, refers to one of these titles, the *Essai sur l'architecture chinoise*, which is bound in two albums. However, archival documents dated 3 October 1773 contain the text copied into the albums of the *Essai*, providing the approximate dates between which the text on the *Plafonds Chinois* would have been composed.[24] The two pages of text copied into the album of *Plafonds Chinois*, however, are selected from the original manuscript sent to France, a manuscript that begins with a reference to what is surely the *Essai sur l'architecture chinoise*: "You must have seen in the shipment from last year the exterior and interior form of Chinese buildings."[25] This then dates the composition of the article on *Plafonds Chinois* and the *Essai sur l'architecture chinoise* to approximately the years 1772–1773.

Only a selection from the document appears in the bound album of *Plafonds Chinois*, the text that would be read by those who viewed the album in Bertin's "Cabinet chinois," but it does lay out the context for large-scale paintings that decorate the interiors, specifically the ceilings, of notable Chinese buildings. These statements are followed by remarks on the history of Chinese painting and the assertion that contemporary Chinese painters would not have the skills or the media to produce such monumental painted ceilings—nor the skills to create paintings equivalent to the important models which the European trade has brought to Canton, to the imperial court, and the collections of those who might be interested in such works. However, current European judgments on the lack of talent and taste among the Chinese to produce great paintings are belied by the history of Chinese painting dating back to the references to painters and paintings in the official histories of the dynasties of the Eastern Jin (266–420 CE), the Southern Song (1127–1279), the Han (206 BCE–220 CE) and the Tang (618–907 CE). To counter such opinions that the missionaries have heard, they would instead refer to the information contained in a treatise in 12 volumes that had recently fallen into their hands which entirely refutes these accusations. The text is mostly focused on historical narratives and lists of paintings, the majority of which date to the ninth century with many going back to the third and fourth centuries, but the critical details and observations it contains would surely astonish European readers. It is not clear what text the missionary author is referring to, but it is possible that it is the *Lidai minghua ji* 歷代名畫記 (Record of famous painters of history, completed 847 CE), compiled by Zhang Yenyuan 張彥遠 (active ca. 840–after 874 CE), one of the most important early histories of Chinese painting.[26] The book in 10 *juan* or chapters might have been accompanied by supplemental texts, leading to the Jesuits' description of a book in "12 volumes." The text contains three *juan* on various topics in painting, including a list of 370 famous painters from earliest times to the Tang dynasty, as well as the subjects of paintings, connoisseurship, collecting, and appreciation. It also includes seven *juan* with biographies of the 370 painters, along with lists of titles, from the Jin through the Six Dynasties (220–589 CE) and the Tang. The details of the contents of the *Lidai minghua ji* correspond in many ways to the brief description of the volumes examined by the Jesuit missionary author or authors of the text in the album of *Plafonds Chinois*.

The manuscript text that is the source of the selected commentary in the album of *Plafonds Chinois*, however, continues with a further discussion of Chinese painting, which is not reproduced in the album. The document goes on with a criticism of the present dynasty in the context of the failures of the policies of the Qing government, citing two traditional Chinese texts which remain, unfortunately, impossible to identify, which would support family values and good social order.[27] The blame is placed in part on the bad effects of "illustrations" (most likely a reference to paintings with improper or licentious subjects) by both Chinese and foreign (no doubt European) artists. The author or authors condemn the excessive spending on useless display that such paintings and statues inspire as well as their ill effects on the love of country, conjugal unions, filial piety, and especially social virtues, faith, and religion. They exclaim:

> Alas! How many souls have been corrupted by corrosion from paintings or engravings which natural modesty would have thrown on the fire if the Fame of the brush or the Burin of those who made them and not been an object of curiosity or Commerce.[28]

The comments, which continue in this vein to the end of the manuscript, would not have been as widely read as what was copied into the album, but they anticipate the kinds of moralistic judgments that characterize later texts on Chinese painting sent to Bertin and subsequently published in the *Mémoires concernant les Chinois*. The text ends with the admission that it has moved away from the subject of Chinese painted ceilings:

> But where have we strayed from the subject of two small paintings of Chinese ceilings? Please excuse us this fervor for our love of country and of religion. The history of China makes us fearful for the future of our France if the Wisdom and the example of our good ancestors does not return public opinion back to a taste for the real, the solid, and the useful which alone can provide the abundance and the innocence on which public peace depends. Alas! having come to sacrifice ourselves at the end of the world for Foreigners, what would we not do for our Compatriots?[29]

This is the most fervent expression of such moralistic concerns on the part of the Jesuit missionaries—clearly reflecting their role as proselytizers of the Christian faith—but it is not unique.

Chinese paintings are rarely qualified as "art" in the European sense of the term in the documents sent to Bertin, although there is at least one important exception to this judgment. This was the album of paintings described in Chapter 1 illustrating the flooding of Yanzhou fu in 1742 and the emperor's response in support of the victims of the disaster. The translation of a Chinese commentary and the relatively simple engravings based on the paintings were published in the *Mémoires*, Volume 9 (1783).[30] The album was described as a Chinese manuscript with 16 colored paintings on silk depicting the flooding of Yanzhou fu, 12 of which were chosen for reproduction, accompanied by the explanations of the 12 plates by Amiot, noting especially the gratitude of the Chinese people to their emperor. The album was described as an original work, something a Chinese would purchase in the same way a European would purchase paintings by great masters, as one of the most beautiful parts of his heritage:

> The missionary who had this precious album sent to France informed us that "it is an original work of which there exists no copy; and that in China one who wished to know such things would purchase such a masterpiece as in Europe we purchase the original paintings of the great masters; and that he would leave it to his children as one of the most important parts of his estate; and that his family would rather sell their lands and their homes than relinquish it."[31]

The translation of the original inscription written for the album by a scholar of the Hanlin Academy named Songnan, dated June 1744 and discussed briefly in Chapter 1, reflects on the quality of the paintings as an emblem of the gratitude of the people of Yanzhou fu to the emperor:

> But painting can present to the eyes the history of these events worthy of everlasting memory, making them known throughout the empire and preserving the details for future generations; it is beyond all the efforts of this sublime art to present a faithful image and one which is equal to the truth. Let at least these paintings be an eternal monument to the gratitude of those who have requested them, and inspire in all those who see them the feelings of respect and love for the greatest of Princes with which they are filled![32]

While the paintings are described as not the equivalent of witnessing the actual events, something that is beyond the power of painting, still they provide testimony to history and the actions of a benevolent ruler, a characterization of the emperor of China often echoed in the Jesuits' own texts.

However, the most extensive accounts of the history of Chinese painting are contained in Volume 2 of the *Mémoires*, which appeared in 1777, in the "Remarks" (*Remarques*) refuting the many false assertions about China published by Cornelius de Pauw in 1773.[33] These are discussed in Chapter 2, in reference to the subject of Chinese gardens. The first "Remark" that raises the question of Chinese painting responds to de Pauw's assertion that tea makes Chinese women pale.[34] The Jesuit missionaries question what kind of Chinese women are described here and how they might be portrayed if not by paintings. This leads to the recitation of how the missionary-artists are embarrassed—humiliated—by the traditional depictions of nudity in European painting, which are offensive to Chinese morals. Even in religious images, bare feet and arms, and even the breast partly exposed, must be avoided. One of the missionary-artists states, in a direct quotation,

> The fanciful ideas that fill our heads in the Occident are so insistent on this issue that I would probably still cling to them if the necessity of abandoning them in

our paintings for the Emperor had not opened up my understanding and let [his requirements] take the upper hand.[35]

This is not the only occasion on which the Jesuit missionaries condemn nudity in the European artistic tradition as immoral, evoking the distance between their training and knowledge as artists and their Christian mission.

Another "Remark" countering the assertion that Chinese painters become only what their fathers were—mere "daubers" (*barbouilleurs*)—dismisses the criticism as that of someone who would only know Chinese painting from the decoration on porcelains produced in Canton.[36] But in order to make any informed judgment, one would have to have read the books that teach the theory and rules of painting—books more ancient than those found in Europe—and to have seen the works of the finest masters, and as well to have listened to the opinions of the connoisseurs of Chinese painting. The emperor, the nobility, and others have collections of paintings by great masters, and the scholar-officials of the Hanlin Academy have written works on what is worthy of praise in Chinese painting. Chinese painters are especially skilled in the portrayal of flowers, birds and animals, and landscapes, if perhaps not in figure painting. For court painters, accuracy in rendering flowers and other subjects is the highest value. Painting manuals illustrated with prints in four or five colors are part of a long tradition, which are well in advance of similar European manuals (although they are not identified), and a number of these illustrated texts were to be found in the Jesuit libraries.[37] A subsequent "Remark" responds to an assertion immediately following the previous one by de Pauw, that Chinese painters are badly paid for their work, which raises the subject of reverse painting on glass produced in Canton.[38] Reverse paintings on glass were an important element in the trade in paintings between China and Europe, one that is described in detail in another article from the *Mémoires concernant les Chinois*, which is discussed below. In the present text, such painters are again dismissed as "daubers" producing paintings for European merchants who hope to make great profits from their sale, but the Jesuit authors of the "Remark" turn the discussion to the subject of the enormous prices paid in the past for paintings by great masters, especially of the Yuan and Ming dynasties, although the passion for such paintings has dissipated somewhat in the present Qing dynasty. The historical conditions of Chinese painting are compared to those of Europe, where painting was supposedly reborn three centuries earlier, first in Italy, then France, Flanders, and Germany, and princely galleries or collectors' studios are no longer large enough to hold all of them. This leads again to a moral judgment on painting, that, if an artist has too much competition to distinguish himself by what is "picturesque" or worthy as a subject, he would then turn to subjects that are romantic, cynical, and dissolute in search of financial gain. The same would be true for Chinese painting; the missionary authors, Cibot and Aloïs Ko,[39] wonder what kind of damage such paintings might do in China, which does not have Christian morals to help protect the people from the most seductive and dangerous passions, and they cite as an example the decline and corruption that were embodied in the gradual decline of the Song dynasty, in the tenth, eleventh, and twelfth centuries. Chinese painters are not seen as working in the best interests of the public, of universal abundance, and the innocence of morals, again applying Christian missionary judgments to the practice of painting in general.

De Pauw's assertion that the Chinese did not know the techniques of true fresco painting, which would have been used in the decoration of Buddhist and Daoist temples, leads to a discussion of the history of mural painting, which dates back to the reign of the first emperor, Qin Shi Huangdi (r. 221–210 BCE), and the Eastern Han dynasty (25–220 CE).[40] These included paintings so accurate and naturalistic that they were mistaken for real animals or architecture, an assertion supposedly based on ancient texts that leads to a description of a trompe-l'oeil scene created in the European Palaces of the Yuanming yuan for the Qianlong emperor.[41] The European Palaces were a suite of buildings constructed in a hybrid Sino-European style, set among European-style fountains and gardens; construction probably began in 1747 and was generally complete by 1751. The emperor almost immediately ordered the construction of an extension of the European Palaces, and work on this section began as early as 1753 and was largely complete by 1759. One additional building was added in 1768.[42] The second extension to the European Palaces ended in a monumental garden construction, effectively a trompe-l'oeil European stage set depicting a street in a European town, entitled the Hudong xianfa hua 湖東綫法畫 or "Perspective Painting East of the Lake."[43] The authors of the "Remarks" link the history of Chinese painting to mural painting, to ancient texts, and to the construction in the European Palaces:

> If painting was a subject interesting and useful enough to deserve research, we could send to the West many details that would perhaps better help to understand and explain that they do not do only what is found among the authors on the ancients. The emperor today has in his park [the Yuanming yuan] a European village painted in fresco with scenes that seek to fool the eyes. The wall represents a landscape and hills that end so beautifully, as seen in the mountains that are behind in the far distance, that it is difficult to imagine anything of this type that could be more beautifully designed and executed. Our Chinese painters have completed this fine work according to the designs and under the direction of a *poor grinder of colors*.[44]

The final reference to the Jesuit missionary-artist in charge of the fresco decoration of the "Perspective Painting East of the Lake" as a "poor grinder of colors" is likely an ironic reference to de Pauw's general denigration of painting in China—a surprising comment, perhaps, in a published text, but de Pauw's original book was severely criticized by the Jesuits. The description of the "Perspective Painting" is especially important in the transfer of knowledge of imperial China to Europe given the fact that the European Palaces would be represented in an album of 20 engravings produced for the Qianlong emperor—an album of which copies reached Europe at a surprisingly early date—but which was commissioned in 1783 and not officially completed until 1787, a decade after the description of this remarkable construction was sent to Bertin.[45] The album of the "20 Engravings of the European Palaces" is discussed later in the context of the commensurability of Chinese and European civilization.

Important elements of the history and practice of Chinese painting are contained in additional "Remarks," including comments on the lack of sculpture in ancient China, which is linked to the idolatry of the Chinese.[46] The only other sculptures on a scale comparable to European sculpture known to the missionaries are the statues of officials and soldiers on the avenue and in the halls associated with the Ming imperial tombs northwest of Beijing, sculptures which are effectively invisible to the general public. De Pauw's assertion that the Chinese only like bright colors is countered with the observation that the best Chinese painters use light colors, emphasizing expressive brushwork, the charm of the proportions, and grace of the composition.[47] Such paintings, likened to drawings rendered in ink wash or watercolor by European masters, are created by the literati (referred to as the *Gens des Lettres*), who paint in ink on paper in the same way the great painters of Europe would prepare their drawings. Awareness of the expressive qualities of literati ink painting, of scholar-painters expressing themselves on paper, and of the skill in brushwork such paintings represent surely reflects the missionaries' direct contact with the officials of the Qing court. The criticism of de Pauw's lack of knowledge is summarized at the end of this "Remark," again stating that he is only acquainted with low-quality export paintings from Canton:

> We would have to go on much too long if we put ourselves to raising everything that the Author advances that is false, guesswork, or meaningless concerning our [Chinese] painting, which he seemed to know only by fans or screens from Canton.[48]

In a very different context, in the second part of a history of Chinese characters, published in 1783 in Volume 9 of the *Mémoires*, Cibot links the origins of Chinese characters to paintings, although paintings are limited in that they can only present what the eyes see while characters—writing—can express what the mind alone can distinguish.[49] This history would effectively demonstrate the antiquity of Chinese painting, which is once again judged in moral terms, with Chinese painting described as having retained a decorum and modesty that European painting should emulate, since European painting cannot help but be seduced by nudity, which should never be represented in paintings sent to China. The voluptuous, scandalous, and lascivious contents of European painting are features that must be concealed if the paintings are to be shown to the emperor. However, the role of the Jesuit missionary-artists in the Qing court might indeed prevent Chinese painting from following the path of European art, and the text continues:

> May we be permitted to add here that if genius and good taste could draw Chinese painting out of its languor, then the brothers Castiglione and Attiret would have succeeded by means of the fine works in all genres that they produced for the Emperor. The history of their works and their lives would deserve to be included in that of painting.[50]

Asserting that Castiglione and Attiret might somehow save Chinese painting from the moral failings that the Jesuit missionaries often portray is an exaggeration of their admittedly important role in the production of paintings for the Qing court and the training of court painters in European techniques. However, the position of Castiglione and Attiret in the court workshops is raised in the discussion of a particular kind of Chinese painting well-known in Europe in the later eighteenth century, reverse painting on glass.

One of the "Remarks" discussed earlier introduces the subject of reverse paintings on glass, also referred to as mirror paintings, which are objects of the China export trade that were well-known and widely circulated in late eighteenth-century Europe. As such, they became emblems of Chinese painting in general, and even the Jesuit missionaries' writings use them as key examples of what is good—and bad—about Chinese painting. The technique was originally European, probably developed in Venice and then spread to other countries. It may first have been introduced in China, to workshops in Canton serving the export market, at the time of the Ming-Qing transition.[51] In general, the paintings are rendered in oil colors applied to a sheet of glass, to be viewed through the glass, which obliges the painter to work in reverse order from an ordinary painting: first outlining the final details of the image and then filling in the colors that render the faces and costumes as well as architecture and landscape backgrounds. Alternatively, the paintings were produced on paper, cut out, and then applied face-down to the sheet of glass. Open spaces, such as the sky or water, are silvered—the standard technique for producing European mirrors. For Chinese and European reverse paintings, either the unpainted glass was silvered after the finished image or a pre-prepared mirror had the areas for the painting carefully outlined and the silvering then scraped off, leaving the space to be painted. In Volume 11 of the *Mémoires*, published in 1786, a text by the late Father Cibot (d. 1780) on the "practical arts" of China described Chinese ironwork, paintings produced on pieces of soapstone (used to decorate such things as folding screens), and the art of painting on glass or mirrors.[52]

Cibot's text states that the secret of painting on glass came to China from Europe, and he will give a summary of what the missionary-artists know about the technique. On their arrival in Beijing, they were often sent by the emperor to wait for him in the painting workshop in order to present their own designs as well as to answer questions posed by the court painters, providing ample opportunity to observe imperial workshop practice. The workshop was divided into three large studios along with another space reserved for the European painters, and in one of the Chinese studios were painters from Canton producing reverse-glass paintings for the emperor. In the studios, the Jesuit painters did not closely observe or question the glass painters on their techniques, although they did note their skill, and only spoke to them on occasion in their role as "missionaries." However, the emperor ordered Castiglione and Attiret to paint on a number of large panes of glass (or mirrors—the term is not entirely clear),[53] and they wanted to more closely observe the Canton glass painters, whose skill in working effectively in reverse order from ordinary painting practice they much admired. What follows in Cibot's text is a detailed description of the techniques involved, including first removing the silvered part of the mirror. The Canton painters worked in oil on prepared paper or the kind of silk normally used for painting (referred to as *kiuen*, i.e., *jian* 縑), and there were also those who worked in tempera or watercolors, cutting out the image and applying it face-down on the cleared space on the mirror. The same technique is used for paintings on panes of glass that are silvered after the image has been applied—all of these procedures were described to the missionary-artists, who may not have seen them practiced in person.

But the discussion quickly turns to the European market for reverse paintings on glass, to the small paintings purchased by European merchants for resale at the highest price, and the obscene subjects produced by Chinese painters simply for money:

> The Chinese have only too well succeeded in painting, on both large and small mirrors, the filth and the cynical infamies that have been given to them as models.

> It wasn't sufficient to inspire the talent of true Painters by luring them with gold and silver, it was further necessary to embolden them against the laws of the Empire, to hire them to work in hidden and secret places in order not to expose them and their families; and this was achieved by means of small sums.[54]

Indeed, published reproductions of reverse glass paintings from the China export trade often show images of Chinese women with partly exposed breasts or in what would be considered intimate scenes, and a number of Chinese paintings are based on European prints that depict nudes.[55]

Bertin's particular knowledge of Chinese glass and mirror production is revealed in the context of the gifts he sent to China with Ko and Yang, an international diplomatic episode discussed in Chapter 1.[56] The gifts included a case of 12 very large panes of glass, which were to be silvered as mirrors in China. There was originally some confusion on what the case contained, since Ko and Yang first assumed that the contents, referred to as *glaces*, a term which in eighteenth-century French can mean both a mirror or a pane of glass intended to be made into a mirror, were mirrors.[57] However, Bertin had ordered the glass to be sent to China to be silvered there, since he understood that this process was accomplished much better by the Chinese.[58] Specifically how Bertin knew about this particular artisanal skill in China is unknown, but one goal of the presents was to encourage a Chinese market for European goods. Bertin made an annotation on a document sent to Ko and Yang in 1765, repeating that it would be most beneficial for both France and China if the emperor, the nobles of the court, and the Chinese nation should develop a taste for the arts of France. In the future, they would be sent descriptions of French products and detailed price lists for such things as panes of glass.[59]

"A General Idea of China"

While the Jesuit missionaries' evaluation of Chinese painting was presented in a rather haphazard manner, other subjects were dealt with in more coherent presentations. The published texts aimed to provide a broadly based view of China, some being more focused than others, varying from short notes on very specific subjects to longer treatments in biographical, technical, and historical studies, all ultimately aimed at a comparison between civilizations. The *Avertissement*, the introduction, to Volume 5 of the *Mémoires* announced the first article in this volume, published in 1780, entitled "A General Idea of China and its First Relations with Europe," which consists of an abbreviated history of China, including its revolutions, religion, laws, way of life, and customs, on the premise that it "would be useful and enjoyable for the large number of readers who would thereby be in a better position to compare the subjects that are thus compared, and to judge Europe by China, and China by Europe."[60] The author is anonymous (referred to only as M. **), but he was not one of the Jesuit missionaries in Beijing, and the writer remains unidentified. The article is relatively short, given the scope envisioned by the title, effectively dealing with only a select few subjects divided into three sections. The first part focuses on the narratives of early voyages to China.[61] In an extended description of the knowledge of China brought to Europe by Marco Polo (1254–1324), and with an awareness of the questions raised by his travel accounts, the author cites the beginnings of a long-standing image of China as an empire ruled by a wise monarch. Describing the rule of Kublai Khan as the Shizu emperor (世祖, r. 1260–1294) of the Mongol Yuan dynasty, the writer maintains that "still today, when we speak of China and the way in which this family governed the Empire, we call it *wise government*."[62] Not surprisingly, much of the narrative of early European contacts with China focuses on the arrival of Jesuit missionaries and their initial attempts to use scientific instruments and other valuable European objects as gifts to be presented to the imperial officials at Canton with the hope of achieving access to the imperial court.[63] The "General Idea of China" cites in particular the gifts taken to China by Alessandro Valignano (1539–1606), the Jesuit founder of St. Paul's College in Macao in 1594, including watches, clocks, astronomical quadrants, globes, and mathematical instruments.[64] This practice was well established in diplomatic approaches to Qing China and was followed in the selection and presentation of gifts entrusted by Bertin to Aloys Ko and Étienne Yang for their return journey to China in 1765, which is discussed in Chapter 1.

The second part of the "General Idea" describes the education of the Chinese, their studies in history and other subjects, Chinese morals or customs, filial piety as a fundamental principle of government, the sciences, and Chinese astronomy.[65] The superior qualities of the Chinese system are emphasized a number of times, in statements such as "Of all the models of Government which have come down to us from the ancients, there is none that encompasses as much perfection as the Chinese Monarchy."[66] Part three, the last part of the text, takes up the subjects of the chronology, the history, and the religions of China.[67] The official compilation of detailed memorials and chronological records—with paragraphs dedicated to each of the historical dynasties—testifies implicitly to the European view of China as a nation with a historical record comparable only to that of Europe. Accounts of Chinese religion, however, clearly reflect the prejudices of Christian missionaries, which are shared by the anonymous author, and the description of Buddhism here, directly attributable to the missionaries as in other texts, is particularly dismissive. The section, however, also contains a brief history of Christianity in China, one which deals in some detail with the controversies among the different missions. It ends abruptly with brief notes on Islam in China.

Commensurability, or the Equivalence of Nations

As briefly noted in Chapter 1, Bertin sent plans or maps to China with the Chinese Christian priests Ko and Yang that were intended to be presented to the emperor of China. The maps would show the distance between France and China. Plans of Paris, the Louvre, Versailles, and other royal residences are briefly described in Bertin's "Instructions to Ko and Yang," where he specifically stated that they would present to the emperor an idea of the magnificence of Louis XV:

> The geographical maps that Ko and Yang are taking with them will serve to demonstrate the distance that separates the empire of China from that of France which French shipping is able to traverse in order to maintain commercial trade with the Chinese, the size of China compared with that of France, and with that of the other powers of Europe. The plans of Paris, the Louvre, Versailles, and the other royal houses will give an idea of the magnificence of the King.[68]

The text then continues, directly linking the support for the sciences and the arts maintained by the king of France with the parallel patronage believed to be practiced by the emperor of China:

> The papers on astronomy and geometry that the Royal Academicians have published and which Ko and Yang are [also] bringing with them will make known the special protection that the King gives to the scholarship, sciences and the arts, as does the Emperor of China, for whom they are broadly endorsed.[69]

The text of the "Instruction," as discussed in Chapter 1, ends with an exhortation to Ko and Yang to take every opportunity to demonstrate the correspondence between the French and Chinese national characters that they might observe, given that the two nations can be considered among the most well-ordered and naturally civilized in the world.

Clearly a key issue in Bertin's interest in China was the comparison of China and Europe, in the context of what could be seen as the two great world civilizations. Implicit in the comparison is the equivalence of China and Europe, signaled by the use of *comparer* in relevant texts, which in eighteenth-century usage implies a comparison of equals,[70] beginning with the Préface to Volume 1 of the *Mémoires*:

> If, in the time since China has been sending explanations and details to Europe, they had always been carefully collected and presented to the public more or less as they were, we would be in a better position than we are now to compare the Chinese with ourselves, in relation to the arts, industry, traditions, and government. We would have seen long ago that this nation, so far from us in so many respects, has not been less rich nor less content than we are; that it had perhaps been more so; and we could have drawn this useful result, that a certain middle ground between gross ignorance and the refinements of the sciences and of knowledge is perhaps the element that best suits the human species; and this as well, that the paternal Government, from which the Chinese Emperors have rarely deviated, and of which they are constantly reminded by the general tone of the customs and principles of the Chinese nation, is one that most surely informs the happiness of the people and the true glory of their rulers.[71]

The statement is truly inclusive in the range of subjects to be compared, and it helps to lay out the goals of the publication of the *Mémoires concernant les Chinois* to bring to an educated public the specific knowledge of China from which France could profit.

Many of these objectives had already been laid out a decade earlier in the "Instruction" from Bertin that was to guide Ko and Yang's training before their return to China. As discussed previously, section nine of the "Instruction" reiterates Bertin's hope that what Ko and Yang will have learned in their studies in France can be mutually beneficial to both France and China.[72] On the uses of what they have learned, the text states:

> [B]ut as they would not know themselves how to fulfil everything they need to know to complete these objectives, they must carefully seek to form different connections similar to the knowledge of a different but comparable form that is essential for them to acquire in China to compare with what they have learned in France.[73]

The text here is completed by a long note in Bertin's own handwriting, stating that Ko and Yang should be prepared, too, to collect knowledge of particular things (*objets*) and techniques which they might not have already heard of and which might be lacking in France, that Bertin, in his own words, would be grateful for whatever knowledge they might provide, and that they will "always be provided with instructions on where Europe stands relative to these subjects."[74]

In a very thoughtful article, Greg M. Thomas discusses the ways in which Europeans—and Chinese—presumably only the elites of both nations, viewed each other with a kind of "intercultural curiosity."[75] The French royal palace at Versailles and the Chinese imperial garden-palace, the Yuanming yuan, provided parallels between the two great mid-eighteenth-century nations, and the Yuanming yuan was often referred to as the "Versailles de Pékin." Maps and plans of the palace and gardens of Versailles, like the images of the Yuanming yuan in the Qianlong emperor's album of the "40 Views of the Yuanming yuan," are cited as embodiments of royal or imperial power. The gardens of the original Yuanming yuan were well-known from Attiret's letter of 1743, describing the gardens, a crucial document in the history of gardens that is discussed in Chapter 2. In addition to versions of the "40 Views" sent to Europe in the eighteenth century, one of the sets of the Qianlong imperial album of "20 Engravings of the European Palaces" was also sent to Europe.[76] In 1786, Father Bourgeois, the administrator of the French Jesuit mission in Beijing, had sent a number of Chinese objects and images to Louis-François Delatour (1727–1807), including a set of the prints from the album of the "20 Views of the European Palaces" along with a map of the European Palaces.[77] The map was a kind of schematic diagram of the layout of the European-style constructions and gardens, which are briefly described in Chapter 3. It is labeled with the names of the 20 sites of the European Palaces according to the titles engraved on the "20 Views," and pasted to it is a note in Delatour's handwriting stating that he had received the plan in October 1787.[78] The European Palaces of the Yuanming yuan were depicted in an album of engravings commissioned by the Qianlong emperor, and an early version of the prints, most likely printers' proofs, had been sent to Delatour, who was, among other things, an author, printer and bookseller, and a secretary to Louis XVI after 1779. The project for the engraved album illustrating the Qianlong emperor's European Palaces was begun in 1781 and completed in February 1787, under the supervision of the Manchu court official and artist Ilantai (伊蘭泰, act. ca. 1749–1793), one of the last surviving students of Giuseppe Castiglione.[79] Delatour was a colleague of Henri Bertin, and the two men shared a keen interest in China. Delatour himself also apparently maintained a direct correspondence with the French Jesuit missionaries in Beijing, sending them money for the acquisition of objects, texts, and books, as well as to commission drawings and paintings for his personal collection.[80] Like Bertin, Delatour published a substantial selection of what the missionaries had sent him along with extensive information on Chinese architecture, gardens, medicine, and other subjects in his *Essais sur l'architecture des Chinois, sur leurs jardins, leurs principes de médecine, et leurs moeurs et usages. . . .*[81] Delatour's publication, however, had little of the impact or influence of the *Mémoires concernant les Chinois*, given that it appeared anonymously in 1803, in an edition of only 36 copies.[82] Delatour, nevertheless, published the story of his reception of a set of the "20 Engravings" in the *Essais sur l'architecture des Chinois*, and it is clear from what he wrote that this is the set now in the John Rylands Library, Manchester.[83]

In the *Essais*, in the section on Chinese gardens, Delatour turns to the subject of Chinese greenhouses, *serres chinoises*, which are discussed in detail in Chapter 3.[84] He states specifically at the beginning that his chapter on the subject is taken from Father Cibot's article (*mémoire*) on greenhouses, that is, most likely the manuscript text that was sent to Bertin by Father Bourgeois in 1777 and subsequently published in Volume 3 of the *Mémoires* in 1778.[85] At the end of his chapter, Delatour describes having seen the paintings that comprise the album *Serres chaudes des Chinois et fleurs qu'ils y conservent*, which are also discussed and illustrated in Chapter 3:

> In 1776, we saw in the hands of M. [Charles] Batteux, of the Académie Française, the publisher of the first seven volumes of the *Mémoires* of the French missionaries in Beijing, four drawings of the fine greenhouses of the Emperor, colored with an infinite skill. We should have to call these drawings paintings: they had been sent as gifts by the missionaries to M. Bertin, and would in no way detract from the rich collection of Chinese curiosities that comprise his study.[86]

Bertin's Chinese study, his Chinese collection, is described at the beginning of the present Conclusion. In Delatour's remarks, Charles Batteux (1713–1780) is accurately identified as one of the editors of the *Mémoires concernant les Chinois*, although he apparently makes a mistake on the date when he would have seen the superb paintings of the *Serres chaudes des Chinois*, since the album itself contains a note that it was received in 1777.[87] Delatour continues, describing the paintings as the work of painters of the imperial court and providing extensive detail on the greenhouses and their contents, and, citing a review of the article in Volume 3 of the *Mémoires* in a contemporary journal, emphasizes that the description of Chinese greenhouses provides simple and economical means that characterize the genius of the Chinese people. However, with the somewhat different tastes of Europeans one should not expect to find many Chinese greenhouses in French gardens.[88]

The Dispersal of Bertin's Chinese Collection

Delatour's chapter on Chinese gardens ends with a comment on Bertin's Chinese study, its ultimate fate, and the end of Bertin's life:

> The splendid studio of M. Bertin, formed by the missionaries in China, who had in him a generous and dedicated protector, always ready to seek financial assistance from the government to facilitate their access, and to be useful to the nation, and close to the Nobility of the court and the Sovereign himself, must be considered according to their efforts as Missionaries and men of letters. This studio, which contained so many objects of refinement and curiosity, passed into the hands of others before 1791 by dispersal or by the sale that the former minister, stripped of his pensions and fortune, was forced to make. A foreign land provided him with an asylum where, shortly afterwards, he ended his days.[89]

Bertin was well aware that historical events would lead to the end of the French monarchy; he sold his chateau at Chatou and disposed of other properties, leaving France for Aix-la-Chapelle (the German city of Aachen), most likely in the summer of 1791.[90] He had written to Father Bourgeois in Beijing in January 1790 comparing the unfolding "disaster" in France to the fall of the Roman Empire.[91] Bertin ultimately went to Spa, in Belgium, where he died on 16 September 1792.[92] Significant parts of his collection entered the Bibliothèque nationale in February 1794, confiscated in the course of the nationalization of the possessions of the citizens who had fled France, the so-called *émigrés*.[93] The political process of nationalization, however, was a complex one which began with a decree in September 1792.[94] Under the supervision of the Commission des arts, established on 18 December 1793 and effective until December 1795, works of art and other properties from the possession of the *émigrés* and others were collected, housed in state properties (*dépôts*), and meticulously catalogued.[95] The minutes of the meetings of the Commission des arts were carefully compiled, and transcripts were published in two annotated volumes, providing a detailed record of the paintings and objects seized from Bertin's collection, among many others.[96] The first recorded discussion of Bertin's collection took place on 24 January 1794, in reference to the earliest efforts to examine and inventory Chinese paintings or prints which had been entrusted to "an engraver" in 1785 and 1789.[97] This is surely a reference to works in the hands of Isidore-Stanislas Helman, who reproduced a number of Chinese images after originals in Bertin's collection. Authorization to transport Bertin's Chinese paintings to the Bibliothèque nationale was given on the same day, 24 January.[98] The minutes of the Commission for 28 February 1794 note the official reception of 17 Chinese paintings from Bertin's collection, which had been deposited in the Cabinet des Estampes of the National Library on 14 February 1794.[99] An archival document in the Bibliothèque nationale de France, also bearing the date of 14 February, is entitled "Condition of 17 articles from the émigré Bertin"; it is described as a duplicate of the receipt presented to the Commission des arts.[100] The document consists of two pages, the first listing paintings and albums numbers 1 to 8 and the second listing numbers 9 to 17. A few of these are images that have been discussed in the present volume, including numbers 4 and 5, the *Essai sur l'architecture chinoise*, the two albums discussed in detail in Chapter 3, and number 10, the album of *Serres chaudes des Chinois*, also discussed in Chapter 3. All of the albums and paintings listed here are currently in the BnF.[101] One document is entitled "Condition of the 44 articles mentioned in the preceding piece,"[102] but it is unclear what the preceding document referred to here might be. Another lists pieces from the collection of the émigré Bertin from the deposit (the official collection of the objects) on 14 February 1794, the same date as the list of the aforementioned 17 paintings, but the document, totaling five pages, lists some 98 paintings and scrolls (*rouleaux*), each of which is assigned an estimated value, apparently in view of their being resold, although again this is not clear.[103] A further document is described as a "Note on the Chinese curiosities from the study of Mr. Bertin," and the four pages list another 98 objects, such as paintings, scrolls, including sets of paintings of vases, plans of gardens, and temples, at least one painting that appears to be mounted in Chinese style, and books or albums of paintings, along with letters and articles grouped in notebooks (*cahiers*).[104] Although later notes from the BnF describe this list as a duplicate of the preceding list—and both contain 98 entries—the contents are very different.[105] These various lists merit further study, which would link documents and paintings especially with what we already know from Bertin's collection and help identify other objects whose current location is unknown.

In addition, equally unclear is the status of a large number of objects seized from Bertin's collection, which are also inventoried in a document in the BnF, in the archives of the Cabinet des Médailles, which provides a catalogue of objects for a proposed Museum of Antiques to be housed in the Bibliothèque nationale.[106] The proposal in 1795 for the Museum brought together objects that would now be considered ethnographic for display in direct comparison with the antiquities already in the Cabinet des Médailles, and these included objects seized from Bertin's collections.[107] An early, detailed history of the Muséum des Antiques also refers to the objects seized from Bertin, which had been stored for cataloguing by the Commission des art in the Hôtel de Nesle in Paris.[108] Bertin's Chinese collections added to the very broad range of objects proposed for the Museum.[109] The inventory in the Cabinet des Médailles, which contains four pages, is dated in accordance with 3 September 1797.[110] It includes Chinese scientific and musical instruments, boxes, lacquer objects—a whole range of what would rightly be called "Chinese curiosities." Among these objects, whose locations are not presently known, is no. 10, a "Bâton de Vieillesse" given to Father Amiot by the Qianlong emperor, now in three pieces, which is most likely a *ruyi* 如意 scepter, a ceremonial object often made of precious materials that would indicate the status of the person holding it.[111]

Another object, however, provides more complex links between Bertin's collection and works that may be more precisely identified. It is described in the list in the Cabinet des Médailles as follows: "No. 42. Cup made in the Emperor's workshop. It bears a poem that the emperor made while hunting, under a tree that pleased him; damaged."[112] Kei Il Choi, in a thoughtful and provocative essay, has linked a group of Qing imperial porcelain cups inscribed with a poem by the Qianlong emperor to two specific references to such cups sent to Bertin in the 1760s.[113] Choi has translated this citation: "[no. 4] 2 cups and their covers, on which are poems composed by the Emperor himself, in the 11th year of his reign, and which I have translated into French as best as I could."[114] What is effectively the same listing appears in two places in another list of objects sent from China.[115] Choi correctly points out that one of these cups appears in the catalogue of the first auction sale of objects from Bertin's collection in 1815.[116] The catalogue entry, no. 20, describes a cup with its cover, decorated with three trees in the bottom of the cup, for which the Qianlong emperor wrote verses that are "engraved" (*sic*) on the cup. The entry adds the citation of Amiot's transcription at the end of his translation of *L'Éloge de la Ville de Moukden*, published in 1770.[117] Amiot's translation provides the date for the Qianlong emperor's poem: in the *xiao[yang]chun* 小陽春 month of the *bingyin* 丙寅 year (equivalent to the tenth month of 1746).[118] It is Choi's thesis that the cups had been presented to Amiot by the Qianlong emperor and were then forwarded by the French Jesuit missionary to Bertin, becoming the first Qing imperial porcelains to reach Europe.[119] The cup inventoried to the proposed Muséum des Antiques in the Cabinet des Médailles, the imperial cup seized from Bertin's collection, is indeed described in terms that would appear to identify it as one of the cups sent by Amiot, and it is incidentally described as "damaged" (*mutilée*). However, no specific example of such a Qianlong imperial porcelain cup can apparently be located in a French public collection at present.

According to the Avertissement, the 1815 sale catalogue contains listings for some 500 objects, and the entries provide an astonishing inventory of Bertin's former collection. These include musical instruments such as jade chimes, lacquer boxes, a *bitong* 筆筒 or brush holder, imperial porcelains, objects carved in jade and other hardstones, two sets of the 12 animals of the Chinese zodiac, two "Mandarin scepters" (no doubt the same type as the *baton de vieillesse*, the *ruyi* scepter discussed earlier), and natural specimens, including a sample of kaolin for the manufacture of porcelain accompanied by a note written by Father Amiot,[120] along with many other objects whose very brief descriptions suggest their quality and value. While only a couple of these can be identified with objects in the "Catalogue des objets chinois" seized by the Republican government (such as the "Bâton de Vieillesse" given to Father Amiot by the Qianlong emperor, and the porcelain cup inscribed with the Qianlong emperor's poem), others are nevertheless highly significant parts of Bertin's collection. One is a nine-panel screen decorated with painted stone inlay mounted in hard wood, referred to as *acajou*—mahogany, with the stone described as "steatite" in the sale catalogue.[121] The entry states that it was decorated with different views of the landscape with pagodas, figures, and animals. The screen was supposedly sent to Bertin by the emperor of China, and it is the only example of its kind in Europe. Archival documents provide some of the history of this screen. A letter from Bertin to Ko and Yang, dated 20 January 1767, acknowledges the receipt of a case containing a screen of painted stone.[122] A letter from Étienne Yang, dated 14 November 1765, contains a long description of the screen, which he would send to Bertin.[123] In the center of the scene is a country house or palace (Maison de Campagne) of an emperor named Han, which suggests that the scenes represented on the screen are conventional views of figures and buildings in a garden setting usually entitled "Springtime in the Han Palace." And a letter from Father Cibot, replying to questions in a letter from Bertin received in 1777 provides some additional detail on the screen, which Cibot only vaguely remembers, although Ko and Yang had spoken of it to him at length.[124] The painter was apparently a novice, but he had learned from painters who had worked for the court at Suzhou, although the specific technique had been developed by this particular artist. Like many of the objects associated with Bertin's collection, the present location of this noteworthy screen is unknown.

The section on Chinese manuscripts and paintings in the 1815 catalogue lists two highly important sets of paintings from Bertin's collection. One of these is an album of 105 plates representing the principal events of the life of Confucius, which was sent to Bertin by Father Amiot.[125] This is clearly the album of which 18 images were selected for reproduction in the *Mémoires concernant les Chinois*, Volume 12, to accompany the "Life of Confucius" authored by Amiot, which is discussed previously and in Chapter 4. Another entry in this brief section of the auction catalogue describes in detail a manuscript with 16 colored drawings on silk accompanying the text in Chinese that describes the flooding of *Yen-Tcheou-Fou* (Yanzhou fu), an album which is discussed in Chapter 1.[126] The entry states that the manuscript is accompanied by Amiot's notes and that the paintings were engraved in very small scale in the *Mémoires*, which hardly renders the character of the originals.

Ultimately it is unclear how the contents of Bertin's studio came to be auctioned in 1815. A second auction of works from Bertin's collection took place in 1828, where most notably paintings that had belonged to Bertin were offered alongside works associated with other important figures in the history of European connections with Qing China.[127] Among these were works from the collections of Isaac Titsingh (1745–1812), who led an embassy from Holland to China in 1794 to 1795 under the auspices of the Dutch East India Company,[128] and Andreas Everardus Van Braam Houckgeest (1739–1801), who accompanied the Dutch embassy, during which he made numerous original sketches of China and kept a journal of the voyage, which was later published.[129] The listings for paintings from Bertin's collection, which are introduced with a note emphasizing their quality, which is superior to those imported in the general China trade from Canton, raise questions about what is actually being offered for sale. Number 3 is given the title "Palais et maison d'un oncle de l'empereur Kien-Long, *situés à Pékin*" (Palace and residence of an uncle of the Qianlong emperor in Beijing), presented in a wooden frame at the top of which Bertin had placed an inscription in black on a gold background. However, a Chinese painting from Bertin's collection with the same title, "Palais de l'oncle de Qian Long à Péking," and of approximately the same proportions and size as the painting in the 1828 catalogue, remains in the Bibliothèque nationale de France, where it was acquired as part of the confiscation of Bertin's collection as of 14 February 1794.[130] The framed painting auctioned in 1828 might have been a copy of the original painting in Bertin's collection, but like so many other objects listed for sale at auction from Bertin's collection its identity is not clear. And the fact that so many of these objects and paintings can no longer be located underscores the regret expressed by Delatour at the dispersal of Bertin's incomparable collection.

Amiot's Last Thoughts on Confucius

The Confucian values embodied in Bertin's *cabinet chinois*, the supposedly authentic Chinese-style construction planned for his chateau at Chatou, are discussed in detail in Chapter 4. Bertin's knowledge of Confucius was deeply informed, of course, by the texts sent to him by the missionaries in Beijing, most especially Father Amiot. Much of the detail of the proposed *cabinet chinois* is outlined in Amiot's letter of 16 October 1790, which included a number of objects as well as a diagram for Bertin's Chinese studio at Chatou and fulfilled promises that Amiot had made in a long letter dated just one year earlier, on 10 October 1789. That letter contains Amiot's personal reflections on the life of Confucius, his teachings on morality, his decisive influence in forming the principles of Chinese society, and how these might be received by Bertin himself.[131] Amiot believed that the more Bertin reflected on Confucius' life the more he would see him as a model in opposition to the ignorant prejudices of others, implying perhaps contemporary European prejudices about China in general, although Amiot's reference is not clear. But Amiot realizes that fortunately there are wise men in every age who can see the wisdom of the sages of the past, ideally in transporting themselves to the times or the places where these ancient sages lived. The sentiment echoes Amiot's wish, expressed in the letter of October 1790, that he could transport himself in his imagination to Bertin's *cabinet chinois*, where they might discuss the life of Confucius, among other matters. A posthumous engraved portrait of Amiot, based on a painting by Giuseppe Panzi, is accompanied by inscriptions that celebrate his achievements and character (Figure 5.3). The inscription around the edge of the portrait describes Amiot as a missionary in Beijing, delegated by

> His Most Christian Majesty to the Emperor of China, who appointed him a Mandarin. He translated from the Chinese the History of famous Men and others found in the *Mémoires concernant les Chinois*; he died after 42 year of residence in Peking in 1973, at the age of 74.

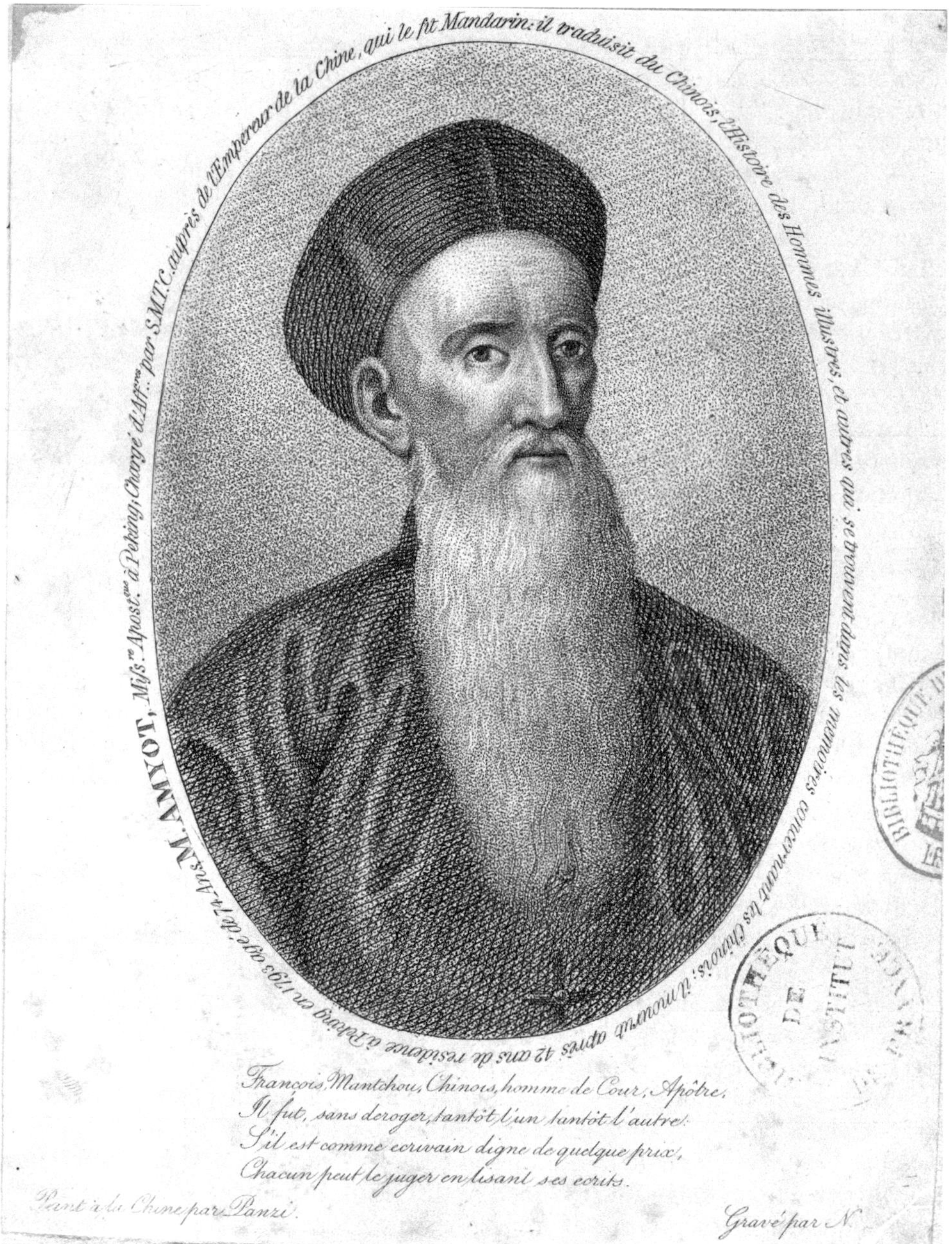

Figure 5.3 Portrait of Jean-Joseph-Marie Amiot, engraved by "N" after a portrait by Giuseppe Panzi, ca. 1790. Paris, Bibliothèque de l'Institut de France, Ms 1522, fol. II.

Source: Photo ©RMN-Grand Palais (Institut de France)/Stéphane Maréchalle.

And the four lines below the portrait celebrate him as:

> French, Manchu, Chinese, man of the Court, Apostle
> He was, without fail, either one or the other
> If he is a writer who merits a certain value,
> Each may judge him in reading his writings.[132]

In reflecting on Confucius' "humanism," Amiot distinguishes his teachings from what would be characterized as religious beliefs and puts them into a moral context, in statements that reflect his deep understanding of Confucian principles apart from any particular religious judgment. He sees Confucius motivated not by a specifically mystical relationship with *Tian* (天, Heaven) but as an agent of this concept of Heaven who should bring men back to the observation of *Li* 禮, a Confucian term that can be translated as "ritual" as well as "principle" or "propriety" in the sense of proper personal conduct.[133] Confucius is described by Amiot as an ideal for Bertin in finding happiness in the present life:

> It is more than likely that it is only that portion of happiness to which one can aspire in the course of their mortal life on earth, and that it is up to the justice and goodness of Heaven to reward or punish them in another life, depending on whether they deserve one or the other. For this reason, [Confucius] preferred the path of education that instructs and directs, and of the example that persuades, to the path of laws that order or forbid. Moreover, nothing is exalted in him: he proposes, he directs, he instructs, he exhorts, he acts; but always with discretion, and without passion, etc.[134]

Bertin would have received this letter at the end of his time in France, perhaps just before he sold his estates and left for Aix-la-Chapelle in the summer of 1791. In the publication of the *Mémoires concernant les Chinois* and in the presentation of his unsurpassed Chinese collections, Bertin embodied the ideals that Amiot attributed to Confucius. In this he was truly a pioneer in the encounters and exchanges between China and Europe in the eighteenth century.

Notes

1. Silvestre de Sacy, *Sillage*, Chap. XIII, "La Retraite à Chatou (1780–1792)," 149–155.
2. Luc-Vincent Thiéry, *Guide des amateurs et des étrangers voyageurs à Paris, ou Description raisonnée de cette ville, de sa banlieue et de tout ce qu'elles contiennent de remarquable*, 2 vols. (Paris: Hardouin et Gattey, 1787). See vol. 1, 134–136: "Le Cabinet de M. Bertin . . . est riche sur-tout en raretés des Indes, & particulièrement de la Chine. Une correspondance suivie que M. Bertin entretient depuis plus de vingt ans avec des François résidens à Pékin lui a facilité les moyens de se procurer ce que ce pays produit de plus curieux & de plus intéressant, soit dans les Arts, soit pour l'Histoire naturelle. . . . Mais ce qui rend encore ce Cabinet plus intéressant c'est la collection considérable des Peintures que M. Bertin a reçues de la Chine, & qui mettent sous les yeux les moeurs, les usages, les productions & les arts de ce grand Empire, qui nous est jusqu'à présent si peu connu. M. Bertin se fait un plaisir non-seulement de laisser voir ce Cabinet, mais même d'en communiquer les différens objets aux Savans & aux Artistes qui espèrent retirer quelque utilité de leur examen." The two volumes contain numerous descriptions of "cabinets" which held works of art, natural specimens, and the other collections. I would like to

thank Vincent Droguet, Director of Heritage and the Collections at the Château de Fontainebleau, for bringing this important source to my attention.

3. Bib. Inst. Ms 1522, fol. 54 recto: "puisque je suis déterminé premièrement à faire imprimer chaque année tout ce que vous nous envoyés, afin que le public joüisse sur le champs des richesses littéraires dont les sciences et les arts ne sauroient profiter trop tôt. Secondement j'ai formé un cabinet ou tout ce que vous m'envoyés de la Chine est conservé prétieusement pour en donner communication à tout ceux qui ayant aquis vos mémoires et seront curieux de voir, de comparer, d'analyser même les originaux." Part of this text is cited in Bienaimé and Michel, "Portrait du singulier monsieur Bertin," in de Rochebrune and others, *La Chine à Versailles*, 155–156, n. 30, on the formation of Bertin's *Cabinet chinois*. My thanks to Philippe Pons, Centre de recherche sur les civilisations de l'Asie orientale (CRCAO), for making the entire document available to me.
4. Bib. Inst. Ms 1522, fols. 58 verso–60 recto.
5. Panzi's dates are given in slightly different form in different sources. The information here follows Dehergne, *Répertoire*, p. 194, noting that Panzi was born in Florence, 2 May 1734, arrived in China in 1771 and Beijing in 1773, and died in Beijing before 1812. French documents from the period refer to him as Joseph Panzi. Paul Pelliot reconstructed Panzi's Chinese name from the transcription *Pan-ting-tchang* in the *Lettres Édifiantes*, Édition du Panthéon Littéraire, vol. IV, passim., which Pelliot assumes is P'an T'ing-tchang (Pan Tingzhang) 潘廷璋; see "Les 'Conquêtes de l'Empereur de la Chine'," *T'oung Pao* 1921, 187–188, n. 1; Pelliot here notes that other sources, e.g., Henri Cordier, mistakenly cite the name P'an Jo-chö (Pan Ruose) 潘若瑟.
6. Bib. Inst. Ms 1515, see esp. fols. 20 verso–21 verso.
7. Panzi's design was reproduced in two forms at the royal manufactory at Sèvres, as an overglaze enamel painting on a porcelain plaque and as a full-figure unglazed portrait sculpture. See Kee Il Choi, Jr., "*Portraits of Virtue*: Henri-Léonard Bertin, Joseph Amiot and the 'Great Man' of China," *Transactions of the Oriental Ceramic Society* 80 (2015–16), 49–65. My thanks to Kee Il Choi for providing a copy of this article.
8. *Mémoires*, vol. 1 (1776), frontispiece: "Occupé sans relâche à tous les soins divers / D'un Gouvernement qu'on admire / Le plus grand Potentat qui soit dans l'Univers / Est le meilleur Lettré qui soit dans son Empire."
9. See the discussion of the flooding of Yanzhou fu in Chap. 1.
10. See Chap. 4, n. 66, for references to Chao-Ying Lee's thoughtful and informative publications on this visual conversion. References and lists of the plates (*planches*) in the individual volumes of the *Mémoires* are found in Dehergne, "Grande Collection."
11. On Helman's many illustrations of Chinese subjects, see Niklas Leverenz, "Isidore-Stanislas Helman and J. Pélicier," *Print Quarterly* 37, no. 1 (2020), "Notes," 75–76. Helman produced many images of events associated with the French Revolution; see BnF, https://catalogue.bnf.fr/ark:/12148/cb149542077, accessed 29 September 2019, which includes links to some 340 images; the website also gives the date of his death as 1806 or 1809.
12. *Mémoires*, vol. 12, *Avertissement*, iii: "II. Il nous a fait passer plus de cent Dessins relatifs aux diverses circonstances de la vie de Confucius; nous n'avons employé que les plus intéressans, & nous les avons fait graver par un Artiste d'autant plus propre à saisir & à rendre ce qui les caractérise, qu'il travaille depuis plusieurs années fur des Dessins de Chine, dont il a publié des suites avec succès." All of the plates include Helman's signature, "Helman sculp[sit]" (engraved by Helman), at the bottom right-hand corner of the plate. See also the discussion of Helman's illustrations in Chap. 4.
13. *Mémoires*, vol. 12: "*AVIS*. On a été obligé d'augmenter le prix de ce Volume, à cause du grand nombre de Figures qui y sont insérées, & des soins qu'il a fallu apporter à leur gravure."
14. On the albums, see Kee Il Choi, Jr., "Ancien vs Antique: Henri-Léonard Bertin's Albums of the Qianlong Emperor's 'Vases Chinois'," *Journal18*, no. 6, "Albums" (Fall 2018), www.journal18.org/issue6/ancien-vs-antique-henri-leonard-bertins-albums-of-the-qianlong-emperors-vases-chinois/, accessed 3 October 2019.
15. *Recueil. Vases anciens et diverses porcelaines de Chine*. BnF, Département des Estampes et de la photographie, Réserve OE-42-PET FOL.
16. The text is recorded in both Bréquigny 123, fols. 213–214, and Bréquigny 126, fols. 96–99; both versions include the date 1777.

17. Bib. Inst. Ms 1522, fols. 57–58: "4 volumes magnifiques qui contiennent les gravures ou impressions des vases chinois de la plus haute antiquité."
18. The information appears in a list of the contents of crates sent to Bertin in 1767, which appears to have been compiled some time after that date. See Bib. Inst. Ms 1524, fols. 130, 133.
19. On Bertin's copy of the *Xiqing gujian*, now in the BnF, see Monique Cohen and Nathalie Monnet, *Impressions de Chine* (Paris: Bibliothèque nationale de France, 1992), cat. 86; see also Nathalie Monnet, *Chine: l'Empire du trait*, cat. 99, *Qinding Xiqing gujian*, 1755.
20. *Xiqing gujian, juan* 17, p. 19, Zhou *huanliang you* no. 6.
21. Bib. Inst. Ms 1522, letter to Ko and Yang, fol. 57 verso: "J'ai fait exécuter cette année deux de ces vases dans la manufacture du Roy, ils ont été très goutés à la cour et le Roy en a fait présent à l'un de ses petits fils."
22. See Charlotte Vignon's remarks cited in the archived press release from the Frick Collection, first published in 2011, www.frick.org/sites/default/files/pdf/press/Fall2011NewAcquisitionsRelease_Archived.pdf, accessed 3 October 2019, which are the source for many of the details here. The Vase Japon is illustrated and discussed at length in Kristel Smentek, "China and Greco-Roman Antiquity: Overture to a Study of the Vase in Eighteenth-Century France," *Journal18*, no. 1, "Multilayered" (Spring 2016), www.journal18.org/issue1/china-and-greco-roman-antiquity-overture-to-a-study-of-the-vase-in-eighteenth-century-france/, accessed 3 October 2019. In addition to the examples of the Vase Japon produced in 1774, Smentek refers to an order from Bertin in 1785, in which he wanted two additional examples, possibly with a variant decoration imitating metal vessels, to send to the emperor of China; see Smentek, "China and Greco-Roman Antiquity," 4, nos. 20–24.
23. Inscriptions in the albums themselves also support the connections among them. See Chap. 3, n. 61, for the links between the four albums; see also the discussion of their contents.
24. See Chap. 3, n. 87, for the reference to Fonds Bréquigny 126, fols. 19–22. On fol. 17, the last page of the first section on architecture is the date: "a pe-king ce 3. oct. 1773." What is apparently the identical text also appears in BnF Fonds Bréquigny 123, fols. 221–223.
25. BnF Fonds Bréquigny 123, fol. 221 recto: "On a dû voir dans l'envoi de l'année dernière la forme extérieure et intérieure des Bâtiments Chinois."
26. For a concise description of the book and its contents, see Hin-cheung Lovell and John C. Ferguson, *An Annotated Bibliography of Chinese Painting Catalogues and Related Texts*, Michigan Papers in Chinese Studies 16 (Ann Arbor: University of Michigan, 1973), 99–101.
27. BnF Fonds Bréquigny 123, fol. 223 recto, while the handwriting is sometimes difficult to read, refers to the names or titles as He-Le-Sieou, Ha-La-Tchi, and Hiao Tchang (all underlined in the original).
28. BnF Fonds Bréquigny 123, fol. 223 verso (capitalization as in the original manuscript): "Hélas! combien d'ames ont été gangrenées de l'usure par des peintures et des gravures que la pudeur naturelle eut fait jetter dans les flames si la Célébrité du pinceau ou du Burin qui les avoit faites n'en avoit pas fait un objet de curiosité ou de Commerce."
29. BnF Fonds Bréquigny 123, fol. 223 verso: "mais où nous égarons nous à propos des deux petites peintures de plafonds Chinois? qu'on nous pardonne cette follie à notre amour pour la patrie et pour la religion. l'histoire de la Chine nous effraye sur les avenirs que se prépare notre France si la Sagesse et l'exemple de nos bons ayeux ne ramenent pas les idées publiques vers le goût du vrai, du solide, de l'utile qui peuvent seuls procurer l'abondace et l'innocence dont dépend la tranquilité publique. Hélas! nous étant venus sacrifier au bout du monde pour des Etrangers que ne ferions-nous pas pour nos Compatriotes?"
30. *Mémoires*, vol. 9 (1783), 454–470, followed by the twelve plates chosen for reproduction. See Lee Chao-Ying, 'L'enjeu politique', 89–92.
31. Ibid., 454: "Le Missionnaire qui a fait passer en France ce recueil précieux, avertit que 'c'est une pièce originale dont il n'existe point de copie; qu'en Chine un curieux acheteroit un pareil monument, comme on achète en Europe les tableaux originaux des plus grands maîtres; qu'il le laisseroit à ses enfans, comme une des plus belles portions de son héritage; & que sa famille vendroit plutôt ses terres & ses maisons que de s'en dessaisir.'" This is followed by a reference to what is also said about the paintings on p. 458.

32. Ibid., p. 458: "Mais si la peinture peut raconter aux yeux l'histoire de ces faits dignes d'un éternel souvenir, les faire connoître à tout l'Empire & en conserver les détails aux races futures; il est au-dessus de tous les efforts de cet art sublime d'en présenter une image fidelle & qui égale la vérité. Puissent au moins ces peintures être un monument eternel de la reconnoissance de ceux qui les ont demandées, & inspirer à tous ceux qui les verront, les sentimens de respect & d'amour dont ils sont pénétrés pour le meilleur des Princes!"
33. *Mémoires*, vol. 2 (1777), 365–574, "Remarques sur un Écrit de M. P**. . .," a text dated 27 July 1775 which severely criticized de Pauw's *Recherches philosophiques sur les Egyptiens et les Chinois.*
34. Ibid., 426–428, XXXIIIe REM.
35. Ibid., 427, italics in the original: "*Les idées pittoresques dont on nous remplit la tête en Occident sont si folles sur cet article, que j'y tiendrois encore probablement, si la nécissité de les abandonner, dans nos peitures pour l'Empereur, n'avoit pas mis ma raison au large, & ne lui avoit pas fait prendre le dessus.*"
36. Ibid., XLe REM., 436–439, countering a claim made in de Pauw's original text covering all "Oriental" art, Section IV, "De l'état de la peinture & de la sculpture chez les Égyptiens & les Chinois & tous les Orientaux en général."
37. One likely source for the titles referred to here would be Verhaeren and others, *Catalogue de la Bibliothèque du Pé-T'ang.*
38. Mémoires, vol. 2 (1777), XLIIe REM., 442–445.
39. Dehergne, "Grande Collection," 274, names Cibot and Ko as the authors of the "Remarques," citing a letter from Bertin to Cibot, dated 30 September 1777, and the text of the "Remarques," 365; as well as citing Louis Pfister, *Notices biographiques et bibliographiques sur les Jésuites de L'ancienne Mission de Chine, 1552–1773* (Shanghai: Imprimerie de la Mission catholique, 1932, 1934), no. 924, n. 3.
40. *Mémoires*, vol. 2, XLIXe REM., 459–460.
41. See the discussion of the introduction of European linear perspective in China in Chap. 3 in the context of the creation of trompe-l'oeil painted ceilings.
42. This was the Yuanyingguan 遠瀛觀, the View of Distant Seas, which was constructed to house a set of Beauvais tapestries presented to the emperor by Louis XV. The tapestries had arrived in China in 1766 but were delayed at customs by the governor of Canton, where they became part of the maneuvering between the Jesuits at Beijing and the imperial government. See Henri Cordier, "Les Correspondants de Bertin, VII, Michel Benoist," *T'oung Pao*, 2e série, 18 (1917), 303 ff. The Yuanyingguan also held numerous other European objects in the Qianlong emperor's collection. See George R. Loehr, "The Sinicization of Missionary Artists and Their Work at the Manchu Court during the Eighteenth Century," *Cahiers d'histoire mondiale* 7, no. 4 (1963), 795–816; see esp. 812–813. Louis-François Delatour, *Essais sur l'architecture des Chinois, sur leurs jardins, leurs principes de médecine, et leurs moeurs et usages . . .* (Paris: Impr. de Clousier, 1803), 165, notes that a building had recently been built for the set of "Gobelin" (*sic*) tapestries sent by Louis XV in 1767, housed in a room 70 feet long, filled with "machines."
43. See Finlay, "The Qianlong Emperor's Western Vistas"; esp. 163–168.
44. *Mémoires concernant les Chinois*, vol. 2, 459–460, italics in the original: "Si la peinture etoit un sujet assez intéressant & assez utile pour mériter des recherches, nous pourrions envoyer en Occident bien des détails qui aideroient peut-être à mieux entendre & à mieux expliquer qu'on ne fait ce qu'on trouve dans les Auteurs sur celle des Anciens. L'Empereur a actuellement dans son parc un village européen peint à fresque & en scènes, de manière à tromper les yeux. La muraille représente un paysage & des collines qui se terminent si heureusement au point de vue des montagnes éloignées qui sont derrière, qu'il est difficile d'imaginer rien en ce genre de plus heureusement inventé & exécuté. Nos peintres Chinois ont exécuté ce bel ouvrage d'après les dessins & sous la direction d'un *misérable broyeur de couleurs.*"
45. On versions of the "20 Engravings of the European Palaces" and their arrival in Europe, see Finlay, "Henri Bertin (1720–1792) and Images of the Yuanmingyuan in Eighteenth-century France," 129–131.
46. *Mémoires*, vol. 2, L^e^ REM., 460–461.
47. Ibid., LXVIe REM., 488–489.

48. Ibid., 489: "Nous en aurions trop long à dire, si nous nous mettions à relever tout ce que l'Auteur avance de faux, de hasardé & d'inconséquent sur notre peinture, qu'il ne paroît connoître que par des éventails ou des paravents de Canton."
49. *Mémoires*, vol. 9 (1783), "Essai sur la langue et les caractères des Chinois," 282–430; the remarks discussed here are contained in note 16 on pp. 363–364, referring to p. 296 of the text.
50. Ibid., 364: "Qu'on nous permette d'ajouter ici que si le génie & le bon goût pouvoient tirer la peinture chinoise de sa langueur, les frères Castiglioné & Attiret y auroient réussi par les belle choses en tout genre qu'ils ont faites pour l'Empereur. L'histoire de leurs ouvrages & de leur vie mériteroit d'entrer dans celle de la peinture."
51. For basic introductions to reverse painting on glass, also called "back-painting" as well as mirror painting, see Margaret Jourdain and R. Soame Jenyns, *Chinese Export Art in the Eighteenth Century* (Feltham, Middlesex: Country Life Ltd., 1950; reprint, Spring Books, 1967), esp. Chap. III, "Paintings on Glass," 33–39, figs. 53–66; and Emily Byrne Curtis, *Glass Exchange between Europe and China, 1550–1800: Diplomatic, Mercantile and Technological Interactions* (Farnham, Surrey, and Burlington: Ashgate, 2009), Chap. 4, "Panes of Glass: Windows and Paintings," 41–55; see esp. "Reverse Glass Paintings," 50–52.
52. *Mémoires*, vol. 11 (1786), "Diverses remarques de feu M. Cibot, missionnaire à Péking, sur les arts-pratiques en Chine," 361–370; see no. II. *De l'art de peindre sur les glaces*, 363–366.
53. The term *glace* in eighteenth-century French can mean both a mirror as well as a pane of clear glass; see n. 57 below.
54. *Mémoires*, vo. 11, 365–366: "Les Chinois n'ont que trop bien réussi à peindre, sur de grandes & de petites glaces, les saletés & les infames cyniques dont on leur avoit donné des modeles. Il ne suffisoit pas d'exciter le talent des vrais Peintres par l'appât de l'or & de l'argent, il falloit encore les enhardir contre les loix de l'Empire, les engager à travailler dans des lieux cachés & inconnus, pour ne pas exposer leurs personnes & leurs familles; & l'on en est venu à bout à force des piastres." This text is also referenced in Jourdain and Jenyns, *Chinese Export Art*, 38, n. 1, although the page number cited and the attribution to Amiot are incorrect.
55. See Jourdain and Jenyns, *Chinese Export Art*, figs. 53–68, for a representative selection.
56. See also Finlay, "Henri Bertin and the *Présents* from Louis XV to the Qianlong Emperor."
57. Dictionnaire Littré online, http://littre.reverso.net/dictionnaire-francais/: *glace*, [10] Plaques de verre, de cristal dont on fait des miroirs. Couler une glace. Étamer une glace. Il se dit particulièrement des miroirs de grande dimension.
58. A letter from Bertin to Ko and Yang, dated 16 January 1765, details his "Instruction pour Mr. Ko et Mr. Yang" on what they should do with the gifts that the King of France had ordered delivered to them to take back to their homeland. Bib. Inst. MS 1521: fols. 60–71; see also the notes in Bertin's handwriting in the margins of this document.
59. Ibid.: fol. 62 verso.
60. *Mémoires*, vol. 5 (1780), *Avertissement*, n.p.: "Ce cinquième Volume des *Mémoires* sur les Chinois, contient, 1°. une *Idée générale de la Chine, & de ses premières relations avec l'Europe*. On a pensé qu'une exposition abrégée de l'Histoire de la Chine, de ses révolutions, de sa Religion, de ses Loix, de ses mœurs, de ses usages, &c. seroit utile & agréable au grand nombre des Lecteurs qui par-là seront plus en état de faire la comparaison des objets ainsi rapprochés, & de juger l'Europe par la Chine & la Chine par l'Europe. Ce morceau n'a point été envoyé de Pékin: c'est l'ouvrage de M. **." The article appears on pp. 1–68. Note that nothing in the Table Générale des Matières, vol. 10 (1784), indicates who the author might be; and there is no reference in Dehergne, "Une grande collection."
61. Ibid., "Première Partie," *Extraits des Voyages faits à la Chine*, 1–25.
62. Ibid., 6: ". . . encore aujourd'hui, lorsqu'on parle à la Chine de la manière dont cette famille gouverna l'Empire, on l'appelle *le sage gouvernement*." The voyages, discoveries, and accounts of Marco Polo are described on pp. 4–10 and referenced on subsequent pages.
63. The text cites the establishment of a Jesuit mission at Macao in 1573, under the reign of the Ming Wanli emperor (萬曆, r. 1572–1620), giving his name inexplicably as *Chin-tsong II*; ibid., 15–16.

64. Ibid.: "Le Père Valignan eut soin de se procurer des curiosités de l'Europe, comme des montres, des horloges, des quarts de cercle, des globes, toutes sortes d'instrumens de mathématiques, & autres choses de prix, afin de les présenter au Mandarins de Canton, & de les engager de les faire recevoir favorablement à la Cour de Pékin."
65. Ibid., 25–45, "Seconde Partie," *Education, Etudes, Mœurs, Gouvernement, Sciences & Astronomie des Chinois.*
66. Ibid., 32: "De tous les modèles du Gouvernement qui nous sont venus des anciens, il n'en est aucun qui renferme autant de perfection que la Monarchie Chinoise."
67. Ibid., 45–68, "Troisième Partie," *De la Chronologie, de l'Histoire & des Religions de la Chine.*
68. Bib. Inst. Ms 1521, fol. 71 verso, end of "Instruction" section no. IX: "Les cartes géographiques que le Sr. Ko et le Sr. Yang emportent avec eux leur serviront à démontrer la distance qui sépare l'empire de la Chine de celuy de la France et que la navigation françoise sçait franchir pour entretenir un commerce avec les Chinois, la grandeur de la Chine comparée avec celle de la France et avec celle des autres puissances de l'Europe, les plans de Paris, du Louvre, de Versailles et des autres maisons royales donneront une idée de la magnificence du Roy."
69. Ibid.: "Les mémoires d'astronomie et de géométrie que les académiciens du Roy on publié et qu'ils que les Srs. Ko et Yang emportent feront connoitre la protection particulière que le Roy accorde aux lettres, aux sciences et aux arts, comme l'empereur de la Chine auprès duquel ils sont en grande recommandation."
70. See the Dictionnaire Littré online, http://littre.reverso.net/dictionnaire-francais/: *comparer*.
71. *Mémoires*, vol. 1 (1776), *Préface*, xiii–xiv: "Si depuis que la Chine envoie en Europe des observations & des faits, on les eût toujours recueillis soigneusement, & donnés au public à peu près tels qu'ils étoient, nous serions plus en état que nous ne le sommes de comparer les Chinois avec nous, quant aux Arts, à l'Industrie aux Mœurs, au Gouvernement. Nous aurions vu il y a long-tems que cette Nation, éloignée de nous à tant d'égards, n'a pas été moins riche, ni moins heureuse que nous; qu'elle l'a peut-être été davantage: & nous aurions pu en tirer cette conséquence utile, Qu'un certain milieu entre la grossière ignorance & les rafinemens des Sciences & du Goût est peut-être l'élément qui convient le mieux à l'espèce humaine: & celle-ci encore, Que le Gouvernement paternel, dont les Empereurs Chinois se sont rarement écartés, & où ils sont rappellés sans cesse par le ton général des mœurs & des principes de la Nation Chinoise, est celui de tous qui produit le plus sûrement le bonheur des Peuples & la vraie gloire des Souverains."
72. See Chap. 1, n. 62; the text in question is found in Bib. Inst. Ms 1521, fols. 66 verso—69 verso.
73. Bib. Inst. Ms 1521, section IX, fols. 66 verso—67 verso: "mais comme ils ne sauroient suffire d'eux-mêmes à la connoissance de tout ce qui leur est nécessaire pour remplir ces objets, ils doivent chercher soigneusement à former des liaisons différentes et analogues aux connoissances de différente espèce qu'il leur est essentiel d'acquérir à la Chine pour les comparer avec celle qu'ils on pris en France."
74. Bib. Inst. Ms 1521, fol. 67 recto: ". . . on leur fera les instructions toujours de l'état ou en est l'Europe relativement à ces mêmes objets."
75. Greg M. Thomas, "Yuanming yuan/Versailles: Intercultural Interactions between Chinese and European Palace Cultures," *Art History* 32, no. 1 (February 2009), 115–143.
76. Ibid., 129–130; see also Finlay, "Henri Bertin (1720–1792) and Images of the Yuanmingyuan in Eighteenth-century France."
77. Ibid., 135–136. Thomas is the first modern scholar to discuss the map, which was until recently unidentified in the collections of the BnF.
78. BnF, Département des Estampes et de la photographie, call no. AG-187-GRAND ROUL; the label reads: "Plan d'une grande partie du Parc d'Yuen-ming-yuen, appellé par les Européens le Versailles de la Chine / Et des Palais ou Maisons de plaisance de l'Empereur Kien-Long, / contenus dans les XX. Planches gravées en taille douce à Peking que j'ai recues en Octobre 1787. de M. Bourgeois Missionnaire Francois de la Résidence de Péking." According to the BnF, the map first appears in the sale catalogue *Catalogue des livres imprimés et manuscrits, composant la bibliothèque de feu M. L.-M.-J. Duriez (de Lille),*

dont la vente se fera du 22 janvier au 1er avril 1828 (Paris, J.-S. Merlin, 1827); the listing is cat. no. 1353, on p. 137, "Plan d'une grande partie du parc de Yuen-Min-Yuen. . . ."

79. For a recent, concise discussion of the 20 engravings and Ilantai's role in their production, see Kleutghen, *Imperial Illusions*, Chap. 5, Staging Europe. See esp. 194 ff., "Engraving and viewing the *Pictures of the European Palaces and Waterworks*," where Qing archival documents are cited for the dates of the project.
80. See the preface to the catalogue of the first posthumous sale of Delatour's collections, *Premier Catalogue des Livres, la plupart précieux, du Cabinet de feu M. L.-F. Delatour* (Paris: Tilliard Freres; J.-G. Mérigot, 1808).
81. Delatour, *Essais sur l'architecture des Chinois*, Chapter V, on Chinese gardens, refers a number of times to Delatour's correspondence with Bourgeois; Delatour cites the prints that Bourgeois had sent him, and these are listed in the inventory of shipments from Beijing in 1786, Bib. Inst. Ms 1524, fol. 192. They included Chinese impressions of the 16 engravings of the "Conquests" of the Qianlong emperor, which were engraved in France; the 20 views of the European palaces, mistakenly described as the first copper-plate engravings made in China; the woodblock prints of the "40 Views of the Yuanming yuan," again mistakenly described as 50 plates; and six paintings of the palace of the emperor along with the six woodblocks on which they were based. For these paintings, see Finlay, "Henri Bertin (1720–1792) and Images of the Yuanmingyuan in Eighteenth-century France."
82. See Pelliot, "Les 'Conquêtes de l'empereur de la Chine'," note 4 on pp. 227–229, see esp. 228, where Pelliot cites the posthumous sale catalogue of 1808.
83. The Rylands Library holds the Special Collections of the University of Manchester Library. See Finlay, "Henri Bertin (1720–1792) and Images of the Yuanmingyuan in Eighteenth-century France."
84. Delatour, *Essais sur l'architecture des Chinois*, Des Jardins Chinois, chap. 6, *Des serres chinoises et de leurs formes, etc.*, 221–229.
85. For Delatour's selections from Cibot's text, see ibid., 221–227.
86. Delatour, *Essais sur l'architecture des Chinois*, 228: "En 1776, nous avons vu entre les mains de M. l'abbé Batteux, de l'Académie françoise, Editeur des sept premiers volumes des Mémoires des Missionnaires françois de Pékin, quatre dessins des belles serres de l'Empereur, colorés avec une propreté infinie. On doit appeler ces dessins des peintures: elles avoient été envoyées en présent par les Missionnaires, à M. Bertin, et ne déparoient pas la riche collection de curiosités chinoises qui formoient son cabinet."
87. See Chap. 3, n. 2; it is not clear who wrote the note, which mentions six paintings, while the album only contains five.
88. Delatour, *Essais sur l'architecture des Chinois*, 229, quoting the weekly journal *Affiches, Annonces, et Avis Divers . . . Feuille Hébdomadaire*, no. 26 (1 July 1778), 102.
89. Delatour, *Essais sur l'architecture des Chinois*, 244, note (*o*) in reference to p. 228: "Le riche cabinet de M. Bertin, formé par les Missionnaires de la Chine, qui avoient en lui un protecteur généreux et zélé, toujours disposé à solliciter, auprès du gouvernement, des secours pécuniaires, pour faciliter leur accès, et être utiles à la nation, près des Grands de la cour et du Prince même, doivent être considérés par leurs travaux, comme Missionnaires et littérateurs. Ce cabinet qui contenoit tant d'objets de goût et de curiosité, est passé, avant 1791, en d'autres mains par dispersion, ou par la vente que l'ancien ministre, dépouillé de ses pensions et de sa fortune, a été obligé de faire. Une terre étrangère lui a présenté un asile où, peu de temps après, il a terminé ses jours."
90. Silvestre de Sacy, *Sillage*, 154–155.
91. Ibid., 154, citing Cordier, "Correspondants de Bertin," *T'oung Pao* 17 (1916), 620.
92. Silvestre de Sacy, *Sillage*, 155; see also Laure Beaumont-Maillet, *Les collectionneurs au Cabinet des estampes* (Paris: Nouvelles de l'estampe, December 1993), no. 132, 5–27; Bertin, no. 12; which cites Bertin's death date as 12 September 1792. See also Bussière, *Bulletin du Périgord*, vol. 36 (1909), 238–239, citing the date as 16 September 1792.
93. Beaumont-Maillet, *Les collectionneurs au Cabinet des estampes*, loc. cit.
94. Irène Aghion, "Le Musée révolutionnaire," in *Histoires d'archéologie: De l'objet à l'étude* (Paris: Institut national d'histoire de l'art, 2009), 1, http://journals.openedition.org/inha/2789, accessed 8 October 2019.

95. See the data page on the BnF website, "France. Convention nationale. Commission des arts," https://data.bnf.fr/fr/13533855/france_convention_nationale__commission_des_arts/, accessed 8 October 2019. The carefully detailed instructions for cataloguing appear in Félix Vicq-d'Azyr, Thomas Lindet, and Bouquier (aîné) [*sic*], *Instruction sur la manière d'inventorier et de conserver, dans toute l'étendue de la République, tous les objets qui peuvent servir aux arts, aux sciences et à l'enseignement, proposée par la Commission temporaire des arts* . . . (Paris: Imprimerie nationale, an II [1793].
96. Louis Tuetey, comp. and ed., *Procès-verbaux de la Commission temporaire des arts*, 2 vols. (Paris: Imprimerie Nationale, 1912), vol. 1, vol. 2 (1917). Many of relevant original documents are now housed in the Archives Nationales, Paris; others are kept in the Cabinet des Medailles of the BnF; on these, see Aghion, "Le Musée révolutionnaire," 4.
97. Tuetey, *Procès-verbaux de la Commission temporaire des arts*, vol. 1, p. 54, n. 1. Tuetey's note cites the catalogue number in the Archives Nationales, F^{17} 1231.
98. Ibid., 56; Bertin is consistently named as the "émigré Bertin."
99. Ibid., 87, n. 4; the note records the receipt from the librarian, dated in accordance with 14 February 1794, which included the current condition of the 17 paintings, a document in the Archives Nationales, F^{17} 1047, no. 7.
100. "État des 17 articles provenant de l'émigré Bertin. . .," BnF, Département des Estampes et de la photographie, Réserve, document no. 399; I am grateful to the staff of the Department for allowing me to examine the documents in the BnF relevant to paintings and objects from Bertin's collections.
101. The document no. 399 has been annotated in pencil with the call numbers, most of them held in the Réserves of the Département des Estampes et de la photographie.
102. BnF, Département des Estampes et de la photographie, Réserve, doc. no. 398, "Etat des 14 articles mentionnés dans la pièce précédente."
103. BnF, Département des Estampes et de la photographie, Réserve, doc. no. 400, the values are listed as an "Estimation."
104. BnF, Département des Estampes et de la photographie, Réserve, doc no. 401, "Note des Curiosités Chinoises provenant du cabinet de Mr. Bertin."
105. These notes, effectively a brief inventory included with the documents in the Département des Estampes et de la photographie, are entitled "Dossier de l'Émigré Bertin" and simply record the titles of six documents, the lists numbered 397 to 402.
106. Entitled "Catalogue des objets chinois provenant du cabinet du citoyen Bertin, enlevé à la maison de Nêle le dix-sept fructidor an cinq [3 September 1797] de la République, pour le Muséum des antiques de la Bibliothèque nationale"; call no. 5 AMC 74. See also the following note.
107. Bertrand Daugeron, "Entre l'antique et l'exotique, le projet comparatiste oublié du 'Muséum des Antiques' en l'an III," *Annales historiques de la Révolution française* 356 (April–June 2009), 143–176, http://ahrf.revues.org/10629, accessed 8 October 2019; see esp. 165 and n. 97, which refers to the "Catalogue des objets chinois provenant du cabinet du citoyen Bertin. . ." in the Cabinet des Médailles; call no. 5 AMC 74, as in the previous note. The call no. is apparently no longer current.
108. Théophile Marion Dumersan, *Histoire du Cabinet des médailles, antiques et pierres gravées avec une notice sur la Bibliothèque Royale, et une description des objets exposés dans cet établissement* (Paris: chez l'auteur, 1838), 164.
109. Ibid., 165; n. 95 on this page refers to Tuetey, *Procès-verbaux de la Commission temporaire des arts*, a source cited many times by Dumersan.
110. "[L]e dix-sept fructidor an cinq de la République."
111. "10. Bâton de Vieillesse donné au P. Amiot par l'Empereur. Il est en trois pièces."
112. "42. Tasse faite à la Manufacture de l'Empereur. Elle porte un poème que l'empereur a fait à la chasse sous un arbre qui lui plut. mutilée."
113. Kee Il Choi, Jr., "Father Amiot's Cup," in Gerritsen and Riello, eds., *Writing Material Culture History*; see esp. 24, nn. 8 and 9.
114. Ibid., 34, n. 8; the citation in Bib. Inst. Ms 1522, fols. 2–3, reads: "4°: 2 tasses avec leur couvercles sur lesquels sont des vers faits par l'Empereur lui-même, la 11e Année de son règne, et que j'ay traduits en français le moins mal que j'ay pû." The 11th year of the Qianlong reign is equivalent to 1746; Choi also cites here the entry in Bernard[-Maître], "Catalogue des objets envoyés de Chine," 125.

115. Ibid., 34, n. 9, citing Bib. Inst. Ms 1524, fol. 133, a list that happens to be dated 1769 but contains an entry essentially identical to another on a previous page in the same manuscript, fol. 129, which reads: "Deux tasses avec leurs couvercles, sur lesquels sont des vers faits par l'Empereur lui-même, la onzième année de son règne, et que j'ai traduit en françois." A note on fol. 127 identifies the lists on the following pages: "Objets venus de Chine."
116. *Notice des articles curieux composant le Cabinet chinois du feu M. Bertin, Ministre et Secrétaire d'État sous Louis XV et Louis XVI*, H. Delaroche; Moreau, commissaire-priseur (Paris: l'Imprimerie de Crapelet, 1–4 February 1815); the entry in question is on p. 9, no. 20. I would like to thank Kee Il Choi for providing me with a scanned copy of this catalogue.
117. This identification is central to Choi's discussion of the inscribed porcelain cup in "Father Amiot's Cup." See Amiot, trans., *Éloge de la ville de Moukden et de ses environs; poème composé par Kien-Long, empereur de la Chine & de la Tartarie, actuellement régnant*, Josesph de Guines, pub. (Paris: N.M. Tilliard, 1770); the Qianlong emperor's poem, entitled "Vers sur le thé" (Poem on tea) is described, transcribed, and translated on pp. 329–337. The principal content of the book is the book is Amiot's translation of the Qianlong imperial poem celebrating the city of Mukden, the heart of the Manchu Qing dynasty.
118. Amiot's transcription, *Éloge de la Ville de Moukden*, 336–337, reads: ". . . au petit printems de la dixième lune de l'anée *Ping-yn* (c), de mon regne *Kien-long*"; note (c), provided by the editor, gives the equivalent of the cyclical date *bingyin* as 1746.
119. Choi, "Father Amiot's Cup," 36–37.
120. *Notice des articles curieux composant le Cabinet chinois du feu M. Bertin*, 1815, cat. no. 125.
121. Ibid., cat. no. 157. The screen is noted in Bernard[-Maître], "Catalogue des objets envoyés de Chine par les missionnaires de 1765 à 1786," 154–155, no. 32–1777; no. 35 here further refers to Henri Cordier, *La Chine en France au XVIIIe siècle* (Paris: Henri Laurens, 1910), 103–105, where the screen is described with relevant citations.
122. Bib. Inst. Ms 1521, fols. 93–96: "J'ai reçu enfin, Messieurs, les trois caisses que vous m'avés addressé contenant la premiere un paravant de pierre peinte. . . ."
123. Bib. Inst. Ms 1524, fols. 127 recto-verso, and fol. 129.
124. Ibid., fol. 168.
125. *Notice des articles curieux composant le Cabinet chinois du feu M. Bertin*, cat. no. 164, "Recueil de 105 planches, représentant le principaux traits de a vie de Confucius; envoyées par le P. Amiot, pour accompagner sa vie de ce philosophe." The entry notes the publication of 18 images in the *Mémoires*, vol. 12, but says that they are much reduced, only imperfectly rendering the original designs.
126. Ibid., cat. no. 165.
127. *Catalogue de Peintures chinoises et persanes . . ., de Bronzes, Lacques et Porcelaines de la Chine, ...* (Cat. published Paris: M. Nepveu, 22–26 April 1828). Titsingh's name is spelled "Titzingh" in the *Avertissement*, p. 2, which also lists Bertin's collection and that of Van Braam; the sale included "Persian" and numerous European works of art, books and documents, as well.
128. See Jacques Marx, "Mandarins hollandais à la cour de Qianlong: l'ambassade Titsingh (1795) dans le système tributaire," http://jacquesmarx.be/pdfs/be509e1b37.pdf, accessed 23 October 2013.
129. *Voyage de l'ambassade de la Compagnie des Indes orientales hollandaises vers l'empereur de la Chine dans les années 1794 et 1795. . .*, 2 vols. (Paris: Moreau de Saint-Méry, 1798; and Philadelphia, 1797–1798).
130. BnF, Département des Estampes et de la photographie, Réserve AG-35-Roul, noted as: "Provient de la confiscation révolutionnaire de la collection Bertin (26 pluviôse an II, 14 février 1794)." Document 399 in the Réserve of the Département des Estampes et de la photographie lists the painting as no. 16.
131. Bib. Inst. Ms 1517, fols. 65–86; the relevant text from Amiot's letter is at the end, on fols. 85 verso–86 recto.
132. "M. AMYOT, Mys^{re}. Apost^{que}. à Peking, Chargé d'Aff^{res}. par S.M.T.C. auprès de l'Empereur de la Chine, qui le fit Mandarin. il traduisit du Chinois, l'Histoire des Hommes illustres, et autres qui se trouvent dans les memoires concernant les Chinois; il mourut après 42

ans de residence à Peking en 1793 agé de 74 Ans." S.M.T.C. is a conventional abbreviation for the title "Sa Majesté Très Chrétienne." The poem reads: "François, Mantchou, Chinois, homme de Cour, Apôtre / Il fut, sans deroger, tantôt l'un tantôt l'autre / S'il est comme ecrivain digne de quelque prix, / Chacun peut le juger en lisant ses ecrits."

133. For a brief discussion, emphasizing the importance of *Li* as "principle" in neo-Confucian philosophy, see Wing-tsit Chan, comp. and trans., *A Source Book in Chinese Philosophy* (Princeton: Princeton University Press, 1963; paperback ed., 1969, 1973), 519–520. Chan also cites *Tianli* (*t'ien-li* 天理) as a neo-Confucian concept for the Principle of Nature, and of Natural Law.

134. Bib. Inst. Ms 1517, fol. 86 recto, p. 43 of Amiot's letter: "Il est plus que probable qu'il ne s'agit icy que de cette portion de bonheur à laquelle ils pouvoient aspirer dans le cours de leur vie mortelle sur la terre, et qu'il laissoit à la justice et à la bonté de ce même tien de les récompenser ou de les punir dans une autre vie, suivant qu'ils auroient mérité l'un ou l'autre. C'est pour cette raison qu'il préféra la voie de l'enseignement qui instruit et indique, et de l'exemple qui persuade, à la voie de la magistrature qui ordonne ou défend. D'ailleurs rien n'est exalté chez lui: il propose, il indique, il instruite, il exhorte, il agit; mais toujours avec discrétion, et sans enthousiasme, &c. &c."

Bibliography

Archival Sources

Bréquigny, Louis George Oudard Feudrix de (1714–1795). *Collection de manuscrits constituée de la correspondance et des travaux historiques de L.-G. de Bréquigny*. Acquired by the Bibliothèque royale in 1815, 165 volumes. Bibliothèque nationale de France. Département des manuscrits. http://catalogue.bnf.fr/ark:/12148/cb144688432/PUBLIC, accessed 24 August 2015. Cited in the present volume as: BnF Fonds Bréquigny.

Correspondance des RR. PP. Jésuites missionnaires en Chine avec H.-L.-J.-B. Bertin. Twelve volumes of Bertin's papers and correspondence, acquired by the publisher and bookseller Auguste Nepveu (act. ca. 1804–1837), sold to François-Marie Delessert (1780–1868), and bequeathed in 1874 to the Bibliothèque de l'Institut de France; referred to in the present volume as: Bib. Inst. Mss 1515–1526. See the website of the Institut de France, www.calames.abes.fr/pub/institut.aspx#details?id=IF2B12091, accessed 18 October 2019.

Albums From Henri Bertin's Collection

Essai sur l'architecture chinoise. 2 vols. Ca. 1773. BnF, Département des Estampes et de la photographie, Réserve OE-13-PET FOL, and Réserve OE-13 (A)-PET FOL.

Haitien. Maison de Plaisance de l'Empereur de Chine. Ca. 1750–1792. BnF, Département des Estampes et de la photographie, Réserve OE-21-PET FOL.

Paysages Chinois [Tirés des Jardins de l'Empereur, et autres]. BnF, Département des Estampes et de la photographie, Réserve OE-26-FT 4.

Pierres employées pour ornemens [sic] dans les jardins chinois. BnF, Département des Estampes et de la photographie, Réserve OE-44-PET FOL.

Portraits de quelques uns d'entre les principaux chinois qui se sont rendus célèbres . . . . Bibliothèque nationale de France, Département des Manuscrits, Chinois 1236.

Recueil. Arcs de triomphe et berceaux chinois. Ca. 1772. BnF, Département des Estampes et de la photographie, Réserve OE-24-FT 4.

Recueil Historique des Principaux Traits de la Vie des Empereurs Chinois. 2 vols. BnF, Département des Estampes et de la photographie, Réserve OE-5-BOITE FOL, Réserve OE-5 (A)-BOITE FOL.

Recueil. Paysages Chinois [Recueil Relatif à l'Architecture Chinoise]. BnF, Département des Estampes et de la photographie, Réserve OE-31-4.

Recueil. Plafonds Chinois. BnF, Département des Estampes et de la photographie, Réserve OE-25-FT 5.

Recueil. Plans relatifs à l'essai sur l'architecture chinoise. Ca. 1773. BnF, Département des Estampes et de la photographie, Réserve OE-15-FT 4.

Recueil. Vases anciens et diverses porcelaines de Chine. BnF, Département des Estampes et de la photographie, Réserve OE-42-PET FOL.

Serres chaudes des Chinois et fleurs qu'ils y conservent. Ca. 1777. BnF, Département des Estampes et de la photographie, Réserve OE-30-FOL.

Yuzhi Gengzhi tu. Text by the Kangxi emperor; prints after Jiao Bingzhen. 1696. BnF, Département des Estampes et de la photographie, Réserve OE-89-4.

Yuzhi Gengzhi tu. Text by the Kangxi emperor; prints after Jiao Bingzhen. 1696. BnF, Département des Estampes et de la photographie. Réserve OE-90-PET FOL.

Bibliography

Aghion, Irène. "Le Musée révolutionnaire." In *Histoires d'archéologie: De l'objet à l'étude*. Paris: Institut national d'histoire de l'art, 2009.

Amiot, Jean-Joseph-Marie, S.J., trans. *Art militaire des Chinois, ou Recueil d'anciens traités sur la guerre, composés avant l'ere chrétienne, par différents généraux chinois . . . .* Edited by Joseph de Guignes. Paris: Didot l'Ainé, 1772.

Amiot, Jean-Joseph-Marie, S.J., trans., and Josesph de Guines, ed. *Éloge de la ville de Moukden et de ses environs; poeme compose par Kien-Long, empereur de la Chine & de la Tartarie, actuellement régnant*. Paris: N.M. Tilliard, 1770. Reprint; Milton Keynes, UK: Lightning Source UK Ltd., 2010.

Attiret, Jean-Denis. "Lettre du frère Attiret, de la Compagnie de Jésus, peintre au service du l'Empereur de la Chine, à M. d'Assaut." *Lettres édifiantes et curieuses* 27 (1749): 1–57.

Attiret, Jean-Denis. *A Particular Account of the Emperor of China's Gardens Near Pekin . . . .* Translated from the French by Sir Harry Beaumont [Joseph Spence]. London: R. Dodsley, 1752.

Bailey, Gauvin Alexander. *Art on the Jesuit Missions in Asia and Latin America, 1542–1773*. Toronto: University of Toronto Press, 1999.

Baridon, Laurent, Jean-Philippe Garric, and Martial Guédron. *Jean-Jacques Lequeu: bâtisseur de fantasmes*. Paris: Bibliothèque nationale de France; Éditions Norma, 2018.

Barrier, Janine, Monique Mosser, and Che Bing Chiu, comp. *Aux Jardins de Cathay: l'imaginaire anglo-chinois en Occident, William Chambers*. Besançon: Éditions de l'Imprimeur, 2004.

Beaumont-Maillet, Laure. "Les collectionneurs au Cabinet des estampes." In *Nouvelles de l'estampe*, Vol. 132: 5–27. Paris, December 1993.

Bernard, Auguste. *Histoire de l'imprimerie royale du Louvre*. Paris: Imprimerie impériale, 1867.

Bernard-Maître, Henri, S.J. "Le voyage du père de Fontaney au Siam et à la Chine, 1685–1687, d'après des lettres inédites." *Bulletin de l'Université l'Aurore* (1942): 227–280.

Bernard-Maître, Henri, S.J. "Le Frère Attiret au service de K'ien-long (1739–1768): Sa premiére Biographie écrite par le P. Amiot, rééditée avec notes explicatives et commentaires historiques par Henri Bernard, S.J." *Bulletin de l'Université l'Aurore* (1943), series III, 4, no. 1 (2013): 30–82; 4, no. 2 (2014): 435–474.

Bernard[-Maître], Henri, S.J. "Catalogue des objets envoyés de Chine par les missionnaires de 1765 à 1786." *Bulletin de l'Université l'Aurore*, Series III, 9, (January–April 1948): 119–206.

Bernard-Maitre, Henri, S.J. "Le 'petit Ministre' Henri Bertin et la correspondance littéraire de la Chine à la fin du XVIIIe siècle." *Comptes-rendus des séances de l'Académie des Inscriptions et Belles-Lettres*, 92nd year, no. 4 (1948): 449–451.

Bernard-Maître, Henri, S.J. "Deux Chinois du XVIIIème siècle à l'école des physiocrates français." *Bulletin de l'Université l'Aurore* (1949): 151–197.

Bernard-Maitre, Henri, S.J. *Les Tapisseries chinoises de Boucher au Palais Yuen-Min-Yuen de Pékin*. Variétés d'orientalisme 1. Paris: Lille: Editions Cathasia, n.d., 1950.

Beurdeley, Michel. *Peintres jésuites en Chine au XVIIIe siècle*. Arcueil: Anthèse, 1997.

Bienaimé, Constance. "Les objets 'de la Chine' dans les collections des ducs de Chaulnes." In *L'Extrême-Orient dans la culture européenne des XVIIe et XVIIIe siècles*, edited by Florence Boulerie and others: 151–165. Tübingen: Narr, 2009.

Bienaimé, Constance, and Patrick Michel. "Portrait du singulier monsieur Bertin, ministre investi dans les affaires de la Chine." In Rochebrune, *La Chine à Versailles: Art et diplomatie au XVIIIe siècle*, edited by Marie-Laure de Rochebrune: 150–177. Paris: Somogy Éditions d'Art, 2014.

Blondel, Jacques-François. *Discours sur la nécessité de l'étude de l'architecture: Prononcé à l'ouverture du cinquième cours public* . . . . Paris: C.-A. Jombert, 1754.

Bray, Francesca. "Agricultural Illustrations: Blueprint or Icon?" In *Graphics and Text in the Production of Technical Knowledge in China: The Warp and the Weft*, edited by Francesca Bray, Vera Dorofeeva-Lichtmann, and Georges Métailié: 521–567. Leiden and Boston: Brill, 2007.

Budde, Hendrik, and others, eds. *Europa und die Kaiser von China (1240–1816)*. Frankfurt am Main: Insel-Verlag, 1985.

Cahill, James. "A Group of Anonymous Northern Figure Paintings from the Qianlong Period," http://jamescahill.info/the-writings-of-james-cahill/a-group-of-anonymous-northern-figure-paintings-from-the-qianlong, accessed 31 October 2015.

Cahill, James. *Pictures for Use and Pleasure: Vernacular Painting in High Qing China*. Berkeley: University of California Press, 2010.

The Cambridge History of China: Volume 8, the Ming Dynasty, Part 2: 1368–1644. Edited by Denis C. Twitchett and Frederick W. Mote. Cambridge, UK: Cambridge University Press, 1998.

Carmontelle (Louis Carrogis, 1717–1806). *Jardin de Monceau, près de Paris, appartenant à S. A. S. Mgr. le duc de Chartres*. Paris: Delafosse, 1779.

Catalogue de Peintures chinoises et persanes . . ., de Bronzes, Lacques et Porcelaines de la Chine, . . ., 22–26 April 1828. Paris: M. Nepveu.

Catinat, Jacques. *Les Châteaux de Chatou et le nymphée de Soufflot*. Chartres: S.O.S.P., 1974.

Chambers, Sir William. *Designs of Chinese Buildings, Furniture, Dresses, Machines and Utensils* . . . . London: Published for the Author . . ., 1757.

Chambers, Sir William. *Desseins des édifices, meubles, habits, machines, et ustenciles [sic] des Chinois* . . . . London: J. Haberkorn, 1757.

Chambers, Sir William. *Traité des édifices, meubles, habits, machines et ustensiles des Chinois* . . . . Paris: Chez le Sieur Le Rouge, 1776.

Chan, Wing-tsit, comp. and trans. *A Source Book in Chinese Philosophy*. Princeton: Princeton University Press, 1963; paperback ed., 1969, 1973.

Chiu, Che Bing. *Yuanming Yuan: Le jardin de la Clarté parfaite*. Besançon: Les Éditions de l'Imprimeur, 2000.

Choi, Kee Il, Jr. "Father Amiot's Cup: A Qing Imperial Porcelain Sent to the Court of Louis XV." In *Writing Material Culture History*, edited by Anne Gerritsen and Giorgio Riello, Chap. 3: 33–41. London and New York: Bloomsbury Academic, 2014.

Choi, Kee Il, Jr. "*Portraits of Virtue*: Henri-Léonard Bertin, Joseph Amiot and the 'Great Man' of China." *Transactions of the Oriental Ceramic Society* 80 (2015–16): 49–65.

Choi, Kee Il, Jr. "Ancien vs Antique: Henri-Léonard Bertin's Albums of the Qianlong Emperor's 'Vases Chinois'." *Journal18*, "Albums,", no. 6 (Fall 2018), www.journal18.org/issue6/ancien-vs-antique-henri-leonard-bertins-albums-of-the-qianlong-emperors-vases-chinois/, accessed 3 October 2019.

Chung, Anita. *Drawing Boundaries: Architectural Images in Qing China*. Honolulu: University of Hawai'i Press, 2004.

Clunas, Craig, and Jessica Harrison-Hall. *Ming: 50 Years That Changed China*. London: British Museum Press, 2014.

Cohen, Monique, and Nathalie Monnet. *Impressions de Chine*. Paris: Bibliothèque nationale, 1992.

Cojannot, Alexandre, and Alexandre Gady. *Dessiner pour bâtir: le métier d'architecte au XVIIe siècle*. Paris: Archives Nationales; Paris: Le Passage, 2017.

Cordier, Henri. *Catalogue des albums chinois et ouvrages relatifs à la Chine conservés au Cabinet des estampes de la Bibliothèque nationale*. Extrait du Journal asiatique, Septembre–Octobre 1909: 209–262. Paris: Impr. nationale, 1909.

Cordier, Henri. *La Chine en France au XVIIIe siècle*. Paris: Henri Laurens, 1910.

Cordier, Henri. "La Suppression de la Compagnie de Jésus et la mission de Peking." *T'oung Pao*, Second Series, 17, no. 3 (July 1916): 271–347, and *Suite*, *T'oung Pao*, Second Series, 17, no. 4/5 (October–December 1916): 561–623.

Cordier, Henri. "Les Correspondants de Bertin, Secrétaire d'État au XVIIIe siècle." *T'oung Pao*, 18, no. 4/5 (October–December 1917): 295–379.

Cordier, Henri. "Les Chinois de Turgot." In *Mélanges d'histoire et de géographie orientales*, Vol. 2: 31–39. Paris: J. Maisonneuve, 1920.

Corsi, Elisabetta. "Envisioning Perspective: Nian Xiyao's (1671–1738) Rendering of Western Perspective in the Prologues to 'the Science of Vision'." In *A Life Journey to the East: Sinological Studies in Memory of Giuliano Certuccioli (1923–2001)*. Kyoto: Italian School of East Asian Studies, 2002.

Corsi, Elisabetta. *La fábrica de las ilusiones: los Jesuitas y la difusión de la perspectiva lineal en China (1698–1766)*. Mexico City: El Colegio de México, 2004.

Courant, Maurice. *Catalogue des livres chinois, coréens, japonais*, 3 vols. Paris: Ernest Leroux, 1902, 1910, 1912.

Curmer, Albert. *Les Seigneurs de Chatou*. Versailles: Impr. de J. Aubert, 1919.

Curtis, Emily Byrne. *Glass Exchange between Europe and China, 1550–1800: Diplomatic, Mercantile and Technological Interactions*. Farnham, Surrey and Burlington: Ashgate, 2009.

Dardess, John W. *A Political Life in Ming China*. Lanham, MD: Rowman & Littlefield, 2013.

Daugeron, Bertrand. "Entre l'antique et l'exotique, le projet comparatiste oublié du 'Muséum des Antiques' en l'an III." *Annales historiques de la Révolution française* 356 (April–June 2009): 143–176.

Dehergne, Joseph, S.J. "Voyageurs chinois venus à Paris au temps de la marine à voiles et l'influence de la Chine sur la littérature française du XVIIIe siècle." *Monumenta Serica* 23 (1964): 372–397.

Dehergne, Joseph, S.J. *Répertoire des Jésuites de Chine de 1552 à 1800*. Roma: Institutum Historicum; Paris: Letouzey & Ané, 1973.

Dehergne, Joseph, S.J. "Une grande collection: Mémoires concernant les Chinois (1776–1814)." *Bulletin de l'Ecole française d'Extrême-Orient* 72 (1983): 267–298.

Delatour, Louis-François. *Essais sur l'architecture des Chinois, sur leurs jardins, leurs principes de médecine, et leurs moeurs et usages . . . .* Paris: Impr. de Clousier, 1803.

Demattè, Paola. "A Confucian Education for Europeans." *The Art Bulletin* 98, no. 1 (March 2016): 43–71.

de Pauw, Cornelius. *Recherches philosophiques sur les Égyptiens et les Chinois, par l'auteur des recherches sur les Amériquains*, 2 vols. Berlin: C.J. Decker, 1773.

Descriptions des arts et métiers, faites ou approuvées par messieurs de l'Académie royale des sciences de Paris, avec figures en taille douce, 113 vols. Paris, 1761–1788.

De Verboden Stad: Hofcultuur van de Chinese Keizers (1644–1911)/The Forbidden City: Court Culture of the Chinese Emperors (1644–1911). Edited by J.R. ter Molen and Ellen Uitzinger. Rotterdam: Museum Boymans—van Beuningen, 1990.

Diderot, Denis, and others, comp. *Encyclopédie, ou Dictionnaire raisonné des sciences, des arts et des métiers, par une Société de gens de lettres. Mis en ordre et publié par M. Diderot, et, quant à la partie mathématique, par M. d'Alembert*, 35 vols. Paris: Briasson, 1751–1780.

Différents palais & temples de l'Empereur de la Chine: dessinés et gravés à la Chine. Ex. col. Michel-Ferdinand d'Albert d'Ailly (duc de Chaulnes, 1714–1769). Bibliothèque nationale de France, Département des Estampes et de la photographie, Réserve OE-21 (C)-PET FOL.

Duboÿ, Philippe. "Jean Jacques Lequeu Architecte?" PhD Diss., Istituto Universitario di Architettura di Venezia (IUAV), Venice, 1972.

Duboÿ, Philippe. *Jean Jacques Lequeu: une énigme*. Paris: Hazan, 1987.

Duboÿ, Philippe. *Jean Jacques Lequeu: dessinateur en architecture*. Paris: Gallimard, 2018.

Du Halde, Jean-Baptiste. *Description géographique, historique, chronologique, politique et physique de l'Empire de la Chine et de la Tartarie chinoise* . . ., 4 vols. Paris: P.-G. Le Mercier, 1735.

Dumersan, Théophile Marion. *Histoire du Cabinet des médailles, antiques et pierres gravées avec une notice sur la Bibliothèque royale, et une description des objets exposés dans cet établissement*. Paris: chez l'auteur, 1838.

Dumoulin-Genest, Marie-Pierre. "L'Introduction et l'acclimatation des plantes chinoises en France au XVIIIe siècle." PhD diss., EHESS, Paris, October 1994.

Ecke, Gustave. "A Group of Eighteenth-Century Paintings of Beijing Interiors." *Journal of the Chinese Classical Furniture Society* 4, no. 3 (Summer 1994): 60–70.

E'ertai 鄂爾泰, and others. *Guochao gongshi* 國朝宮史 (History of the Palaces of the Present [Qing] Dynasty), 1769; reprint, Beijing: Guji chubanshe, 2000.

Elliott, Mark C. "The Limits of Tartary: Manchuria in Imperial and National Geographies." *The Journal of Asian Studies* 59, no. 3 (August 2000): 603–646.

Eng, Clarence. *Colours and Contrast: Ceramic Traditions in Chinese Architecture*. Leiden: Brill, 2014.

Explication des peintures, sculptures, et autres ouvrages de Messieurs de l'Académie royale . . . ., Jean-Baptiste Reydellet, comp. Paris: Jacques Colombat, 1742.

Fatica, Michele, and Yue Zhuang. "Copperplates Controversy: Matteo Ripa's *Thirty-Six Views of Jehol* and the Chinese Rites Controversy." In *Entangled Landscapes: Early Modern China and Europe*, edited by Yue Zhuang and Andrea M. Riemenschnitter: 144–186. Singapore: National University of Singapore Press, 2017.

Finlay, John. "The Qianlong Emperor's Western Vistas: Linear Perspective and Trompe l'Oeil Illusion in the European Palaces of the Yuanming yuan." *Bulletin de l'Ecole française d'Extrême-Orient* 94 (2007): 159–193.

Finlay, John. "'40 Views of the Yuanming yuan': Image and Ideology in a Qianlong Imperial Album of Poetry and Paintings." PhD diss., Yale University Press, New Haven, CT, 2011.

Finlay, John. "Between France and China in the Late 18th Century: Henri Bertin and the Commerce in Images." In *Qing Encounters: Artistic Exchanges between China and the West*, edited by Petra Chu and Ning Ding: 79–94. Los Angeles: Getty Institute, 2015.

Finlay, John. "Henri Bertin (1720–1792) and Images of the Yuanmingyuan in Eighteenth-century France." In *Collecting and Displaying China's "Summer Palace" in the West: The Yuanmingyuan in Britain and France*, edited by Louise Tythacott: 123–137. Abingdon, UK and New York: Routledge, 2018.

Finlay, John. "Henri Bertin and Louis XV's Gifts to the Qianlong Emperor." In *Des arts diplomatiques: Échanges de présents entre la Chine et l'Europe, XVIIe-XVIIIe siècles*, edited by Zhao Bing, Isabelle Landry-Deron, and Fabien Simon. *Extrême-Orient Extrême-Occident*, Vol. 43, 2019.

Finlay, John. "Constructing an Authentic China: Henri Bertin and Chinese Architecture in 18th-Century France." In *Rhetorics of Landscape: Articulating Authority in the Early Modern World*, edited by Stephen Whiteman. Forthcoming, 2020.

Gall, Anne. *Inventaire avec indication de provenance des collections d'albums, d'estampes et de peintures chinoises du Département des Estampes*. Paris: Bibliothèque nationale de France, 1990; available only as a photocopy in the Département des Estampes et de la photographie.

Giès, Jacques. "*Perspectiva* ou *Science de la vision* de Nian Xiyao (?-1739): Le paradoxe récurrent de la rencontre Chine-Occident." In *Les Très Riches Heures de la Cour de Chine: Chefs-d'oeuvre de la peinture impériale des Qing, 1662–1796*, edited by Marie-Catherine Rey: 13–43. Paris: Éditions de la Réunion des musées nationaux, 2006.

Golvers, Noël. *Libraries of Western Learning for China: Circulation of Western Books between Europe and China in the Jesuit Mission (ca. 1650—ca. 1750). Part 3: Of Books and Readers*. Leuven Chinese Studies XXX. Leuven: Ferdinand Verbiest Instituut KU Leuven, 2015.

Grimm, Friedrich Melchior, and Denis Diderot. *Correspondance littéraire, philosophique et critique de Grimm et de Diderot depuis 1753 jusqu'en 1790*, Vol. 12, 1784–1785. Edited by Jules-Antoine Taschereau. Paris: Furne, 1830.

Grosier, Jean Baptiste Gabriel Alexandre (1743–1823). *De la Chine, ou description générale de cet empire . . . .*, Third Edition, 7 vols. Paris: Pillet Ainé, 1818–20.

Hammers, Roslyn Lee. "Perspectives in Early Qing-Dynasty *Pictures of Tilling and Weaving* and *Pictures of Cotton*." *Historia Scientiarum* 21, no. 1 (2011): 3–19.

Hammers, Roslyn Lee. *Pictures of Tilling and Weaving: Art, Labor and Technology in Song and Yuan China*. Hong Kong: Hong Kong University Press, 2011.

Hargett, James M. "Huizong's Magic Marchmount: The Genyue Pleasure Park of Kaifeng." *Monumenta Serica* 38 (1988–89): 1–48.

Harrist, Robert E., Jr. *Painting and Private Life in Eleventh-Century China: Mountain Villa by Li Gonglin*. Princeton: Princeton University Press, 1998.

He, Li, and Michael Knight. *Power and Glory: Court Arts of China's Ming Dynasty*. San Francisco: Asian Art Museum, 2008.

He, Zhongyi, and Zeng Zhaofen. *Yuanming yuan yuanlin yishu* (Garden Art of the Yuanming yuan). Beijing: Kexue chubanshe, 1995. 何重义, 曾昭奋著. 圆明园园林艺术. 北京: 科学出版社, 1995.

Hearn, Maxwell K., ed. *Landscapes Clear and Radiant: The Art of Wang Hui (1632–1717)*. New York: Metropolitan Museum of Art; New Haven: Yale University Press, 2008.

Helman, Isidore-Stanislas. *Suite des seize estampes représentant les conquêtes de l'empereur de la Chine . . . .* Paris: Chez l'Auteur, 1785–86.

Helman, Isidore-Stanislas. *Faits mémorables des Empereurs de la Chine, Tirés des Annales Chinoises, Dédiés à Madame, Ornés de 24 Estampes en 4o*. Gravées par Hellman, d'après les Desseins Originaux de la Chine, tirés du Cabinet de Mr. Bertin, Mtre. et ancien Sre. d'Etat. A Paris: Chez l'Auteur, . . ., 1788.

Helman, Isidore-Stanislas. *Abrégé historique des principaux traits de la vie de Confucius, Célèbre Philosophe Chinois . . . .* Paris, 1786–88(?).

Hu, Philip K., ed. *Visible Traces: Rare Book and Special Collections from the National Library of China*. New York: Queens Borough Public Library; Beijing: National Library of China, 2000.

Hucker, Charles O. *A Dictionary of Official Titles in Imperial China*. Stanford, CA: Stanford University Press, 1985.

Hummel, Arthur W., ed. *Eminent Chinese of the Ch'ing Period (1644–1912)*, 2 vols. Washington, DC: U.S. Government Printing Office, 1943.

Jacob, François. "Kien-Long, poète d'empire." *Text Presented on Academia.edu*, www.academia.edu/14040787/Kien-Long_po%C3%A8te_dempire, accessed 24 November 2016.

Jourdain, Margaret, and R. Soame Jenyns. *Chinese Export Art in the Eighteenth Century*. Feltham, Middlesex: Country Life Ltd., 1950; reprint, Spring Books, 1967.

Kaufmann, Emil. "Three Revolutionary Architects, Boullée, Ledoux and Lequeu." *Transactions of the American Philosophical Society*, New series, 42, part 3 (1952): 431–564.

Kleutghen, Kristina. *Imperial Illusions: Crossing Pictorial Boundaries in the Qing Palaces*. Seattle and London: University of Washington Press, 2015.

Lach, Donald. "Leibniz and China." *Journal of the History of Ideas* 6, no. 4 (1945): 436–455.

Lach, Donald. *The Preface to Leibniz' Novissima Sinica: Commentary, Translation, Text*. Honolulu: University of Hawai'i Press, 1957.

La Chine en miniature, ou Choix de costumes, arts et métiers de cet Empire, ... Edited by Jean Baptiste Joseph Breton de La Martinière. Paris: Nepveu, 4 vols., 1811; 2 vols. 1812.

Laffitte, Marie-Pierre, ed. *1789, le patrimoine libéré: 200 trésors entrés à la Bibliothèque nationale de 1789 à 1799*. Paris: Bibliothèque nationale, 1989.

Lagerwey, John, and Pierre Marsone, eds. *Modern Chinese Religion I: Song-Liao-Jin-Yuan (960–1368 AD)*. Leiden: Brill, 2015.

La Lande, Jérôme de. *Art de faire le papier*. Paris: Saillant et Nyon, 1761.

Landry-Deron, Isabelle. "Les Mathématiciens envoyés en Chine par Louis XIV en 1685." *Archive for History of Exact Sciences* 55, no. 5 (April 2001): 423–463.

Landry-Deron, Isabelle. *La preuve par la Chine: la "Description" de J.-B. Du Halde, jésuite, 1735*. Paris: Éd. de l'École des hautes études en sciences sociales, 2002.

Landry-Deron, Isabelle. "La curiosité de Turgot à l'égard de la Chine: Regard sur ses cinquante-deux questions à Ko et Yang." *Paper for the Colloque International Turgot (1727–1780), notre contemporain? Économie, Administration et Gouvernement au Siècle des Lumières*. Université de Caen, 14–16 May 2003.

Landry-Deron, Isabelle. "'Pour la perfection des sciences et des arts': La mission jésuite française en Chine sous le patronage de l'Académie royale." In *L'œuvre scientifique des missionnaires en Asie*, edited by Pierre-Sylvain Filliozat, Jean-Pierre Mahé, and Jean Leclant: 77–96. Paris: Académie des Inscriptions et Belles-lettres; de Boccard, 2011.

Laugier, Marc-Antoine. *Essai sur l'Architecture*. Paris: Chez Duchesne, 1753; idem, *Nouvelle édition, Revue, corrigée, & augmentée . . . .* Paris: Chez Duchesne, 1755.

Laugier, Marc-Antoine. *An Essay on Architecture by Marc-Antoine Laugier*. Translated by Wolfgang and Anni Herrmann. Los Angeles: Hennessey & Ingalls, 1977.

Le Bitouzé, Corinne. "'Un très curieux recueil': Les dessins de Jean-Jacques Lequeu dans les collections du Département des estampes et de la photographie de la BnF." In *Jean-Jacques Lequeu: Bâtisseur de fantasmes*, edited by Laurent Baridon and others: 173–177. Paris: Bibliothèque nationale de France; Éditions Norma, 2018.

Lee, Chao-Ying. "L'enjeu politique et religieux des modes de représentation dans les *Mémoires concernant les Chinois* (1776–1791)." *Histoire de l'Art* 51 (November 2002): 87–99.

Lee, Chao-Ying. "L'enjeu politique dans les *Mémoires concernant les Chinois* (1776–1791)." *Croisements* 4 (2014), Atelier des cahiers voyages/voisinages: 190–208.

Lee, Chao-Ying. *Visions de l'Empire du Milieu au 18e siècle en France: Illustrations des* Mémoires concernant les Chinois *(1776–1791)*. Paris: L'Harmattan, 2016.

Legge, James. *The Works of Mencius Translated, with Critical and Exegetical Notes, Prolegomena, and Copious Indexes by James Legge*. The Chinese Classics, Vol. 2. Oxford: Clarendon Press; reprint, New York: Dover Publications, 1970.

Legge, James, trans. *Confucius: Confucian Analects, the Great Learning & the Doctrine of the Mean*. The Chinese Classics, Vol. 1. Oxford: Clarendon Press; reprint, New York: Dover Publications, 1971.

Lequeu, Jean-Jacques. *Architecture civile de Jean Jacques Le Queu contenant nombre d'édifices de diférents peuples disséminés sur la terre . . . .*, 2 vols., 1777–1825. Bibliothèque nationale de France, Département des Estampes et de la photographie, Réserve HA-80 (1)-FOL and HA-80 (2)-FOL.

Leroy, Paul. "Notes sur les relations artistiques entre la France et la Chine aux XVIIe et XVIIIe siècles." *Réunion des sociétés des beaux-arts des départements*, Salle de l'hémicycle, à l'École nationale des beaux-arts, 24th session (1900): 413–430.

Lettres édifiantes et curieuses, écrites des Missions étrangères, par quelques missionnaires de la Compagnie de Jésus, Vols. 1–34. Paris: Nicolas Le Clerc, and others, 1703–1776. See the BnF website https://catalogue.bnf.fr/ark:/12148/cb328061927.public, accessed 18 October 2019, for details on the publication of the first series.

Leverenz, Niklas. "Isidore-Stanislas Helman and J. Pélicier." *Print Quarterly* 37, no. 1 (2020), "Notes," 75–76.

Levesque, Pierre-Charles, ed. *Pensées morales de Confucius, recueillies et traduites du latin par M. Levesque*. Paris: chez Didot l'aîné et De Bure l'aîné, 1782.

Li, Weiwen 李纬文. *Lun Zhongguo jianzhu: 18 shiji Faguo chuanjiaoshi bixia de Zhongguo jianzhu* 论中国建筑: 18 世纪法国传教士笔下的中国建筑. Preface by Antoine Gournay. Beijing: Publishing House of Electronics Industry电子工业出版社, 2016.

Liang Shizheng 梁詩正, and others, comp. *Qinding Xiqing gujian* (40 *juan*) 欽定西清古鑑 (四十卷). Beijing: Wuying dian 武英殿, Qianlong 16 (1751). Bibliothèque nationale de France,

Département des manuscrits, Chinois-1139 (*juan* 6–12), Chinois-1140 (*juan* 1–5, 13–19), Chinois-1141 (*juan* 20–26), Chinois-1142 (*juan* 27–33), Chinois-1143 (*juan* 34–40).

Littré, Émile (1801–1881). *Dictionnaire de la langue française*, 4 vols. Paris: L. Hachette, 1863–1872. Dictionnaire de la langue française "Littré", http://littre.reverso.net/dictionnaire-francais/

Liu, Cary Y. "Architects and Builders of the Qing Dynasty Yuanming Yuan Imperial Garden-Palace." *The University of Hong Kong Museum Journal* 1 (September 2002), in English and Chinese: 38–59, 151–161.

Loehr, George R. "The Sinicization of Missionary Artists and Their Work at the Manchu Court during the Eighteenth Century." *Cahiers d'histoire mondiale* 7, no. 4 (1963): 795–816.

Lovell, Hin-cheung, and John C. Ferguson. *An Annotated Bibliography of Chinese Painting Catalogues and Related Texts*. Michigan Papers in Chinese Studies 16. Ann Arbor: University of Michigan, 1973.

Lu, Wensheng, and Julia K. Murray. *Confucius: His Life and Legacy in Art*. New York: China Institute Gallery, 2010.

Marin, Catherine. "La mission française de Pékin après la suppression de la compagnie de Jésus en 1773." *Transversalités* 107 (2008/3): 9–28.

Marx, Jacques. "Mandarins hollandais à la cour de Qianlong: l'ambassade Titsingh (1795) dans le système tributaire," http://jacquesmarx.be/pdfs/be509e1b37.pdf, accessed 23 October 2013.

Mathews, R.H. *Mathews' Chinese-English Dictionary*, Revised American Edition. Cambridge, MA: Harvard University Press, 1943.

Mémoires concernant l'histoire, les sciences, les arts, les moeurs, les usages, &c. des Chinois: Par les missionnaires de Pekin, Joseph Amiot, François Bourgeois, Pierre-Martial Cibot, Aloys Kao, Aloys de Poirot, et al., comp., 15 vols. Paris: Nyon, 1776–1791. Referred to in the present volume as: *Mémoires concernant les Chinois*.

Meynard, Thierry, S.J., trans. and ed. *Confucius Sinarum Philosophus (1687): The First Translation of the Confucian Classics*. Monumenta Historica Societatis Iesu Nova Series, Vol. 6. Rome: Institutum Historicum Societatis Iesu, 2011.

Monnet, Nathalie. *Le Gengzhitu: Le livre du riz et de la soie*. Paris: J.C. Lattès, 2003.

Monnet, Nathalie. *Chine: l'Empire du trait: calligraphies et dessins du Ve au XIXe siècle*. Paris: Bibliothèque nationale de France, 2004.

Monnet, Nathalie. "Le Jeune duc du Maine, Protecteur des premières missions françaises en Chine." In *La Chine à Versailles: Art et diplomatie au XVIIIe siècle*, edited by Marie-Laure de Rochebrune: 36–43. Paris: Somogy Éditions d'Art, 2014.

Monval, Jean. *Soufflot, sa vie, son oeuvre, son esthétique (1713–1780)*. Paris: A. Lemerre, 1918.

Morris, Edwin T. *The Gardens of China: History, Art, and Meanings*. New York: Charles Scribner's Sons, 1983.

Morvan, Frédéric. "Jean Jacques Lequeu." In Appendix in Philippe Duboÿ, *Jean Jacques Lequeu: dessinateur en architecture*: 233–261. Paris: Gallimard, 2018.

Mowry, Robert D., with contributions by Claudia Brown, and others. *Worlds within Worlds: The Richard Rosenblum Collection of Chinese Scholars' Rocks*. Cambridge, MA: Harvard University Art Museums, 1997.

Mungello, David E. *Leibniz and Confucianism: The Search for Accord*. Honolulu: University of Hawai'i Press, 1977.

Mungello, David E. "Some Recent Studies on the Confluence of Chinese and Western Intellectual History." *Journal of the History of Idea* 40, no. 4 (October–December 1979): 649–661.

Mungello, David E. *The Great Encounter of China and the West, 1500–1800*, Fourth Edition, Revised. Plymouth: Rowman & Littlefield, 2013.

Musillo, Marco. "Bridging Europe and China: The Professional Life of Giuseppe Castiglione (1688–1766)." PhD diss., School of World Art and Museology, University of East Anglia, United Kingdom, 2006.

Musillo, Marco. *The Shining Inheritance: Italian Painters at the Qing Court, 1699–1812*. Los Angeles: Getty Research Institute, 2016.

Naquin, Susan. *Peking: Temples and City Life, 1400–1900*. Berkeley: University of California Press, 2000.

Needham, John Turberville. *De Inscriptione quâdam Ægyptiacâ Taurini inventâ, et Characteribus Ægyptiacis, olim Sinis communibus* . . . . Rome: Nicolai, 1761.

Nieuhof, Johan. *Journaal van zommige voorvallen, inde voyagie vande E. Heeren Pieter de Goyer en Jacob Keyser, ambassadeurs, aande grootmachtige keizer van Chyna en Tartaryen, inde jaaren 1655, 56 & 1657*. Travel journal, 1659. Paris: Société de Géographie, held in the Bibliothèque nationale de France.

Nieuhof, Johan. *Het gezantschap der Neêrlandsche Oost-Indische Compagnie aan den grooten tartarischen Cham, den tegenwoordigen keizer van China*. Dutch Edition. Amsterdam: Jacob van Meurs, 1665.

Nieuhof, Johan. *Die Gesandschaft der Ost-Indischen Gesellschaft in den Niederlanden an den Tartarischen Cham und nunmehr auch Sinischen Keiser. Ber. durch . . . Peter de Gojer u. Jacob Keiser mit 150 Kupferstükken*. German Edition. Amsterdam: Moers 1666; Amsterdam: Moers, 1669.

Nieuhoff, Jean. *L'ambassade de la Compagnie orientale des Provinces Unies vers l'empereur de la Chine, ou grand cam de Tartarie, faite par les Srs. Pierre de Goyer, & Jacob de Keyser*. French Edition. Leiden: Pour J. de Meurs, 1665.

Notice des articles curieux composant le Cabinet chinois du feu M. Bertin, Ministre et Secrétaire d'État sous Louis XV et Louis XVI. H. Delaroche; Moreau, commissaire-priseur, 1–4 February, 1815. Paris: l'Imprimerie de Crapelet.

Owen, Stephen. *The End of the Chinese 'Middle Ages': Essays in Mid-Tang Literary Culture*. Stanford, CA: Stanford University Press, 1996.

Paléologue, Maurice. *L'Art Chinois*. Paris: Alcide Picard & Kaan, 1887.

Parr, Adam. "John Clarke's *Military Institutions of Vegetius* and Joseph Amiot's *Art Militaire des Chinois*: Translating Classical Military Theory in the Aftermath of the Seven Years' War." PhD diss., University College London, 2016, http://discovery.ucl.ac.uk/1485839/7/Adam%20Parr%20Translating%20Classical%20Military%20Theory%202016.pdf, accessed 30 November 2016.

Pelliot, Paul. "Les 'Conquêtes de l'Empereur de la Chine'." *T'oung Pao* 20 (1921): 183–274.

Perrault, Claude. *Les dix Livres d'architecture de Vitruve, corrigez et nouvellement traduits en françois, avec des notes et des figures*. Paris: J.-B. Coignard, 1673.

Pfister, Louis. *Notices biographiques et bibliographiques sur les Jésuites de l'ancienne mission de Chine, 1552–1773*, 2 vols. Variétés Sinologiques 59–60. Shanghai: Imprimerie de la Mission catholique, 1932, 1934.

Pinot, Virgile. "Documents inédits relatifs à la connaissance de la Chine en France de 1685 à 1740." PhD diss., Université de Paris, P. Geuthner, Paris, 1932; Reprint: Slatkine, Geneva, 1971.

Pirazzoli-t'Serstevens, Michèle, ed. *Le Yuanmingyuan: jeux d'eau et palais européens du XVIIIème siècle à la cour de Chine*. Paris: Editions Recherche sur les civilisations, 1987.

Poivre, Pierre. *Oeuvres complettes de P. Poivre, . . . Précédées de sa vie, et accompagnées de notes*. Paris: Fuchs, 1797.

Pozzo, Andrea, and Vincenzo Mariotti. *Perspectiva Pictorum et Architectorum Andreae Putei*. Rome: Joannis Jacobi Komarek, 1693. English Edition, *Rules and Examples of Perspective Proper for Painters and Architects*. London, 1707; reprint, *Perspective in Architecture and Painting*. New York: Dover Books, 1989.

Premier Catalogue des Livres, la plupart précieux, du Cabinet de feu M. L.-F. Delatour. Paris: Tilliard Freres; J.-G. Mérigot, 1808.

Rado, Mei Mei. "Qing Court's Encounters with European Tapestries: The *Tenture Chinoise* and Beyond." In *Arachné: un regard critique sur l'histoire de la tapisserie*, edited by Pascal-François Bertrand and Audrey N. Maupas. Rennes: Presses Universitaires de Rennes, 2017.

Recueil de planches, sur les sciences, les arts libéraux et les arts mechaniques: avec leur explication . . . . Paris: Briasson, David, Le Breton, Durand, 1762.

Recueil de voyages au nord: contenant divers mémoires très utiles au commerce & à la navigation, Jean-Frédéric Bernard, ed., Vol. 10. Amsterdam: Jean Frédéric Bernard, 1738.

Rinaldi, Bianca Maria. *The "Chinese Garden in Good Taste": Jesuits and Europe's Knowledge of Chinese Flora and Art of the Garden in the 17th and 18th Centuries.* Munich: Martin Meidenbauer, 2006.

Rinaldi, Bianca Maria, ed. *Ideas of Chinese Gardens: Western Accounts, 1300–1860.* Penn Studies in Landscape Architecture. Edited by John Dixon Hunt. Philadelphia: University of Pennsylvania Press, 2016.

Rochebrune, Marie-Laure de, ed. *La Chine à Versailles: Art et diplomatie au XVIIIe siècle.* Paris: Somogy Éditions d'Art, 2014.

Rochebrune, Marie-Laure de. "Les porcelaines de Sèvres envoyées en guise de cadeaux diplomatiques à l'empereur de Chine par les souverains français dans la seconde moitié du XVIIIe siècle." In *Extrême-Orient Extrême-Occident.* Des arts diplomatiques: Échanges de présents entre la Chine et l'Europe, XVIIe-XVIIIe siècles, edited by Zhao Bing, Isabelle Landry-Deron, and Fabien Simon, Vol. 43, 2019.

Rochemonteix, Camille de, S.J. *Joseph Amiot et les derniers survivants de la mission française à Pékin (1750–1795), avec quelques relations nouvelles des missions, et des notes géographiques et historiques.* Paris: Librairie Alphonse Picard et fils, 1915.

Roi, Jacques. "Les Missionnaires de Chine et la botanique." *Collectanea Commissionis Synodalis in Sinis* 6, nos. 7–8 (July–August 1938).

Royet, Véronique, and others, comp. *Georges Louis Le Rouge: Jardins anglo-chinois.* Paris: Bibliothèque nationale de France, 2004.

Ruitenbeek, Klaas. *Carpentry and Building in Late Imperial China: A Study of the Fifteenth-Century Carpenter's Manual Lu Ban jing.* Leiden, New York and Cologne: E.J. Brill, 1993.

Schafer Edward H. *Tu Wan's Stone Catalogue of Cloudy Forest: A Commentary and Synopsis.* Berkeley: University of California Press, 1961; reprint, Warren, CT: Floating World Editions, 2005.

Shaw, Shiow-jyu Lu. *The Imperial Printing of Early Ch'ing China, 1644–1805.* Taipei: Chinese Materials Center, 1983.

Silvestre de Sacy, Jacques. *Henri Bertin dans le sillage de la Chine: 1720–1792.* Paris: Editions Cathasia; les Belles lettres, 1970.

Sirén, Osvald. *China and Gardens of Europe of the Eighteenth Century.* New York: Roland Press, 1949; reprint, Washington, DC: Dumbarton Oaks Research Library and Collection, 1990.

Smentek, Kristel. "China and Greco-Roman Antiquity: Overture to a Study of the Vase in Eighteenth-Century France." *Journal18*, no. 1 (Spring 2016), "Multilayered", www.journal18.org/issue1/china-and-greco-roman-antiquity-overture-to-a-study-of-the-vase-in-eighteenth-century-france/, accessed 3 October 2019.

Smentek, Kristel. "Chinoiseries for the Qing: A French Gift of Tapestries to the Qianlong Emperor." *Journal of Early Modern History* 20 (2016): 87–109.

Strassberg, Richard. "The Landscape of Intercultural Citation: The Chinese-Style Garden in Europe." In *China on Paper: European and Chinese Works from the Late Sixteenth to the Early Nineteenth Century*, edited by Marcia Reed and Paola Demattè: 121–132. Los Angeles: Getty Research Institute, 2007.

Strassberg, Richard. "War and Peace: Four Intercultural Landscapes." In *China on Paper: European and Chinese Works from the Late Sixteenth to the Early Nineteenth Century*, edited by Marcia Reed and Paola Demattè: 89–137. Los Angeles: Getty Research Institute, 2007.

Strassberg, Richard E. "Yizuo Qingdai yuyuan zhi chuanbo: Kangxi Bishu shanzhuang sanshiliu jing qi zai xifang de chuanbo licheng" (一座清代御苑之传播康熙避暑山庄三十六景及其在西方的传播历程); "Transmitting a Qing Imperial Garden: Kangxi's Thirty-Six Views of Bishu shanzhuang and Their Journey to the West." *Fengjing yuanlin* 风景园林 (*Landscape Architecture*) 83 (June 2009): 93–103.

Szambien, Werner. *Symétrie, goût, caractère: Théorie et terminologie de l'architecture à l'âge classique 1550–1800*. Paris: Picard, 1986.

Thiéry, Luc-Vincent. *Guide des amateurs et des étrangers voyageurs à Paris, ou Description raisonnée de cette ville, de sa banlieue et de tout ce qu'elles contiennent de remarquable*, 2 vols. Paris: Hardouin et Gattey, 1787.

Thomas, Greg M. "Yuanming yuan/Versailles: Intercultural Interactions between Chinese and European Palace Cultures." *Art History* 32, no. 1 (February 2009): 115–143.

Tuetey, Louis, comp. and ed. *Procès-verbaux de la Commission temporaire des arts*, 2 vols. Paris: Imprimerie Nationale, 1912, 1917.

Turgot, Anne-Robert-Jacques, *Oeuvres de M. Turgot, ministre d'État, ... Précédées et accompagnées de Mémoires et de Notes sur sa Vie, son Administration, et ses Ouvrages*, edited by Pierre Samuel Du Pont de Nemours, 9 vols. Paris: Imprimerie de Delance, 1808–1811.

Uitzinger, Ellen. "For the Man Who Has Everything: Western-Style Exotica in Birthday Celebrations at the Court of Ch'ien-lung." In *Conflict and Accommodation in Early Modern East Asia: Essays in Honour of Erik Zurcher*, edited by Leonard Blussé and Harriet T. Zurndorfer. Sinica Leidensia XXIX: 206–239. Leiden, New York, and Cologne: E.J. Brill, 1993.

Van Braam Houckgeest, Andreas Everardus. *Voyage de l'ambassade de la Compagnie des Indes orientales hollandaises vers l'empereur de la Chine dans les années 1794 et 1795 . . .*, 2 vols. Paris: Moreau de Saint-Méry, 1798; Philadelphia, 1797–1798.

van Campen, Jan. "A Chinese Collection in the Netherlands." *The Magazine Antiques*, September 2000: 360–371.

Verhaeren, Hubert Germain and Mission catholique des Lazaristes à Pékin. *Catalogue de la Bibliothèque du Pé-T'ang*. Beijing: Mission catholique des Lazaristes à Pékin, 1949. Reprint: Paris: Société d'Edition Les Belles Lettres, 1969.

Vicq-d'Azyr, Félix, Thomas Lindet, and Bouquier (aîné) [sic]. *Instruction sur la manière d'inventorier et de conserver, dans toute l'étendue de la République, tous les objets qui peuvent servir aux arts, aux sciences et à l'enseignement, proposée par la Commission temporaire des arts . . . .* Paris: Imprimerie nationale, an II, 1793.

Vitruvius: The Ten Books on Architecture. Translated by Morris Hicky Morgan. Cambridge, MA: Harvard University Press, 1914; reprint, New York: Dover Books, 1960.

Voltaire (François-Marie Arouet). *Dictionnaire philosophique, portatif*. "Liberté de Penser": 224–228. London, 1765.

Voyage et Séjour en France, par Ordre du Roi, de deux particuliers chinois, les Sieurs Kô & Yang, 1765. Bibliothèque de l'Institut de France, Ms 1520, fols. 50–55.

Wakeman, Frederic, Jr. "The Chinese Mirror." *Proceedings of the Academy of Political Science* 31, no. 1, China's Developmental Experience (March 1973): 208–219, www.jstor.org/stable/1173495, accessed 30 July 2016.

Watelet, Claude-Henri. *Essai sur les Jardins*. Paris: Impr. de Prault, 1774.

Whately, Thomas. *Observations on Modern Gardening, Illustrated by Descriptions . . . .* London: Printed for T. Payne, at the Mews-gate, 1770.

Whately, Thomas. *L'Art de former les jardins modernes, ou L'art des jardins anglois . . . .* Translated by François de Paule Latapie. Paris: Charles-Antoine Jombert, Père, 1771.

Wilkinson, Endymion. *Chinese History: A Manual*. Harvard-Yenching Institute Monograph Series 52. Cambridge, MA: Harvard University Asia Center, Harvard-Yenching Institute; Harvard University Press, 2000.

Zhuang, Yue. "Hatchings in the Void: Ritual and Order in *Bishu Shanzhuang Shi* and Matteo Ripa's *Views of Jehol*." In *Qing Encounters: Artistic Exchanges between China and the West*, edited by Petra ten-Doesschate Chu and Ning Ding: 142–157. Los Angeles: Getty Research Institute, 2015.

Zhuang, Yue. "Fear and Pride: Sir William Chambers' *Dissertation on Oriental Gardening*, Burke's Sublime and China." In *Entangled Landscapes: Early Modern China and Europe*, edited by Yue Zhuang and Andrea M. Riemenschnitter: 56–114. Singapore: National University of Singapore Press, 2017.

Zhuang, Yue, and Andrea M. Riemenschnitter, eds. *Entangled Landscapes: Early Modern China and Europe*. Singapore: National University of Singapore Press, 2017.

Zou, Hui. "Jesuit Perspective in China." *Architectura* 31 (2001): 145–168.

Zou, Hui. "The *jing* of a Perspective Garden." *Studies in the History of Gardens and Designed Landscapes* 22, no. 4 (October–December 2002): 293–326.

Index

Page numbers for Figures and Plates are in italics.

For Product Safety Concerns and Information please contact our EU representative GPSR@taylorandfrancis.com Taylor & Francis Verlag GmbH, Kaufingerstraße 24, 80331 München, Germany

Batch number: 10758087

Printed by Printforce, the Netherlands